COVENANT

John Murray's and Meredith G. Kline's Response to the Historical Development of Federal Theology in Reformed Thought

Jeong Koo Jeon

University Press of America,® Inc.
Lanham · Boulder · New York · Toronto · Oxford

Copyright © 1999 by
University Press of America,® Inc.
4501 Forbes Boulevard
Suite 200
Lanham, Maryland 20706
UPA Acquisitions Department (301) 459-3366

PO Box 317
Oxford
OX2 9RU, UK

All rights reserved
Printed in the United States of America
British Library Cataloging in Publication Information Available

Library of Congress Cataloging-in-Publication Data

Jeon, Jeong Koo.
Covenant theology : John Murray's and Meredith G. Kline's
response to the historical development of federal theology in
reformed thought / Jeong Koo Jeon.
p. cm.
Includes bibliographical references.
1. Covenant theology—History of doctrines—20th century.
2. Murray, John, 1898-1975—Contributions in covenant
theology. 3. Kline, Meredith G.—Contributions in covenant
theology. 4. Reformed Church—Doctrines. I. Title.
BT155.J46   1999   230'.52'0922—dc21   99—43550 CIP

ISBN 0-7618-3062-6 (paperback : alk. ppr.)

∞™ The paper used in this publication meets the minimum
requirements of American National Standard for Information
Sciences—Permanence of Paper for Printed Library Materials,
ANSI Z39.48—1984

*To the memory of my father Kee Dae Jeon (1914-1976)
and mother Heon Yim Lim (1921-1988), who raised me and taught me
to live a life of generosity, patience and love.*

TABLE OF CONTENTS

FOREWORD	ix
INTRODUCTION	1
CHAPTER ONE: THE HISTORICAL DEVELOPMENT OF FEDERAL THEOLOGY: MAIN STREAM REFORMED TEACHING IN LIGHT OF MODERN CRITICISM	11
A. John Calvin (1509-1564)	14
B. Caspar Olevianus (1536-1587)	29
C. Robert Rollock (1555-1599)	33
D. The Westminster Confession of Faith (1643-1648)	40
E. John Owen (1616-1683)	46
F. Francis Turretin (1623-1687)	56
G. Charles Hodge (1797-1878)	69
H. Geerhardus Vos (1862-1947)	79
I. Summary	94
CHAPTER TWO: JOHN MURRAY'S RESPONSE TO FEDERAL THEOLOGY	103
A. The Adamic Administration instead of the Covenant of Works	105
B. The Covenant of Grace	116
1. The Noahic Covenant	118
2. The Abrahamic Covenant	120
3. The Mosaic Covenant	126
4. The Davidic Covenant	127
5. The New Covenant	128
C. The Mosaic Covenant	131
D. Justification	144

1. The Antithesis between Law and Gospel in Relation to Justification by Faith Alone	145
2. The Antithesis between Adam and Christ	170
3. Justification and Good Works	175
E. Summary	186

CHAPTER THREE: MEREDITH G. KLINE'S RESPONSE TO FEDERAL THEOLOGY — 191

A. The Covenant of Creation	194
1. Man as *Imago Dei*	196
2. The Sabbath	199
3. The Creation Motif	202
4. The Parallel between the First and Second Adams	202
5. The Presence of the Glory-Spirit	203
6. The Marriage Motif	204
7. The Eschatological Sanctions	205
a. The Sacramental Tree	206
b. The Probation Tree	208
8. The Eschatological Judgment After the Fall	211
B. The Covenant of Redemption	213
1. The Intratrinitarian Covenant	213
2. The Inauguration of the Covenant of Redemption	215
3. The Prediluvian Noahic Covenant	219
4. The Postdiluvian Noahic Common Grace Covenant	221
5. The Abrahamic Covenant	222
6. The Mosaic Covenant	231
7. The Davidic Covenant	233
8. The New Covenant	234
C. The Mosaic Covenant	235
D. Justification	257
1. The Antithesis between Law and Gospel in relation to Justification by Faith Alone	257
2. The Antithesis between Adam and Christ	261
3. Justification and Good Works	270
E. Summary	272

CHAPTER FOUR: CRITICAL ASSESSMENT — 279

A. The Reaffirmation of the Antithesis between	280

the Covenants of Works and Grace: The Adamic
　　Administration versus The Covenant of Creation
　B. The Mosaic Covenant　　　　　　　　　　　307
　C. Justification　　　　　　　　　　　　　　314
　D. Summary　　　　　　　　　　　　　　　326

CONCLUSION　　　　　　　　　　　　　　　329

BIBLIOGRAPHY　　　　　　　　　　　　　　335

FOREWORD

Nothing is more important to Christianity than the Gospel. The good news of the saving work of Jesus the Christ stands at the center of the life and ministry of the Christian church. Throughout the history of the church serious struggles have arisen over the exact nature and meaning of the Gospel. At the heart of the great sixteenth-century movement known as the Reformation was a debate about what the Scriptures taught the Gospel to be. The Reformers faithfully and effectively derived the Gospel from the Scriptures in the face of great opposition and carefully enshrined in the remarkable confessions of that period. As Luther wrote in his best known hymn, "And though this world, with devils filled, should threaten to undo us, we will not fear, for God hath willed His truth to triumph through us."

That Gospel truth recovered by the Reformation is threatened still today. Old enemies continue to attack or compromise it while new challenges have emerged. On the scholarly level the theologian Karl Barth and those influenced by him as well as the Biblical scholar E. P. Sanders and his advocates have rejected the Protestant consensus of the Reformation on the Gospel. They have rejected the historic evangelical distinction between the law and the Gospel and have dismissed the idea of a covenant of works which Reformed theology had developed as a key foundation for understanding the work of Christ and justification by faith alone. On a more popular level preachers, teachers and laity seem often to confuse the Gospel with either legalism or antinomianism.

In the midst of this confusion Jeong Koo Jeon's study is very timely and helpful. While at first glance it may appear to be quite narrowly focused on two important but not very popular Reformed theologians, in fact it illumines central aspects of the current debate on the Gospel. Both John Murray and Meredith G. Kline were educated in and well acquainted with historic Reformed theology. Both wrote as confessional, orthodox Reformed theologians, but also with creativity and originality seeking to advance the Reformed cause. Both were careful students of the Bible as well as of contemporary theological developments. Dr. Jeon's analysis of their work, their disagreements and more fundamental agreements will aid the serious reader to think more clearly about the Gospel. The theologies of Murray and Kline and the debates between them open up the essential issues in discussions of justification in our time and demonstrate the critical theological concerns that cluster around that debate. They show that covenant theology is a great help to proper Biblical and systematic theology and that crucial questions with respect to the covenant of works and the Mosaic covenant must be answered appropriately in order to have a stable doctrine of the covenant of grace.

Dr. Jeon's work is very interesting simply as a study of two significant Reformed theologians of the twentieth century. But the theological issues that Murray and Kline address are so basic to the health and life of the church and its ministry in our time that this study needs to be widely read and carefully pondered.

W. Robert Godfrey, Ph.D.
President and Professor of Church History
Westminster Theological Seminary in California

INTRODUCTION

Many scholars in the twentieth century have paid close attention to the development of federal theology[1] which culminated in the antithesis between the covenants of works and grace. Barth, for example, claims that the development of a federal theology among Calvinists was the product of *dualism and historicism*, which are inadequate applications of biblical revelation. According to Barth, only the covenant of grace and not the covenant of works can be justified from a *Christomonistic perspective*:

> Their doctrine of a purely intertrinitarian pact did not enable them to give an unequivocal or binding answer to the question of the form of the eternal divine decree as the beginning of all things. The result was that for all their loyalty to Scripture they inherited the notion that the covenant of grace fulfilled and revealed in history in Jesus Christ was perhaps only a secondary and subsequent divine arrangement (the foundation and history of a religion?) and not the beginning of all the ways of God. Their view of the covenant became dualistic. The idea of a basic and always determinative and concurrent covenant of nature or works was superimposed on their conception of the covenant of grace. Yet this could have been avoided–even though as children of their time they were exposed to the temptation of humanism–if they could have determined to know the eternal and therefore the only basis of the

---

[1] Federal theology or covenant theology which developed in the Reformed tradition, expounds biblical truth around three covenants, namely, the covenant of works, a covenant of redemption, and a covenant of grace. Our major interest in the development of this thesis is to evaluate the function and importance of the contrast between the *foedus operum* and the *foedus gratiae* in relation to the *ordo salutis* and the *historia salutis*. We will use the term federal theology or covenant theology interchangeably. Donald Macleod, "Covenant Theology," in *Dictionary of Scottish Church History & Theology*, ed. Nigel M. De S. Cameron (Downers Grove, Illinois: InterVarsity, 1993), 214-18.

divine work in the work itself, in its temporal occurrence, to know the eternal divine Logos in His incarnation. And on this basis they might well have overcome the other weaknesses in their doctrine: the abandonment of an original universalism in the conception of the covenant; and finally the radical historicism of their understanding of Scripture.[2]

G. C. Berkouwer, rejecting the antithesis between Law and Gospel as a hermeneutical principle, is also critical of covenant theology. He argues that there is no antithesis between the covenants of works and grace. Moreover, he rejects the historical order of *law and grace*:

> Vainly do we search the Scriptures for any such antithesis in the covenants of works and grace. Certainly there is a chasm between *works* and *grace* as those two terms are used by the Apostle Paul. But we find no indication that these terms point to alternative paths which were once laid out by God. Rather they point us to a much more radical antithesis. The way of works is condemned by God because it is *not the way of God*.[3]

John Murray and Meredith G. Kline have played a significant role in the discussion of covenant theology in the twentieth century within Reformed circles and broader circles of evangelicalism. Robertson properly summarizes their contribution to covenant theology by noting that their approaches manifest several divergences:

> Yet from the perspective of the historical and theological succession of John Calvin and the reformers, 'covenant theology' has been central in thought and practice. In the light of this unbroken line of biblical and theological concern with the covenants, it is particularly significant to note the most recent probings into the concept of the covenant from a reformed perspective. These current probings are best summarized in the works of two men: John Murray and Meredith G. Kline. The contribution of these two men to reformed thinking on the matter of the covenants is immense indeed. Together they have led the church into a deeper level of understanding of the biblical concept of the divine

---

[2] Karl Barth, *Church Dogmatics*, trans. G. W. Bromiley, vol. 4/1 (Edinburgh: T. & T. Clark, 1974), 66.

[3] G. C. Berkouwer, *Studies in Dogmatics: Sin*, trans. Philip C. Holtrop (Grand Rapids: Michigan, 1971), 208.

covenant in Scripture. Yet divergences of judgment between the two are quite significant.[4]

The historical development of covenant theology in the Reformed tradition is crucial to both Murray and Kline. Murray claims to be a *revisionist* while Kline, elaborating upon a biblical covenant theology, identifies himself as a *classic covenant theologian*. In view of this, a careful analysis of the development of covenant theology is necessary, especially in the antithesis between the covenants of works and grace, along with the discontinuity between Law and Gospel. Further, we will pay special attention to the doctrine of justification in relation to covenant theology. Robertson shows the importance of understanding the historical development of covenant theology as a background for understanding the covenant theology of Murray and Kline:

> It should be plain that Murray and Kline have much in common in their treatment of the divine covenants of Scripture. They both are building on the contributions of covenant theologians of the past, while at the same time offering fresh insights. However, it should be apparent that these two men diverge from one another at some most basic points. While the areas of agreement are significant, the areas of disagreement also have far-reaching implications.[5]

Although Murray and Kline share the common heritage of covenant theology, their approaches to the original covenant of works and to the Mosaic Covenant are quite divergent as Willem A. VanGemeren points out:

> The ambivalent relation between law and grace has come to the fore during the latter half of this century in the writings of John Murray and Meredith G. Kline. In defining the relationship between the Abrahamic covenant and the Mosaic covenant, Murray is more sympathetic to continuity, whereas Kline favors discontinuity.[6]

---

[4] O. Palmer Robertson, "Current Reformed Thinking on the Nature of the Divine Covenants," *Westminster Theological Journal* 40 (1977): 63.

[5] Robertson, "Divine Covenant," 66.

[6] Willem A. VanGemeren, "The Law is the Perfection of Righteousness in Jesus Christ: A Reformed Perspective," in *Five Views on Law and Gospel*, ed., Wayne G. Strickland (Grand Rapids, Michigan: Zondervan Publishing House, 1996), 48.

When tracing and evaluating John Murray's and Meredith G. Kline's covenant theology in the light of the development of federal theology, we may have a fundamental question about the legitimacy of comparing and contrasting the two, since the former is a systematic theologian and the latter a biblical theologian specializing in the Old Testament. But this question can be easily handled since Murray identifies his systematic theology as a *biblico-systematic theology*, wherein he develops his theology based upon biblical theology. Kline makes it clear that his biblical theology stands in the line of *classic covenant theology*.[7]

---

[7] The two articles written as *Systematic Theology* in *The Westminster Theological Journal* in 1963 manifest Murray's desire and willingness to integrate biblical theology with systematic theology. For his comprehensive analysis of the intimate relationship between biblical and systematic theology over against modernity and a stereotyped dogmatics, see *Collected Writings of John Murray* (Edinburgh / Carlisle: The Banner of Truth Trust, 1982), 4:1-21.

Murray emphasizes the *correlation* of biblical and systematic theology although the two are different in terms of *methodology*. What is pertinent in Murray's analysis is that the *logical nature* of systematic theology and the recognition of the truly *historical* character of biblical history in biblical theology stand or fall together in opposition to modern critical scholarship in which biblical history is *dehistoricized* in its pursuit of biblical theology: "Biblical theology deals with the data of special revelation from the standpoint of its history; systematic theology deals with the same in its totality as a finished product. *The method of systematic theology is logical, that of biblical theology is historical* [emphasis mine]. The definition of Geerhardus Vos puts this difference in focus. 'Biblical Theology is that branch of Exegetical Theology which deals with the process of the self-revelation of God deposited in the Bible.'" Ibid., 4:9.

Thus, systematic theology, according to Murray, is to be rooted and developed in biblical theology: "Systematic theology is tied to exegesis. It coordinates and synthesizes the whole witness of Scripture on the various topics with which it deals. But systematic theology will fail of its task to the extent to which it discards its rootage in biblical theology as properly conceived and developed." Ibid., 19. Moreover, Edward J. Young as the colleague of Murray and predecessor of Kline in the Old Testament department of Westminster classifies the necessity of the coherent relationship of biblical and systematic theologies over against modern tendency which ignores and depreciates systematic theology at the expense of biblical theology: "Old Testament theology serves as a useful handmaid to the discipline of Systematic Theology. There has appeared a tendency to Systematic Theology at the expense of what some would call biblical theology.

Our thesis will prove that federal theology, while culminating in the antithesis between the covenants of works and grace, does not fall into *legalism* or *dualism* as critics have often claimed. Conversely, it plays a key role in expounding the doctrine of justification by faith alone against *legalism*. Moreover, covenant obligation is required according to the logic of the *bilateral* covenant of grace. Furthermore, the antithesis between the covenants of works and grace, along with the antithesis between Law and Gospel, is a necessary hermeneutical tool to expound the rich ingredients of *eschatology* revealed in Scripture. Although *union with Christ (unio cum Christo)* is the controlling motif of the *ordo salutis* in covenant hermeneutics, justification by faith alone is safeguarded, since it is rightly understood in the light of the antithesis between Law and Gospel. Murray and

---

Systematic Theology, however, is simply the formal statement of the teaching of the Bible." Edward J. Young, *The Study of Old Testament Theology Today* (Westwood, New Jersey: Fleming H. Revell Company, 1959), 110.

For the extensive and comprehensive discussion of the mutual dependence and relationship between systematic and biblical theology from the vantage point of covenant hermeneutics, see Oswald T. Allis, *Prophecy & The Church* (Phillipsburg, New Jersey: Presbyterian and Reformed Publishing Company, 1947); Edmund P. Clowney, *Preaching and Biblical Theology* (Nutley, New Jersey: Presbyterian and Reformed Publishing Company, 1975); idem, *The Unfolding Mystery: Discovering Christ in the Old Testament* (Phillipsburg, New Jersey: Presbyterian and Reformed Publishing, 1988); John M. Frame, *The Doctrine of the Knowledge of God* (Phillipsburg, New Jersey: Presbyterian and Reformed Publishing Company, 1987), 207-14; Richard B. Gaffin, Jr., "Systematic Theology and Biblical Theology," *The New Testament Student and Theology*, vol. 3. ed. John H. Skilton (New Jersey: Presbyterian and Reformed Publishing Company, 1976), 32-50; Vern S. Poythress, *God-Centered Biblical Interpretation* (Phillipsburg, New Jersey: Presbyterian and Reformed Publishing Company, 1999); Cornelius Van Til, *An Introduction to Systematic Theology* (Phillipsburg, New Jersey: Presbyterian and Reformed Publishing Company, 1974), 1-20; Geerhardus Vos, *Biblical Theology: Old and New Testaments* (Grand Rapids, Michigan: Eerdmans Publishing Company, 1948; reprint, 1988), 3-18; Young, *Study*, 5-112.

For the *dehistorization* of biblical history in doing biblical theology among critical scholars, see Walther Eichrodt, *Theology of the Old Testament*, trans. J. A. Baker (Philadelphia: The Westminster Press, 1961), 25-35; Gerhard von Rad, *Theologie Des Alten Testaments*, Band I & II. (München: Chr. Kaiser Verlag, 1958 & 1965).

Kline, despite different approaches to covenant theology, affirm both justification by faith alone and sovereign grace in divine election, because both theologians apply the antithesis between Law and Gospel.

As we trace the historical development of federal theology from John Calvin to Geerhardus Vos in chapter one, we will pay close attention to Calvin's role in the later development of the antithesis between the covenants of works and grace. We will substantiate that Calvin applies the antithesis between Law and Gospel as a key reference point to depict the principle of grace in salvation and justification, manifested in the dictums of *sola fide* and *sola gratia* in the one covenant of grace. In other words, the development of federal theology does not reject Martin Luther's Law and Gospel contrast. Rather, it affirms the hermeneutical principle shared by the Protestant reformers, depicted justification by faith alone apart from good works as a corrective of *legalism*. Moreover, the believer's application of the law producing good works through the power of the Holy Spirit is required in opposition to *antinomianism*. As develop our thesis, we will show that while Calvin interprets salvation history in the postlapsarian state in the light of one covenant of grace as the means of salvation and justification, he sees *discontinuity* between the Old and New Covenants and designates the Mosaic Covenant as the *foedus legale*. The notion of the *foedus legale* is vital to the *eschatological* understanding of the Old Covenant, since the principle of the law was operative in the administration of blessings or curses for the nation of Israel. The administration of blessings or curses on the nation of Israel points to the eschatological, heavenly blessing and everlasting hell. The eschatological interpretation of the Old Covenant is progressively developed among later covenant theologians as seen in the application of *typology*.[8] Although Calvin does not use the term *foedus operum* for

---

[8] An adequate understanding of *typology* and its application to biblical theology and systematic theology is vitally important for avoiding the two extremes of allegorism on the one hand, and literalism on the other hand. cf. Allis, *Prophecy*, 16-54; Clowney, *Biblical Theology*, 100-21; Jonathan Edwards, *The Works of Jonathan Edwards: Typological Writings*. vol. 11, ed. Harry S. Stout (New Haven and London: Yale University Press, 1993); Patrick Fairbairn, *The Revelation of Law in Scripture* (Phillipsburg, New Jersey: Presbyterian and Reformed Publishing Company, 1996); idem, *The Typology of Scripture* (Grand Rapids, Michigan: Zondervan Publishing

the prelapsarian state, he posits it from the vantage point of an *eschatology* governed by the principle of the law, which signifies the ultimate goal of God's creation. Thus it will be suggested that Calvin affirms the historical order of *law and grace* as the means of attaining eschatological heavenly blessings. We will seek to demonstrate that Calvin's covenant idea is fully congruous with the later development of the antithesis between the covenants of works and grace. Thus we

---

House, 1952); Duane A. Garrett, "Type, Typology," in *Evangelical Dictionary of Biblical Theology*, ed. Walter A. Elwell (Grand Rapids, Michigan: Baker Book House, 1996), 785-7; W. Edward Glenny, "Typology: A Summary of the Present Evangelical Discussion," *Journal of the Evangelical Theological Society* 40 (1997): 627-38; Mark W. Karlberg, "Justification in Redemptive History," *Westminster Theological Journal* 43 (1981): 213-46; G. R. Osborne, "Type, Typology," in *Evangelical Dictionary of Theology*, ed. Walter A. Elwell (Grand Rapids, Michigan: Baker Book House, 1984), 1117-9; Vern S. Poythress, *The Shadow of Christ in the Law of Moses* (Phillipsburg, New Jersey: Presbyterian and Reformed Publishing Company, 1993); John H. Stek, "Biblical Typology Yesterday and Today," *Calvin Theological Journal* 5 (1970): 133-62; Geerhardus Vos, *The Teaching of the Epistle to the Hebrews* (Phillipsburg, New Jersey: Presbyterian and Reformed Publishing Company, 1956), 55-87. The following quote from the elegant pen of Clowney is significant: "Clearer understanding of biblical theology and sharper discernment of the theological horizons of the periods of revelation will aid us in appreciating the symbolism of Scripture. The reverse is also true. If we proceed to construct the line of typology only when we have first clarified the symbolism we will be able to work in confidence. We honor the Word of God when we recognize the principle of organic connection between promise and fulfillment. Such a method does not commend itself to those who deny or de-emphasize the primary authorship of Scriptures. Only the lack of hermeneutical method can shut us up to recognizing types only where the New Testament itself explicitly recognizes them. Such caution is then admirable. But a better grasp of biblical theology will open for us great riches of revelation. We need not lack the sound method to find these and bring them to the people of God." Clowney, *Biblical Theology*, 111-12. Oswald Allis rightly points out this balanced approach to biblical theology: "The question of literal versus figurative interpretation is, therefore, one which has to be faced at the very outset. And it is to be observed at once that the issue cannot be stated as a simple alternative, either literal or figurative. No literalist, however thoroughgoing, takes everything in the Bible literally. Nor do those who lean to a more figurative method of interpretation insist that everything is figurative. Both principles have their proper place and their necessary limitations." Allis, *Prophecy*, 17.

will refute the contention that there is a sharp contrast between Calvin and Calvinists. Therefore the classic covenant theology developed in the Reformed tradition affirms the antithesis between the covenants of works and grace. We have selected seven covenant theologians and the Westminster Confession of Faith to show the development of federal theology. Some of them have directly influenced Murray and Kline. Our major reason for selecting them, however, is to trace the *general* pattern of the development of federal theology among the Continental and English Puritans including a Scottish covenant theologian, and the *Old Princeton* covenant theologians.

In chapter two, we will deal with Murray's revision of covenant theology. In doing so, we will trace his historical and biblical-theological logic to deny the *foedus operum*. In the final analysis, we will prove that Murray's theological logic, however, is compatible with the antithesis between the covenants of works and grace, since he preserves the historical order as *law and grace* in interpreting the Adamic administration from the vantage point of *eschatology*. Murray explains the Mosaic Covenant exclusively from the perspective of *continuity* in relation to the Abrahamic and New Covenants, and fails to apply the *foedus legale* in respect to the administration of the typological nation of Israel. We will argue that Murray's approach obscures the rich concept of *eschatology* revealed in the Old Covenant. We could assume that Murray rejects the antithesis between Law and Gospel since he rejects the covenant of works. But this is not the case. We will endeavor to demonstrate that he utilizes the antithesis between Law and Gospel to expound justification by faith alone apart from good works while opposing *legalism*, whereas he urges the application of the law in the process of the believer's sanctification in opposition to *antinomianism*.

Kline, as a student and colleague of Murray at Westminster Theological Seminary in Pennsylvania, who will be visited in chapter three, is critical of Murray's revision of covenant theology. The weaknesses and strengths revealed by Murray indeed provide a good opportunity for Kline's biblical covenant theology to mature and flower, although we still see a need for minor modifications. Against the contention that Kline's hermeneutics has an affinity to Lutheranism or Dispensationalism, we will fully demonstrate that Kline is a thoroughly covenant theologian. Kline stands in the rich tradition of classic covenant theology, which interprets the *ordo salutis* and *historia salutis* in the light of the antithesis between the covenants of works and grace, along with the antithesis between Law and Gospel. The distinctiveness of Kline's biblical theology is that he integrates covenant and kingdom motifs together and points to the goal of the eschatological kingdom. Believers under the Old Covenant were saved and justified by the principle of the *foedus gratiae* according to the logic of covenant *continuity* between the Old and New Covenants. The typological kingdom of Israel, which points to the eschatological heavenly kingdom blessing, was administered by the principle of the *foedus legale*, which contrasts the Old and New Covenants. In other words, Kline brilliantly avoids *legalism* by maximizing the concept of *typology*, which is vital to the *eschatological* interpretation of the Old Covenant. Furthermore, Kline vigorously defends the doctrine of justification by faith alone in opposition to *legalism* by utilizing the hermeneutical principle of the antithesis between Law and Gospel along with the antithesis between the covenants of creation and redemption. The application of the law by believers in the process of sanctification is required by the principle of covenant obligation and is applied against *antinomianism*.

Our final chapter will be devoted to the critical evaluation of Murray and Kline from the vantage point of historical and biblical theology. In doing so, we will reaffirm the antithesis between the covenants of works and grace together with the antithesis between Law and Gospel. As we affirm the historical order of *law and grace* over against *grace and law*, covering creation, fall and redemption, we will provide the logic of biblical theology to expound the original covenant of works *judicially* or *forensically*. Certainly the *forensic* interpretation of the original covenant of works, illumined by the antithesis between the first and second Adams, will be seen as a contribution of Kline's biblical covenant theology. Moreover, the *forensic* standing of the first Adam qualifies Adam's meritorious position as the representative covenantal head. Therefore, the concept of *merit* will be limited to the first and second Adams since our definition of *merit* is applicable only to perfect obedience to the requirements of the law. Thus we will suggest that the Israelites' obedience under the Mosaic Covenant was *not meritorious*, in the strict sense, although the *foedus legale* was operative in the administration of the earthly typological kingdom. Murray and Kline agree on the doctrine of justification by faith alone, since both apply the antithesis between Law and Gospel as their key hermeneutical principle. Now, we turn to our first chapter to trace the development of federal theology which provides a good historical theological background for understanding the thought of John Murray and Meredith G. Kline.

Chapter One

THE HISTORICAL DEVELOPMENT OF FEDERAL THEOLOGY: MAINSTREAM REFORMED TEACHING IN LIGHT OF MODERN CRITICISM

In recent historical theological scholarship, Barth and others have argued the "'Calvin against the Calvinists' approach" concerning the development of federal theology. They see Calvin "as a theologian of grace to be distinguished from the legalism of later 'Calvinist' covenantal or federal theology."[1] The scrutinized critique of the Reformed development of federal theology by Barthians is an attempt to infuse their own theological reference point into Calvin's theology, radically separating the Calvinists from Calvin. Muller adequately summarizes the problem of the neoorthodox interpretation of Calvin *against* Calvinists: "Typical here is the attempt to identify Calvin as the direct ancestor of neoorthodox Christocentrism and to discredit theologically the Reformed orthodox teaching as incompatible both with Calvin and with Barth."[2] Therefore, neoorthodox proponents harshly criticize the antithesis between the covenants of works and grace within Reformed orthodoxy, as well as the antithesis between Law and Gospel as it relates to justification by faith alone (i.e. excluding good works). Thus, they create an erroneous contrast between Calvin and the Calvinists. These critics contend that federal theology changed the biblical order of *grace and law* into *law and grace*. Thus, in their historical theological point of view, they stress

---

[1] Richard A. Muller, "Calvin and the 'Calvinists': Assessing Continuities and Discontinuities Between the Reformation and Orthodoxy," *Calvin Theological Journal* 30 (1995): 349.
[2] Ibid., 353.

the priority of *grace over law* and identify themselves with Calvin, to whom the distinction between the covenants of works and grace and the antithesis between Law and Gospel are allegedly unknown.[3] Rolston, for example, asserts, "Indeed, it has seldom been realized by persons otherwise well versed in the Reformed tradition that the twin covenant tectonics which dominates the substructure of all later Reformed dogmatics is totally absent from Calvin. Worse than that, its fundamental incompatibility with Calvin's thought has gone all but unnoticed."[4] Likewise, James B. Torrance asserts that "this distinction between a Covenant of Works and a Covenant of Grace was unknown to Calvin and the Reformers–nor indeed would Calvin ever have taught it."[5] Supporting this contention, Bruggink maintains,

---

[3] Paul Althaus, *Die Prinzipien der deutschen reformierten Dogmatik im Zeitalter der aristotelischen Scholastik* (Leipzig, 1914; reprint, Darmstadt: Wissenschaftliche Buchgesellschaft, 1967), 148-52; Barth, *Church Dogmatics*, 4/1:54-66; Donald J. Bruggink, "Calvin and Federal Theology," *The Reformed Review* 13 (1959-60): 15-22; August Lang, *Der Heidelberger Katechismus und vier verwandte Katechismen* (reprint, Darmstadt: Wissenschaftliche Buchgesellschaft, 1967), LXIV-LXVII; Jürgen Moltmann, "Föederaltheologie," in *Lexikon für Theologie und Kirche*, 1960; Otto Ritschl, *Dogmengeschichte des Protestantismus* (Göttingen: Vandenhoeck & Ruprecht, 1926), 3:416-18; Holmes Rolston, III, "Responsible Man in Reformed Theology: Calvin Versus the Westminster Confession," *Scottish Journal of Theology* 23 (1970): 129-56; idem, *John Calvin versus the Westminster Confession* (Richmond: John Knox, 1972); Gottlob Schrenk, *Gotesreich und Bund im älteren Protestantismus vornehmlich bei Johannes Cocceius* (Gutersloh: Bertelsmann, 1923), 48-9; James B. Torrance, "Covenant or Contract ? A Study of the Theological Background or Worship in Seventeenth-Century Scotland," *Scottish Journal of Theology* 23 (1970): 51-76; idem, "The Covenant Concept in Scottish Theology and Politics and Its Legacy," *Scottish Journal of Theology* 34 (1981): 225-43; idem, "Calvin and Puritanism in England and Scotland - Some Basic Concepts in the Development of 'Federal Theology,'" in *Calvinus Reformator* (Potchefstroom: Potchefstroom University for Christian Higher Education, 1982), 264-277; idem, "Strengths and Weaknesses of the Westminster Theology," in *The Westminster Confession,* ed. Alisdair Heron (Edinburgh: St. Andrews, 1982), 40-53; David N. J. Poole, *The History of the Covenant Concept from the Bible to Johannes Cloppenburg "De Foedere Dei"* (San Francisco: Mellen Research University Press, 1992).

[4] Rolston, *Calvin versus the Westminster Confession*, 11.

[5] James B. Torrance, *Covenant or Contract*, 61-2.

"Nevertheless, even in this brief glimpse of the system, it becomes evident that despite its popularity, federal theology was not a logical development of Calvin's theology. Rather it was a perversion of great seriousness, for it introduced a covenant of works as a valid relationship between man and God, and then carried works into the very covenant of grace."[6] However, the bottom line is to reject the antithesis between Law and Gospel, which was a common theological denominator used by all the major Reformers in their focus on justification by faith alone; and this was set in opposition to the medieval schoolmen's legalistic and moralistic notions of salvation. Ironically, neoorthodox theologians condemn the orthodox Reformed distinction between the covenants of works and grace. In so doing, neoorthodox theologians create the key problem that leads into a moralistic and legalistic religion.

In his theology, which we shall later discuss, Calvin used three theological reference points as the background for the later development of the twofold covenants. They are (1) an absolute antithesis between Law and Gospel in expounding the doctrine of justification by faith alone; (2) one covenant of grace in God's redemptive history in the postlapsarian state; (3) and the governing principle of the law in the prelapsarian state. Also, he identified the *foedus legale* under the Mosaic Covenant as the *contrast* between The Old Covenant and New Covenant, in which the principle of the law was implied in the former with regard to the earthly blessing and curse in the nation of Israel. This earthly, national administration of the law ultimately pointed to the everlasting heavenly blessing for believers in Christ Jesus and eternal curse for unbelievers. Believers under the Sinaitic Covenant were justified and saved by the covenant of grace in Christ Jesus, who would come later. These hermeneutical tools decisively contributed and gradually permeated in the thinking that led to the development of the antithesis between the covenants of works and grace hermeneutics in Reformed orthodoxy.

In this connection, we will pay special attention to some scholars' suggestion that even though Calvin does not use the term *foedus operum*, referring to Adam's original situation, his biblical theological concept is fully congruous with the later developed doctrine of the covenant of works. The Reformed orthodox formulation of the

---

[6] Bruggink, *Calvin and Federal Theology*, 22.

prelapsarian covenant of works was gradually developed from Calvin's federal notion of the prelapsarian Adamic administration of law. Therefore, there is a covenantal theological continuity between Calvin and the following Reformed covenant theologians, respecting the antithesis between the covenant of works and grace.[7] Upon careful historical theological analysis, we will show that the antithesis between the covenants of works and grace is an important hermeneutical principle that is fully compatible with Calvin's covenantal theological concept, and that has been progressively developed by Reformed orthodox theologians.

A. John Calvin (1509-1564)

John Calvin's application of the hermeneutical principle of the antithesis between Law and Gospel was evidenced in his doctrine of justification by faith alone. Luther's struggle to discover the Gospel finally concluded when he also used this important hermeneutical tool, the antithesis between Law and Gospel. In his treatise, 'Sermon on the Twofold Righteousness,' on April 13, 1519, Luther articulated

---

[7] Mark W. Karlberg, "The Mosaic Covenant and the Concept of Works in Reformed Hermeneutics: A Historical-Critical Analysis with Particular Attention to Early Covenant Eschatology" (Ph.D. diss., Westminster Theological Seminary, 1980), 74-85; idem, "Reformed Interpretation of the Mosaic Covenant" *Westminster Theological Journal* 43 (Fall, 1980): 13; Peter A. Lillback, "Ursinus' Development of the Covenant of Creation: A Debt to Melanchthon or Calvin," *Westminster Theological Journal* 43 (1981): 247-88; idem, "The Binding of God: Calvin's Role in the Development of Covenant Theology" (Ph.D. diss., Westminster Theological Seminary, 1985), 7-11, 446-497; Richard A. Muller, "The Covenant of Works and the Stability of Divine Law in Seventeenth-Century Reformed Orthodoxy: A Study in the Theology of Herman Witsius and Wilhelmus À Brakel," *Calvin Theological Journal* 29 (1994): 88-89. The precise nature and importance of the bipolar covenants has been addressed by Mark Karlberg: "Chapters three and four develop the importance of the law-gospel distinction and its application to the doctrine of the two covenants, the covenant of works and the covenant of grace. The biblical concept of works (law) is crucial to the Reformed theological system, especially with regard to the doctrine of the atonement of Christ and of justification by faith. Communion with God is possible only on the ground of faithful (sinless) covenant obedience, for God cannot look upon sin. This demand was met exclusively by Christ on behalf of the sinner redeemed by grace. Justification is by faith, not works." Karlberg, *Mosaic Covenant and Works*, 7.

justification by faith alone, stating that "alien righteousness" (*iustitia aliena*) excludes the moralistic and ethical concepts of justification, for "through faith in Christ," the righteousness of Christ which is "infinite righteousness", becomes "our righteousness."[8] Calvin used this vital

---

[8] Martin Luther, *Luther's Works*, vol. 31. ed. Harold J. Grimm (Philadelphia: Muhlenberg Press, 1957), 297-306. We adopt the thesis that despite the theological difference and disagreement between Lutherans and Reformed, both agree on the doctrine of justification by faith alone, and it is because both adopt a hermeneutical principle which assumes the antithesis between the principle of Law and Gospel in relation to justification. cf. Louis Berkhof, *The History of Christian Doctrines* (Grand Rapids, Michigan: Baker Book House, 1995), 217-21; idem, *Systematic Theology* (Grand Rapids, Michigan: Eerdmans Publishing Company, 1938; reprint, 1988), 510-26; D. Clair Davis, "A Challenge to Theonomy," in *Theonomy:A Reformed Critique*, eds. William S. Barker & W. Robert Godfrey (Grand Rapids, Michigan: Zondervan Publishing House, 1990), 398-402; idem, "How Did the Church in Rome Become Roman Catholicism," in *Roman Catholicism: Evangelical Protestants Analyze What Divides and Unites Us*, ed. John Armstrong (Chicago: Moody Press, 1994), 45-62; idem, "Inerrancy and Westminster Calvinism," in *Inerrancy and Hermeneutic: A Tradition, A Challenge, A Debate*, ed. Harvie M. Conn (Grand Rapids, Michigan: Baker Book House, 1990), 35-46; W. R. Godfrey, "Law and Gospel," in *New Dictionary of Theology*, eds. Sinclair B. Ferguson & David F. Wright (Downers Grove, Illinois / Leicester, England: InterVarsity Press, 1988), 379-80; idem, "What Really Caused the Great Divide," in *Roman Catholicism: Evangelical Protestants Analyze What Divides and Unites Us*, ed. John Armstrong (Chicago: Moody Press, 1994), 65-82; Charles Hodge, *Systematic Theology* (reprint, Grand Rapids, Michigan: Eerdmans Publishing Company, 1995), 3: 114-212; Michael Horton, "What Still Keeps Us Apart?" in *Roman Catholicism: Evangelical Protestants Analyze What Divides and Unites Us*, ed. John Armstrong (Chicago: Moody Press, 1994), 245-66; J. Gresham Machen, *What is Faith* (New York: The Macmillan Company, 1925); Thomas R. Schreiner, *The Law and Its Fulfillment: A Pauline Theology of Law* (Grand Rapids, Michigan: Baker Books, 1993), 14-6; R. C. Sproul, *Faith Alone: The Evangelical Doctrine of Justification* (Grand Rapids, Michigan: Baker Book House; reprint, 1996); Robert B. Strimple, "Roman Catholic Theology Today," in *Roman Catholicism: Evangelical Protestants Analyze What Divides and Unites Us*, ed. John Armstrong (Chicago: Moody Press, 1994), 85-117; Cornellius Van Til, *The Sovereignty of Grace: An Appraisal of G. C. Berkouwer's View of Dordt* (Phillipsburg, New Jersey: Presbyterian and Reformed Publishing Company, 1969), 8-9, 12. Louis Berkhof, for example, rightly states that Luther and Calvin agreed on the important doctrine of

motif in his theological system. Calvin, in his final edition of *'Institutes of the Christian Religion'* of 1559 and in his commentaries, clearly expounded justification by faith alone, employing the Law and Gospel hermeneutical principle which Luther developed. Man is justified by faith, Calvin points out, excluding "the righteousness of

---

justification which was a common denominator of evangelical consensus of the Protestant Reformation although they had many different aspects of theological disagreement: "But however Calvin may have differed from Luther as to the order of salvation, he quite agreed with him on the nature and importance of the doctrine of justification by faith. In their common opposition to Rome they both describe it as an act of free grace, and as a forensic act which does not change the inner life of man but only the judicial relationship in which he stands to God. They do not find the ground for it in the inherent righteousness of the believer, but only in the imputed righteousness of Jesus Christ, which the sinner appropriates by faith. Moreover, they deny that it is a progressive work of God, asserting that it is instantaneous and at once complete, and hold that the believer can be absolutely sure that he is for ever translated from a state of wrath and condemnation to one of favour and acceptance." Berkhof, *Christian Doctrines,* 220. Recently, the Protestant Reformation consensus on the *articulus stantis et cadentis ecclesiae* is summarized in the acute pen of Michael Horton: "It is the *articulus ecclesiae stantis et cadentis*, the 'article by which the church stands and falls,' the Reformers declared of the doctrine of justification. 'As long as a person is unaware of this doctrine' and the distinction between the law and the gospel, Luther insisted, 'he is no different than a Jew, a Turk [Moslem] or a Heathen.' ... It was not enough for the Reformers to say that we were saved by grace. Nor, indeed, was it even enough to say that we were saved by grace alone. Thus far they would not have said anything that a typical Augustinian would not have affirmed in his day. What Luther and the other Reformers insisted on was grace alone through faith alone. In medieval doctrine, justification was considered what evangelicals call 'regeneration' or the new birth. In baptism, the child received his or her 'first justification,' and this began the process of sanctification. Thus, justification was seen as the beginning of moral change, and only at the end of the process—assuming one made proper use of the sacraments, confessed one's sins verbally to a priest, and died without having committed a mortal sin—could one hope to be justified. In fact, the process actually continued beyond the grave, in purgatory, where the remaining corruptions and transgressions were purged. The whole process may indeed be ascribed to 'grace alone,' and yet the way one received this 'grace' was, in effect, by meriting." Horton, "What Still Keeps Us Apart?" 254-5.

works." Man embraces "the righteousness of Christ through faith, and clothed in it, appears in God's sight not as a sinner but as a righteous man. Therefore, justification is the acceptance by which God receives us into his favor as righteous men. It consists in the remission of sins and the imputation of Christ's righteousness".[9] Contrary to this, the medieval Sophists held that man is justified by *fide et operibus*, by "both faith and works." Their major theological problem, according to Calvin, was a failure to admit a radical contrast between the principle of Law and Gospel, elaborated by Paul in Romans 10:5-9 and Galatians 3:11-12:

> Still they do not observe that in the contrast between the righteousness of the law and of the gospel, which Paul elsewhere introduces, all works are excluded, whatever title may grace them [Gal. 3:11-12]. For he teaches that this is the righteousness of the law, that he who has fulfilled what the law commands should obtain salvation; but this is the righteousness of faith, to believe that Christ died and rose again [Rom. 10:5,9].[10]

The Law and Gospel distinction excludes all concepts of works in Calvin's doctrine of justification by faith alone since *faith* embraces the righteousness of God. Calvin points out how Paul clearly analyzes this in his Epistles:

> For in comparing the law and the gospel in the letter to the Romans he says: "the righteousness that is of the law" is such that "the man who practices these things will live by them" [Rom. 10:5]. But the "righteousness that is of faith" [Rom. 10:6] announces salvation "if you believe in your heart and confess with your mouth that Jesus is Lord and that the Father raised him from the dead" [Rom. 10:9 p.]. Do you see how he makes this the distinction between law and gospel: that the former attributes righteousness to works, the latter bestows free righteousness apart from the help of works? This is an important passage, and one that can extricate us from many difficulties if we

---

[9] John Calvin, *Institutes of the Christian Religion*, ed. John T. McNeill, trans. Ford Lewis Battles, *Library of Christian Classics*, vol. 20-21 (Philadelphia: The Westminster Press, 1975), 3.9.2.

[10] Ibid., 3.11.14. In Calvin's hermeneutics, it is pertinent to notice that the principles of the promises of the law and the gospel are antithetical, which is manifested in Leviticus 18:5, Romans 10:5-9 and Galatians 3:11-12. Ibid., 3:17:3.

understand that that righteousness which is given us through the gospel has been freed of all conditions of the law. Here is the reason why he so often opposes the promise to the law, as things mutually contradictory: "If the inheritance is by the law, it is no longer by promise" [Gal. 3:18]; and passages in the same chapter that express this idea. Now, to be sure, the law itself has its own promises. Therefore, in the promises of the gospel there must be something distinct and different unless we would admit that the comparison is inept. But what sort of difference will this be, other than that the gospel promises are free and dependent solely upon God's mercy, while the promises of the law depend upon the condition of works?[11]

Thus, the antithesis between Law and Gospel is a biblical theological reference point upon which Calvin develops the doctrine of justification by faith alone, excluding human merit. This point is placed against the background of the medieval Schoolmen's meritorious concept of salvation, which was embraced in *meritum de congruo et meritum de condigno*. Commenting on another Pauline passage, Galatians 3:11-12, Calvin separates the two opposing principles of works and faith. "Law righteousness" is distinguished from "faith righteousness," based upon the antithesis between Law and Gospel:

The law, he [Paul] says, is different from faith. Why? Because works are required for law righteousness. Therefore it follows that they are not required for faith righteousness. From this relation it is clear that those who are justified by faith are justified apart from the merit of works–in fact, without the merit of works. For faith receives that righteousness which the gospel bestows. Now the gospel differs from the law in that it does not link righteousness to works but lodges it solely in God's mercy.[12]

In other words, law righteousness seeks to be justified by the merit of works *in opposition to* faith righteousness. Works righteousness, states Calvin, is only possible "in perfect and complete observance of the law." From this biblical logic, man cannot be justified by the merit of works, unless one reaches "to the highest peak of perfection."[13] While Calvin rejects the meritorious concept of works and salvation in the

---

[11] Ibid., 3.11.17.
[12] Ibid., 3.11.18.
[13] Ibid., 3:15:1

fallen state, he, nevertheless, affirms the merit of works in the prelapsarian state, quoting Augustine's *On the Predestination of the Saints*, 15:31: "For in one place Augustine speaks thus: 'Let *human merits, which perished through Adam* [emphasis mine], here keep silence, and let God's grace reign through Jesus Christ.' Again: 'The saints attribute nothing to their merits; they will attribute all to thy mercy alone, O God.'"[14] Good works in the Christian life are necessary, as Paul demonstrates in 2 Timothy 3:16-17. However, good works are not meritorious, since salvation is based on the principle of *sola gratia*, a principle which excludes human merit. In other words, the

---

[14] Ibid., 3:15:2. Thus, Calvin's point in respect to the law is that if man fulfills the requirement of the law, it is meritorious in relation to salvation and justification, which is not possible in the fallen state: "So also ought we to recognize that God's benevolence has been set forth for us in the law, if we could merit it by works, but it never comes to us by this merit." Ibid., 3:17:2; "We assuredly do not question that the righteousness of the law consists in works, and not even that righteousness consists in the worth and merits of works. But it has not yet been proved that we are justified by works unless they produce some one man who has fulfilled the law." Ibid., 3:17:13.

As observed in the above quotation, we may draw a legitimate conclusion from Calvin's analysis that works in the *foedus legale* are meritorious in an ideal situation. This notion of merit is applied by Charles Hodge and Meredith G. Kline later in the covenant hermeneutics especially in respect to the original covenant of works in the light of the complete antithesis between the covenants of works and grace.

Merit can be identified as "the value or worth of a good or obedient act or the act itself." In this respect, the problem of the medieval concept of merit is that human works contribute to salvation in the notion of *meritum de congruo et meritum de condigno*. In opposition to this, the Protestant scholastics suggest that human acts or acts of obedience are not meritorious in the fallen world. As such, good works, flowing from the divine grace, are God's acts in us and cannot do anything for man's salvation. According to this view, "only perfect righteousness can be meritorious, only Christ merits life in and of himself, not for himself, but vicariously for us." Thus, *meritum Christi* is the fundamental ground of salvation. Richard A. Muller, *Dictionary of Latin and Greek Theological Terms: Drawn Principally from Protestant Scholastic Theology* (Grand Rapids, Michigan: Baker Book House, 1985), 190-92. We will show that if the absolute distinction between the covenants of works and grace is a legitimate principle in the light of biblical and systematic theology, then Adam's perfect obedience in the original covenant of works would have been *merited*.

principle of *soli Deo gloria* of Matthew 5:16 is the ultimate point of reference of believers' good works, over against the Schoolmen's anthropocentric notion of salvation culminating from the merit of human works. "Christ's merit alone" (*meritum Christi*) is the only foundation of believers' justification, and it is the concrete reason why justification by faith alone, excluding the merit of human works, is valid.[15]

The problem of *meritum de congruo et meritum de condigno* in the medieval scholastics lies in the fact that it fails to distinguish between Law and Grace in the discussion of justification and salvation. In this respect, Calvin properly denotes that merit is only possible based on perfect obedience and can be predicated only of Christ's obedience and Adam's prefall obedience, although in the latter case this did not happen. Thus, there is a logical connection from the distinction between Law and Grace to the antithesis between merit and grace. In other words, the Schoolmen fail to grasp justification by faith alone apart from good works since they do not make a legitimate distinction between Law and Grace along with the antithesis between merit and grace. For an incisive discussion into the problem of merit in Roman Catholic theology and the Reformers' reaction to it, see Sproul, *Faith Alone*, 135-51. Here, Sproul properly argues that merit and grace are antithetical in the Reformers' discussion on the doctrine of justification and salvation; and this is set over against the Schoolmen's concept of *gracious merit*: "Rome's view of merit and grace contains an unresolved paradox. On the one hand Rome insists on speaking of merit, while on the other she insists that this merit is rooted in grace. The Germans expressed this paradox by coining the term *Gnadenlohn*, 'gracious merit.' ... In common language *merit* is usually understood in distinction from grace. The two are polar opposites. To conjoin them paradoxically in certain contexts into a concept of 'gracious merit' sounds like an oxymoron. The New Testament sharply distinguishes between grace and debt. The Reformers made every effort to keep this distinction clean ... For Rome grace makes human merit possible. For the Reformers grace makes such merit impossible. If we do what we do by grace, then it is seriously misleading to speak of merit at all." Ibid., 148-49. For a further discussion on the concept of merit, its diverse development from the early Church to the Reformation, and its adaptation and refutation, see: Alister McGrath, *Iustitia Dei: A History of the Christian Doctrine of Justification* (Cambridge, London: Cambridge University Press, 1986), 1:109-118; Heiko A. Oberman, "The Tridentine Decree on Justification in the Light of Late Medieval Theology," in *Journal for Theology and the Church 3: Distinctive Protestant and Catholic Themes Revisited*, ed. Robert W. Funk (New York: Harper & Row, 1967), 28-54.

[15] Ibid., 3:16:3.

Thus, in discussing justification by faith, the principles of law and faith are contrasted, without any amalgam, between Law and Gospel. Calvin, in his commentary, states this issue: "The major is proved by the difference in the methods of justification. The law justifies him who fulfills all its precepts, while faith justifies those who are destitute of the merit of works, and who rely on Christ alone. To be justified by our own merit, and to be justified by the grace of another, are two schemes which cannot be reconciled: one of them must be overturned by the other."[16] Calvin goes on to say, "the contradiction between the law and faith lies in the matter of justification."[17] The presupposition of justification by faith alone, through the imputation of Christ's righteousness, is that there is no amalgam between Law and Gospel. To state in another way, we cannot discuss the imputed righteousness of Christ in justification without the theological framework provided by the antithesis between Law and Gospel.

Because of Christ's active and passive obedience, his righteousness is imputed to us apart from good works. The imputation of Christ's righteousness is the ultimate basis of our justification, since Christ was once for all the "atoning sacrifice of sin." Therefore, our righteousness is an alien righteousness which is only in Christ.[18] In this sense, faith is "merely passive" and the "instrumental cause" in our justification, because it is a free gift of God whereby Christ's righteousness is imputed to us.[19] No one, however, is justified by works, because "works righteousness" is possible only in "perfect and complete observance of the law."[20] Good works, in this sense, are only the fruit of faith.[21] Indeed, although believers are justified by faith alone in respect to the principle of the covenant of grace, God requires

---

[16] John Calvin, *Commentaries on the Epistles of Paul to the Galatians*, trans. William Pringle (Edinburgh: Calvin Translation Society, 1843; reprint, Grand Rapids, Michigan: Baker Book House, 1996), 3:11.

[17] Ibid., 3:12

[18] Calvin, *Institutes*, 3.11.19-21, 3.14.10.

[19] Ibid., 3.13.5, 3.14.17.

[20] Ibid., 3.15.1.

[21] cf. W. Stanford Reid, "Justification by Faith According to John Calvin," *Westminster Theological Journal* 42 (1980): 296-307; Calvin, *Institutes*, 3.11.5-20

"uprightness and sanctity of life" for believers admitted to "the fellowship of the covenant."[22]

Union with Christ is the controlling motif of all redemptive blessings, including the blessings given in justification. In this respect, a justified believer is "clothed with Christ's righteousness." Accordingly, believers' good works are acceptable to God although they are imperfect, since they are covered by the perfection of Christ.[23] Moreover, good works in believers will be applied to their heavenly reward by the principle of the adopted sons' right of inheritance as written in Matthew 25:35-37, but their heavenly reward is not by "the merit of works" as the Sophists argue, because it is the outworking of the free covenant of God's mercy. It is the divine promise with respect to good works.[24] Thus, Calvin's understanding of good works, produced in progressive sanctification as the law is applied, provides a concrete biblical theological answer to *antinomianism*. On the other hand, the antithesis between Law and Grace is a definite hermeneutical principle necessary for justification by faith alone, apart from good works, providing an answer to *legalism*.

As we have demonstrated, Calvin's use of the Law and Gospel antithesis was a decisive theological framework used to safeguard justification by faith alone against the background of the medieval Schoolmen's notion of meritorious salvation. In understanding God's redemptive history from a covenantal perspective, hermeneutical principle of Law / Gospel was applied under the rubric of one covenant of grace in the postlapsarian state: "The covenant made with all the patriarchs is so much like ours in substance and reality that the two are actually one and the same. Yet they differ in the mode of dispensation. But because no one can gain a clear understanding from such a statement, a fuller explanation is required if we wish to make any progress."[25] This one covenant of grace was also identified as a "spiritual covenant", covering all of redemptive history since Adam's fall. This covenant continuity provided a theological rationale for standing against the Anabaptists and Servetus. It signified the redemptive spiritual covenant continuity between the Old and New Covenants, in which the believers in the Old Testament as well as

---

[22] Ibid., 3:17:5.
[23] Ibid., 3:17:8.
[24] Ibid., 3:18:1-8.
[25] Ibid., 2.10.2.

those in the New Testament were saved by God's grace in Christ. Once again in Calvin's words:

> But my readers may prefer to have testimonies cited from the Law and the Prophets, to prove to them that, as we have heard from Christ and the apostles, the spiritual covenant was also common to the patriarchs .... Adam, Abel, Noah, Abraham, and the other patriarchs cleaved to God by such illumination of the Word. Therefore I say that without any doubt they entered into God's immortal Kingdom. For theirs was a real participation in God, which cannot be without the blessing of eternal life.[26]

Calvin demonstrates that the *protevangelium* of Genesis 3:15 is the beginning of God's redemptive covenant of grace and this covenant of grace is progressively revealed and unfolded in the Scripture:

> The Lord held to this orderly plan in administering the covenant of his mercy: as the day of full revelation approached with the passing of time, the more he increased each day the brightness of its manifestation. Accordingly, at the beginning when the first promise of salvation was given to Adam [Gen. 3:15] it glowed like a feeble spark. Then, as it was added to, the light grew in fullness, breaking forth increasingly and shedding its radiance more widely.[27]

Calvin made a great theological point when he demonstrated that there is only one covenant of grace which unifies redemptive history. Even the Old Testament believers were justified by faith alone in Christ, in whom they had everlasting hope and spiritual life, while they enjoyed earthly blessings when they faithfully complied with God's law:

> The Old Testament fathers (1) had Christ as pledges of their covenant, and (2) put in him all trust of future blessedness. These I shall not labor to prove because they are less controversial and clearer. Let us, therefore, boldly establish a principle unassailable by any stratagems of the devil: the Old Testament or Covenant that the Lord had made with the Israelites had not been limited to earthly things, but contained a promise of spiritual and eternal life.[28]

---

[26] Ibid., 2.10.7.
[27] Ibid., 2.10.20.
[28] Ibid., 2.10.23.

For several decades, many scholars have argued that there are two traditions of the covenant of grace within the continental Reformation. One was developed by the Rhinelanders such as Zwingli, Bullinger, John Oecolampadius, and Martin Bucer, and the other tradition was forwarded by the Genevan Reformers such as Calvin and Beza. The former has been identified as *bilateral*, and the latter as *unilateral*.[29] However, some, such as Bierma, Karlberg, and Lillback conclude that there is only one covenant tradition, which was *bilateral*, originating with Zwingli in Zürich and developed by the Rhinelanders, especially Bullinger. It was well received by Calvin, and utilized in his covenant theology. In short, Calvin used a bilateral notion of covenant to harmonize double predestination and a *bilateral* covenant of grace.[30] Lillback rightly concludes:

---

[29] Charles S. McCoy and Wayne J. Baker, *Fountainhead of Federalism: Heinrich Bullinger and the Covenant Tradition* (Louisville, Kentucky: Westminster / John Knox Press, 1991); Joseph C. McLelland, "Covenant Theology–A Re-Evaluation," *Canadian Journal of Theology* 3 (1957): 182-88; Jens Møller, "The Beginning of Puritan Covenant Theology," *Journal of Ecclesiastical History* 14 (1963): 46-67; Leonard Trinterud, "The Origins of Puritanism," *Church History* 20 (1951): 37-57.

[30] Lyle D. Bierma, "Federal Theology in the Sixteenth Century: Two Traditions?" *Westminster Theological Journal* 45 (1983): 304-21; Peter A. Lillback, "The Continuing Conundrum: Calvin and The Conditionality of the Covenant," *Westminster Theological Journal* (1994): 42-74. However, the Reformed biblical covenant theologian Geerhardus Vos errs when he says that the covenant idea is not dominant in the theology of Calvin because his theology was deeply rooted in the concept of Trinity rather than that of covenant. In this regard, he argues that the development of the covenant theology of Reformed orthodoxy was influenced by the Rhinelanders instead of Genevan Reformers: "In Calvin, too, mention is frequently made of the covenants. However, his theology was built on the basis of the Trinity, and therefore the covenant concept could not arise as a dominant principle in his case. He is the forerunner of such Reformed theologians who allocate to it a subordinate place as a separate locus. Even his *Geneva Catechism*, where one would most expect this idea to be elaborated, bypasses it. The theologians of Zürich, on the other hand, are to be regarded as the forerunners of federal theology in the narrower sense insofar as the covenant for them becomes the dominant idea for the practice of the Christian life. Both Olevianus and Ursinus, the well-known Heidelberg theologians, stood in the closest connection to the Zürich theologians." Geerhardus Vos, *Redemptive History*

There is no basis for the thesis that pits the Rhineland Reformers, Bullinger and Zwingli, against Calvin in terms of the mutuality and conditionality of the covenant of grace. There clearly is a difference of emphasis and difference of rationale for stating the distinctive doctrines of predestination and covenant in each of these Reformed theologians. But foundationally, all three affirm a conditional, mutual covenant of grace that is worked out in the context of a sovereign predestination that includes reprobation.[31]

Briefly, Calvin's and the Rhinelanders' *bilateral* covenant of grace, the mutuality and conditionality of the covenant, was harmonized splendidly with double predestination, providing a balance between covenant and predestination[32].

While Calvin recognizes one bilateral covenant of grace after the Fall, he stipulates that the Mosaic Law was in a sense "the covenant of law" or the *foedus legale*. But, did Calvin use the term *foedus legale* of the Mosaic Covenant accidentally, or did he intend for a significant theological meaning? Calvin, in a limited sense, regards the Moasic Covenant as a *foedus legale,* contrasting it with the New Covenant. This is because the Mosaic Covenant was an administration of temporary ceremonies and sacrifices which were applied to the earthly nation of Israel. It was called a temporary covenant, whereas the Abrahamic Covenant was an everlasting covenant, finally fulfilled in the New Covenant:

> Here we are to observe how *the covenant of the law compares with the covenant of the gospel, the ministry of Christ with that of Moses* [emphasis mine]. For if the comparison had reference to the substance of the promises, then there would be great disagreement between the Testaments. But since the trend of the argument leads us in another direction, we must follow it to find the truth. Let us then set forth the covenant that he once established as eternal and never-perishing. Its fulfillment, by which it is finally confirmed and ratified, is Christ ... The Old Testament of the Lord was that covenant wrapped up in the shadowy and ineffectual observance of ceremonies and delivered to the

---

and Biblical Interpretation, ed. Richard B. Gaffin, Jr. (Phillipsburg, New Jersey: Presbyterian and Reformed Publishing Company, 1980), 236.

[31] Lillback, "The Continuing Conundrum," 73-4.

[32] Ibid., 58-73; cf. Calvin, *Genesis,* 17:1-27; idem, *Leviticus,* 26:40-3.

Jews; it was temporary because it remained, as it were, in suspense until it might rest upon a firm and substantial confirmation.[33]

Carefully reflecting on Jeremiah 31 and 32, Calvin contrasts the *foedus legale* and the New Covenant because, while the former was temporal, being governed by the principle of works for the Israelites' earthly blessings and curses and signifying the temporal nature of Israel, the latter was an everlasting covenant. In the Mosaic Covenant, the Israelites tasted exile due to their general corporate disobedience, so that the *foedus legale* was void. Based upon the Abrahamic Covenant of promise, however, the Israelites returned to the promised land from the curse of exile:

> We must notice *the contrast between the covenant of the Law, and the covenant of which the Prophet now speaks* [emphasis mine]. He called it in the thirty-first chapter a new covenant, and gave the reason for it, because their fathers had soon fallen away after the Law was proclaimed, and because its doctrine was that of the letter, and deadly, and also fatal. But he now calls it a *perpetual covenant*. That the covenant of the Law was not valid, this was accidental to it; for the Law would remain in force, were we only to keep it; but through men's fault it happened that the covenant of the Law became void and immediately vanished .... We must, at the same time, bear in mind that this covenant peculiarly belongs to the kingdom of Christ. For though it was a part of God's grace, which was manifested in delivering his people from captivity, yet the continued stream of his grace ought to be extended to the coming of Christ. The Prophet then, no doubt, brings Christ before us, together with the new covenant; for without him there is not the least hope that God would make another covenant, as it appears evident from the whole Law and the teaching of the Prophets. Then Christ is here opposed to Moses, and the Gospel to the Law. It hence follows, that the Law was a temporary covenant, for it had no stability, as it was that of the letter; but that the Gospel is a perpetual covenant, for it is inscribed on the heart.[34]

The *foedus legale* was not the means of justification even in the Abrahamic Covenant because Abraham was justified by faith alone, not by works. Faith was imputed to Abram for his justification. In this sense, Abraham's circumcision, as an element of the *foedus legale*,

---

[33] Calvin, *Institutes*, 2.11.4.
[34] Calvin, *Jeremiah*, 32:40.

was not the means of justification, but rather, his circumcision was the sign of the covenant. Calvin's point is that the law cannot be the way of justification in the postlapsarian state:

> I also grant, that Paul, for this reason, contends that works are not meritorious, except under the covenant of the law, of which covenant, circumcision is put as the earnest and the symbol .... Both arguments are therefore of force; first, that the righteousness of Abram cannot be ascribed to the covenant of the law, because it preceded his circumcision; and, secondly, that the righteousness even of the most perfect characters perpetually consists in faith; since Abram, with all the excellency of his virtues, after his daily and even remarkable service of God, was, nevertheless, justified by faith.[35]

The earthly nation of Israel, pointing ultimately to the eternal heaven, was administered by types and figures, and at last abolished by Christ's eternal priesthood in which the law was fulfilled. In this regard, Calvin contrasts the Old and New Covenants: "The second difference between the Old and New Testaments consists in figures: that, in the absence of the reality, it showed but an image and shadow in place of the substance; the New Testament reveals the very substance of truth as present. This difference is mentioned almost wherever the New Testament is contrasted with the Old."[36] Israel's blessings and curses in the Land of Canaan, administered by the Mosaic law, was a mirror and type of the heavenly blessing and eternal curse. On this Calvin states:

> We contend, on the contrary, that, in the earthly possession they enjoyed, they looked, as in a mirror, upon the future inheritance they believed to have been prepared for them in heaven .... He [God] willed that, for the time during which he gave his covenant to the people of Israel in a veiled form, the grace of future and eternal happiness be signified and figured under earthly benefits, the gravity of spiritual death under physical punishments.[37]

Calvin, meanwhile, does not regard the prelapsarian situation as the *foedus naturale*, *foedus legalis* or *foedus operum* Nevertheless,

---

[35] Calvin, *Genesis*, 15:6.
[36] Ibid.
[37] Calvin, *Institutes*, 2.11.1, 3.

he attaches the motif of natural law to it, which was an important step toward the *foedus operum* as developed by Reformed scholastic orthodoxy.[38]

Adam in his original state was waiting for glorious creation eschatology. In doing so, the means of eschatological blessing was the law. In this regard, the principle of law informs "the order of creation" in Calvin's thought.[39] At this point, Rolston fails to see the law as the road to eschatological consummation before the fall, making a polar distinction between Calvin and the Calvinists: "Calvinism failed to understand and retain Calvin's concept of the grace of God as primary even in this primal and general relation between God and man; very soon the principle of it was no longer grace, but law."[40] However, Calvin writes, "In this integrity man by free will had the power, if he so willed, to attain eternal life .... Therefore Adam could have stood if he wished, seeing that he fell solely by his own will. But it was because his will was capable of being bent to one side or the other, and was not given the constancy to persevere, that he fell so easily."[41] Adam would have passed into eschatological life, had he obeyed God's law.[42] Thus, the principle of law was a principle of eschatological glorification in the prelapsarian state. Commenting on Genesis 2:16, Calvin observes that "a law is imposed upon him in token of his subjection; for it would have made no difference to God, if he had eaten indiscriminately of any fruit he pleased. Therefore, the prohibition of one tree was a test of obedience."[43] The law written in man's heart was a rule of life in the Garden of Eden. Calvin writes, "Therefore, abstinence from the fruit of one tree was a kind of first lesson in obedience, that man might know he had a Director and Lord of his life, on whose will he ought to depend, and in whose commands

---

[38] Muller, "The Covenant of Works and the Stability of Divine Law," 88-9.

[39] Karlberg, "Reformed Interpretation of the Mosaic Covenant," 13.

[40] Rolston, *Calvin versus the Westminster Confession*, 36. Likewise, James B. Torrance interprets Calvin the same way as Rolston does: "For Calvin, all God's dealings with men are those of grace, both in Creation and in Redemption. They flow from the loving heart of the Father. The two poles of his thought are grace and glory–from grace to glory." James B. Torrance, *Covenant or Contract?*, 62.

[41] Calvin, *Institutes*, 1.15.8.

[42] Ibid., 3:19.

[43] Calvin, *Genesis*, 2:16.

he ought to acquiesce."[44] Furthermore, Calvin closely correlates the law which governed the prelapsarian state as the law written in men's heart and the moral law, written on the two stone Tables.[45]

B. Caspar Olevianus (1536-1587)

After his dramatic rescue from a river, Caspar Olevianus extensively studied Calvin's works and Reformation theology as he dedicated his life in service to the Kingdom of God. He personally studied theology in Geneva with Calvin, and in Zürich with Peter Martyr Vermigli and Heinrich Bullinger.[46] In this regard, it is not surprising that Olevianus developed Calvin's and Bullinger's *bilateral* covenant of grace, designating the prelapsarian state as the *foedus creationis, primum foedus* and the *foedus naturale,* and using his contemporary Zachary Ursinus' idea of the *foedus naturale* and the *foedus in creatione* which was employed in his *magnum opus, Summa Theologiae,* in 1584.[47]

Like Calvin and the Rhinelanders, Olevianus conceives all redemptive history covenantally, beginning with the *protevangelium* in Genesis 3:15, and embraces both the Old and New Covenants, qualifying them as one covenant of grace in which all believers are justified and saved by God's redemptive grace through one Mediator,

---

[44] Ibid.

[45] Calvin, *Institutes,* 2.8.1, 4.20.16.; cf., Karlberg, "Reformed Interpretation of the Mosaic Covenant," 13.

[46] Lyle D. Bierma, "The Covenant Theology of Caspar Olevian" (Ph.D. diss., Duke University, 1980), 2-3.

[47] Zacharius Ursinus, *"Summa Theologiae,"* in *Der Heidelberg Kathechismus,* ed. August Lang (Leipzig, 1907; Darmstadt: Wissenschaftliche Buchgesellschaft, 1967), Q.36, Q.135. Detailed discussion of Ursinus' covenant theology and his contribution to Reformed covenant theology can be seen in Bierma, "Covenant Theology," 77-90; Lillback, "Ursinus' Development," 247-88. Geerhardus Vos states that Ursinus, the contemporary of Olevianus, in his Larger Catechism develops the distinction between the covenants of works and grace, identifying it covenantally with the antithesis between the Law and the Gospel, and applies the law as the means of progressive sanctification: "The contrast of law and gospel is brought to bear on the contrast between the covenant of works and the covenant of grace ... Also the law is considered as a rule of life for those who stand in a covenantal relation to God, those who are already in the covenant." Vos, *Redemptive History,* 237.

Christ Jesus.[48] The covenantal promise, made to Adam and Eve by God's grace through Christ Jesus, was the same in substance in the Abrahamic Covenant, except for a change in the *forma foederis gratuiti*.[49] Distinct to Olevianus' thought is his portrayal of the New Covenant administration from the perspective of "the Kingdom of Christ," "the Kingdom of God, and the Kingdom of Heaven," in which all the benefits of salvation are received in Christ, the ultimate King, against the background of the Kingdom of darkness.[50] Olevianus confirms the mutuality and conditionality of the covenant of grace while informing that God sovereignly initiates and fulfills the requirements of the covenant through Christ, and all this is based upon God's free grace. The covenantal blessings, however, are contingent on our faith and obedience. Nevertheless, the fulfillment and benefits of the conditions of the covenant are God's free gift. This *bilateral* covenant of grace does not jeopardize the Gospel of grace, namely justification by faith alone, although the justified person will practice the Christian life by applying God's law in his life through the outworking power of the Holy Spirit.[51]

While Olevianus understood all of redemptive history as one covenant of grace, signifying salvation by God's grace alone in the blood of Christ, he identifies the Mosaic Covenant as the *foedus legale* and as the inscripturation of the norm of eternal righteousness (*aeterna norma iustitiae*). The Mosaic Covenant is characterized as the inscripturated reinstatement of the *foedus creationis* in which God required perfect obedience to the Law (*perfecte obedientiam Legi*) for passage into glorious eschatological life.[52] Principally, God required,

---

[48] Caspar Olevianus, *De Substantia Foederis Gratuiti inter Deum et Electos*, Geneva, 1585, 295; Ibid., 231.

[49] Ibid., 230.

[50] Caspar Olevianus, *An Exposition of the Symbole of the Apostles*, trans. John Fielde (London: H. Middleton, 1581), 43-8.

[51] See Lyle D. Bierma, "The Covenant Theology of Caspar Olevian" (Ph.D. diss., Duke University, 1980), 119-24.

[52] Bierma in his dissertation argues that Olevianus' *foedus creationis* does not include the principle of eschatological life and reality and "the promise of eternal life as the reward of obedience." Ibid., 176-77. Murray, however, correctly interprets the eschatological goal in Olevianus' *foedus creationis*: "After the pattern of what we find in Calvin, Olevianus speaks of the legal covenant as the eternal rule of righteousness to which man is obligated and to which is annexed the promise of life on the fulfillment of perfect obedience

in the *foedus legale,* perfect obedience to the law as the standard of everlasting life (*vita aeterna*). Therefore, either life or curse would be granted according to their perfect obedience or transgression of the law, respectively.[53] The designation of the *foedus legale* in the Mosaic Covenant establishes an antithesis between the principles of the Law and Gospel. The Mosaic Covenant as the *foedus legale,* reveals the principle of law and condemns human sins. But, when we are in the principle of faith, the condemnatory function of the *foedus legale* is canceled because we are in the promise of the gracious covenant *per Christum.*[54] The promised land of Canaan typified God's covenantal promise as the Israelites' eternal, spiritual, heavenly blessing. The sacrificed animals in the earthly Kingdom of Israel were for the atonement of sins and prefigured Jesus Christ, who would come as Messiah as the once for all sacrifice.[55]

Olevianus uses the terms *foedus creationis, foedus primum, foedus naturale* and *ius creationis,* in referring to the Adamic prelapsarian state. This original covenantal arrangement signifies that man as the *imago Dei* had union and communion with God. God required conformity to righteousness and holiness in his original covenant with man due to the creation of man as the *imago Dei*. Through the internal *imago Dei* and God's revelation, God required continuing obedience for honor and glorification.[56] However, Adam broke God's law, or the *foedus creationis* through Satan's temptation. But, the incarnated Christ fulfilled the requirement of the *foedus creationis* through his atoning sacrifice, which was the foundation of the *foedus gratiae,* and restored the *imago Dei* .[57] Thus, we may consider Olevianus as the forerunner of the antithesis between the covenants of works and grace hermeneutics, because he understood creation, fall and redemption covenantally and correctly identified the historical order of law and grace. The antithetical character between the covenants of works and grace in Olevianus' thought has been expressed well by Geerhardus Vos: "Olevianus speaks of the covenant of law, the covenant of nature,

---

and the threat of death in the event of transgression." Murray, *Covenant Theology*, 201. cf. Karlberg, *The Original State of Adam*, 295-97.

[53] Olevianus, *De Substantia,* 12-13.
[54] Ibid., 90, 252.
[55] Ibid., 65, 115-16.
[56] Ibid., 2, 12-13, 251, 254.
[57] Ibid., 9, 12, 26, 270.

the covenant of creation in contradistinction to the covenant of grace."[58]

Olevianus, in his use of the antithesis between Law and Gospel, measured justification by faith alone against the principle of inherent law devoid of the Gospel:

> The Law is a doctrine that God has implanted in human nature and has repeated and renewed in His commandments. In it He holds before us, as if in a manuscript, what it is we are and are not to do, namely, obey Him perfectly both inwardly and outwardly. He also promises eternal life on the condition that I keep the law perfectly my whole life long. On the other hand, He threatens eternal damnation if I do not keep every provision of the law my whole life long but violate it in one or more of its parts. As God says in Deuteronomy 27[:26] and Galatians 3[:10], "Cursed is everyone who does not continue in all things which are written in the book of the law, to do them." And once the law has been violated, it has no promise that by the help of the law, that is, by works of the law, our sins might be forgiven. Rather, the sentence of condemnation is imposed upon us.
>
> The gospel or good news, however, is a doctrine of which even the wisest knew nothing by nature but which is revealed from heaven. In it God does not demand but rather offers and gives us the righteousness that the law requires. This righteousness is the perfect obedience of the suffering and death of Jesus Christ, through which all sin and damnation, made manifest by the law, is pardoned and washed away (Rom. 5; Gal. 3). Furthermore, God does not give us forgiveness of sins in the gospel on the condition that we keep the law. Rather, even though we never have kept it nor will ever be able to keep it perfectly, He still has forgiven our sins and given us eternal life as an unmerited gift through faith in Jesus Christ. John 1[:17] says, "The law was given through Moses, but grace and truth come through Jesus Christ." And Romans 8[:3,4]: "What for the law was impossible in that it was weak through the flesh, God did by sending His Son in the likeness of sinful flesh, and condemned sin in the flesh through sin, that the righteousness required by the law might be fulfilled in us, who do not walk according to the flesh but according to the Spirit." Finally, Galatians 3:[12-14]: "The law is not of faith but 'The man who does it

---

[58] Vos, *Redemptive History*, 237-8.

shall live by it.' Christ, however, redeemed us from the curse of the law when He became a curse for us.[59]

Olevianus concludes that we are justified "on account of an alien righteousness," as a result of the absolute antithesis between Law and Gospel hermeneutics, and our righteousness is imputed righteousness, a free gift, "through faith." Therefore, God declares that we, as wicked sinful men, are righteous "on account of an alien righteousness" in Christ, not in ourselves.[60] There is no amalgam between Law and Gospel in Olevianus' thought with reference to justification by faith alone. "If we were to mix our own works together with the merits of Christ, we would not have a peaceful conscience. Believers' obedience and good works are still sullied with the stains of the flesh and are imperfect; much that is sinful still clings to their good works."[61] We are clothed with Christ's righteousness though faith, and this is the only basis of our justification. Romans 5 sets forth a parallel between man's disobedience and Christ's perfect obedience. Through "the obedience of the death of Christ," God's righteousness is imputed to us, by which we receive the forgiveness of sins as Christ bestows on us "everlasting righteousness."[62]

Christians inherit "the eternal blessing of the Father and are heirs of "the Kingdom of God" through Jesus Christ's merit alone. In this sense, good works are the evidence of "a true, not a counterfeit faith," demonstrating justification through the imputation of the righteousness of Christ.[63]

C. Robert Rollock (1555-1599)

Robert Rollock, a Scottish theologian, fully developed the antithesis between the covenants of works and grace hermeneutics, and applied it to the doctrine of justification by faith alone. Robert Howie, another Scotsman who had studied under Piscator and Olevianus, was deeply

---

[59] Caspar Olevianus, *A Firm Foundation: An Aid to Interpreting the Heidelberg Catechism*, trans. and ed. Lyle D. Bierma (Grand Rapids, Michigan: Baker Book House, 1995), 9-10.
[60] Ibid., 108-11.
[61] Ibid., 115. cf. Ibid., 116, 119-20.
[62] Caspar Olevianus, *An Exposition of the Symbole of the Apostles*, trans. John Fielde. H. Middleton, 1581, 162-3, 202-3.
[63] Olevianus, *A Firm Foundation*, 84-6. cf. Ibid., 101, 116-117, 121-22.

impressed by Olevianus' "covenant teaching." Howie was one of the major figures who introduced covenant theology to Rollock.[64] Robert Letham summarizes the development of covenant theology in the Reformation context of the sixteenth century.[65] He misunderstands, however, that Rollock's dichotomy between the covenants of works and grace was based on the philosophical adaptation of Ramist dichotomy.[66] In fact, we need to recognize that the dichotomy between the covenants of works and grace is nothing fundamentally different from the antithesis between Law and Grace, which was developed by the Reformers and applied to the doctrine of justification by faith alone. The antithesis between Law and Gospel was similar to the antithesis between the covenants of works and grace. In other words, Rollock's dichotomy between the covenants of works and grace is, at the same time, a covenantal application of the antithesis between Law and Grace.

Rollock published *Tractatus de vocatione efficaci* in 1597 and it was translated into English in 1603. In this representative work, Rollock argues that the relationship between God and man is thoroughly covenantal since "God speaks nothing to man without covenant."[67] Although John Murray as a distinguished systematic theologian in the Westminster School rejects the *foedus operum*, he agrees with the importance of Rollock's role in the development of the doctrine of the covenant of works:

> The concept of legal covenant, found in Calvin but not applied by him to the Adamic administration, is here in Rollock clearly utilized in the interpretation and construction of the Adamic institution. From this time on the rubric of the Covenant of Works is part of the staple of covenant theology.[68]

As such, in Rollock, the covenantal structure is divided in two, namely the covenants of works and grace. The *foedus operum* is a legal

---

[64] Robert Letham, "The *foedus Operum:* Some Factors Accounting for its Development," *The Sixteenth Century Journal* 14/4 (1983): 464.

[65] Ibid., 457-67.

[66] Ibid., 464-67.

[67] Robert Rollock, "A Treatise of our Effectual Calling," in *Select Works of Robert Rollock,* vol. 1 ed. W. M. Gunn (Edinburgh: Woodrow Society, 1849), 33.

[68] Murray, *Covenant Theology*, 202

covenant because God's law was engraved on the human heart at the time of creation. Because man was created as the *imago Dei*, God's law was written in his heart. God characteristically made a covenant with humanity, "wherein he promised him eternal life, under the condition of holy and good works, which should be answerable to the holiness and goodness of their creation, and conformable to his law."[69] Perfect obedience was the condition of the covenant of works because God created man "pure and holy," engraving his law on man's heart, so that good works might operate as the governing principle of the covenant. In the original covenant of works, there is "a double righteousness." One is man's "original justice," bestowed by God as the *imago Dei*; and this is the basic ground of the covenant of works. The second righteousness is *eschatological and forensic righteousness*, which could be fulfilled through good works. Based upon good works, God might declare man's eschatological justification, imputing righteousness based on good works. Then, everlasting life might be given to him.[70] The principle summary of the covenant of works is found in Leviticus 18:5, and it is confirmed by Jesus' discourse with a certain young man: *"Do this, and thou shalt live."* Rollock indicates, however, that glorious eschatological life in the original covenant of works could not be meritorious because man's good works were only his duty as a creature in the presence of the Creator, "as pledges of thankfulness in man to his Creator, for that excellent work of his creation, and to glorify God his Creator."[71]

---

[69] Rollock, *Effectual Calling*, 34. We need to notice here that the antithesis between the covenants of works and grace is in the foreground of Rollock's theology as the result of his articulation of the *foedus operum*. Thus Geerhardus Vos correctly says that "the doctrine of the covenant of works is already notably clearer than with Olevianus." Vos, *Redemptive History*, 239. Vos also correctly remarks that the antithesis between the covenants of works and grace in Rollock is the best way to articulate the idea of the covenant of grace and defines the role of the Mediator: "Rollock already demonstrates how the work of the Mediator with respect to the covenant of grace was nothing but a carrying through in him of the covenant of works broken in Adam." Ibid., 249.

[70] Rollock, *Effectual Calling*, 34-5.

[71] Ibid., 36-7. In this respect, Vos correctly remarks that in Rollock's thought "good works in the first covenant were not strictly meritorious, but were richly rewarded by free favor." Vos, *Redemptive History*, 240.

Jesus Christ as our Mediator satisfied God's justice and wrath, fulfilling the requirement of the broken covenant of works. God's grace and mercy were made possible by the Mediator's shed blood. Because of the sinfulness of man, it must be God's free mercy that is the "first immediate ground of the Covenant of Grace." In other words, Christ's redemptive blood and God's grace in Christ are the foundation of the covenant of grace. The primary promise in the covenant of grace is "the righteousness of our Mediator Jesus Christ" which comes "by faith, and by the imputation of God." Thus, we are justified in the presence of God only by the imputation of the righteousness of Christ. There is another promise in the covenant of grace after justification, namely "inherent justice." This term could be identified as progressive sanctification, which begins in us but will be perfected in heaven. In the covenant of works, compliance to God's law was the condition of eschatological glory and justification. In the covenant of grace, however, faith, given by God's free grace in Christ is the only condition.[72]

Christ as "God and the Son of God" did not stand "under the covenant of works or of grace." Christ as man, however, stood "under the covenant of works in respect of us," and Christ's divine and human nature were united together as our Mediator. Therefore, Christ was under the covenant of works, perfectly fulfilling "the condition of the covenant of works" through his active and passive obedience. Fulfilling the requirements of the covenant of works, Christ satisfied God's justice and wrath for us, meriting God's mercy, "reconciliation, righteousness, and life eternal for us."[73]

Christian "faith and holiness" are incomplete in the present life, so that we need "the terrible glass of the law, and of the covenant of works," ... "as a continual severe schoolmaster, which, ever casting many fears before us, may drive us to the faith of Christ, and to

---

[72] Rollock, *Effectual Calling*, 38-40. It is important to realize that faith as the condition of the covenant of grace does not prejudice the principle of divine grace in salvation and justification in Reformed thought. As such, Murray correctly comments that Rollock does not hinder the principle of grace, while formulating that faith as the condition of the covenant of grace: "The viewpoint here set forth is essentially the same as that of Rollock's predecessors mentioned above, but faith as the condition is brought into clearer focus and its relation to the covenant carefully defined so as in no way to prejudice free mercy and grace." Murray, *Covenant Theology*, 207.

[73] Rollock, *Effectual Calling*, 52-3.

Historical Development

sanctimony of life." The covenant of works as "a condemning tyrant" is canceled for those who are under God's grace in Christ. It is operative, however, as "a schoolmaster to chasten us, and with terrors to drive us unto Christ."[74] Thus, the moral law under the gospel of grace functions to give the Christian rules for "the works of grace, and attendeth not on the covenant of works, but of grace and of the gospel, so far it resteth in use for the servants of Christ."[75] In this respect, Rollock affirms the believers' usage of moral law as against the background of *antinomianism*.

The Reformers' distinction between Law and Gospel grew into a distinction between the covenants of works and grace hermeneutics in Rollock's thought, as seen in his discussion of the second use of the law (*usus elenchticus sive paedagogicus*):

> This is the use then of the covenant of works, to work in us the sense of sin and misery, and to prepare men to receive grace. Therefore the doctrine of the gospel begins with the legal doctrine of works and of the law moral; for the gospel should preach and promise in vain righteousness and life to the believers, if they were not first prepared by feeling their own corruption and miserable condition, to hear and receive grace by the gospel. For this cause Christ himself first (Matt. 5:17, and after) freeth and restoreth the law as pure from the leaven of the Pharisees, expounding the perfection and exact severity thereof, for this very cause, that men by this light of the covenant of works and law moral, might acknowledge how miserable they be by nature, and so might hereby be prepared to embrace the Covenant of Grace. So did Christ prepare that rich young man (which came unto him to be schooled, as he made show) to entertain the Covenant of Grace. *Wilt thou* (saith he)*enter into life? Keep the commandments.* Paul begins his doctrine in the Epistle to the Romans, from the law and covenant of works, and spends near his three first chapters of his Epistle in this doctrine, to this end, that he might conclude all under sin and condemnation, and so might prepare men to the doctrine of grace, which begins, Rom. 3:21. So (Gal. 4:21) he teacheth the Galatians that would be under the law, (as he speaketh,) their miserable servitude, which be in that condition, and how at the last they are cast out of God's kingdom, for this very cause, that the Galatians, renouncing all confidence in that righteousness which is by the law and covenant of

---

[74] Ibid., 48-9.
[75] Ibid., 51.

works, might lay hold on that righteousness which is by faith and grace.[76]

What is pertinent in Rollock's thought is that the antithesis between the covenants of works and grace is a biblical hermeneutical principle which establishes the doctrine of justification by faith alone and salvation by God's grace alone. It excludes good works in the doctrine of justification.

Rollock clarifies that Paul fought against the Jewish concept of legalistic salvation in Romans 1-3 by the antithetical principle between the covenants of works and grace, teaching justification by faith alone:

> I grant he doth expressly fight against that justification and salvation, which is by the works of nature required in the covenant of works, and for the justification of faith, which is required in the Covenant of Grace; but by one and the self-same disputation he concludes both against nature and the covenant of works, and for Christ and for God's grace in him- that is, for the Covenant of Grace.[77]

Accordingly, the Jews' misunderstanding in the Pauline context was "justification and salvation by works, and according to the form of the covenant of works." This is clearly "against the Covenant of Grace, and against justification and salvation of men, which is according to the Covenant of Grace" through God's grace in Christ. The fundamental misconception of the Jews was that they did not explicate the total depravity of man in the postlapsarian state; they did not consider Christ as the Mediator; they did not conceive that "the covenant of works was abolished in Christ"; they did not understand that the covenant of grace was made with man in Christ Jesus; lastly, they did not consider that good works were "duties only, and testimonies of thankfulness, according to the first institution of that covenant" and not meritorious virtue.[78]

At the same time, the Papists misunderstood salvation, interpreting it from a meritorious perspective. They held, "The covenant of works, and the works which proceed from free-will, justification by works of free-will, meritorious also according to the covenant of works; for they say, the ground of every merit, whether it be of congruity or

---

[76] Ibid., 43-4.
[77] Ibid., 56-7.
[78] Ibid., 57.

condignity–to use their own terms–is free-will." This concept of salvation is "against the only Covenant of Grace, against justification which is by Christ only, by the grace of God only, by faith only."[79] Thus, Rollock's distinction between the covenants of works and grace is a decisive hermeneutical reference point to expound upon the sovereign gracious character of salvation against the background of the Jewish and Papist legalistic concepts of salvation in the period of the sixteenth century.

Rollock discerns that God repeated the *foedus operum* to the Israelites on Mount Sinai, giving the law written on two stone tablets. When God made the Sinaitic Covenant, the terms of the covenant could be summarized with *"do these things, and ye shall live."* In this sense, the principle requirement of the covenant of works was "not Christ, nor the grace of God in Christ, but the nature of man in the first creation holy and perfect, endued also with the knowledge of the law."[80] In the Mosaic Covenant, therefore, the *foedus operum* operated in a limited sense because God's law was administered as a pedagogical function, whereas people were saved by God's grace in Christ by the covenant of grace, as administered by types and figures:

> For that the Old Testament did serve specially to prepare men to receive Christ, which in his appointed time was to come. For the law was a schoolmaster unto Christ (Gal. 3:24). Therefore the greatest part of the Old Testament is spent in propounding, repeating, and expounding the covenant of works. And because Christ was not as yet manifested in the flesh, therefore the doctrine of the Covenant of Grace is more sparingly and darkly set forth in it. Finally, as touching the faithful in the Old Testament, which embraced Christ the Mediator of the Covenant of Grace, howsoever then but shadowed before their eyes in types and figures–to them, I say, being justified in him which was to come, and regenerate by his grace.[81]

The *foedus operum* was the means of Adam's justification in the prelapsarian state. After the fall, however, the covenant of works cannot justify men because of their sinfulness which pointedly condemns them (Rom. 8:3). Unbelievers, therefore, feel divine condemnation in themselves because God's law reveals continual

---

[79] Ibid.
[80] Ibid., 34.
[81] Ibid., 46.

condemnation and death. Rollock further argues that "in the elect, the acknowledgment of sin and condemnation which they have by the covenant of works, is unto them a preparative to embrace the Covenant of Grace; but in the reprobate it is the way to extreme desperation."[82] Thus, since the fall, the covenant of works is operative as a schoolmaster or tutor to lead the elect to Christ for everlasting salvation. The same covenant of works condemns the reprobate.

D. The Westminster Confession of Faith (1643-1648)

Geerhardus Vos rightly points out the importance of the Confession, asserting that "the Westminster Confession is the first Reformed confession in which the doctrine of the covenant is not merely brought in from the side, but is placed in the foreground and has been able to permeate at almost every point."[83] The Confession's formula of the bi-polar distinction between the covenants of works and grace and the historical order of *law and grace* have been objects of severe criticism; for the critics believe that the two covenant schemes are not compatible with Calvin's theology in that they reverse the biblical order of *grace and law*. For example, Rolston writes, "All this talk of covenants and orders instituted with Adam has, of course, to be demythologized for the modern Christian. But after the symbols are broken, as well as before, those who take the Westminster Confession seriously will find it has running through it a dualism between law and grace to which Calvin would have strenuously objected."[84] We have

---

[82] Ibid., 47.

[83] Vos, *Redemptive History*, 239. Furthermore, Vos makes an important comment on the major influences behind the Westminster Assembly's covenant theology, namely, John Ball's *Treatise on the Covenant of Grace* (1645) and James Ussher's *Irish Articles* (1615). Ibid., 240-41.

[84] Rolston, *Calvin versus the Westminster Confession*, 37. An identical argument has been found in James B. Torrance, who is perhaps the most acute critic of the covenant theology of the Confession: "This distinction between a covenant of works and a covenant of grace–the covenant of nature and the covenant of the Gospel–was unknown to Calvin and the earlier Reformers, but was expounded in the Westminster Confession of Faith." James B. Torrance, *Covenant Concept*, 235. Torrance asserts that the covenant theology of the Confession teaches that "the two covenants of Works and Grace (Law and Grace) are the two stages by which God executes the eternal decrees and brings the elect to salvation." Torrance argues that this order of *Law and Grace* found in the Confession is totally foreign to both the Bible and Calvin.

proved our thesis, however, that Calvin's thought is fully compatible with the later development of antithesis between the two covenants. As such, the distinction between the covenants of works and grace hermeneutics was used by the Westminster divines in a confessional form. "The first covenant made with man was a covenant of works, wherein life was promised to Adam, and in him to his posterity, upon condition of perfect and personal obedience."[85] In the covenant of works, glorious eschatological life was based upon perfect obedience of the representative head, Adam. He and Eve as the *imago Dei*, "having the law of God written in their hearts" had the capability to fulfill it. The original covenant blessing and curse was dependent upon their obedience to the law: "God gave to Adam a law, as a covenant of works, by which He bound him, and all his posterity, to personal, entire, exact, and perpetual obedience, promised life upon the fulfilling, and threatened death upon the breach of it, and endued him with power and ability to keep it."[86] The Larger and Shorter Catechisms express this original covenant of works as "a covenant of life," based on the condition of perfect obedience.[87] In addition to that, Adam and Eve received "a command, not to eat of the tree of the knowledge of good and evil, which while they kept, they were happy

---

This critical stricture of Torrance and other critics is a fundamental misrepresentation of Reformed theology as a whole in that it rejects the hermeneutical principle of antithesis between the Law and the Gospel in order to confirm justification by faith alone and exclude the legalistic notion of salvation in Medieval theology. Torrance states: "The federal scheme is built thus on the *priority of Law over Grace*. Calvin, in the 1536 edition of his *Institutes*, followed the pattern of Law-Grace in Luther's *Short Catechism*, but subsequently abandoned it as not true to the Bible. Law is the gift of grace, spelling out the obligations of grace and leads to grace–its fulfillment in Christ. That is the inner meaning of *Torah*. That is true not only in the life of Israel, *but in Creation*. So Calvin never taught any 'covenant of works' nor would have. But the English Puritan tradition, in its practical concern to use the law as a schoolmaster to bring men to Christ, universalised from that use of the law ('law-work'), read it back into Creation and into the doctrine of God, and grounded the Two Covenants on it. But this is to go back to the Medieval *ordo salutis* (of Alexander of Hales, etc.) of Man-Law-Sin-Repentance-Grace." idem, *The Westminster Theology*, 48-9.
[85] The Westminster Confession of Faith, 7.2.
[86] Ibid., 19.1.
[87] The Larger Catechism, Q.A. 20. The Shorter Catechism, Q.A. 12.

in their communion with God, and had dominion over the creatures."[88]

Thus, the confession established that the primary principle of the prelapsarian state was governance by the law, or the covenant of works. In this sense, the definition of sin "both original and actual," was identified as "being a transgression of the righteous law of God, and contrary thereunto."[89] The confession, however, is careful in stating that Adam did not stand as the representative head *autonomously*, marking a careful note of the radical distinction between the Creator and creature. Rather, creatures "could never have any fruition of Him [Creator] as their blessedness and reward, but by some voluntary condescension on God's part, which He hath been pleased to express by way of covenant."[90] In other words, the expression of "voluntary condescension on God's part" signifies the distinction between the Creator and creature. Although McWilliams describes the difference between the covenants of works and grace in his analysis of the Confession, he fails to see in it the prelapsarian priority of *law over grace*. He states that "the idea of the covenant of works, at least as it is presented in the *WCF*, does not prioritize law over grace." But, we must understand that the Confession teaches us the law *as the means of the eschatological blessing in the original covenant of works* while at the same time it requires a careful distinction between the Creator and creature.[91]

---

[88] Confession, 4.2.

[89] Ibid., 6.6.

[90] Ibid., 7.1.

[91] David B. McWilliams, "The Covenant Theology of the *Westminster Confession of Faith* and Recent Criticism," *Westminster Theological Journal* 53 (1991): 120.

Although A. A. Hodge accidentally designates the covenant of works as the covenant of grace, in a real sense he makes an absolute distinction between the covenants of works and grace in respect to the two different means of eschatological salvation. A. A. Hodge, *The Confession of Faith*, (1869; reprint, Edinburgh/Carlisle: The Banner of Truth Trust, 1983), 222: "Thus, it is called the 'covenant of works,' because perfect obedience was its condition, and to distinguish it from the covenant of grace, which rests our salvation on a different basis together. It is also called the 'covenant of life,' because life was promised on condition of the obedience. It is also called a 'legal covenant,' because it demanded the literal fulfillment of the claims of the moral law as the condition of God's favour. This covenant was *also in its*

Man, however, broke the original covenant of works, so that God revealed another covenant, namely the covenant of grace:

> Man by his fall having made himself incapable of life by that covenant, the Lord was pleased to make a second, commonly called the covenant of grace: whereby he freely offereth unto sinners life and salvation by Jesus Christ, requiring of them faith in him, that they may be saved; and promising to give unto all those that are ordained unto life his Holy Spirit, to make them willing and able to believe.[92]

God's entering into the covenant of grace was founded upon his election, in that he delivered the elect from sin and misery through a

---

essence a covenant of grace [emphasis mine], in that it graciously promised life in the society of God as the freely-granted reward of an obedience already unconditionally due. Nevertheless it was a covenant of works and of law with respect to its demands and conditions."

Accordingly, A. A. Hodge makes a clear distinction between the covenants of works and grace. In doing so, he asserts that the condition of eschatological life and justification in the original covenant of works was "perfect obedience," whereas faith in Christ is the only condition of the covenant of grace. However, Arminians fail to make a distinction between the two covenants, observing that "perfect obedience" was the condition of the covenant of works, while "faith and evangelical obedience" is the condition of the covenant of grace. In opposition to this view, A. A. Hodge affirms that works and faith are antithetical conditions of eschatological salvation and blessing. Ibid., 121-30.

In this respect, we can conclude that A. A. Hodge designates the covenant of works as *a covenant of grace* in an *accidental sense*. Furthermore, he asserts that Adam's standing as the representative covenantal head was *meritorious*: "That Adam did so act as the representative of his descendants, in such a sense that they were equally interested with himself in *all the merit or the demerit* [my emphasis], the reward or the penalty, attaching to his action during the period of probation, has already been proved to be the doctrine both of our Standards and of Scripture." Ibid., 122.

Accepting the forensic view of justification, A. A. Hodge affirms justification by faith alone, which excludes evangelical obedience. In doing so, he applies the antithesis between the covenants of works and grace along with the antithesis between works and faith. Moreover, justification by faith alone is a common denominator between Lutheran and Reformed Theology, and opposes the Romanists, the Socinians and the Arminians, for whom works and faith are mixed with the doctrine of justification. Ibid., 179-88.

[92] Confession, 7.3.

Redeemer.[93] Christ had to fulfill the broken covenant as the second Adam. This was accomplished as he was "made under the law, and did perfectly fulfill it" through his active and passive obedience to the law, thus satisfying God's justice. And in doing so, he "purchased, not only reconciliation, but an everlasting inheritance in the kingdom of heaven, for all those whom the Father hath given unto Him."[94] The moral law, however, continuously condemns unbelievers' sins, driving them to Christ. But for believers it ceases to be "a covenant of works" and becomes the rule of obedience.[95]

In the postlapsarian state there is only one covenant of grace, the same in substance, but differently administered during the epochs of the law and the gospel. Although the Confession does not designate the Mosaic Covenant as the *foedus legale* or *foedus operum*, it describes well the administration of the earthly nation of Israel through the principle of works, such as sacrifices and types, thus signifying and pointing to Christ Jesus who would come later as the Messiah:

> Under the law it was administered by promises, prophecies, sacrifices, circumcision, the paschal lamb, and other types and ordinances delivered to the people of the Jews, all foresignifying Christ to come; which were, for that time, sufficient and efficacious, through the operation of the Spirit, to instruct and build up the elect in faith in the promised Messiah, by whom they had full remission of sins, and eternal salvation; and is called the Old Testament. Under the gospel, when Christ, the substance, was exhibited, the ordinances in which this covenant is dispensed are the preaching of the Word, and the administration of the sacraments of Baptism and the Lord's Supper: which, though fewer in number, and administered with more simplicity, and less outward glory, yet, in them, it is held forth in more fullness, evidence, and spiritual efficacy, to all nations, both Jew and Gentiles; and is called the New Testament.[96]

In the postlapsarian state, the moral law continues as a "perfect rule of righteousness," and as thus it is eventually delivered on Mount Sinai by God, even as it is neatly summarized by God in the ten

---

[93] Shorter Catechism, Q. A. 20.
[94] Confession, 8.4,5.
[95] Larger Catechism, Q. A. 96-97.
[96] Ibid., 12. 5-6. cf. Larger Catechism, Q. A. 33-35.

commandments. And in addition to the Decalogue, God bestowed ceremonial laws which included diverse typical ordinances such as the types of Christ in the earthly Kingdom of the Israelites. These types were abrogated in the New Covenant. The judicial laws which governed the nation of Israel expired with the termination of the Kingdom of Israel but continue with the implication of "the general equity."[97]

Justification is possible not because of our evangelical obedience, but by the imputation of Christ's obedience and the satisfaction that God has with Christ. Faith, resting on Christ's righteousness, is the only instrument of justification since Christ satisfied God's justice through his active and passive obedience.[98] Thus, justification is "an act of God's free grace unto sinners," pardoning our sins and accepting us as righteous in God's sight, based upon the perfect obedience of Christ. In this way Christ's righteousness is imputed to us.[99] Believers are not "under the law, as a covenant of works" as a means of justification and condemnation because Christ fulfilled the requirement of the covenant of works. Yet it is "a rule of life," and a dictum against antinomianism, namely the third use of law, expecting God's blessings upon "God's approbation of obedience."[100] According to this logic, good works which are manifested in believers' lives by obedience to God's law are "the fruits and evidences of a true and lively faith," and thus serve in the capacity of strengthening their assurance. And of course, the ultimate goal and direction of believers' good works is *soli Deo gloria*.[101] Good works done by believers are imperfect. Nevertheless, God accepts them through Christ. In other words, God looks upon believers' good works in Christ, and rewards them in His eternal heaven despite their weaknesses and imperfections, and this is the covenant hermeneutics' solution to the problem of good works, in opposition to the Romish dogma of *meritum de condigno*.[102] Thus, we see the application of the distinction between the covenants of works and grace in the doctrine of justification by faith alone, which excludes good works as is stated in the Confession.

---

[97] Ibid., 19. 2-4.
[98] Ibid., 11, 1-3.
[99] Larger Catechism, Q. A. 70. cf. Shorter Catechism, Q. A. 33.
[100] Confession, 19.6. cf. Larger Catechism, Q. A. 96.
[101] Confession, 16. 2. cf. Larger Catechism, Q. A. 32, 73.
[102] Confession, 16. 5-6.

E. John Owen (1616-1683)

John Owen, possessor of one of the greatest Puritan minds, developed and expounded his theology on the basis of the distinction between the covenants of works and grace hermeneutics. One common theological denominator of all Puritan theologians was that the "covenant was coming to be recognized as a fundamental theme of redemptive history and biblical doctrine."[103] Owen thinks of God's revelations and unfolding plan under the rubric of the covenants, namely the covenants of works and grace.[104] The distinction between the covenants of works and grace is a decisive hermeneutical foundation for the biblical theological understanding of creation, fall and redemption. Owen identifies the Adamic administration as a covenant because it contains all the elements and nature of a covenant.

> There was an *original covenant* made with Adam, and all mankind in him. The rule of obedience and reward that was between God and him was not expressly called covenant, but it contained the express nature of a covenant; for it was the agreement of God and man concerning obedience and disobedience, rewards and punishments. Where there is a law concerning these things, and an agreement upon it by all parties concerned, there is a formal covenant.[105]

In the original covenant made with Adam, "there was no mediator" for there was no enmity between God and man.[106] In this respect, the original covenant was "immediate" without the introduction of a mediator; and the governing principle of the original covenant[107] was the law. "The law was the moral instrument or rule of the covenant

---

[103] Sinclair B. Ferguson, *John Owen on the Christian Life* (Edinburgh / Carlisle: The Banner of Truth Trust, 1987), 20.

[104] John Owen, *Biblical Theology*. trans. Stephen P. Westcott (Pittsburg, PA: Soli Deo Gloria Publications, 1994), 45. An acute and concise discussion of John Owen's covenant theology respecting the distinction between the covenants of works and grace, is found in Sinclair B. Ferguson, *John Owen*, 20-32.

[105] John Owen, *An Exposition of the Epistle to the Hebrews*. vol. 6. ed. W.H. Goold (London: Johnstone & Hunter, 1855; reprint, Grand Rapids, Michigan: Baker Book House, 1980), 60.

[106] Ibid., 57.

[107] Owen designates this original covenant as the covenant of the law, works, nature, or creation. cf. Owen, *Exposition*, 2:387-8.

that was made immediately between God and man: but it could not continue to be so after the entrance of sin; that is, so as that God might be glorified thereby, in the obedience and reward of men. Wherefore he 'sent his Son in the likeness of sinful flesh;' that is provided a mediator for a new covenant."[108] The promises and rewards of the covenant of works was based on "Do this, and live," so that eschatological life was promised for perfect obedience.[109]

Owen asserts that Adam, as the *imago Dei*, was an upright person who had dominion over God's creatures. The account that God required perfect obedience from Adam "under the penalty of eternal death, and with the promise of eternal reward and felicity, establishes at once for us that Adam was fully furnished with the wisdom and moral light required to enter into this relationship."[110] The covenant of works was "coeval with mankind," and Adam had a duty to obey voluntarily as "a means of signing and sealing it." "The proposed reward of obedience" consisted of experiencing and having God's eternal glory and enjoyment. Owen further states that "such is the voice of the law down to our own times, 'Do this and live.' Neither did God offer any other reward for obedience when the covenant was revealed to Adam."[111] While the governing principle of the covenant of works was the law, the original covenant was based upon God's "infinite holiness, wisdom, righteousness, goodness, and grace."[112] Owen indicates that God annexed "promises and threatenings of reward and punishment; the first of grace, the other of justice." It is important to notice that although the covenant of works was controlled by the principle of the law, the promise of the covenant was derived from God's grace based on the logical distinction between Creator and creature.[113] In this sense, Owen conceives that "every covenant

---

[108] Ibid., 6:59.
[109] Owen, *Works*, 6:473.
[110] Owen, *Biblical Theology*, 24
[111] Ibid., 25.
[112] Owen, *Works*, 6:472.
[113] The distinction between the Creator and creature in the prefall state of Adam can be seen in Owen's penetrating discussion on "the theology of Adam" and is based on natural theology where the law was a controlling motif in the covenant of works and Adam's eschatological life was dependent upon his perfect obedience to the law. Therefore, the covenant of works was based upon "God's gracious will" and "His free choice" because God is absolutely sovereign over all things. Owen, *Biblical Theology*, 20-4. Therefore, based

between God and man must be founded on and resolved into *'promises.'* Hence a promise and a covenant are essentially all one; and God calls an absolute promise, founded on an absolute decree, his covenant, Gen. 9:11."[114] Owen continues:

> The expression of these promises and threatenings in external signs; the first in the tree of life, the latter in that of the knowledge of good and evil. By these did God establish the original law of creation as a covenant, gave it the nature of a covenant. On the part of man, it was required that he accept of this law as the rule of the covenant which God made with him.[115]

By virtue of the covenant of law, Sabbath observation was "prescribed and required, as a token and pledge of God's rest in that covenant, in the performance of the works whereon it was constituted, and of the interest of man in that rest, as also to be a means of entrance into it."[116]

The covenant of works, affirms Owen, is in an absolute sense "the old, or first covenant." "The tree of life, and that of the knowledge of good and evil" were the signs and pledges of the covenant of works.[117] The eschatological life and blessings in the covenant of works was promised upon "personal, perfect, sinless obedience, as the condition of life."[118] After the fall, the covenant of works was canceled as the means of salvation and justification, as it only continually offered "the terror of threatened punishment" for unbelievers.[119]

Meanwhile, Owen carefully explains that there is an absolute antithesis between the covenants of works and grace. Because of the "corruption of natural theology" through Adam's fall, "super natural theology" was inaugurated in the *protevangelium* of Genesis 3:15.

---

upon the distinction between Creator and creature, Owen employs the concept of grace in the original status of Adam and this grace is not soteric: "The creation of man in original righteousness was an effect of divine grace, benignity, and goodness; and the reward of eternal life in the enjoyment of God was of mere sovereign grace." idem, *Works*, 5:277.

[114] Owen, *Exposition*, 6:65.
[115] Ibid., 6:60. cf. Ibid., 2:337-38.
[116] Ibid., 2:385.
[117] Ibid., 6:61.
[118] Ibid., 6:62
[119] Owen, *Biblical Theology*, 45.

Although בְּרִית is used for the first time in Genesis 6:18, Owen asserts that we must identify the Adamic covenantal administration from the beginning of the world. As soon as the covenant of works was broken by Adam, God entered "into a new covenant with fallen Adam" ... "with its own special commands and requirements, backed up by gracious promises." We call this a covenant of grace "because it is graciously grounded in the person of another–the mediator of the covenant." What is pertinent in Owen's double covenant thought is the absolute distinction between the principles of the covenants of works and grace:

> Any other sort of covenant, say one that might be completed by right obedience, and rewarded as a matter of right, would be a covenant of works and not of grace. This covenant was then a matter of pure grace alone, and was founded upon one who bound himself to take on all its conditions. In a word, this new phase of theology consisted of the teachings and promises of the covenant.[120]

Thus, the covenant of grace, inaugurated after Adam's fall, is:

> In opposition unto that of 'works,' which was made with us in Adam; for these two, *grace* and *works*, do divide the ways of our relation unto God, being diametrically opposite, and every way inconsistent, Rom. 11:6. Of this covenant the Lord Christ was the mediator from the foundation of the world, namely, from the giving of the first promise, Rev. 13:8; for it was given on his interposition, and all the benefits of it depended on his future actual mediation.[121]

The New Covenant, as a promise, "was opposed unto the covenant of works; as a covenant, it was opposed unto that of Sinai" since in the Old Covenant God's promise was administered through "types and shadows," whereas in the New Covenant it was "now solemnly sealed, ratified, and confirmed, in the death and resurrection of Christ."[122] The original covenant of works was focused on eschatological life and blessings, founded on "the accomplishment of perfect obedience." Conversely, in the covenant of grace, it is well harmonized between present and eschatological promises: "In the covenant of grace all

---

[120] Ibid., 170-71.
[121] Owen, *Exposition*, 6:63. cf. Ibid., 2:78.
[122] Ibid., 6:64-5.

things are founded in promises of present mercy, and continual supplies of grace, as well as of future blessedness."[123]

The Sinai Covenant, made with "the church of Israel," was "not as absolutely the covenant of grace, but as actually established in the death of Christ, with all the worship that belongs unto it." In this respect, it stands as the continuity of the previous promissory covenant. Thus, the Old Covenant cannot be identified as "the original covenant of works, made with Adam and all mankind in him" because the original covenant of works is a radically different covenant "in the essence and substance of it from the new." The Old and New Covenants, however, were "not indeed two distinct covenants, as unto their essence and substance, but only different administrations of the same covenant."[124] In this regard, Owen argues that "the church under the Old Testament had the same promise of Christ, the same interest in him by faith, remission of sins, reconciliation with God, justification and salvation by the same way and means, that believers have under the new."[125]

Against the background of the old Pelagian contention, Owen affirms that even under the Sinaitic Covenant, men were saved by God's grace in Christ, so that "no man was ever saved but by virtue of the new covenant, and the mediation of Christ therein."[126] God's gracious promise as "the only way and means of salvation of sinners," inaugurated after man's fall, was not abrogated by the introduction of the Sinaitic Covenant since the promise was given for "the whole church." In this sense, The Mosaic Covenant did not disannul the Abrahamic promissory covenant. Rather, the Mosaic Covenant

---

[123] Ibid., 6:68.

[124] Ibid., 6:70.

[125] Ibid., 6:71. Owen observes that the Mosaic Covenant depicts salvation and justification which are based upon God's sovereign grace in Christ Jesus, and which absolutely excludes human merits and good works: "Mosaic theology taught a gratuitous justification and eternal salvation to be realized through the merits and mediation of Messiah. In the passage of time, this great truth became obscured, and then replaced by a soul-destroying error concerning justification through the works of the law and correct observance of ceremonies and rites. The result was that this deluded people, naturally stubborn, became puffed up into a boundless regard for themselves, as if they and they alone could ever be worthy of God's regard." idem, *Biblical Theology*, 487.

[126] Owen, *Exposition*, 6:70.

confirmed that "the commands of the covenant of works, requiring perfect, sinless obedience, under the penalty of the curse" cannot be the way "for sinners to seek life and salvation by." Therefore, the way of salvation and justification through Christ's sacrificial death was "typed by the tabernacle and temple."[127] From a *heilsgeschichte* perspective, Owen believed that the continual efficacy of the Sinaitic Covenant relied on the covenant of grace which was inaugurated after Adam's fall and that this Sinaitic Covenant was essentially patterned after the Abrahamic Covenant.

Owen maintains, however, the legitimate discontinuity between the Old and New Covenant administrations. In the New Covenant:

> Our access now to God is immediate, by Jesus Christ, with liberty and boldness, as we shall afterwards declare. Those under the law were immediately conversant, in their whole worship, outward, typical things,-the tabernacle, the altar, the ark, the mercy-seat, and the like obscure representations of the presence of God. Besides, the manner of the making of the covenant with them at mount Sinai filled them with fear, and brought them into bondage, so as they had comparatively a servile frame of spirit in all their holy worship.[128]

In addition to this, in the Old Covenant, God appointed a large number of "outward rites, ceremonies, and observances" which were legal, administering "severe penalties" in cases of disobedience. However, "the way of worship, ... under the gospel is spiritual, rational, and plainly subservient unto the ends of the covenant itself; so as that the use, ends, benefits, and advantages of it are evident unto all."[129]

Owen admits that in a sense the Sinaitic Covenant was "a distinct covenant, and not a mere administration of the covenant of grace," in contrast to the New Covenant. In this respect, the Sinai covenant "re-enforced, established, and confirmed" the covenant of works, given by God "in the law of creation," although it was not given as a means of salvation and justification on Mount Sinai.[130] In the earthly Kingdom of Israel, "the covenant of the law, or of works," was renovated in a twofold sense, in its "framing and constitution." In this regard, the

---

[127] Ibid., 6:79.
[128] Ibid., 6:73.
[129] Ibid.
[130] Ibid., 6:77.

earthly Kingdom Covenant was the "especial covenant" of the church of Israel because "it was not absolutely a new covenant, nor is it so called, but is everywhere called the old, and hence the Sabbath became peculiarly theirs."[131] The Old Covenant revived the promise and curse of the original covenant of works. The sentence of promise of eternal life on perfect obedience was reinstituted as "that the man which doeth those things shall live by them" in Leviticus 18:5 and Romans 10:5. This is the revival of the covenant of works, summarized in "Do this, and live." On the other hand, the sentence of the curse of the covenant of works was restated as "cursed be he that confirmeth not all the words of this law to do them" in Deuteronomy 27:26 and Galatians 3:10. Because of this principle of works or law, Paul disputes against a background of "justification by the law, or by the works of the law," which were "the works of the first covenant," on which "the promise of life" was dependent.[132] In this sense, "the original covenant of works" was freshly presented to the people of Israel and exemplified, for example, in the precise observation of the seventh day Sabbath. Thus, the strict observation of the seventh day Sabbath by the Israelites was due in respect to the covenant of works:

> Because it was a moral pledge of the rest of God in the first covenant; for this the instructive part of the law of our creation, from God's making the world in six days, and resting on the seventh, did require. The observation of this day, therefore, was still continued among the Israelites, because the first covenant was again presented unto them. But when that covenant was absolutely, and in all respects as a covenant, taken away and disannuled, and that not only as to its formal efficacy, but also as to the manner of the administration of God's covenant with men, as it is under the gospel, there was a necessity that the day of rest should also be changed, as I have more fully showed elsewhere.[133]

Referring to Hebrews 8:13, Owen reckons that there is a radical difference between the Old and New Covenants. The Mosaic Covenant was the *revival* of "the first covenant made with Adam." The Sinaitic Covenant solemnly revived and represented the covenant of works and "its sanction, whereby it had life and power given it to keep the people

---

[131] Ibid., 2:387.
[132] Ibid., 6:78.
[133] Ibid., 2:391-92.

in bondage all their days." In this respect, the New Covenant took away "the legal administration" of the Old Covenant.[134] "Reviving the commands of the covenant of the works, with the sanction of the death," the Sinaitic Covenant "shut up unbelievers," in order that they might not seek salvation by the principle of the covenant of works, convincing them of and condemning them in their sins, and ultimately leading and pointing them to Christ.[135]

In this sense, the Sinaitic Covenant was "a particular, temporary covenant," which applied to the Israelites. Through "the renovation of the rule of the covenant of works," the typical sacrificial system and law were "to be made effectual, namely, in the mediation and sacrifice of Jesus Christ; which was the end of all their ordinances of worship. And the outward law thereof, with the observance of its institution, they looked on as their only relief when they came short of exact and perfect righteousness."[136] The Sinaitic Covenant was "typical, shadowy, and removable" according to Hebrews 10:1 whereas "the new covenant is substantial and permanent, as containing the body, which is Christ." Therefore, the typical ordinances of the Old Covenant were to "typify, shadow, and the heavenly, substantial things of the new covenant, or the Lord Christ and the work of his mediation."[137]

Interpreting Hebrews 8:6, Owen remarks that the Old Covenant or the Sinaitic Covenant is *contrasted* with the New Covenant. The principle of gracious salvation, however, was operative in the Sinaitic Covenant because of the continuing effect of the Abrahamic promissory covenant:

> The *church of Israel* was never absolutely under the power of that covenant as a covenant of life; for them the days of Abraham, the promise was given unto them and their seed. And the apostle proves that no law could afterwards be given, or covenant made, that should disannul that promise, Gal. 3:17. But had they been brought under the old covenant of works, it would have disannulled the promise; for that covenant and the promise are diametrically opposite. And moreover, if they were under that covenant, they were all under the curse, and so perished eternally: which is openly false; for it is testified of them that they pleased God by faith, and so were saved. But it is evident that the

---

[134] Owen, *Works*, 6:471-72.
[135] Owen, *Exposition*, 6:81.
[136] Ibid., 6:86.
[137] Ibid., 6:96.

covenant intended was a covenant wherein the church of Israel walked with God, until such time as this better covenant was solemnly introduced. This is plainly declared in the ensuing context, especially in the close of the chapter, where, speaking of this former covenant, he says, it was 'become old,' and so 'ready to disappear.' Wherefore it is not the covenant of works made with Adam that is intended, when this other is said to be a 'better covenant.'[138]

We have seen that the distinction between the covenants of works and grace is foundational in Owen's covenant hermeneutics. This important theological motif is applied to the doctrine of justification *by faith alone* in Owen's theology. Referring to Romans 11:6, Owen expresses that there is an absolute antithesis between the principles of works and grace in relation to justification and salvation. In "the first covenant of works," man could be justified before God based upon personal obedience and righteousness, i.e. perfect and sinless obedience without any mediator. In the New Covenant of Grace, however, our obedience cannot be the "rule and cause of our acceptance and justification" before God because it absolutely excludes good works as "the cause of our justification." In the New Covenant of Grace, because of the "mediator and surety," who performed the requirements of the law of the covenant of works, our

---

[138] Ibid., 6:62. Owen suggests that the Abrahamic Covenant is a typical example of the covenant of grace, as it is a *bilateral* promissory covenant which is sovereignly executed by the Almighty God in Christ Jesus and in which God requires faithful obedience in response to his sovereign act of free salvation and justification: "There was added to this unfolding of the promise a richer demonstration and clarification of covenant grace. In conversing with Abraham about obedience, not only does the Lord make mention of His covenant. 'I am Almighty God: walk before Me, and be thou perfect' (Genesis 17:1); and then proceeds in solemn dialogue to reiterate the terms on which God covenants, 'I will establish My covenant between Me and thee, and thy seed after thee, in their generations, for an everlasting covenant, to be a God unto thee and thy seed after thee' (Genesis 17:7). In all of this, the very title of GOD ALMIGHTY is directly linked with covenant promise, that all would be eternally well with Abraham and his seed through the promised covenant seed, Christ. The promise of that seed is the foundation of all grace. Having already been promised, it was now specifically and graciously renewed to Abraham that, in and by his seed, God would show Himself to be a merciful, sanctifying, justifying, and saving God, and that freely and unchangeably, requiring in return faith and obedience." idem, *Biblical Theology*, 366.

good works cannot be "the means of justification."[139] Thus, in Owen's discussion of salvation and justification, the principles of works and grace along with the covenants of works and grace are *absolutely antithetical*.[140] In the original covenant of works, there was no surety of the covenant because "God and men were immediate covenanters." In this respect, the covenant of works was a breakable covenant. The New Covenant of Grace, however, is unbreakable because Christ Jesus is "a surety of the covenant" who underwent all the punishments of human sins, thus redeeming sinners through "a propitiatory sacrifice."[141] The radical distinction between the covenants of works and grace safeguards Owen's teaching of justification by faith alone, in which an alien righteousness (*iustitia aliena*) achieved by Christ Jesus is imputed to believers:

> Instead of our own righteousness, we have the 'righteousness of God;' instead of being righteous in ourselves before God, he is 'the Lord our Righteousness.' And nothing but a righteousness of another kind and nature, unto justification before God, could constitute another covenant. Wherefore, the righteousness whereby we are justified is the righteousness of Christ imputed unto us, or we are still under the law, under the covenant of works.[142]

Referring to Romans 2:13 and 10:5, Owen states that man cannot be justified by the law because man cannot fulfill the requirements of the law, since the law will justify man only "by perfect obedience." Therefore, all good works are excluded in man's justification, even when performed by believers after their regeneration.[143] In the covenant of grace, however, God requires obedience and good works from believers as the fruits of justifying faith according to the terms of the *bilateral* covenant. The *bilateral* covenant of grace does not invalidate justification by faith alone, although it concretely requires obedience and good works. In this respect, Owen's thought on the Christian life after one's justification by faith alone accentuates the believers' "practice of holiness and obedience" according to the principle of the covenant:

---

[139] Owen, *Works*, 5:276.
[140] cf. Ibid., 5:277.
[141] Ibid., 5:186-88.
[142] Ibid., 5:277.
[143] Ibid., 5:283-84.

The whole mind is now diverted to the practice of communion with God in Christ, and a diligent and willing offering of obedience to the covenant of grace, which makes men true and wise theologians. To sum up: the man who is wise in the mystery of the gospel is the one who has been brought to understand the counsel, design, love, and grace of God in and through Christ according to the revelation of the Scriptures, and who, by the powerful operation of the Spirit, comes to willingly surrender himself in obedience to God. Certainly this is the practice of holiness and obedience according to the covenant. Without this, anything advanced under the name of 'wisdom' is nothing but an empty name, a shadow, a ghost of wisdom.[144]

F. Francis Turretin (1623-1687)

We may consider the thinking of Francis Turretin "as representative of the more detailed expositions" of covenant theology.[145] Turretin deepened the important hermeneutical principle, namely, a radical distinction between the covenants of works and grace, so as to embrace biblical and redemptive history. He points out that the two covenants are *antithetical*, being "nature and of grace; of works and of faith; legal and evangelical." In the covenant of works, "God as Creator" requires "perfect obedience" from Adam with the promise of *eschatological life and blessings*. In the covenant of grace, however, "God as Father promises salvation in Christ" to the sinful man through the means of faith. The *foedus operum* depends upon man's work and obedience whereas the *foedus gratiae* relies on *sola gratia*. "The former upon a just Creator; the latter upon a merciful Redeemer. The former was made with innocent man without a mediator; the latter was made with fallen man by the intervention of a

---

[144] Owen, *Biblical Theology*, 646. Owen states that Christians as they grow in Christ grow more and more into the *imago Dei*; and that this is characteristically based upon the covenant of grace: "The faithful soul, pouring out without ceasing those prayers which are supplied to us by God's Spirit in gracious provision for our infirmities, enjoys communion with God Himself as he shares in the understanding of the things of the gospel. By practice in prayer, he increases daily in fellowship with his Lord while his soul within him testifies to the extent of its progress, while assurance of saving knowledge waxes stronger daily. Such a soul—such a gospel student— is gradually admitted in the secrets of God's covenant, plighted to the saints in Christ Jesus, while all the time it is growing more and more into the image of Him who is our Head and is Lord of all." Ibid., 702.

[145] Murray, *Covenant Theology*, 203.

mediator."[146] Thus, Turretin asserts that the eschatological justification, life and glory of the prelapsarian state of man was dependent upon man's perfect obedience according to the terms of the covenant.[147] "Do this and live" was the principle of the promise of the covenant of works while "cursed is he who continueth not" was the principle of the curse of the original covenant.[148] Against Episcopius and the Remonstrants who rejected the covenant of works between God and Adam, Turretin affirms the covenant of works upon sound biblical and exegetical grounds.[149]

The distinction between the covenants of works and grace, as a hermeneutical reference point, was a decisive apologetical tool for Turretin to fight back against any misconstrued theology within the seventeenth century continental theological context. Indeed, Socinians and Amyraldians denied that the reward and promise of the covenant of works was *eschatological heavenly glory and life*; they exclusively limited it to the earthly life and paradise since they limited "the promise of eternal life to the blessings of the New Testament." Turretin, however, affirms that the promise of the covenant of works according to Leviticus 18:5; Matthew 19:16, 17 and Romans 7:10 was "the promise of heavenly and eternal life." The eschatological understanding of the prelapsarian state, argues Turretin, was of the Reformed tradition and consistent with Calvin's interpretation of Genesis 2:17. Turretin proves the eschatological character of the

---

[146] Francis Turretin, *Institutes of Elenctic Theology*. vol. 1. trans. George Musgrave Giger and ed. James T. Dennison, Jr. (Phillipsburg, New Jersey: Presbyterian and Reformed Publishing Company, 1992), 575.

[147] Turretin designates this original covenant as the covenant of nature, works and law: "The covenant of nature is that which God the Creator made with innocent man as his creature, concerning the giving of eternal happiness and life under the condition of perfect and personal obedience .... It is also called 'legal' because the condition on man's part was the observation of the law of nature engraved within him; and of 'works' because it depended upon works or his proper obedience." Ibid. On another occasion, he designates it as "the covenant of friendship" because the original covenant was ratified without mediator between God and man. Francis Turretin, *Institutes of Elenctic Theology*. vol. 2. trans. George Musgrave Giger and ed. James T. Dennison, Jr. (Phillipsburg, New Jersey: Presbyterian and Reformed Publishing Company, 1994), 190.

[148] Ibid., 2:174.

[149] Ibid., 1:575-76.

promise of the covenant of works through the distinctions and comparisons between the covenants of works and grace:

> Christ alone gives us promises of eternal life in the state of sin. Yet in the state of nature, Adam might have had them by his own obedience, according to God's pact ...The covenant of works promises life only to the man perfectly just and deserving; but the covenant of grace promises not only life, but also salvation to man altogether undeserving and unworthy (namely to the sinner). Although this covenant of nature was without a mediator, still no less could it promise and confer upon Adam (persevering) heavenly life.[150]

In the covenant of works, Adam was the representative covenantal head of all mankind. "As the first covenant had been made with Adam and in Adam with his whole posterity-which pleases many because the promises are said to have been made to him (Gal. 3:16) and because, as the head and prince of his people, he holds the first place among all, so that nothing can be obtained except in him and from him."[151] In this respect, the covenant of works was "*universal*" because it was "made with all men in Adam," whereas the covenant of grace is "*particular*" because it was "made with the elect alone and those to be saved in Christ."[152]

In Turretin's mind, it is important to see a historical order, namely, *law and grace* according to the historical order of the covenants of works and grace:

> As to order, the covenant of works precedes and the covenant of grace follows. From this to that, there is granted an appeal from the throne of justice to the throne of mercy. Hence the violator of the covenant of grace has no further remedy or hope of pardon because there is no other covenant by which he can be reconciled to God. On this account, the sin against the Holy Ghost is unpardonable because it is committed against the covenant of grace.[153]

There is a twofold sanction of the covenant of nature (*foedus naturale*), namely, the eschatological blessing and curse: "It consisted both in the promise of reward and gain and in the threatening of

---

[150] Ibid., 1:583-85.
[151] Ibid., 2:177.
[152] Ibid., 2:191.
[153] Ibid.

punishment. The promise was of the highest happiness (of eternal life) to be passed not on earth but in heaven. The threatening was of death and whatever in Scripture comes under the name of death to express punishment of all kinds."[154]

Due to the distinction between the Creator and creature, Turretin asserts that the covenant of nature was "gratuitous, as depending upon a pact or gratuitous promise," from God's perspective.[155] Based upon this careful analysis, Turretin designates the benefits of the original covenant as *merit*, in a limited sense, to be applied if Adam had fully obeyed the terms of the covenant, whereas in the covenant of grace, man's justification and eschatological life depends absolutely upon the *meritum Christi*:

> If therefore upright man in that state had obtained this *merit*, it must not be understood properly and rigorously. Since man has all things from and owes all to God, he can seek from nothing as his own by right, nor can God be a debtor to him–not by condignity of work and from its intrinsic value ..., but from the pact and the liberal promise of God ... and in comparison with the covenant of grace (which rests upon the sole merit of Christ, by which he acquired for us the right to life). However, this demanded antecedently a proper and personal obedience by which he obtained both his own justification before God and life, as the stipulated reward of his labors.[156]

---

[154] Ibid., 1:578.

[155] Ibid.

[156] Ibid. Turretin is very careful in saying that the prefall state was *meritorious* and that this notion was drawn from the distinction between the principles of the covenants of works and grace: "In the end, the legal condition has the relation of a meritorious cause (at least congruously and improperly) of the promised thing (namely, of life)–'Do this and live.' Thus life is granted to him because he has done and on account of his obedience; but the evangelical condition cannot properly be called the cause of salvation, much less merit, because it is the pure gift (χάρισμα) of God (Rom. 6:23). It may be called an instrument by which the thing promised is apprehended (Acts 26:18; Rom. 5:17) and without which it cannot be obtained (Heb. 11:6)." Ibid., 2:186. "Faith accepts by a reception of the promises; obedience keeps by a fulfillment of the commands. 'Be ye holy, for I am holy.' And in this way legal and evangelical obedience are not confounded because the legal is prescribed for the *meriting of life* [emphasis mine], the evangelical, however, only for the possession of it. The former precedes as the cause of life ('Do this and thou shalt live'); the latter follows as its fruit, not that you may live but because

The tree of the knowledge of good and evil in Genesis 2:16-17 was "the special law," given to Adam. If Adam had fully obeyed it, he would have proved that he had recognized God's dominion and subjected his own will to God's "will and voice." Meanwhile, "the tree of life" was "a sacrament and symbol of the immortality" which could have been granted to Adam if he had perfectly obeyed God's law. With respect to *eschatological life*, it was a definitive sign of glorious life to "be passed in paradise and to be changed afterwards" into an eschatological life, if he had continuously obeyed. Meanwhile, in relation to the covenant of grace, "the tree of life" was "an illustrious type" of the eschatological heavenly blessings. "Also a type of Christ himself who acquired and confers it upon us and who is therefore called 'the tree of life in the midst of the paradise of God' (Rev. 2:7); 'the tree of life yielding her fruit twelve times every month, whose leaves are for the healing of the nations' (Rev. 22:2)."[157] Turretin states that the two trees in paradise are mysterious, for the tree of the knowledge of good and evil was "a sacrament of trial," prescribing man's duty while the tree of life was "a symbol of the reward." In this respect, the distinction between Law and Gospel was mysteriously manifested in the "double symbol" at the Garden of Eden. "For the law (as the tree of the knowledge of good and evil) is given to us as a trial of obedience and by sin (no less than that) is made the occasion of death and the minister of condemnation. The gospel, however, is the saving and quickening tree of life because it is 'the word of life' (Jn. 6:68)."[158]

Standing in the tradition of Reformed covenant thought, Turretin affirms that the *foedus gratiae*[159] was inaugurated in the so called

---

you live. The former is not admitted unless it is perfect and absolute; the latter is admitted even if imperfect, provided it be sincere. That is only commanded as man's duty; this is also promised and given as the gift of God." Ibid., 2:189. On another occasion, however, Turretin, in a strict sense, rejects the covenant of works as meritorious: "It is gratuitously and falsely supposed that the promises of God are regulated according to the proportion of our merit." Ibid., 1:585. "For if innocent man could merit nothing with God, how much less the guilty sinner?" Ibid., 2:175.

[157] Ibid., 1:578-81.

[158] Ibid., 1:582.

[159] Turretin also designates the covenant of grace as "the covenant of reconciliation" because "a mediator was necessarily required to make peace and reconcile men to God and God to men." Ibid., 2:190.

protevangelium, saying that it contains "the bare promise made to Adam" in Genesis 3:15. Thus, the Old Testament should not be restricted only to the typological promise of the promised land. Rather, in the progressive revelation of the covenant of grace, God revealed "the complete nature of the Old Testament," administering the heart of the gospel through types and ceremonial laws in the promised land and, even, from the beginning of the world.

In the covenant of grace, Christ perfectly fulfilled the requirement of the covenant as "a full consummation of the covenant of grace." Turretin clearly believes that the covenant of grace is *bilateral* since God demands "faith in the promises and obedience to his commands" as the believer's duties, and in response he promises the covenant blessings. "On God's part, the promised blessings; on the part of men, the duties prescribed to them. Both are set forth in general or in particular. In general, they are contained in the formula of the covenant in which God promises to be our God and demands that we should be his people."[160] The statement "I will be their God, and they shall be my people" in Jeremiah 31:33 designates the *bilateral* character of the covenant of grace:

> Here the relation between God and us is designated, implying a mutual exchange of benefits and duties, so that if God is our husband, we should be his chaste and faithful spouse; if he is our Father, we should be sons; if a King and Redeemer, we should be his peculiar people who live as the ransomed of the Lord. However as all God's blessings towards us are comprehended in this one promise alone, so all man's duties towards God are prescribed in this single condition.[161]

Of those who belong to the covenant of grace, God requires faithful worship and obedience along with faith and repentance. Thus, "walk before me, and be thou perfect" in Genesis 17:1 is the representative command of "the evangelical law."[162]

Over against "the Socinians, Anabaptists and Remonstrants" who rejected that "the fathers of the Old Testament" were saved by God's grace through faith in Christ who would come later, Turretin affirms that believers in the Old Testament were saved by looking to Christ

---

[160] Ibid., 2:179.
[161] Ibid., 2:183.
[162] Ibid., 2:184.

and "the hope of his coming." The Socinians, Anabaptists, and Remonstrants, on the other hand, limited the blessings of the Old Covenant to "earthly happiness," to "only temporal goods and earthly promises;" thus they radically exclude *the eschatological heavenly blessings*.[163] Turretin, however, affirms the unity of the covenant of grace between the Old and New Covenants, asserting that:

> Christ was not only predicted but also promised to the fathers and by his grace they were saved under the Old Testament no less than we are saved under the New; nor was any other name given under heaven even from the beginning from which salvation could be hoped for (Acts 4:12) and that too according to the inviolable promise of the gratuitous covenant.[164]

The covenant of grace is not conditional since it is entirely gratuitous, depending on God's absolute will and excluding human merit; and salvation is based upon God's sacred faithfulness, Christ's infinite merit and "the righteousness of Christ alone" (*sola iustitia Christi*). From another perspective, however, faith as "the instrumental cause," can be the condition of the covenant, "uniting man to Christ and so bringing him into the fellowship of the covenant" as it is described in John 3:16,36; Romans 10:9; and Mark 16:16. Furthermore, "faith and repentance" are the conditions of the covenant , related not to the *means* of "the promises of the covenant but to the *end*." [165] The *bilateral* character of the covenant of grace, however, does not vitiate the principle of the Gospel of justification *by faith alone* in Turretin's theology, for he is careful not to mix the Law and Gospel in his discussion of justification and salvation:

> Although the covenant of grace be conditional, the promises of the law and the gospel are not therefore to be confounded. There always remains a manifold difference: (1) in the matter, because the legal condition is an entire and perfect obedience to the law (Rom. 10:5), but the evangelical is faith (Rom. 10:9; Jn. 3:16) - not perfect and free from all blemish, but living and sincere (1 Tim. 1:5; Jam. 2:14).[166]

---

[163] Ibid., 2:192-93.
[164] Ibid., 2:194.
[165] Ibid., 2:185-86.
[166] Ibid., 2:186.

The Mosaic Covenant belongs to the covenant of grace in the light of redemptive historical *continuity*, and the covenant of grace is first revealed in the *protevangelium*, and then progressively unfolded in successive covenantal epochs, such as from Adam to Abraham and from Abraham to Moses. "Then was the Israelite republic reared by Moses for whose benefit the covenant of grace had not only the relation of promise and covenant, but a more perfect and testamentary form which was ratified by the blood of victims (Ex. 24:6-8), as the symbol of the blood of Christ (Mt. 26:28)."[167] The Mosaic Covenant, "from solemn confirmation and ratification alluded to in Ex. 24:8,9 where mention is made of the sprinkling of the blood of victims and the approach of the elders to God," anticipates the covenant of grace. Although principally the Mosaic Covenant reveals the *foedus operum*, it is impossible to fulfill the requirement of the law since man is totally corrupt. Therefore, in this respect, it belongs to the *foedus gratiae*. Thus, Turretin argues that it is not:

> The decalogue had nothing in common with the covenant of grace and was nothing else than the covenant of works itself, renewed for the purpose of recalling the people to it, that they might seek life from it. For since the law was made weak in the flesh after sin (Rom. 8:3), the way to life by it became altogether impossible for man. Hence Paul testifies that the law was not given that it might give life (Gal. 3:21) or that the promise first given might be abrogated (Gal. 3:17), but 'on account of transgressions,' that sin being uncovered by it, the necessity of grace might be the more clearly seen.[168]

The decalogue has two functions. One is as a schoolmaster who condemns human sins, leading men into Christ, structurally summarized as an absolute distinction between *law and grace*, without amalgam between the two and properly understood as the *foedus operum*. The other is the rule of the Christian life, which is a good indication of the *bilateral* character of the covenant of grace:

> Thus it is rightly said that the decalogue belonged to the covenant of grace ... Both antecedently as a schoolmaster, by convincing of sin, bringing to it men smitten with fear of death and despairing of

---

[167] Ibid., 2:224.
[168] Ibid., 2:226.

themselves; and consequently as a rule, prescribing the measure of obedience and holiness demanded by God in the covenant of grace.[169]

Thus in a sense, the Mosaic Covenant belongs to the covenant of grace which is "evangelical," for it administers heavenly blessings and salvation through ceremonial laws which are the types and shadows of Christ Jesus.[170]

John Cameron and Amyrald propagated the threefold covenant thesis, identifying the covenants of works and grace and citing the Mosaic Covenant as a third *legal covenant*. But in opposition to this, Turretin affirms that there are only two covenants, the covenants of works and grace, which cover the whole biblical history of creation, fall and redemption:

> However, we recognize only two covenants mutually distinct in species (to wit, the covenant of works, which promises life to the doer; and the covenant of grace, which promises salvation to believers). Although we confess that the Sinaitic covenant as to mode of dispensation was different from both, still as to substance and species we deny that it is constituted a third covenant and hold that it was nothing else than a new economy of the covenant of grace. It was really the same with the covenant made with Abraham, but different as to accidents and circumstances (to wit, clothed as to external dispensation with the form of a covenant of works through the harsh promulgation of the law; not indeed with that design, so that a covenant of works might again be demanded with the sinner [for this was impossible], but that a daily recollection and reproaching of the violated covenant of works might be made; thus the Israelites felt their sin and the curse of God besides hanging over them and acknowledged the impossibility of a legal righteousness; driven away from that hope, they so much the more ardently thirsted for the righteousness of redemption and were led along by the hand to Christ). Hence in it there was a mixture of the law and the gospel: the former to strike into sinners and press upon the neck of the stiff-necked (*schlerotragelou*) people; the latter to lift up and console the conscience contrite and overpowered by a sense of sin.[171]

---

[169] Ibid.
[170] Ibid., 2:227.
[171] Ibid., 2:262-63.

"Under the external dispensation" of the Mosaic Covenant, the internal blessing embraced all "the substance of the covenant of grace and of the gospel promise." It included Christ's redemptive blessings, wonderfully manifested in Christ's redemptive sacrifice and glory. Thus, God administered the covenant of grace in the Mosaic Covenant through temporal and spiritual blessings:

> Temporal, as the inheritance of the land of Canaan and the earthly blessings (given in detail, Dt. 28) which were promised in it to the faithful worshippers of God; less principally and secondarily on account of the disposition of the Israelite people (still children and more affected by carnal than spiritual things); but spiritual primarily and principally, as absolutely necessary to salvation.[172]

Meanwhile, the Mosaic Covenant, in an accidental or supplemental sense, is the *foedus operum*, since the decalogue, received on Mount Sinai, reveals the principle of the law, which radically condemns human sins and ultimately points to redemptive heavenly eschatological blessings through the temporal blessings of the promised land. The curse in the land of Canaan pointed to eschatological judgment for unbelievers. Moreover, Paul makes a diametric distinction between "the law of works" and "the law of faith" in his thought, on the principle of the decalogue in contrast to that of the promise of grace:

> But in the decalogue, no mention either of a surety or promise of salvation to be given to sinners occurs; but a bare promise of life to those doing and a threatening of death to transgressors. Hence the law of works (comprised in the decalogue) is everywhere contradistinguished by Paul from the law of faith and the promise of grace (Rom. 3:27; Gal. 3:17, 18) for as the law is not of faith (Gal. 3:12), so neither is faith of the law. So great is the contrariety between these two means that they are wholly incompatible (*asystata*) with each other.[173]

The administration of the law in the Mosaic Covenant reveals the perfect requirements of the law, decisively condemning human sins and regarding us as the "children of death." In doing so, Turretin

---

[172] Ibid., 2:230.
[173] Ibid., 2:226.

affirms that the Mosaic Covenant is a legal covenant, namely, the covenant of works:

> The one legal, more severe, through which by a new promulgation of the law and of the covenant of works, with an intolerable yoke of ceremonies, he wished to set forth what men owed and what was to be expected by them on account of duty performed. In this respect, the law is called the letter that kills (2 Cor. 3:6) and the handwriting which was contrary to us (Col. 2:14), because by it men professed themselves guilty and children of death, the declaration being written by their own blood in circumcision and by the blood of victims.[174]

The external administration of the entire law in the Mosaic economy belongs to the covenant of works. In its administration, God pointed to heavenly blessing and rest through the blessings of Israel in the land of Canaan:

> The matter of that external economy was the threefold law-moral, ceremonial and forensic ... The form was the pact added to that external dispensation, which on the part of God was the promise of the land of Canaan and of rest and happiness in it; and, under the image of each, of heaven and the rest (σαββατισμός) in him (Heb. 4:3,9); or of eternal life according to the clause, 'Do this and live.' On the part of the people, it was a stipulation of obedience to the whole law or righteousness both perfect (Dt. 27:26; Gal. 3:10) and personal and justification by it (Rom. 2:13). But this stipulation in the Israelite covenant was only *accidental* [my emphasis], since it was added only in order that man by its weakness (*adynamian*) might be led to reject his own righteousness and to embrace another's, latent under the law.[175]

Turretin applies an important hermeneutical reference point, namely, the absolute distinction between the covenants of works and grace to the doctrine of justification by faith alone, which radically excludes good works. In this respect, the roads to justification between the covenants of works and grace are *absolutely antithetical*. As such, the legal covenant with Adam required a perfect obedience of the law, while only faith in Christ is the instrument of justification in the covenant of grace:

---

[174] Ibid., 2:227.
[175] Ibid.

For as there are two covenants which God willed to make with men–the one legal and the other of grace–so also there is a twofold righteousness-legal and evangelical. Accordingly there is also a double justification or a double method of standing before God in judgment–legal and evangelical. The former consists in one's obedience or a perfect conformity with the law, which is in him who is to be justified; the latter in another's obedience or a perfect observance of the law, which is rendered by a surety in the place of him who is to be justified-the former in us, the latter in Christ. Concerning the first, Paul says, 'Not the hearers, but the doers of the law shall be justified' (Rom. 2:13); and 'Moses describeth the righteousness which is of the law. That the man which doeth those things shall live by them' (Rom. 10:5). Concerning the other, he says, 'The gospel is the power of God unto salvation to every one that believeth, for therein is the righteousness of God revealed from faith to faith: as it is written, The just shall live by faith' (Rom. 1:16-17); and 'Being justified freely by his grace through the redemption that is in Christ Jesus' (Rom. 3:24). Concerning both, he says, 'That I may be found in Christ, not having my own righteousness, which is of the law, but that which is through the faith of Christ' (Phil. 3:9; cf. also Rom. 9:30,31). Hence a twofold justification flows: one in the legal covenant by one's own righteousness according to the clause, 'Do this and live'; the other in the covenant of grace, by another's righteousness (Christ's) imputed to us and apprehended by faith according to the clause, 'Believe and thou shalt be saved.' Each demands a perfect righteousness. The former requires it in the man to be justified, but the latter admits the vicarious righteousness of a surety. The former could have place in a state of innocence, if Adam had remained in innocence. But because after sin it became impossible to man, we must fly to the other (i.e, the gospel), which is founded upon the righteousness of Christ.[176]

Man is justified by faith alone, excluding good works since it is obvious that there are only two modes of justification; "by faith and by works." The latter, however, must be excluded in the covenant of grace. Thus, Turretin, citing Romans 3:28; Galatians 2:16; and Ephesians 2:8, affirms that Paul eagerly emphasizes "an antithesis between faith and works" in the matter of justification.[177] Because of the antithetical character between works and faith, Turretin argues that Paul excludes good works in justification. Hence Turretin confirms that "the thing itself proves this also for he antithetically

---

[176] Ibid., 2:637.
[177] Ibid., 2:677

opposes faith to works in this matter. Hence it appears that all works entirely of whatsoever kind and not some particular ones are excluded."[178] As a matter of fact, Paul and James are not opposing each other on the issue of justification. Paul argues against the Pharisees, who radically emphasize meritorious justification, whereas James opposes "the Libertines and Epicureans," who are satisfied with a mere profession of faith while denying the necessity of good works. "Against the former, Paul rightly urges faith alone for justification. Against the latter, James properly commends the necessity of works for the confirmation of justification."[179]

Out of the *distinction* between the principles of the covenants of works and grace, Turretin develops the concept of imputation into justification. Thus, our justification is only possible because Christ's righteousness (*iustitia Christi*) is imputed to us through faith. "For the righteousness of Christ alone imputed to us is the foundation and meritorious cause upon which our absolute sentence rests, so that for no other reason does God bestow the pardon of sin and the right to life than on account of the most perfect righteousness of Christ imputed to us and apprehended by faith."[180]

Faith is not the material but the instrumental cause of justification because "Christ is our righteousness (1 Cor. 1:30; 2 Cor. 5:21)," and we have redemption and salvation based upon the imputation of Christ's righteousness. The principle of justification in the covenant of works has to be works and obedience. In the covenant of grace, however, it is faith alone, because the principles of works and faith are antithetical in justification. Thus, we are received into the covenant of grace by union with Christ, through faith, and Christ is "the foundation of the covenant and the bond of our union with God."[181]

---

[178] Ibid., 2:640-41.

[179] Ibid., 2:682.

[180] Ibid., 2:639.

[181] Ibid., 2:187. Thus, Turretin develops justification by faith alone, which excludes good works, from the *dichotomy* between the principles of works and grace, which are antithetical in character: "If faith is counted for righteousness, we will be justified by works because thus faith cannot but have the relation of a work which justifies. And yet it is clear that in this business Paul always opposes faith to works as incompatible (*aystata*) and two antagonistic (*antidieremena*) means by which man is justified either by his own obedience and in himself, by the law, or by another's obedience by the gospel. Nor does the difference between these modes of justification

Faith alone is the sole condition of the covenant of grace, for "it alone embraces Christ" and his redemptive benefits. Christian "holiness and obedience" are "subsequent" thus being the "fruit" of the covenant of grace and "they are the means and the way by which we arrive at the full blessing of the covenant."[182]

G. Charles Hodge (1797-1878)

Following in the footsteps of the Reformed covenant theology, Charles Hodge adopted the hermeneutical principle respecting the distinction between the covenants of works[183] and grace. Hodge indicates that rationalism discarded covenant theology and Christ's atonement because of its philosophical commitment. In opposition to this, Hodge affirms that God made the covenant of works with Adam and that there is a constant antithesis between the principle of works and faith in the Bible, even though we do not find the term *foedus operum* in Genesis:

> Although the word covenant is not used in Genesis, and does not elsewhere, in any clear passage, occur in reference to the transaction there recorded, yet inasmuch as the plan of salvation is constantly represented as a New Covenant, new, not merely in antithesis to that made at Sinai, but new in reference to all legal covenants whatever, it is plain that the Bible does represent the arrangement made with

consist in this–that in the former a perfect obedience and in the latter an imperfect is accepted of God as perfect, since the mode of justification would be always the same-by works. Rather the difference consists in this–that since in both cases a perfect righteousness is required, in the former from the strictness (*akribodikaio*) of the law God demands a personal righteousness, here from the forbearance (*epieikeia*) of the gospel he admits another's (to wit, the righteousness of Christ). Thus faith cannot be said to justify properly and by itself unless we slide back to the old covenant and return to legal justification." Ibid., 2:671.

[182] Ibid., 2:189.

[183] The original covenant has been named by Hodge as the covenant of works and life: "God then did enter into a covenant with Adam. That covenant is sometimes called a covenant of life, because life was promised as the reward of obedience. Sometimes it is called the covenant of works, because works were the condition on which that promise was suspended, and because it is thus distinguished from the new covenant which promises life on condition of faith." Charles Hodge, *Systematic Theology*. 3 vols. (reprint, Grand Rapids, Michigan: Eerdmans Publishing Company, 1995), 2: 118.

Adam as a truly federal transaction. The Scriptures know nothing of any other than two methods of attaining eternal life: the one that which demands perfect obedience, and the other that which demands faith. If the latter is called a covenant, the former is declared to be of the same nature.[184]

Adam stood as "the head and representative" of the whole human race in the original covenant of works. Accordingly, as the result of Adam's fall, all mankind "fell with him in his first transgression." Since then, the covenant of works has been canceled as the means of life and salvation. Nevertheless, argues Hodge, the principle of the covenant of works is perpetually effective for those who do not belong to the covenant of grace:

> Hence our Lord said to the young man, 'This do and thou shalt live.' And hence the Apostle in the second chapter of his Epistle to the Romans, says that God will reward every man according to his works. To those who are good, He will give eternal life; to those who are evil, indignation and wrath. This is only saying that the eternal principles of justice are still in force. If any man can present himself before the bar of God and prove that he is free from sin, either imputed or personal, either original or actual, he will not be condemned. But the fact is that the whole world lies in wickedness. Man is an apostate race. Men are all involved in the penal and natural consequences of Adam's transgression. They stood their probation in him, and do not stand each man for himself.[185]

The condition of the covenant of works "made with Adam" was "perfect obedience" in "a definite period of probation." The basic theological assumption of the Pauline epistles "to the Romans and to the Galatians" is that God's law requires "perfect obedience." Otherwise, Paul's argument falls entirely to the ground.[186] The promise attached to the covenant of works was *eschatological life* upon the condition of Adam's perfect obedience according to the principle of "This do and thou shalt live" and "The man that doeth them shall live by them." This was based on "the principle of justice." Hence, there is no doubt that if Adam continued to obey God's law, he could have enjoyed life and holiness, which would have flowed from

---

[184] Ibid., 2:117.
[185] Ibid., 2:122.
[186] Ibid., 2:119-20.

God's favour. The promised life was "the happy, holy, and immortal existence of the soul and body." Life as related to Adam's obedience was eschatological "glory, honour, and immortality," as stated in Romans 2:7. And this life from obedience would have eventually sprung from God's favour and fellowship.[187] However, the penalty revealed in the covenant of works was death which was "the opposite of the life promised." Death includes the miseries of life, physical death, and "spiritual and eternal death." The results of Adam's original sin were "the loss of the image and favour of God and all the evils which flowed from that loss."[188]

One of the greatest theological problems for the Pelagians, asserts Hodge, is that there is no clear distinction between the covenants of works and grace, eventually making an amalgam between Law and Gospel in the doctrine of salvation and justification:

> It includes even the Pelagian view of the plan of salvation, which assumes that there is no difference between the covenant of works under which Adam was placed, and the covenant of grace, under which men are now, except as to the extent of the obedience required. God promised life to Adam on the condition of perfect obedience, because he was in a condition to render such obedience. He promises salvation to men now on the condition of such obedience as they are able to render, whether Jews, Pagans, or Christians.[189]

The Adam and Christ parallel, asserts Hodge, is a decisive theological reference point to establish the *distinction* between the covenants of works and grace in the Bible. "As Adam was the head and representative of his posterity, so Christ is the head and representative of his people. And as God entered into the covenant with Adam so He entered into covenant with Christ. This, in Romans 5:12-21, is set forth as the fundamental idea of all God's dealings with men, both in their fall and in their redemption."[190] As the result of the antithesis between the covenants of works and grace, Adam's perfect obedience would have *merited* eschatological blessings, while in the covenant of grace Christ's *meritorious* work is the only ground of our salvation:

---

[187] Ibid., 2:118-19.
[188] Ibid., 2:120.
[189] Ibid., 2:355.
[190] Ibid., 2:360.

> In this sense perfect obedience was the condition of the covenant originally made with Adam. Had he retained his integrity he would have *merited* [emphasis mine] the promised blessing. For to him that worketh the reward is not of grace but of debt. In the same sense the work of Christ is the condition of the covenant of redemption. It was the *meritorious ground* [emphasis mine], laying a foundation in justice for the fulfillment of the promises made to Him by the Father.[191]

This comparison between Adam and Christ on the idea of merit is *a breakthrough* in Reformed covenant thought and is due to Hodge's careful analysis. In Hodge's mind, the concept of merit in the Adamic covenant of works is derived from *the complete distinction* between the covenants of works and grace. He concludes that Adam stood as the meritorious representative covenantal head in the covenant of works, while Christ is the meritorious representative covenantal head in the covenant of grace. In other words, Hodge's meritorious concept in respect to the two Adams is his contribution to covenant theology since it is the result of a careful analysis of the antithesis and parallel between the covenants of works and grace.

In the covenant of grace, Christ wonderfully cancels the death and condemnation brought about as the result of the broken covenant of works.[192] Moreover, Christ is constantly portrayed as "the mediator of the covenant of grace" just as Moses was a mediator of the Old Covenant between God and the Israelites. In this way, Christ is the ultimate surety of our salvation because he was "a federal sacrifice"

---

[191] Ibid., 2:364-65. In dealing with the matter of *merit*, Hodge asserts that there is a close interrelation between merit and divine justice, whereas merit and grace, and law and grace are antithetical. In short, the *foedus operum* is to be understood in the light of divine justice since the principle of the law was operating as the condition of eschatological glorification: "It is, however, clearly recognized in Scripture that a labourer is worthy of his hire. To him that worketh, says the Apostle, the reward is not reckoned of grace, but of debt. It is *something due in justice* [emphasis mine] ... The payment is not a matter of favour; it is not due simply because promised; but because it has been earned. It is a debt. So in the case of Adam, had he remained perfect, there would have been no ground *in justice* [emphasis mine] why he should die, or forfeit the favour of God; which favour is life ... God is just, and being just, He rewards every man according to his works, so long as men are under the law. If not under the law, they are dealt with, not on the principles of law, but of grace." Ibid., 2:243-44.

[192] Ibid., 2:120.

and "His blood was the blood of the covenant." For adults, "faith in Christ" is "the condition of the covenant of grace," receiving Christ Jesus as "the Son of God." Hence, without Christ's work there is no salvation, so that everlasting life comes from the Son of God through faith. "I will be your God, and ye shall be my people" is the representative statement of the promises of the covenant of grace.[193]

Under the Old Covenant, asserted the Socinians, there was no guarantee of *heavenly everlasting life*, so that "the condition of salvation was not faith in Christ." At the same time, the Anabaptists denied that the Abrahamic Covenant belongs to the covenant of grace, and identified it merely as a "national covenant entirely distinct from the covenant of grace." And also, theorizing about the *limbus patrum*, the Romanists affirmed that the Old Testament patriarchs "were not admitted into heaven, but passed into a place and state called the *limbus patrum*, where they remained in a negative condition until the coming of Christ, who after his death descended to hell, *sheol*, for their deliverance."[194] In opposition to these diverse theories, Hodge insists that the way and mode of salvation has always been the same because there is only one covenant of grace after the fall, including "the promise of redemption" revealed to Adam. In other words, *heilsgeschichte* is the history of the covenant of grace in Christ. Thus, Hodge writes, "We learn that the plan of salvation has always been one and the same; having the same promise, the same Saviour, the same condition, and the same salvation."[195] As a result, it has been manifested that the Old Testament believers are now in heaven

---

[193] Ibid., 2:364-65.

[194] Ibid., 2:366-67.

[195] Ibid., 2:367-68. Thus, Hodge concretely affirms the continuity of God's redemptive history within the one covenant of grace in opposition to the Anabaptists and Romanists: "The covenant of grace, or plan of salvation, being the same in all its elements from the beginning, it follows, first in opposition to the Anabaptists, that the people of God before Christ constituted a Church, and that the Church has been one and the same under all dispensations. It has always had the same promise, the same Redeemer, and the same condition of membership, namely, faith in the Son of God as the Saviour of the world. It follows from the same premises, in opposition to the Romanists, that the salvation of the people of God who died before the coming of Christ, was complete. They were truly pardoned, sanctified, and, at death, admitted to that state into which those dying in the Christian faith are now received." Ibid., 2:373.

because they have same eschatological heavenly blessings that we have in the New Covenant.[196]

Hodge affirms that the Mosaic Covenant, from the perspective of redemptive and salvation history in Christ, belongs to the covenant of grace because God's grace in Christ Jesus was wonderfully manifested in the types and symbols of the Gospel of Christ:

> We have the direct authority of the New Testament for believing that the covenant of grace, or plan of salvation, thus underlay the whole of the institutions of the Mosaic period, and that their principal design was to teach through types and symbols what is now taught in explicit terms in the gospel. Moses, we are told (Heb. 3:5), was faithful as a servant to testify concerning the things which were to be spoken after.[197]

The Mosaic Covenant, meanwhile, belongs to the legal covenant in terms of the earthly blessings and curses, based upon the corporate compliance and obedience to the law of the people of Israel:

> Besides this evangelical character which unquestionably belongs to the Mosaic covenant, it is presented in two other aspects in the Word of God. First, it was a national covenant with the Hebrew people. In this view the parties were God and the people of Israel; the promise was national security and prosperity; the condition was the obedience of the people as a nation to the Mosaic law; and the mediator was Moses. In this respect it was a *legal covenant* [emphasis mine]. It said, 'Do this and live.'[198]

The Mosaic Covenant pronounced and revealed God's everlasting principle of justice in which the principle of the covenant of works was freshly manifested, revealing the requirements of the law. In this respect, Hodge writes:

> Secondly, it contained, as does also the New Testament, a renewed proclamation of the original covenant of works. It is as true now as in the days of Adam, it always has been and always must be true, that rational creatures who perfectly obey the law of God are blessed in the enjoyment of his favour; and that those who sin are subject to his wrath

---

[196] Ibid., 2:368-71.
[197] Ibid., 2:375.
[198] Ibid.

and curse. Our Lord assured the young man who came to Him for instruction that if he kept the commandments he should live.[199]

The manifestation of the principle of the covenant of works in the Mosaic Covenant is to show us that if we are not under the covenant of grace in Christ Jesus, then it is necessary to fulfill the requirements of the covenant of works, which is impossible for sinful human beings.[200]

The New Covenant is designated as "the Gospel dispensation" by Hodge, and it is much more spiritual than the Old Covenant, which had been administered through "the types and ceremonies" which pointed to Christ. Even the New Covenant continues to include, however, "a legal element" because "it reveals the law still as a covenant of works binding on those who reject the gospel; but in the New Testament the gospel greatly predominates over the law. Whereas, under the Old Testament, the law predominated over the gospel."[201]

Standing in the tradition of the Reformation consensus, Hodge carefully expounds justification by faith alone which radically excludes works. In this regard, faith is not "the meritorious ground of justification," and our justification is not "on account of " faith. Christ's righteousness, based upon his active and passive obedience (*obedientia activa et obedientia passiva Christi*), is "the ground of justification." Christ perfectly obeyed God's law "as a covenant," and he endured "the penalty of the law" in our place.[202] Hence, "faith is merely the instrumental cause of justification."[203] Christ's righteousness is at the same time God's righteousness "because Christ is God; because God has provided, revealed, and offers it; and it avails before God as a sufficient ground on which He can declare the believing sinner righteous."[204]

The decisive failure of the Remonstrants or Arminians, argues Hodge, lies in the fact that they do not make a clear distinction between Law and Gospel in relation to the doctrine of justification by

---

[199] Ibid., 2:375.
[200] Ibid.
[201] Ibid., 2:376.
[202] Ibid., 3:118.
[203] Ibid., 3:170.
[204] Ibid., 3:152.

faith alone. They confound works and faith, and insert "evangelical obedience" as the condition of justification and salvation:

> According to the Remonstrants or Arminians the works which are excluded from our justification are works of the law as distinguished from works of the Gospel. In the covenant made with Adam God demanded perfect obedience as the condition of life. For Christ's sake, God in the Gospel has entered into a new covenant with men, promising them salvation on the condition of evangelical obedience. This is expressed in different forms. Sometimes it is said that we are justified on account of faith. Faith is accepted in place of that perfect righteousness demanded by the Adamic law. But by faith is not meant the act of receiving and resting upon Christ alone for salvation. It is regarded as a permanent and controlling state of mind. And therefore it is often said that we are justified by a 'fides obsequiosa,' an obedient faith; a faith which includes obedience. At other times, it is said that we are justified by evangelical obedience, *i.e.*, that kind and measure of obedience which the Gospel requires, and which men since the fall, in the proper use of 'sufficient grace' granted to all men, are able to render.[205]

Hodge affirms that all kinds of works are excluded in the doctrine of justification according to Galatians 3:10 and Romans 3:20. Paul assures that both the Jews and Gentiles could not be justified "by the works of the law" because the law requires "perfect obedience." Paul's major thesis to prove justification by faith alone is that there is an absolute antithesis between the principles of works and faith. In other words, justifying faith must be explained and understood in the light of *the antithesis* between works and faith:

> This is still further evident from the contrast constantly presented between faith and works. We are not justified by works, but by faith in Jesus Christ. (Gal. 2:16, and often elsewhere.) It is not one kind of works as opposed to another; legal as opposed to evangelical; natural as opposed to gracious; moral as opposed to ritual; but works of every kind as opposed to faith ... Grace and works are antithetical. 'To him that worketh is the reward not reckoned of grace, but of debt.' (Rom. 4:4) 'If by grace, then is it no more of works: otherwise grace is no more grace' (Rom. 11:6).[206]

---

[205] Ibid., 3:136-37.
[206] Ibid., 3:138.

Thus, the biblical doctrine establishes that "good works are the fruits and consequences" of justification by faith alone in Christ Jesus, and this is due to and out of the grace of God.[207]

Commenting on Romans 10:3 and 4 Hodge indicates that the divine righteousness is "infinitely meritorious." Thus, the folly of the Jews lay in the fact that they did not make a clear distinction between the covenants of works and grace in their understanding of salvation and justification, therefore they vigorously rejected Christ Jesus, who fulfilled the demands of the covenant of works. The Gospel of salvation, however, is provided to sinners, canceling the requirements of the condition of the covenant of works for those who are in Christ.

> The Jews acted under the assumption that the law as a covenant, that is, as prescribing the condition of salvation, was still in force, that men were still bound to satisfy its demands by their personal obedience in order to be saved, whereas Christ had made an end of the law. He had abolished it as a covenant, in order that men might be justified by faith. Christ, however, has thus made an end of the law, not merely setting it aside, but by satisfying its demands. He delivers us from its curse, not by mere pardon, but by being made a curse for us (Gal. 3:13). He redeems us from the law by being made under it (Gal. 4:4-5), and fulfilling all righteousness.[208]

According to "the condition of the covenant," God's perfection requires man's "perfect obedience" in order to have everlasting life, but no one can fulfill the condition of the covenant of works. However, God never forgives sins unless the requirements of justice are met. In other words, God never bestows *everlasting life* unless "perfect obedience" is provided.

> Heaven is always represented as a purchased position. In the covenant between the Father and the Son the salvation of his people was promised as the reward of his humiliation, obedience, and death. Having performed the stipulated conditions, He has a claim to the promised recompense. And this claim insures to the benefit of his people. But besides this, as the work of Christ consisted in his doing all that the law of God, or covenant of works requires for the salvation of men, and as that righteousness is freely offered to every one that believes, every such believer has as valid a claim to eternal life as he

---

[207] Ibid., 3:173.
[208] Ibid., 3:156.

would have had, had he personally done all that the law demands. Thus broad and firm is the foundation which God has laid for the hopes of his people. It is the rock of ages; Jehovah our righteousness."[209]

Accordingly, the distinction between Law and Gospel is the decisive hermeneutical reference point which establishes justification by faith alone apart from works. From this crucial theological motif, following the theological steps of Calvin, Owen, Edwards and Shedd, Charles Hodge informs us that in the Bible, justification is always understood "in a forensic sense," in which God's once for all declaration is involved. The ground of our justification, therefore, is "the imputation of the righteousness of Christ," based upon Christ's active and passive obedience, which wonderfully fulfills the requirements of the law in our place. The forensic character of justification excludes "the moral or subjective" change in us because "the imputation of the righteousness of Christ" is the cornerstone for us to be declared as righteous, completely forgiven of our sin, and bestowed with eternal life.[210] Thus, "the imputation of the righteousness of Christ" is the only foundation of our justification.[211]

The error of the Arminian doctrine of justification is that it rejects the imputation of the righteousness of Christ to believers as the ultimate basis of justification. Thus, Arminians insist that "faith and its fruit, or faith and evangelical obedience" are the real grounds of justification.[212] But the underlying problem with Arminian justification is, according to Hodge, that it fails to make the antithesis between the covenants of works and grace, thereby confusing Law and Gospel, and ultimately, destroying the biblical doctrine of justification by faith alone. Hodge summarizes the Arminian understanding of justification as follows:

> Under the covenant of works as made with Adam, perfect obedience was the condition of acceptance with God and of eternal life; under the Gospel, for Christ's sake, imperfect, or evangelical obedience, is the ground of justification, *i.e*, it is that (*propter quam*) on account of

---

[209] Ibid., 3:164-65.
[210] Ibid., 3:144-50.
[211] Ibid., 3:155.
[212] Ibid., 3:192.

which God graciously grants us the remission of sin and the reward of eternal life.[213]

In opposition to this kind of contention, Hodge asserts in his comment on Romans 3:20 that "good works of every kind" are to be excluded as foundational for justification.[214] For the Romanists, good works are understood in light of *meritum de congruo et meritum de condigno*. Hodge asserts that good works are not meritorious since salvation is founded upon the covenant of grace, in which the *meritum Christi* is the ground of believers' justification and salvation. Nevertheless, the Protestants teach that God rewards believers' good works "on the ground of the merits of Christ" even though their works are imperfect. Moreover, the Bible teaches that there will be *gradations* of heavenly blessings according to the proportion of good works.[215]

H. Geerhardus Vos (1862-1947)

It is evident that both John Murray and Meredith G. Kline were greatly influenced by Geerhardus Vos. In this regard, a careful observation of Vos' biblical covenant theology will be helpful. Vos characteristically developed his biblical covenant theology under the rubrics of *eschatology and the Kingdom of God*, responding to the Ritschlian moralistic Kingdom of God and the dehistoricization of biblical history represented by the Wellhausen school, which emphasized the dynamic historicity of the biblical epochs.

Vos divides special revelation into two historical categories. One is "the pre-redemptive Special Revelation," identified as "the Covenant of works." The other is "redemptive Special Revelation," and is designated as "the covenant of grace." In this manner, the antithesis between the covenants of works and grace is a decisive hermeneutical key for Vos; it embraces the entire biblical theological history both *covenantally* and *eschatologically* in the concept of the Kingdom of God.[216]

---

[213] Ibid., 3:193.
[214] Charles Hodge, *The Epistle to the Romans* (reprint, Edinburgh / Carlisle: The Banner of Truth Trust, 1975), 85.
[215] Hodge, *Systematic Theology*, 3:241-45.
[216] Geerhardus Vos, *Biblical Theology: Old and New Testaments* (Grand Rapids, Michigan: Eerdmans Publishing Company, 1948; reprint, 1988), 23.

"In the second half of the seventeenth century Vlak and Bekker" rejected the doctrine of the covenant of works, arguing that it was an innovation of "the theologians of that period"and not developed among "the older Reformed theologians." They supposed that "Lubbertus, Makkowski, and Cloppenburg" were the first theologians who had invented it. "Just as Coccejus has occasionally been looked upon as the discoverer of the covenant concept in general, so also some wanted to maintain that the doctrine of the covenant of works had been thought up in the period immediately preceding Coccejus."[217] In opposition to this contention, Vos affirms that the doctrine of the covenant of works originally sprouted from the old Reformed school of theologians such as Ursinus and Olevianus in the late sixteenth century.[218]

If Adam already stood in the covenant of works in the prelapsarian state, argues Vos, then it is logical to expect that the covenant concept will also govern God's redemptive history, even in the inter-Trinitarian Covenant of Redemption:

> It was merely the other side of the doctrine of the covenant of works that was seen when the task of the Mediator was also placed in this light. A *Pactum Salutis*, a Counsel of Peace, a Covenant of Redemption, could then be spoken of. There are two alternatives: one must either deny the covenant arrangement as a general rule for obtaining eternal life, or, granting the latter, he must also regard the gaining of eternal life by the Mediator as a covenant arrangement and place the establishing of a covenant in back of it. Thus it also becomes clear how a denial of the covenant of works sometimes goes hand in hand with a lack of appreciation for the counsel of peace.[219]

The condition of the covenant of works, asserts Vos, was perfect obedience to the law, which if carried out, ultimately promised eternal and eschatological glorious life. The principle of the covenant of works may be summarized as "Do this and you shall live" in Leviticus 18:5. However any who are in the covenant of grace, are "exempt from the demand of the law as the condition for eternal blessedness, but not from its demand as being normative for their moral life."[220]

---

[217] Vos, *Redemptive History*, 237.
[218] Ibid.
[219] Ibid., 245.
[220] Ibid., 244.

Between Lutheran and Reformed theologians, there is a crucial difference of emphasis "for the doctrine of the covenant of works" in relation to "the original state of man." The decisive breach is that Lutherans do not have *the eschatological goal* for man before the fall while Reformed covenantal thought places an emphasis on the eschatological heavenly life and realization as the goal of the covenant of works:

> According to the Lutherans man had already reached his destination in that God had placed him in a state of uprightness. Eternal life was already in his possession. In his situation the highest ideal was realized. Nothing more need be added to execute God's purpose in creating man. Man was mutable, that is true, and he could fall away from the state of original uprightness and bliss. But for the Lutheran conception this is not a stage that points forward to something else, but rather that which was usual and normal and to be expected. From this it follows that the same condition returns in the state of grace to which fallen man is brought by Christ. Precisely because mankind's destination had already been reached before the fall in Adam, Christ can do nothing but restore what was lost in Adam.[221]

Reformed covenant theology stresses, however, the magnitude of the goal of the covenant of works as heavenly life and justification, connecting it with the *eschatological goal* of the covenant of grace in the second Adam.

> It was a state of perfect uprightness in which he knew the good and did it consciously. As long as he remained in that state, he could also be sure of God's favor. Up to this point the Reformed view concurs with the Lutheran. But whereas the latter can be satisfied by perpetuating such a state and extending it indefinitely, the Reformed view fixes its

---

[221] Ibid., 242. The magnificent theological fulcrum of the goal of the covenant of works and grace lies in eschatological life and reality. Hence, Vos writes: "But the matter becomes entirely different when eschatology posits an absolute goal at the end of the redemptive process corresponding to an absolute beginning of the world in creation: for then, no longer a segment but the whole sweep of history is drawn into one great perspective, and the mind is impelled to view every part in relation to the whole. To do this means to construct a primitive theological system. Thus eschatology becomes the mother of theology and that first of all theology in the form of a philosophy of redemptive history." Ibid., 193.

gaze on something higher. It sees man not as being placed in eternal bliss from the beginning, but as being placed in such a way that he might attain to eternal bliss. There still hovers above him the possibility of sin and death which is given with his mutable freedom. He is free to do the good out of his good nature, but he has not yet attained the highest freedom which can do good only. The latter is placed before him as an ideal. The means of obtaining it is the covenant of works. Here too the state of grace is again ultimately determined by the idea of man's destiny in the state of original uprightness. What we inherit in the second Adam is not restricted to what we lost in the first Adam: it is much rather the full realization of what the first Adam would have achieved for us had he remained unfallen and been confirmed in his state. Someone placed in that state can never again fall from it. As truly as Christ is a perfect Saviour, so truly must he bestow on us the perseverance of the saints.[222]

The ultimate goal of the covenant of works is not only thoroughly eschatological but also theocentric. It radically eliminates anthropocentric motives, points ultimately to the *gloria Dei*, and displays the *imago Dei* through the religious covenantal relationship and obedience.[223] After the fall, the covenant of works is still effective not as the means of life but as the hypothetical principle to gain

---

[222] Ibid., 243. Vos repeats that the ultimate eschatological goal of both the covenants of works and grace is celestial life, typified by the administration of Sabbath: "Man is reminded in this way that life is not an aimless existence, that a goal lies beyond. This was true before, and apart from, redemption. The eschatological is an older strand in revelation than the soteric. The so-called 'Covenant of Works' was nothing but an embodiment of the Sabbatical principle. Had its probation been successful, then the sacramental Sabbath would have passed over into the reality it typified, and the entire subsequent course of the history of the race would have been radically different. What now is to be expected at the end of this world would have formed the beginning of the world-course instead." idem, 140. Vos carefully notices that there are gracious and merciful ideas introduced in the original covenantal relationship between God and man: "To begin with, we have here the strongest recognition of the antecedent work of God. Man cannot create the good for himself, but he has to develop the divinely given good that lies within him. If his natural goodness is already the creative work of God, the same can be said for the covenantal relationship in which God places him. This too is the product of a free divine deed, a gift flowing out of the condescending mercy of the Lord." idem, *Redemptive History*, 244.

[223] Ibid., 245.

everlasting life and leads ultimately to the Gospel of Christ due to the impossibility of meeting the law's requirement. Furthermore, Vos remarks that the antithesis between Law and Gospel is the fundamental principle in order to comprehend the Gospel of Christ:

> Even after the fall, the law retains something of its covenantal form. The law was not included in the federal relationship without having been affected by it. Even today the call of the law sounds in our ears: such a life I would give you, if only you could fulfill me! God could have wholly eradicated that relation and have taken away the last traces of it from our minds, after the covenant of works was broken. However, He kept its memory alive in us. He has repeated that promise hypothetically and consequently has held up before us constantly the ideal of eternal life to be obtained by keeping the law, a lost ideal though it be. Thus the essential content of the concept of covenant has been kept in our consciousness. When the work of the Spirit by means of the law and the gospel leads to true conversion, in this conversion the longing for this lost ideal of the covenant appears as an essential part.[224]

Vos affirms that the covenant concept is detectable throughout biblical history. It underscores and directs *the historical progress* of redemptive movement and special revelation. Each epoch of God's redemptive history and revelation in the Old Testament is measured by "successive covenants," each plainly introducing "a distinctive character" of its own epoch. The distinction between the covenants of works and grace is ridiculed, however, by critics. In opposition to this, Vos affirms the distinction between the covenants of works and grace as a crucial part of biblical covenantal history which depicts the progressive unfolding of the *historia salutis*. This distinction encompasses the entire scope of creation, fall and redemption from a covenant perspective as this has historically and progressively unfolded:

> Thus the covenant-idea is an eminently historical idea, most intimately associated with the gradual unfolding of God's self-disclosure to His people. This reaches even back of the regime of redemption and characterizes God's dealings with man in the state of rectitude. For, although it is generally considered a dogmatic anachronism to carry the

---

[224] Ibid., 254-55.

covenant-idea back into the original religious status of unfallen man, as the Reformed Theology has done in its doctrine of the covenant of works, a most striking confirmation of the biblical warrant for this view has of late come from an altogether unexpected quarter ... And as the first of these four covenants, it is maintained by Wellhausen and others, the author must have counted the arrangement entered into by God with our first parents in their original state. Thus the much ridiculed 'covenant of works' has been exegetically rehabilitated and it has been shown that the Reformed theologians were not so utterly lacking in historic sense as their critics believed.[225]

Considering the faith of the patriarchs of Hebrews 11, Vos writes that the covenant of grace is *bilateral* for it involves "personal attachment, covenant-loyalty to God" in response to God's sovereign covenantal commitment and execution. Thus, Vos articulates the *bilateral* character of the covenant of grace and follows the Reformed covenant tradition, which carefully balances God's sovereign election in the execution of the covenant of grace with human obligation as a member in the covenant community:

> It is the responsive act on the believer's part to the act of covenant-committal on the part of God. Religion consummates itself in a mutual avowal, the people bearing God's reproach and offering up a sacrifice of praise to Him continually, even the fruit of lips that make confession to His name, and God not being ashamed to be called their God and preparing for them a city. Thus the epistle's idea of faith falls into line with its teaching on revelation and on the priesthood and back of all three equally is seen to lie the covenantal conception of religion.[226]

When the Gospel enters into a man's consciousness, argues Vos, he must deal with "the demand of faith." No one can escape from "that responsibility toward the gospel," the responsibility of being bound by a faithful conscience. Vos further explains the *bilateral* character of the covenant of grace as follows: "Just as man before the fall was obligated to enter into the covenant of works, even so fallen man is obligated to receive grace with a believing heart. Of course, the difference remains that while acceptance was a matter of course in the

---

[225] Ibid., 192-93.
[226] Ibid., 230.

state of rectitude, it cannot take place in the fallen state except for supernatural grace."[227]

Redemptive–historically conceived, the Mosaic Covenant stands in *continuity*[228] with the New Covenant. Even the believers in the Old Covenant were saved by the redemptive provision of Christ Jesus, who is the substance of the Gospel. The Gospel of salvation was characteristically manifested in the types and shadows which anticipated the reality of the New Covenant spiritual blessings:

> For it is in Hebrews that the first age and the first world are identified with the first covenant. When, therefore, the question is raised, how the Old Covenant can be identical in substance with the New, what is the common essence, that notwithstanding the great progress from one to the other, makes them two coherent stages in the expression and conveyance of the same spiritual reality, the answer is immediately forthcoming: the same world of heavenly spiritual realities, which has now come to light in the person and work of Christ, already existed during the course of the Old Covenant, and in a provisional typical way through revelation reflected itself in and through redemption projected itself into the religious experience of the ancient people of God, so that they in their own partial manner and measure had access to and communion with and enjoyment of the higher world, which has now been let down and thrown open to our full knowledge and possession. In other words, the bond that links the Old and the New Covenant together is not a purely evolutionary one, inasmuch as the one has grown out of the other; it is, if we may so call it, a transcendental bond:

---

[227] Ibid., 254.

[228] Vos justifies the idea of continuity between the Old and New Covenants by the proposition that it is only by God's grace in Christ that our salvation is possible. Therefore, grace in Christ applies both to the Mosaic and New Covenants, as revealed in Hebrews 10:21 and 6:13-18: "In this name, 'house of God,' the principle of organic continuity of grace is implied, which elsewhere in the New Testament and throughout the Old appears as one of the important correlates of the covenant-conception ... Apart from the covenant idea the element of continuity is found by the writer inherent in the promises given to Abraham. These promises he does not call a covenant, for the old *diatheke*, with which the new is coordinated, begins according to his representation at Sinai, not with Abraham. But the promise underlies the whole subsequent development; it is the broad basis on which the two successive covenants rest; New Testament believers have an equal interest in it with the saints of the old dispensation, and in this way the uninterrupted continuity of grace is recognized (6:13-18)." Ibid., 226.

the New Covenant in its preexistent, heavenly state reaches back and stretches its eternal wings over the Old, and the Old Testament people of God were one with us in religious dignity and privilege; they were, to speak in a Pauline figure, sons of the Jerusalem above, which is the mother of all.[229]

The author of Hebrews believes that the Old Covenant contains the shadow of heavenly blessings whereas the New Covenant contains the full scope of heavenly blessings. In this regard, we should not create an antithesis by arguing that "there is 'only' a shadow" in the Old Covenant. Rather, the shadow of the spiritual reality exists under the administration of the Old Covenant. If we take Hebrews 7:18 in a strict sense, we would have to argue that the Old Covenant did not contain any "spiritual substance," that the Old Covenant believers enjoyed only the shadows of the New Covenant spiritual substance which the New Covenant believers enjoy. In reality, however, God had "spiritual relations to the people of Israel," who did in fact enjoy "the fount of life and blessedness." Through the administration of "the shadows and ceremonies and all the instrumentalities of the flesh," God surely and sovereignly controlled the religious and spiritual life of each individual of the covenant people in the theocratic Kingdom of Israel; that is, as this pertains to the elect.[230]

Vos asserts that although the Sinaitic Covenant stands in continuation with the covenant of grace and is related to the principle and substance of salvation and justification, in a sense, it was *a revival of the covenant of works*. In this respect, Reformed theologians did not always make a clear distinction between "the covenant of works and the Sinaitic covenant." "At Sinai it was not the 'bare' law that was given, but a reflection of the covenant of works revived, as it were, in the interests of the covenant of grace continued at Sinai."[231] Appealing to Galatians 4:21-31, Vos affirms that there is *a radical contrast* between the Mosaic and New Covenants:

> Here Paul speaks of two contrasting *diathekai*, i.e., two great religious systems operating by diverse methods and with opposite results, the one a Hagar-diatheke, geographically associated with Mount Sinai, the other a Sara-diatheke, having its local center in the heavenly

---

[229] Ibid., 199.
[230] Ibid., 203.
[231] Ibid., 255.

Jerusalem. There is a difference between this and 2 Corinthians 3 insofar as there the old and the new were contrasted in their original God-willed and God-given character, whilst here in Galatians the Sinaitic-Hagar diatheke is the old system as perverted by Judaism.[232]

Paul contrasts "the fundamental bisection" of redemptive and revelational history into the Old and New Covenants, and makes a distinction between the law and faith, the letter and the Spirit, and condemnation and righteousness:

> Thus he speaks not only of the two regimes of law and faith, but even expresses himself in the consecutive form of statement: 'after that faith is come' (Gal. 3:25). It is no wonder, then, that with him we find the formal distinction between the 'New *Diatheke*' and the 'Old *Diatheke*' (2 Cor. 3 :6,14). Here also, to be sure, we have in the first place a contrast between two religious ministrations, that of the letter and that of the Spirit, that of condemnation and that of righteousness. Nevertheless, the idea of difference in revelation, as underlying the difference in ministration between Moses and Paul, clearly enters.[233]

Commenting on Hebrews, Vos contrasts the Old and New Covenants from the eschatological perspective, confirming that "the Epistle distinguishes not only two covenants, but also two worlds or ages, namely *this age*, and *the age to come*. The peculiarity of the old *Diatheke* is that it pertains to this present world, whereas the new *Diatheke* is that of the future eschatological world."[234] The Old Covenant is "terrestrial earthly," finding its expression from the earthly terms whereas the New Covenant has its fulcrum in heaven, finding its expression "in heavenly forms." Another way of distinguishing the two covenants is the *contrast between flesh and spirit*. Moreover, the author of Hebrews contrasts the priesthood of the two covenants. The Old Covenant priesthood was "according to the law of a carnal commandment" while the New Covenant priesthood of Christ was "according to the power of an endless life."[235]

---

[232] Ibid., 163.

[233] Vos, *Biblical Theology*, 301.

[234] Geerhardus Vos, *The Teaching of the Epistle to the Hebrews*, ed. Johannes G. Vos (Phillipsburg, New Jersey: Presbyterian and Reformed Publishing Company, 1956), 50.

[235] Ibid., 62-4.

The observance of the law in the Mosaic Covenant is not, however, "the meritorious ground" of temporal blessings, even though Israel's preservation of the covenant blessings was dependent on obedience. God promised those who do the commandments shall inherit life from them. In opposition to the Judaizers, Paul asserts that the possession of the promised land was not dependent "on previous observance of the law," but on God's grace alone, radically excluding "the meritorious ground of life-inheritance." Now, in Vos' biblical covenant theology, *typology* becomes an important hermeneutical tool to depict the progressive development of the *historia salutis*; thus it anticipates eschatological fulfillment:

> But the Judaizers went wrong in inferring that the connection must be *meritorious*, that, if Israel keeps the cherished gifts of Jehovah through observance of His law, this must be so, because in strict justice they had *earned* them. The connection is of a totally different kind. It belongs not to the legal sphere of merit, but to the symbolico-typical sphere of *appropriateness of expression*. As stated above, the abode of Israel in Canaan typified the heavenly, perfected state of God's people. Under these circumstances the ideal of absolute conformity to God's law of legal holiness had to be upheld. Even though they were not able to keep this law in the Pauline, spiritual sense, yea, even though they were unable to keep it externally and ritually, the requirement could not be lowered. When apostasy on *a general scale* [emphasis mine] took place, they could not remain in the promised land. When they disqualified themselves for typifying the state of holiness, they *ipso facto* disqualified themselves for typifying that of blessedness, and had to go into captivity. This did not mean every individual Israelite, in every detail of his life, had to be perfect, and that on this was suspended the continuance of God's favour. Jehovah dealt primarily with the nation and through the nation with the individual, as even now in the covenant of grace He deals with believers and their children in the continuity of generations. There is solidarity among the members of the people of God, but this same principle also works for the neutralizing of the effect of individual sin, so long as the nation remains faithful. The attitude observed by the nation and its representative leaders was the decisive factor. Although the demands of the law were at various times imperfectly complied with, nevertheless for a long time Israel remained in possession of the favour of God. And, even when the people as a whole become apostate, and go into exile, Jehovah does not on that account suffer the בְּרִית to fail.

After due chastisement and repentance He takes Israel back into favour.[236]

The Prophet Jeremiah presupposes the specific character of "a great bi-section of history," making a distinction between the Old and New Covenants. "The peculiarity of Hebrews," however, is that it highlights the legitimate distinctions "between the present age and the age to come and that between the first covenant and the second covenant." The New Covenant incorporates God's redemptive consummation for his children. The New Covenant believers taste the powers of *the eschatological life* and have come to "the eschatological Mount Zion, the heavenly Jerusalem, the city of the living God." The New Covenant revelation is not only superior to the Old Covenant; it is "final and eternal," on account of its being accomplished by the Son of God: "That the New Covenant actually has this comprehensive eschatological significance, and is not a mere soteriological episode, is easily obscured by the prominent place which the ideas of priesthood and sacrifice with their typical antecedents in the history of Israel occupy."[237] According to Hebrews 10:1, indicates Vos, the Old Covenant administration of the law was the shadow, type and copy of "the good things" of the better Covenant to come; "not the image itself." In addition, the application of typology in the Old Covenant signifies the eschatological direction of the *historia salutis* by anticipating its fulfillment in the New Covenant, and ultimately pointing to the eternal heavenly blessings:

> The Old Testament forms also prefigure what is to follow in the line of historic emergence; they are forecasts in the Pauline sense, but they are this only because first they are reflexes of a heavenly reality which was destined at the end of the ages to come down to earth and fill the New Covenant ... In a somewhat similar sense the author of Hebrews means by shadow the sketch which God drew on the ceremonial canvas of the law of the eternal things that form the object of His vision in the world above. In another passage (8:5) this is said in so many words. Here we read that the Old Testament priests serve that which is a copy and shadow (ὑποδείγματι καὶ σκιᾷ) of the heavenly things. The term 'copy' explains the term 'shadow' and both are equally related to a celestial reality. But perhaps even more strikingly the author's way of

---

[236] Vos, *Biblical Theology*, 127-28.
[237] Vos, *Redemptive History*, 195.

thinking in this respect reveals itself in the peculiar use he makes of the ideas of type and antitype.[238]

The Old Covenant administers "the type," whereas the New Covenant contains "the antitype." Similarly, in 1 Peter 3:21, the apostle Peter demonstrates "the water of deluge as the type, the water of baptism as the antitype." "The author of Hebrews" distinctively denotes, however, that "the Old Testament tabernacle was the antitype, not the type" for "the Old Testament tabernacle was copied, fashioned after the tabernacle in heaven." In this regard, generally speaking, "the Old Testament things" are called "copies of the things in the heavens" as read in Hebrews 9:23-24.[239]

There is an antithetical relationship between law and grace in relation to the Old and New Covenants. The administration of the law in the typological Kingdom of Israel foreshadowed and pointed to the heavenly celestial reality whereas the grace of Christ actually bestows the heavenly life in his person. The author of Hebrews contrasts "the heavenly world" of the New Covenant and the administration of the typological nation of Israel of the Old Covenant in a manner consistent with Hebrews 9:23-24. Moreover, Vos writes:

> And even more closely approaching the view point of Hebrews is the contrast drawn in the prologue between the law given through Moses, and the grace and truth which came through Jesus Christ, for here, it will be observed, the Christian revelation is characterized as 'truth' in distinction from the Mosaic law, to which this predicate does not belong. The meaning is not, of course, that the Mosaic law is untrue or false in the ordinary sense of the word ... 'Truth' here means what it means in Hebrews; it expresses the heavenly character of the Christian realities of revelation and redemption in which the higher world directly communicates itself, and the opposite of 'the true' is the typical, wherein the connection with the heavenly world is present only in a mediated, shadowy form. And Jesus, because He is the center and exponent of this great projection of the supernatural into the lower world, is called 'the Truth.'[240]

Hebrews portrays the characters of the Old Covenant as "looking upward" to the heavenly glorious world, and "looking forward to the

---

[238] Ibid., 200.
[239] Ibid., 201.
[240] Ibid.

New Covenant," as seen, for instance, in "the figure of Melchizedek and about the conception of the promised rest." From the redemptive historical point of view, Christ was "a priest after the order of Melchizedek." This is in accord with the conventional chronology "between type and antitype," with "the former pertaining to the Old, the latter to the New Covenant." Vos also affirms that the earthly rest in the promised land in the Old Covenant was a type of the spiritual and heavenly rest in Jesus in the New Covenant:

> The same observation may be made with regard to the 'rest' promised the people of God. The rest of Canaan given to Israel of old was a type of the supreme rest opened up by Jesus in the New Covenant. But this rest of Canaan was by no means the first or original embodiment of the religious idea of rest. Back of it and above it lay in the heavenly world the σαββατισμὸς of God spoken of in the account of creation, and which is identical with the creation rest, since believers are received by God into the rest that is His own. Generalizing this we may say that according to the teaching of the epistle the Old Testament things are both copies and copied form, and the latter because they are the former.[241]

Thus, the theocratic nation of Israel typified "the perfect Kingdom of God," gloriously consummated in the everlasting Heavenly Kingdom. Moreover, in this ideal realization there will be no distinction between "church and state." This fusion between "the two spheres of secular and religious life" was God's promise to Israel that "Israel will be made 'a kingdom of priests and holy nation' (Ex. 19:6). As priests they are in, nay constitute the kingdom."[242]

The doctrine of justification by faith alone, Vos affirms, is not only forensic but also eschatological in its basic character:

> Justification is a 'δικαίωσιν ζωῆς' (justification of life), and the 'life' thus declared to be its consequent is the endless life, that of which it is promised that the saints 'shall reign' in it, Rom.5:18-21. In general the certainty of salvation so emphatically affirmed by the Apostle with regard to the Christian as such would not be possible, if the central act of the divine saving procedure bore with regard to the future an aspect of relativity ... Ultimately the absoluteness of the divine self-committal

---

[241] Ibid., 202.
[242] Vos, *Biblical Theology*, 126.

inhering in this one aspect of justifying the sinner is due to the feature of its being a 'God-interesting' act in the strongest sense of the word. It is the act in which religion celebrates its triumph, and therefore the act in which the religious and the eschatological are inseparably united. But for this same reason it is in principle capable of being eschatological act in the *exclusive* sense of the word, an act incapable of an anticipation. An experience which was lacking in the *foretaste* of the ultimate enjoyment of God would be to that extent lacking the innermost core of religion itself.[243]

Vos finds that the *forensic* principle of justification, founded upon Christ's fulfillment of the requirements of the law and his resurrection, is the central locus of soteriology. Thus, the foundation of the believers' resurrection springs from "the justification of Christ," which was declared by God through Christ's resurrection (*resurrectio Christi*). The greatest fruit of the justification of Christ (*iustitia Christi*), resulting from his "passive and active obedience," is "the Spirit." Our resurrection comes from Christ's justification, and our justification results from Christ's resurrection. Vos further writes: "Christ's resurrection was the *de facto* declaration of God in regard to his being just. His quickening bears in itself the testimony of his justification. God, through suspending the forces of death operating on Him, declared that the ultimate, the supreme consequence of sin had reached its termination. In other words, resurrection had annulled the sentence of condemnation."[244] In contrast with this, Titius and Holtzmann discredit the forensic character of justification. They solely emphasize "the mystical aspect of the believer's relation to Christ." But, the fulcrum of Pauline theology, according to Vos, lies in its primarily forensic orientation, which subordinates "the mystical aspect of the relation to Christ to the forensic one." "The subjective spiritual changes" in believers are, therefore, the direct result of "the forensic work of Christ applied in justification." "The mystical is based on the forensic, not the forensic on the mystical."[245] This forensic nature of justification has historically been taught in Reformed theology, and has been seen, especially, in the doctrine of the covenant of works.

---

[243] Geerhardus Vos, *The Pauline Eschatology* (Princeton University Press, 1930; reprint, Phillipsburg, New Jersey: Presbyterian and Reformed Publishing Company, 1994), 57-8.
[244] Ibid., 151.
[245] Vos, *Redemptive History*, 384.

Being under this covenant, "Christ by His perfect obedience was just before God, and on the ground of His being just received eternal life."[246]

According to Vos, one of the important theological motifs in Pauline theology is that of *antithesis*. Most prominently, there is antithesis between the first Adam and the last Adam, between Law and Grace. These antithetical principles undergird the forensic character of justification, thus confirming justification by faith alone. Moreover, the eschatological structure becomes clear when we understand it in the light of these antithetical principles:

> What gives dogmatic coloring to his teaching is largely derived from its antithetical structure, as exhibited in the comprehensive antithesis of *the First Adam and the Last Adam* [emphasis mine], sin and righteousness, the flesh and the Spirit, *law and faith* [emphasis mine], and these are precisely the historic reflections of the one great transcendental antithesis between this world and the world-to-come. It is no wonder that such energetic eschatological thinking tended towards consolidation in an orb of compact theological structure. For in it the world-process is viewed as a unit. The end is placed in the light of the beginning, and all intermediate developments are construed with reference to the purpose *a quo* and the terminus *ad quem*.[247]

The Judaistic reliance on the works of the law as the principle of justification was well refuted by Paul in Romans 3:27-28 and 10:3. Paul uses an important hermeneutical principle, namely the antithesis between Law and Gospel, when refuting Jewish legalistic pride. With this he decisively establishes justification *by faith alone* apart from the good works of the law:

> Inspired by such motives, it becomes to him the absolute antithesis to the very idea of religion. Wishing to contrast the gospel of grace with

---

[246] Ibid., 397-98.

[247] Vos, *Pauline Eschatology*, 60-1. Vos consistently cites the antithetical concept in Pauline theology as the background for understanding the gracious character of salvation and justification: "In its soteriological aspect Paul's theology is characterized by the same broad treatment. The great all-embracing contrasts between sin and righteousness, death and life, works and faith, flesh and Spirit will occur to everyone in this connection." idem, *Redemptive History*, 359.

this specific embodiment of the forensic principle, he is willing to stake the entire comparison on the one point, which of the two schemes offers a more effectual safeguard against the cultivation of such detestable pride? 'Where then is the glorying? It is excluded. By what manner of law? Of works? Nay: but by a law of faith. We reckon therefore that a man is justified by faith apart from works of law' (Rom. 3:27,28).[248]

Asserting justification by faith alone and using the hermeneutical principle of the antithesis between Law and Gospel, Vos proceeds to argue that the covenant of grace is *bilateral*. God requires Christians to be active, having "gratitude work on the renewed moral consciousness." The covenant of grace demands "the glorification of God" in the believers' conscience, thus requiring "the active life of the believer." But, this is only true because faith inevitably carries good works (*bona opera*) as "a covenantal obligation in the state of grace." And indeed, this is in contrast with the Roman doctrine of meritorious salvation. If we are united with Christ, then Christ will be active in us, and produce good works in us.[249]

Therefore, according to Vos, the *bilateral* covenant of grace does not mar the principle of justification by faith alone. On the contrary, it excludes evangelical obedience from the doctrine of justification by means of the antithesis between Law and Gospel. On the other hand, good works are the fruits of the application of the moral law in progressive sanctification through the power of the Spirit. The necessity of the application of the moral law in believers, according to Vos, is a definitive biblical theological answer to *antinomianism*.

I. Summary

We have demonstrated one of our theses by arguing that Calvin's covenant concept is fully compatible with the later Reformed Orthodox antithesis between the covenants of works and grace. Calvin maintained an antithesis between Law and Gospel in relation to justification by faith alone; he radically excluded evangelical obedience from this doctrine, and maintained the evangelical consensus of the Protestant Reformation over and against the legalism represented by medieval scholastics. In other words, there is no

---

[248] Ibid., 390-91.
[249] Ibid., 260.

amalgam between Law and Gospel in the doctrine of justification, for we are justified through the imputation of the righteousness of Christ, who fulfilled the requirements of the law.

Calvin states that, as inaugurated in Genesis 3:15, there is but one covenant of grace covering all of *heilsgeschichte* in the postlapsarian state. In regard to this, all of the Old Testament believers were saved and justified in Christ, who was to come later. Calvin's covenant of grace is *bilateral* in its mutuality and conditionality, making for a magnificent balance between the covenant and double predestination. We have seen, however, that Calvin's *bilateral* covenant of grace does not mar justification by faith alone, for he faithfully applied a key hermeneutical principle, namely the antithesis between Law and Gospel. Based on this hermeneutical principle, good works are the fruit of justifying faith in the course of progressive sanctification. Thus, the function of the moral law in the Christian life provides a concrete biblical theological answer to *antinomianism*.

In the Mosaic Covenant, people were saved by the principle of the one covenant of grace. Nevertheless, Calvin, contrasted the Mosaic and New Covenants, and designated the former as the *foedus legale*. The designation of the *foedus legale* for the Mosaic Covenant signifies that the earthly nation of Israel was controlled by types and figures, as they looked up toward the eternal heavenly spiritual kingdom. The national blessings and curses which followed the Israelites' general obedience and disobedience to the law, signified and prefigured the *eschatological* heavenly blessings and the eternal curse. Although Calvin did not use the term *foedus operum* for the prelapsarian Adamic state, he did emphasize that its *eschatological goal* was governed by the principle of the law. Hence, Calvin's theology is fully congruous with the Reformed orthodox hermeneutical principle of the antithesis between the covenants of works and grace.

As a student of Calvin, Olevianus conceived of creation, fall and redemption covenantally, confirming that there is one covenant of grace in which all believers are justified and saved by God's grace in Christ according to and ever since the *protevangelium* of Genesis 3:15. Following in the footsteps of Calvin, Olevianus affirmed that the covenant of grace is *bilateral*, for it manifests the mutuality and conditionality of the covenant. Although the Mosaic Covenant belongs to the covenant of grace in relation to justification and salvation in Christ, Olevianus, in a limited sense, identified the Mosaic Covenant as the *foedus legale*. This designation affirms the antithesis between the principles of Law and Gospel. It simultaneously reveals the principal requirement of the law and condemns human sins. Hence, it points ultimately to the Christ of the New Covenant. The blessings of the promised land typified the Israelites' spiritual heavenly blessings, while the sacrificial animals in the Mosaic Covenant prefigured the sacrificial Lamb, Jesus Christ. We have considered Olevianus as a forerunner of the antithesis between the covenants of works and grace hermeneutics because he applied the terms *foedus creationis*, *foedus primum*, *foedus naturale* and *ius creationis* to the prelapsarian state, thus affirming that the *foedus creationis* had the goal of eschatological life. Olevianus, however, did not apply the antithesis between the covenants of works and grace to the doctrine of justification. Nevertheless, he consistently maintained the antithesis between Law and Gospel, which draws the same conclusion for the doctrine of justification. As a result, he advocates justification by faith alone, which excludes good works. Hence, good works are the fruit of a true faith in the process of sanctification, applying the law in believers' daily life, which is a vital answer to the moral laxity of *antinomianism*.

We have studied Robert Rollock as the theologian who consistently applied the antithesis between the covenants of works and grace, and also to the doctrine of justification by faith alone. This was a result of Rollock's deepening of Olevianus' covenant teaching, to which he had been introduced by Howie. The condition of the *foedus operum* was perfect obedience leading to eschatological life and righteousness according to the principle of the covenant of works revealed in Leviticus 18:5. The eschatological goal and life, however, could not be *meritorious*, for obedience was man's duty as a creature *coram Deo*. Jesus Christ, meanwhile, fulfilled the requirement of the broken covenant of works. Hence, God's redemptive grace in Christ is the foundation of the covenant of grace. In the covenant of grace, faith is the only condition for salvation and comes from the free grace of God as the means through which the righteousness of God is imputed. According to the outworking of the *bilateral* covenant of grace, Rollock affirmed that good works are the result of justifying faith in the Christian life. Even though believers in the Mosaic Covenant were saved according to the covenant of grace as it was administered by types and figures, the *foedus operum* was operative in a limited sense because the law of God was a schoolmaster or tutor pointing to Christ.

Finally, the antithesis between the covenants of works and grace, was adopted by the Westminster Confession of Faith. In the covenant of works, eschatological heavenly life was promised based upon perfect obedience to the law by the representative head, Adam. Death was the punishment upon the breach of the covenant of works. Likewise, the Confession established the law as the governing principle of the prelapsarian state while the covenant was founded upon God's "voluntary condescension." Hence, the covenant of grace was inaugurated, offering life and salvation in Christ, on the basis of God's election. Although the Confession does not designate the Mosaic Covenant as the *foedus operum*, it signifies that the administration of the typical ordinances of the law which governed the earthly nation of Israel was the type and shadow of Christ. Justification is based upon the imputation of Christ's righteousness through faith. Thus, good works are the fruits of a true faith, applying the law as a guiding principle of life.

Owen, one of the greatest minds in Puritan theology, adopted and deepened the antithesis between the covenants of works and grace. The controlling principle of the covenant of works was the law, promising eternal reward and felicity upon perfect obedience according to the principle of "Do this, and live." Owen, however, notes that even though the covenant of works was governed by the principle of the law, the covenantal promise was based upon God's "goodness and grace" due to the distinction between the Creator and creature, and at the same time the threat of punishment was based on God's justice. The covenant of grace, inaugurated in Genesis 3:15, is *antithetical* to the covenant of works in terms of the means of achieving eschatological life. In this respect, works and grace are diametrically opposed to each other. Because the Mosaic Covenant follows Adam's fall, Owen conceives it from the redemptive historical viewpoint of continuity with the covenant of grace. Therefore, under the Mosaic Covenant, believers were saved and justified by virtue of the anticipated New Covenant in Christ. The Mosaic Covenant, nevertheless, reinforced the covenant of works bestowed by God "in the law of creation," even if it was not the means of life and justification on Mount Sinai. The typical ordinances of the Mosaic Covenant, according to the principle of the law, were to typify the heavenly blessings of the New Covenant. Owen consistently applied the diametrical distinction between the covenants of works and grace to the doctrine of justification by faith alone which involves the imputation of an alien righteousness, the righteousness of Christ received by faith. In the covenant of grace, nevertheless, God requires evangelical obedience as the evidence of justification due to the principle of the *bilateral* covenant. Evangelical obedience in the process of progressive sanctification, which applies the moral law, is a vital element of the *ordo salutis* as the fruit of justifying faith.

Turretin further adopted and deepened the radical distinction between the covenants of works and grace by penetrating biblical history *covenantally*. He demonstrated that in the covenant of works *eschatological* life and justification relied on Adam's perfect obedience to the terms of the covenant. "Do this and live" of Leviticus 18:5 was the principle of the covenantal promise in the original covenant, and "cursed is he who continueth not" was also the principle of the condemnation of the covenant of works. The covenant of grace, however, promises not only life, but also everlasting salvation to sinful man in the Mediator, Christ. In addition to this, it is important to notice a historical order in *law and grace*; "the covenant of works precedes and the covenant of grace follows." While recognizing a degree of divine condescension due to the Creator and creature distinction, Turretin asserted that the benefits of the original covenant of works would have been *meritorious* if Adam had fully obeyed the condition of the covenant. The Mosaic Covenant belongs to the covenant of grace in its relation to the principle of salvation and justification. The Mosaic Covenant, however, embodies the *foedus operum* in a limited sense for it reveals the requirements of the law. It condemns sins and looks forward to *eschatological* heavenly blessings through the temporary blessings of the promised land. The curse of the promised land points to the final judgment for unbelievers through the administration of the law. Turretin teaches the antithesis between the covenants of works and grace in the doctrine of justification by faith alone in excluding evangelical obedience. Out of this crucial hermeneutical motif, Turretin establishes that the righteousness of Christ (*iustitia Christi*) is imputed to believers through faith. The *bilateral* character of the covenant of grace does not mar the principle of justification by faith alone to the exclusion of good works because the promises of the law and the gospel must not be confounded. In this respect, good works and holiness are the evidence of genuine Christian life.

Hodge adopted and deepened the antithesis between the covenants of works and grace. The diametrical antithesis between the covenants of works and grace is the hermeneutical background for the comparison between Adam and Christ. As a result, Hodge concludes that the Adamic covenant of works was *meritorious* because the reward was "not of grace but of debt," based upon perfect obedience to the law. On the other hand, Christ's perfect obedience was "the meritorious ground" of the covenant of grace, justifying sinners freely through faith. We have seen the Adam and Christ comparison in the light of *meritorious* ground, and as the foundation of eschatological life. This was *a breakthrough* in Reformed covenant theology. The Mosaic Covenant was a manifestation of the covenant of grace, since believers in that period were saved according to the same principle of Gospel grace as New Covenant believers. The Mosaic Covenant, on the other hand, has the character of "a legal covenant" since theocratic "national security and prosperity" were dependent on the people's obedience "to the Mosaic law," which was administered by the principle of "Do this and live" of Leviticus 18:5. The revelation of the covenant of works teaches that if one is not in Jesus according to the principle of the covenant of grace, then he is still under the principle of the covenant of works. The covenant of works requires perfect obedience, which is impossible. "The imputation of the righteousness of Christ" is the firm ground of the believers' justification. Out of the antithetical distinction between the principles of Law and Gospel, Hodge concludes that justification is by faith alone and excludes good works and evangelical obedience. Evangelical obedience and good works in the Christian life are the fruit of justifying faith. This is analogous to the character of the *bilateral* covenant of grace against *antinomianism*.

Geerhardus Vos stands out as the most influential theological figure in the formulations of biblical covenant theology by John Murray and Meredith G. Kline. Vos, too, adopted the antithesis between the covenants of works and grace as he considered biblical history in the light of its eschatological goal and the concept of the Kingdom of God against the background of the nineteenth century *liberalism*. The fulcrum of the covenant of works lies in the fact that the goal of the covenant was eschatological heavenly life and justification, all ultimately looking up to the *gloria Dei*. Although the original covenant of works was broken, it is still effective as a hypothetical principle for the reception and attainment of everlasting life and justification. Because of the impossibility of keeping the covenant of works, the Spirit of God leads us to genuine conversion by means of the antithesis between Law and Gospel. The covenant of grace, inaugurated in Genesis 3:15, is *bilateral* because it demands "covenant-loyalty" to the sovereign covenantal commitment of God. Therefore, in the light of redemptive historical continuity, Vos argues that the Mosaic Covenant administered heavenly spiritual blessings through "a provisional typical way," and lies in continuity with the New Covenant. Therefore, "the principle of organic continuity of grace" is applied to the believers of that period as well as to New Covenant believers. However, the Mosaic Covenant is *a revival of the covenant of works* since it administers blessings and curses to the Symbolico-Typical Nation of Israel. This is done according to a "general scale" of obedience to the law, and reflects the heavenly blessing and eternal curse. In this light, Vos makes a radical contrast between the Old and New Covenants. The definitive background of our justification stands in the resurrection of Christ through which we are declared by God to be righteous by faith and this forensic character of justification is derived from the antithetical hermeneutical principle between "the First Adam and the Last Adam," between "Law and Faith." Thus, Vos confirms justification by faith alone apart from good works. Although the covenant of grace is *bilateral*, this does not mar the principle of justification by faith alone. God requires evangelical obedience as the fruit of good faith. In this light, evangelical obedience is the fruit of an application of the moral law as it pertains to progressive sanctification through the ongoing work of the Spirit.

We have refuted the Barthian thesis of "Calvin against the Calvinists" which the Barthian alleges to see in the development of the two covenants, namely, the covenants of works and grace. Calvin's covenant concept and theology are fully compatible with the Calvinists' development of the antithesis between the covenants of works and grace. *The antithesis between the covenants of works and grace* along with *the distinction between Law and Gospel* in Reformed orthodox theology has been a key hermeneutical principle in opposition to *legalism*. This antithesis draws out the sovereign principle of salvation and justification, undergirding justification by faith alone apart from the good works of the law. This antithesis between the covenants of works and grace, in the light of the distinction between the First Adam and the Last Adam, underscores the fact that the First Adam's perfect obedience to the law would have been *meritorious* for eschatological life under the covenant of works, providing a clear distinction between the Creator and creature. In doing so, we identified an important concept of *merit*, which may be applied only to "perfect obedience." Thus, we have limited our discussion of the *meritorious* concept of justification and salvation to Adam and Christ, and we have done so from the vantage point of the antithesis between the covenants of works and grace, along with the antithesis between the first and second Adams. On the other hand, when considering the *bilateral* character of the covenant of grace, Reformed theologians have, against the background of *antinomianism*, held that good works are the fruit or evidence of justifying faith through the application of the moral law in the course of progressive sanctification.

From a redemptive historical standpoint, the Mosaic Covenant, as the Old Covenant, lies in continuity with the Abrahamic and New Covenants in terms of salvation and justification, which were applied according to the principle of the *foedus gratiae*. It is, however, the revival of the *foedus legale* or the *foedus operum*, which reveals the principal requirements of the law and governs the earthly Nation of Israel according to the *general* principle of the law. The earthly blessings of the theocratic nation of Israel typify the everlasting heavenly blessing whereas the curse signifies eternal spiritual death as the result of the *general level* of the Israelites' obedience and disobedience to the law. In other words, the limited implication of the *foedus legale* or the *foedus operum* to the administration of blessings or curses to the nation of Israel provides the *eschatological* understanding and direction of the Old Covenant, and applies the principle of the law of Leviticus 18:5 in its economy. This *eschatological* nature of the Old Covenant has been further clarified by *typology*, especially as applied by Geerhardus Vos.

We conclude then, that the antithesis between the covenants of works and grace along with the antithesis between Law and Gospel stand or fall together in the covenant hermeneutics developed by the Reformed tradition. These hermeneutical principles are a candlelight to the understanding of the *historia salutis* and the *ordo salutis*. We, therefore, have established a solid historical theological background of Reformed covenant theology which sets the table for the covenant theology of John Murray and Meredith G. Kline. We now proceed to

Murray and Kline, who are two distinguished Reformed theologians belonging to the Westminster School of the twentieth century.

Chapter Two

JOHN MURRAY'S RESPONSE TO FEDERAL THEOLOGY

John Murray[1] *apparently* does not use the antithesis between the covenants of works and grace that has been a key hermeneutical principle in the Reformed tradition. He does not construe the Adamic administration covenantally. Having said this, we will pay special attention to whether Murray's rejection is linguistic or substantial. Murray's rejection of the *foedus legale* or *foedus operum* in the prelapsarian state is based upon his own historical and biblico-theological conclusions in identifying himself with Calvin. Murray is agnostic about the precise origin of the doctrine of the covenant of works: "But he [Calvin] did not construe this Adamic constitution as a *covenant* of works or of law. It is difficult to discover the genealogy of the doctrine of the Covenant of Works which appeared in fully developed form in the last decade of the 16th century. It may be that the earliest suggestion is found in Caspar Olevianus."[2] Thus, Murray suggests some modifications of the classical Reformed covenant theology of the 17th century because biblico-theological study does not prove the concept of the *foedus operum*: "Biblico-theological study will show that the traditional formulation of covenant theology,

---

[1] See the detailed biographical sketch on Murray written by Iain H. Murray, which is found in *Collected Writings of John Murray*, 4 vols. (Edinburgh / Carlisle: The Banner of Truth Trust, 1976-1982), 3:3-158. For analysis of Murray's theology and location in the history of Reformed thought, see Sinclair B. Ferguson's "John Murray," in *Handbook of Evangelical Theologians* ed. Walter A. Elwell (Grand Rapids: Baker Book House, 1993), 168-81.

[2] Murray, *Collected Writings*, 4:219.

especially that associated with the 17th century, needs modification. This revision does not in the least degree interfere with the centrality of covenant administration in the history of redemption. In fact it only serves to accentuate the significance of the covenant concept."[3] In this regard, Murray is a revisionist covenant theologian. We will see, however, that Murray's theology is fully compatible with the *antithesis* between the covenant of works and grace because he utilizes all the theological benefits and motifs of bipolar covenant distinction hermeneutics, namely the covenant of works and grace even though he rejects the term *foedus operum*. Murray, as a distinguished Reformed systematician, realizes that the antithesis between Law and Gospel is foundational, drawing out justification by faith alone apart from good works, whereas he interprets progressive sanctification as the outworking of the Spirit of God in applying the law in the believers' life, a biblical theological answer to *antinomianism*.

Murray does not like to designate the Mosaic Covenant as the *foedus operum* or *foedus legale* because not only does he not like the idea of the covenant of works or law, but he also understands it exclusively in the light of *continuity* with the Abrahamic and New Covenants. This is his biblical theological answer to the Reformed tradition in which the majority of Reformed theologians have tried to make a balance between *continuity* and *discontinuity*. In general, as we have observed in chapter one, they have expounded the Sinai Covenant, in such a way that it belongs to the covenant of grace in the light of redemptive historical continuity, and that believers in that period were saved and justified under the principle of the covenant of grace, whereas the administration of the law was applied to the theocratic nation of Israel by earthly blessings and curses due to the *general obedience* or *disobedience* of the nation or people to typify the everlasting heavenly life and eternal spiritual death which is clearly enunciated in the New Covenant. Thus, Murray's analysis of the Mosaic Covenant does not interpret it in the light of an *eschatological perspective* because he understands it *exclusively* from the perspective of *continuity* with the Abrahamic and New Covenants. We, however, will observe that the rejection of "the covenant of works" in Murray's covenantal discussion does not tone down the principle of justification by faith alone, for he carefully adopts the Law and Gospel antithesis as

---

[3] Ibid., 4:322-23.

the hermeneutical background of its formulation. Standing in the tradition of Reformed theology, Murray affirms that the antithesis between Law and Gospel in relation to justification does not nullify the Christian implications of the law. Therefore, the law is vital as the rule and guidance of the Christian life, bearing good fruit and good works which will be applied to the eschatological heavenly reward. After all is said and done, we will see that in Murray's theology the antithesis between Law and Gospel is a decisive hermeneutical tool to undergird the *historia salutis* and *ordo salutis*.

A. The Adamic Administration instead of the Covenant of Works

After his own careful analysis, Murray wants to reconstruct the traditional covenant concept in which Reformed orthodox theologians have identified the covenant of works in the prelapsarian state. In opposition to the notion of the covenant of works, he designates it as "the Adamic administration":

> This administration has often been denoted 'The Covenant of Works.' (1) The term is not felicitous, for the reason that the elements of grace entering into the administration are not properly provided for by the term 'works.' (2) It is not designated a covenant in Scripture. Hosea 6:7 may be interpreted otherwise and does not provide the basis for such a construction of the Adamic economy. Besides, Scripture always uses the term covenant, when applied to God's administration to men, in reference to a provision that is redemptive or closely related to redemptive design. Covenant in Scripture denotes the oath-bound confirmation of promise and involves a security which the Adamic economy did not bestow.[4]

---

[4] Murray, *Collected Writings*, 2: 49. In his evaluation of 'The Theology of the Westminster Confession of Faith,' Murray asserts that, if we may use the term, *covenant* in respect to the Adamic administration, the covenant of life is better than the covenant of works because the element of grace is introduced in the Adamic administration: "The term 'covenant of works' to designate the Adamic administration (Chap. VII, Sect. II) is not an accurate designation. If the term 'covenant' is used, the designation in the Shorter Catechism, 'covenant of life,' is preferable." idem, *Collected Writings*, 4:261-62. However, the first generation scholars of Westminster Theological Seminary in Philadelphia, who were Murray's colleagues, recognized *univocally* the antithesis between the covenants of works and grace as an important biblical theological idea, basically agreeing with the development of federal theology in covenant hermeneutics. For a comprehensive discussion of this issue, see:

Oswald T. Allis, "The Covenant of Works," in *Basic Christian Doctrines: Contemporary Evangelical Thought*, ed. Carl F. H. Henry (New York/Chicago/San Francisco: Holt, Rinehart & Winston, 1962), 96-102; J. Gresham Machen, *The Christian View of Man* (Edinburgh / Carlisle: The Banner of Truth Trust, 1937; reprint, 1995); idem, *God Transcendent*, ed. Ned B. Stonehouse (Edinburgh / Carlisle: The Banner of Truth Trust, 1982); Cornelius Van Til, "Covenant Theology," in *New 20th-Century Encyclopedia of Religious Knowledge*, 2d ed., ed. J. D. Douglas (Grand Rapids, Michigan: Baker Book House, 1991); idem, *The Defense of the Faith*, 3rd ed. (Phillipsburg, New Jersey: Presbyterian and Reformed Publishing Company, 1967), 90-5; Edward J. Young, "Confession and Covenant," in *Scripture and Confession: A Book about Confessions Old and New*, ed. John H. Skilton (Phillipsburg, New Jersey: Presbyterian and Reformed Publishing Company, 1973), 31-66; idem, *Genesis 3: A Devotional and Expository Study* (The Banner of Truth Trust, 1983); idem, *The Study of Old Testament Theology Today* (Westwood, New Jersey: Fleming H. Revell Company, 1959), 61-86.

As such, in the shaping of Murray's own attitude toward the *foedus operum*, there is no clear evidence that there was active discussion on the issues at Westminster Theological Seminary. Murray's respected teacher and colleague, J. Gresham Machen adopts the antithesis between the *foedus operum* and *gratiae* in his popular book, *The Christian View of Man* which was published posthumously in 1937. Interestingly, Murray himself wrote a foreword to the British edition in 1965. He remarks that Machen's *The Christian View of Man* and *The Christian Faith in the Modern World* "represent Dr. Machen's maturest thought on the subject of Christian doctrine." Machen, *The Christian View of Man*, 7. Moreover, Machen recognizes that Murray was a *systematic theological adviser* when he prepared *The Christian View of Man*: "Mr. John Murray, who is in charge of the Department of Systematic Theology in Westminster Seminary, to whom I am indebted in a great many ways this autumn and last spring in my preparation for this little series of talks, has called my attention." Ibid., 115.

In addition, Edward J. Young, who was a good friend and colleague of Murray and a prominent Old Testament scholar, adopts the bipolar covenant distinction of the Confession as a proper understanding of Scripture. He accepts Murray's definition of the divine covenant, "sovereign administration of grace and promise" quoting from Murray's popular pamphlet published in 1953, *The Covenant of Grace*. Young, "Confession and Covenant," 31-66. In this respect, we assume that their consensus, perhaps, was that the important issue is the implication of the theological notions of the *foedus operum* and not the usage of its terminology. It does not appear that Murray communicated with them on the *foedus operum* before his rejection of it.

The presupposition of Murray is that the biblical account of the nature of the divine covenant is to be interpreted from God's sovereign administration of grace and promise, understanding it exclusively within the category of redemption. Murray, however, does not ascertain this specific character in the Adamic epoch, for the Adamic economy does not provide the term *foedus*. Murray, therefore, identifies it as "the Adamic administration" and replaces the classical rendering of the covenant of works. Murray's focal point, in the Adamic epoch, is to prove that there is no covenant of works as classical Reformed covenant theologians have rendered it because the Adamic administration was not a covenantal formulation or engagement.

In this regard, Murray criticizes the classical Reformed understanding of the Mosaic Covenant. He emphasizes the uniqueness of the Adamic administration and radically separates it from the Old Covenant, which the Reformed tradition sometimes designated the *foedus legale* or *foedus operum* in relation to the original covenant of works in a limited sense. It applied the law as the governing principle of the Theocratic Kingdom of Israel by blessing and curse, ultimately pointing to the eschatological heavenly spiritual blessing and eternal spiritual death. Murray's thesis is that there is a radical antithesis between "the Adamic administration" and the Mosaic Covenant. The former was governed by the law as the means of *eschatological glory*, whereas the latter was to be understood *only* in the light of the covenant of grace:

> Whether or not the administration is designated covenant, the uniqueness and singularity must be recognized. It should never be confused with what Scripture calls the old covenant or first covenant (cf. Jer. 31:31-34; 2 Cor. 3:14; Heb. 8:7,13). The first or old covenant is the Sinaitic. And not only must this confusion in denotation be avoided, but also any attempt to interpret the Mosaic covenant in terms of the Adamic institution. The latter could apply only to the state of innocence, and to Adam alone as representative head. The view that in the Mosaic covenant there was a repetition of the so-called covenant of works, current among covenant theologians, is a grave misconception and involves an erroneous construction of the Mosaic covenant, as well as fails to assess the uniqueness of the Adamic administration. The Mosaic covenant was distinctly redemptive in character and was continuous with and extensive of the Abrahamic covenants. The

Adamic had no redemptive provision, nor did its promissory element have any relevance within a context that made redemption necessary.[5]

The phrase, 'Do this and you will live' of Leviticus 18:5 is very significant for understanding Murray's covenant theology. He raises a critical question about the implication of Leviticus 18:5: "Could Paul properly have appealed to Lev. 18:5 as an illustration of works-righteousness in opposition to that of faith?" Murray answers that the principle of works-righteousness is operative and active only in the prelapsarian state. As such, the principle of works was the means of eschatological justification and life before the fall of Adam. After the fall, however, the principle of works is not operative as the means of justification and salvation. Accordingly, in the Old Covenant context, the principle of works was *not operative*:

> This principle has the strictest relevance and application in a state of perfect integrity. It is the principle of equity in God's government. Wherever there is righteousness to the full extent of God's demand there must also be the corresponding justification and life ... Perfect righteousness must elicit God's favour or complacency and with this favour goes the life that is commensurate with it. This would have obtained for Adam in sinless integrity apart from any special constitution that special grace would have contemplated. This relationship could have no application to mankind after the fall. It can never again be in operation for man's acceptance with God and for the life that accompanies this acceptance.[6]

In the light of the analogy or parallel between Adam and Christ, however, Murray draws out the crucial concept that eschatological life and justification were an ultimate goal in the prelapsarian Adamic epoch according to obedience to the law. Murray follows the classical Reformed understanding of the *eschatological goal* of God's creation although he eliminates the concept of the *foedus* in it:

> Analogy is drawn between Adam and Christ. They stand in unique relations to mankind. There is none before Adam - he is the first man.

---

[5] Murray, *Collected Writings*, 2:50.

[6] John Murray, *The Epistle to the Romans: The New International Commentary on the New Testament*, 2 vols. (Grand Rapids, Michigan: Eerdmans Publishing Company, 1968), II:249-50.

There is none between - Christ is the second man. There is none after Christ - he is the last Adam (1 Cor. 15:44-49). Here we have an embracive construction of human relationships. We know also that in Christ there is representative relationship and that obedience successively completed has its issue in righteousness, justification, life for all he represents (1 Cor. 15:22). So a period of obedience successfully completed by Adam would have secured eternal life for all represented by him.[7]

Identifying himself with Geerhardus Vos,[8] Murray states that if Adam had passed an intensified period of probation with obedience, he would have been translated into the stage of *non posse peccare* which is the permanent state of eschatological heavenly life. In this regard, we may establish that Murray understands creation, fall and redemption in the light of historical order of *law and grace* although the elements of grace were injected into the Adamic administration from the vantage point of a distinction between the Creator and creature.

The Adamic administration is, therefore, construed as an administration in which God, by a special act of providence, established for man the provision whereby he might pass from the status of contingency to one of confirmed and indefectible holiness and blessedness, that is, from *posse peccare* and *posse non peccare* to *non*

---

[7] Murray, *Collected Writings*, 2:49

[8] The eschatological goal and life in the original covenant of works has been well treated by Vos, *Biblical Theology*, 22: "This is connected with the state in which man was created and the advance from this to a still higher estate. Man had been created perfectly good in a moral sense. And yet there was a sense in which he could be raised to a still higher level of perfection. On the surface this seems to involve a contradiction. It will be removed by closely marking the aspect in regard to which the advance was contemplated. The advance was meant to be from unconfirmed to confirmed goodness and blessedness; to the confirmed state in which these possessions could no longer be lost, a state in which man could no longer sin, and hence could no longer become subject to the consequences of sin. Man's original state was a state of indefinite probation: he remained in possession of what he had, so long as he did not commit sin, but it was not a state in which the continuance of his religious and moral status could be guaranteed him. In order to assure this for him, he had to be subjected to an intensified, concentrated probation, in which, if he remained standing, the status of probation would be forever left behind. The provision of this new, higher prospect for man was an act of condescension and high favour."

posse peccare. The way instituted was that of 'an intensified and concentrated probation,' the alternative issues being dependent upon the issues of obedience or disobedience.[9]

Murray is careful to affirm that the original relationship between God and man was "the ethico-religious bond" which is almost an identical concept to the *foedus*. In other words, Murray wants to preserve all the benefits of the Reformed understanding of the *foedus operum* although he rejects the term itself, understanding that man anticipated the eschatological heavenly glory, executing the cultural mandate as the *imago Dei* from the beginning of the world:

> God placed man on probation and gave commands that were to be consciously and intelligently fulfilled (cf. Gen. 2:15-17). Between God and man there is the ethico-religious bond, a relationship not hinted in the case of the other creatures. For man there is the cultural mandate (cf. Gen. 1:28) co-ordinate with the dominion bestowed upon him. The implications of this mandate make its relevance inconceivable on any lower level than that pertaining to man as defined in Genesis 1:26. And the mandate is given, not as an undertaking to be fulfilled after he has attained a future stage of development, but it is his from the outset. All the powers necessary for the task are conceived of as belonging to him in virtue of his creation in God's image and likeness.[10]

---

[9] Murray, *Collected Writings*, 2:49. At this point, we need to articulate Murray's thought that although the element of grace was introduced at the prelapsarian state, *the means of eschatological justification and life was law*. Therefore, the historical order of creation, fall and redemption may be understood in the light of *law and grace* regarding the means of eschatological life and justification: "The reference is to the original purpose of the law. The purpose of law in man's original estate was not to give occasion to sin but to direct and regulate man's life in the path of righteousness and, therefore, to guard and promote life. By reason of sin, however, that same law promotes death, in that it gives occasion to sin. And the wages of sin is death. The more law is registered in our consciousness the more sin is aroused to action, and law, merely as law, can exercise no restraining or remedial effect. That the law 'was found' to be unto death reflects on the tragedy of Paul's own experience and the disappointment, the disillusionment, which overtook him." idem, *Romans*, 7:10.

[10] Murray, *Collected Writings*, 2:10.

The probation period, Murray asserts, is the period of confirmation in expectation of the eschatological glory: "Man was created in knowledge, righteousness, and holiness. But confirmation of these is a much higher state of blessedness. Confirmation adds to what is good; it does not presuppose evil, the opposite of good."[11]

Man as the *imago Dei*, Murray asserts, had special sovereignty and lordship over the other creatures, ruling over them as the vicegerent of the Creator God according to the principle of Genesis 1:26: "That man's creation is the last in the series, we may regard as correlative with this lordship. The prerogative rests, however, not on the sequence but upon the nature with which man is endowed. He is in the image of God. Since God is sovereign, man's likeness to God involves the exercise of a sovereignty that is correspondent. He is God's vicegerent because he is like God."[12]

Man, "created in the image of God," argues Murray, was a "religious agent," being made "upright and holy and therefore constituted for the demand, endowed with the character enabling him to fulfill all the demands developing upon him by reason of God's propriety in him and sovereignty over him." The logical order of the eschatological stages was that of righteousness, justification, and life while the reverse side of the order according to man's lapse would be unrighteousness, condemnation, and death. Murray is careful to show that although the Adamic administration was not a *foedus operum* or *foedus legale*, it was, nonetheless, governed by the principle of the law, namely "perfect legal reciprocity." This analysis is pertinent in Murray's thought because it is an evidence that Murray understands the historical order as *law and grace* and not vice versa:

> As long as man fulfilled these demands his integrity would have been maintained. He would have continued righteous and holy. In this righteousness he would be justified, that is, approved and accepted by God, and he would have life. Righteousness, justification, life is an invariable combination in the government and judgment of God. There would be a relation that we may call perfect legal reciprocity. As this would be the minimum, so it would be the maximum in terms of the relation constituted by creation in the image of God.[13]

---

[11] Ibid., 2:15.

[12] Ibid., 2:5.

[13] Ibid., 2:47. As Donald Macleod properly observes, Murray's theological analysis of the Adamic administration is congenial to the *foedus operum* of

One of the fatal problems of the *dialectical hermeneutics* propounded by Rudolf Bultmann, argues Murray, is the rejection of the historical order of *law and gospel* along with an antithetical character of Law and Gospel in relation to salvation, which inevitably distorts the Gospel itself. The antithesis and historical order of Law and Gospel to promulgate the Gospel were pertinent to the Reformation as a whole.[14]

Characteristically, man had the ability to fulfill the requirements of the law of God in the prelapsarian state: "In his original state man had plenary ability to fulfill all of God's demands. To maintain otherwise would mean that sin was a necessity of the condition in which he was created. For all failure to meet the full demands of God is sin."[15]

Disobedience, attaching "the threat of death" in Genesis 2:17, would bring "the consequences of the penal judgment," enunciated "in connection with the tree of the knowledge of good and evil." On the other hand, the tree of life in the Garden of Eden in Genesis 3:22 and 24 was "symbolic of life," signifying "the seal of everlasting life." Thus, in the Adamic institution, there was "some provision for eternal life" attached to "the promise of life" and contingent upon obedience

---

covenant theology since Murray carefully reserves the important aspects of the original covenant of works, developed in the covenant hermeneutics although he avoids the term *foedus operum*: "Murray agreed, however, that the divine arrangements with Adam involved both conditions and promises, and traditional federal theologians would probably not have asked for more. He was also thoroughly conservative in his overall view, arguing, for example, that 'the Adamic administration with all its implications for racial solidarity' alone provided an explanation for original sin." Donald Macleod, "Covenant Theology," in *Dictionary of Scottish Church History & Theology*, ed. Nigel M. De S. Cameron (Downers Grove, Illinois: InterVarsity Press, 1993), 217.

[14] Murray, *Collected Writings*, 1:294: "There is the basic fallacy that men apart from the conviction created and conditioned by law and gospel are able to know what their real situation and need are. It is God's judgment respecting sin and misery that must be brought to bear upon men where they are and where they find themselves. When this priority is not observed, then all presumed relevance is a distortion of the gospel–in our day in the hands of its leading exponent, Rudolf Bultmann, such a distortion as denies the central elements of the gospel, the vicarious expiatory blood-shedding of the Saviour and his bodily resurrection from the dead. We must unashamedly and uncompromisingly declare the whole counsel of God, so that men, in conviction, will be *made* relevant to the gospel. This is the relevance Reformation requires and it is the relevance Reformation will bring."

[15] Ibid., 2:83.

according to "the analogy of Genesis 2:17 in respect of disobedience." Hence, the tree of life in Genesis 3:22 was reserved "for the issue of probationary obedience" by providence or revelation while Adam stood as a public head.[16]

Another theological reason that Murray's Adamic administration is fully compatible with the Reformed orthodox view of bipolar covenant hermeneutics is that he understands sin as "the transgression of the law." Murray writes: "And if sin is the transgression of the law, righteousness must be conformity to the law. The law of God which Paul characterizes in this Epistle as Spiritual, that is to say, divine in its origin and nature, and holy and just and good after the pattern of him who is its author (Romans 7:12, 14), must be regarded as the criterion of righteousness no less than it is the criterion of sin."[17] From the vantage point of Pauline theology, the concept of sin, Murray asserts, must be understood in the light of law:

> Since the law is the law of God and its inviolable sanctions are divine, we cannot think of sin and its consequence apart from the law. To this Paul refers in various contexts and in varying ways. Without the law there would be no sinful situation. 'Where no law is, neither is there transgression' (Rom. 4:15). 'Sin is not imputed when there is no law' (Rom. 5:13). 'Without the law sin was dead' (Rom. 7:8). 'The power of sin is the law' (1 Cor. 15:56). And the function of the law in exposing sin arises from this same consideration. 'Through the law is the knowledge of sin' (Gal. 3:20). 'I had not known sin except through the law' (Rom. 7:7). 'I was alive without the law once, but when the commandment came sin revived and I died' (Rom. 7:9). 'I through law died to law' (Gal. 2:19). Also the provoking of the flesh to exercise proceeds from the divinity of the law (cf. Rom. 7:8,11,13).[18]

---

[16] Ibid., 2:48-9.

[17] Murray, *Principles of Conduct*, 191.

[18] Murray, *Collected Writings*, 4:137. Thus, in Murray's thought it is important to notice that the governing principle of the prelapsarian state was *the law* because he understands the concept of sin exclusively from the vantage point of "transgression of law," although the elements of grace were introduced already due to the logic of the distinction between the Creator and creature: "Sin is transgression of law (*anomia*), and law is the expression of all that God is in the moral sphere in relation to man, as absolute and Sovereign Creator and Ruler and righteous Judge. Sin is all along the line of divine perfection a contradiction of each." Ibid., 2:70; "The law that sin violates is the law of God. The categorical imperative binds, demands and

Referring to Romans 5:13-14, Murray asserts that law was present from the beginning of world. That is the reason why sin must be understood in the light of law. As such, Adam's sin was the transgression of revealed law in creation:

> And the thought is that, even though the law had not been promulgated as it was by Moses at Sinai, nevertheless there was law and this is shown by the fact that there was sin-if there had been no law there would have been no sin ... The thought may be paraphrased thus: although it is true that from Adam to Moses sin was in the world and therefore law, though thus there was sin such as would explain the presence of death, yet in that period death reigned not only over those who were violators of expressly revealed law, as was Adam, but also over those who did not sin in that manner, that is, after the pattern of Adam.[19]

Interpreting Romans 5:20-21, Murray argues that Adam's sin was disobedience to the revealed law from God. In this respect, the revelation of the Mosaic Law (*lex Mosaica*) was a clear manifestation of God's law over against the background of human sins: "Adam's trespass was disobedience to expressly revealed commandment. When the law came in through Moses, there was henceforth a multiplication of the kind of transgression exemplified in Adam's trespass, that is to say, transgression of clearly revealed commandment."[20]

God's eschatological heavenly promise was contingent upon Adam's obedience in the Adamic administration. Following the arguments of Shedd[21] and Witsius, Murray argues that the goal of

---

commands because it proceeds from the authority of God, and the authority of God inheres in his being and nature as God. The law of God is simply the expression or transcript of his moral perfection for the regulation of thought and life consonant with his perfection. It is not the law of cosmos, nor the law of reason; it is the law that expresses the nature and will of the supreme personality who has authority over us and propriety in us, to whom we owe complete submission and absolute devotion. We are bound to love the Lord our God with all our heart and soul and strength and mind, and such love is the fulfilling of the law. Herein appears the perverseness of the idea that the moral law may be abrogated and is superseded by love." Ibid., 2:78.

[19] Murray, *Romans*, 5:13-14.
[20] Ibid., 5:20-21.
[21] Although Murray cites Shedd to support his idea that the Adamic administration was based upon "God's faithfulness, not on the basis of

eschatological glory was not based upon *the justice of God* but the faithfulness of God. Accordingly, the ultimate goal of eschatological life was not *meritorious* because it was in a sense "a promise of grace" in the light of the antithesis between the Creator and creature. Murray's thesis is that the eschatological life and justification in the prelapsarian state were upon obedience to the law of God. It was, nevertheless, "a promise of grace" because Murray wants to eliminate the meritorious concept with regard to the prelapsarian state:

> In connection with the promise of life it does not appear justifiable to appeal, as frequently has been done, to the principle enunciated in certain texts (cf. Lev. 18:5; Rom. 10:5; Gal. 3:12), 'This do and thou shalt live.' The principle asserted in these texts is the principle of equity that righteousness is always followed by the corresponding award. From the promise of the Adamic administration we must dissociate all notions of meritorious reward. The promise of confirmed integrity and blessedness was one annexed to an obedience that Adam owed and, therefore, was a promise of grace. All that Adam could have claimed on the basis of equity was justification and life as long as he perfectly obeyed, but not confirmation so as to insure indefectibility. Adam could claim the fulfillment of the promise if he stood the probation, but only on the basis of God's faithfulness, not on the basis of justice. God is debtor to his own faithfulness. But justice requires no more than the approbation and life correspondent with the righteousness of perfect conformity with the will of God.[22]

God threatened death upon Adam's disobedience (Gen. 2:17; 3:17-19). Death, argues Murray, has a threefold perspective: "spiritual (moral and religious), judicial, and psycho-physical." According to the above mentioned passages and Romans 5:12-19, the accent lies on "psycho-physical death." "*Spiritually* our first parents became dead in the day they sinned. Their sin constituted this death; they estranged themselves from God and their mind became enmity against God.

---

justice," we should realize that Shedd confirms that the covenant of works was meritorious while it was based upon "the promise of God": "The merit to be acquired under the covenant of works was pactional. Adam could claim the reward, in case he stood, only by virtue of the promise of God; not by virtue of the original relation of a creature to the creator. Upon the latter basis, he could claim nothing, as Christ teaches in Luke 17:10." William G. T. Shedd, *Dogmatic Theology* (New York: Charles Scribner's Sons, 1888), 2:153

[22] Murray, *Collected Writings*, 2:55-6.

Judicially they also died the day they sinned; they became subject to the curse. *Psycho-physical* death can be said to have befallen them the day they sinned, in that mortality became their lot."[23] Thus, Murray's thought on the Adamic administration is substantially compatible with the classical Reformed concept of the covenant of works because he recognizes the stability of the law as the governing principle of the prelapsarian state, anticipating the heavenly eschatological glory. Murray also analyzes the nature, condition, promise, and threatening of the Adamic administration which have been expounded by Reformed orthodox theologians under the rubric of the *foedus legale* or *foedus operum*.[24]

B. The Covenant of Grace

Murray does not favor the traditional use of the term covenant for the inter-trinitarian covenant, the so called "covenant of redemption" which is presupposed by the covenant of grace. He argues that the term "covenant" in the Bible refers only to "temporal administration" and he goes on to notice that "it is not strictly proper to use a biblical term to designate something to which it is not applied in the Scripture itself. For this reason it is not well, and is liable to be confusing, to speak of this economy in terms of covenant. I prefer some such designation as the inter-trinitarian economy of salvation."[25] In his analysis of the Confession, Murray argues that covenant belongs to the sphere of history and redemption. As such, the grace of the divine election reaches realization and zenith in history through covenantal arrangements: "A confessional statement respecting salvation must be

---

[23] Ibid., 2:56.

[24] In this respect, Murray recognizes that there are four principal elements in the formulation of the covenant: "The formulation of a covenant, therefore, took the form of a four fold division-contracting parties, conditions, promises, threatenings. It was also defined in terms of *stipulation*, denoting the demand of God placed upon man, of *promise* on the part of God to man, of *astipulation*, referring to the acceptance on man's part of the conditions prescribed by God, and , finally, of *restipulation,* whereby man could claim the promise on his fulfillment of the prescribed demands." Ibid., 4:217.

[25] Ibid., 2:130. Murray in his discussion of 'Regeneration,' however, talks about "eternal covenant": "We are dealing with the application of redemption, with the question how men actually become partakers of the blessings of the eternal covenant ratified and sealed by the redemptive work of Christ." Ibid., 2:167.

oriented to God's sovereign election. This, as we found, the Confession does. But the purpose of grace originating in election comes to realization in history in covenantal administration. Biblical theology demonstrates that redemptive revelation and accomplishment are covenantal. Covenant in Scripture denotes administration to men in the sphere of history."[26]

In the Reformed tradition, there is no uniform designation of "the term 'covenant of redemption,'" Murray argues, because it cannot describe sufficiently "the aspects of God's counsel." Because of this, many representative covenant theologians use other terms instead of the covenant of redemption such as "pact", "compact (pactum)", and "counsel of redemption."[27]

Reviewing Samuel G. Craig's *Christianity Rightly So Called*, Murray notes that the essential element of Christianity in opposition to liberalism and modernism, includes the "supernaturalism of Christianity," as Craig rightly suggests. Furthermore, the foundational content of Christianity, Murray asserts, is revealed in the phase of God's election and the covenant of grace. In other words, the fountain of God's redemptive action in history is the divine election and the covenant of grace:

> If, however, Christianity in its essential content is to be stated in terms of that which it really and truly is, there is one phase that is foundational and fontal, giving direction, orientation and character to the whole presentation, which is rather noticeably absent in *Christianity Rightly So Called*. This phase is the truth of God's sovereign purpose of electing love and grace. When we think of Christianity in its objective aspect as the sum total of God's redemptive action and revelation we must not forget that the fountain

---

[26] Ibid., 4:254. Thus, Murray asserts that the concept of covenant is applicable only to the *heilsgeschichte*. In this respect, in his review on G. C. Berkouwer's *Studies in Dogmatics: Divine Election* Murray notices that the biblical concept of covenant refers to the realm of history: "However, in the reviewer's judgment, covenant in Scripture always refers to historical administration and it is a deviation from biblical usage to construct the relations which the persons of the godhead sustained to one another in the counsels of eternity in terms of *covenant*. The *doctrine* of the *pactum* is not thus bereft of any of its significance but it is given a more biblico-theological orientation." Ibid., 4:326.

[27] Ibid., 4:234-38.

from which this whole process of redemptive action springs is God's sovereign purpose of election. Stated in other terms, we should say that the fountain is the covenant of grace. The whole process of redemption, viewed both objectively and subjectively, as once-for-all accomplishment and as continuous progressive application until it reaches its consummation in the glorification of the whole body of the elect, cannot be given proper orientation or adequate exposition except as it is subsumed under the category of the covenant of grace.[28]

1. The Noahic Covenant

The Noahic Covenant after the flood in Genesis 9:9-17, asserts Murray, is the paradigm of the covenant of grace and the pattern for other biblical covenants. It is the reason why Murray begins to discuss the covenant of grace with the postdiluvian Noahic Covenant in his popular pamphlet, *The Covenant of Grace*, which was published originally in 1954. Murray emphasizes that "we may consider, first of all, that instance which, perhaps more than any other in Scripture, assists us in discovering what the essence of covenant is, namely, the post-diluvian Noahic covenant (Gen. 9:9-17)."[29] It is the covenant of

---

[28] Ibid., 3:329-31. This fontal content of Christianity, argues Murray, is deformed and falsified in the Romish and Arminian theologies. As such, the fontal character of Christianity such as supernatural, historical and redemptive action is highlighted and realized in the historical unfolding of divine election and the covenant of grace: "And alas! The very truths which give the only proper orientation and direction to the exposition of Christianity as a supernatural, historical and redemptive movement of divine action and revelation are the very truths which are *falsified* in such deformations of Christianity as Romanism and Arminianism ... In other words, Christianity cannot receive proper understanding, or its exposition proper orientation, unless it is viewed as that which issues from, and is consummated in the accomplishment of, the covenant counsel and purpose of Father, Son and Holy Spirit ... It is on the crest of the wave of God's electing and covenant grace that Christianity as an historical phenomenon realizes itself and it is on the crest of that wave that its overtures break on the shores of lost humanity." Ibid., 3:332.

[29] John Murray, *The Covenant of Grace: Biblical & Theological Studies* (London: Tyndale Press, 1954; reprint, Phillipsburg: Presbyterian and Reformed Publishing Company, 1988), 12. Evaluating Murray's understanding of biblical covenant theology, Robertson correctly states: "In the case of Murray, the covenant with Noah provides the pattern by which the

God established and dispensed by God alone, and its scope is universal. The covenantal promise and its fulfillment are unconditional. Murray goes on to state that "the covenant is intensely and pervasively monergistic. Nothing exhibits this more clearly than the fact that the sign attached to attest and seal the divine faithfulness and the irrevocability of God's promise is one produced by conditions over which God alone has control and in connection with which there is rigid exclusion of human co-operation."[30]

Murray establishes his thesis on the basis of the Davidic Covenant. He argues that the Davidic Covenant passages such as Isaiah 49:8 and 55:3 are proof that the post-diluvian Noahic Covenant is the pattern of God's covenant of grace with his people, and "it is an oath-bound and oath-certified assurance of irrevocable grace and promise."[31] In addition to these, the Noahic Covenant is "an everlasting covenant." From these arguments, Murray tries to confirm the *unilateral* character of the Noahic Covenant. Not only that, but the concept of compact or agreement must be removed.[32] Murray emphasizes that it is a *unilateral* covenant from the beginning to its execution in redemptive history. The next point is whether the pre-diluvian Noahic Covenant in Genesis 6:18-22 is consistent with the post-diluvian Noahic Covenant. Murray recognizes that there is an apparent difference in terms of man's role between the two covenants. Yet, it is a consistent *unilateral* covenant. Murray writes:

> Yet even in this case, where obedience to commandments is the means through which the grace of the covenant is to be realized and enjoyed, we must also take note of the fact that in other respects this covenant exhibits the features of divine initiation, determination, establishment, and confirmation which are so conspicuous in the post-diluvian Noahic

---

rest of the covenants of scripture are to be understood." Robertson, "Divine Covenants," 65.

[30] Ibid., 12-3.

[31] Ibid., 24-5.

[32] Ibid., 14-5: "It is quite apparent that in this covenant we must not take our point of departure from the idea of compact, or contract, or agreement in any respect whatsoever. It is not contractual in its origin, or in its constitution, or in its operation, or in its outcome. Its fulfillment or continuance is not in the least degree contingent even upon reciprocal obligation or appreciation on the part of its beneficiaries."

covenant. The idea of compact or agreement is just as conspicuously absent as in the post-diluvian.[33]

Murray's thesis is that although God's commandments are indispensable "to the blessing of preservation" for Noah, they do not suggest any notion of "mutuality of agreement or compact." Why, then, does God offer the commandments to Noah? Murray answers that "the commandments are added in such a way that they are just as sovereign and unilateral in prescription or dispensation as is the annunciation of the covenant itself. The appended requirements are simply extensions, applications, expressions of the grace intimated in the covenant."[34] Therefore, there is "no deflection from the idea of sovereign dispensation." Noah's co-operation with God in carrying out the covenant provisions must not be understood as the concept of "pact or convention." So, Murray concludes that "it is the co-operation of response which the grace of the covenant constrains and demands."[35]

2. The Abrahamic Covenant

Genesis 15:8-18, Murray points out, is the first incidence of the Abrahamic Covenant. In this passage, he does not employ the traditional interpretation of כרת ברית, in which a covenant was sealed and confirmed by the solemn sanction. Rather, he understands that God confirmed the certainty of his promise to Abraham in which he would inherit the promised land. The solemn sanction, Murray indicates, is that "anthropomorphically, God calls upon Himself the curse of dismemberment if He does not fulfill to Abraham the promise of possessing the land."[36] Of course, Murray intends to avoid imputing a *bilateral* character into the inauguration of the covenant with Abraham.

Murray describes the nature of the Abrahamic Covenant from Genesis 17:9-14: "A covenant is a divine administration, divine in its origin, establishment, confirmation and fulfillment." He goes on to say, after reflecting on the covenantal context of Genesis 15:8-18:

---

[33] Ibid., 15.
[34] Ibid., 16.
[35] Ibid.
[36] Ibid.

It is not Abraham who passes through between the divided pieces of the animals; it is the theophany. And the theophany represents God. The action therefore is divinely unilateral. It is confirmation to Abraham, not confirmation from him. Abraham here does not pledge his troth to God by a self-maledictory oath but God condescends to pledge troth to his promise, a fact which advertises the divine sovereignty and faithfulness as brought to bear upon and as giving character to the covenant constituted.[37]

The Abrahamic Covenant, maintains Murray, was promissory as over against the principle of law. Paul proves this by developing the antithesis between law and promise in order to highlight the concept of the free grace of God as over against obedience to the law. Thus, *the antithesis between law and promise* is synonymous with *the antithesis between works and faith*, and is applied to justification by faith alone. This antithetical principle was used by Paul to confirm that God blessed Abraham on the principle of *promise* in opposition to the principle of law:

> But that the ruling interest is the same is shown by the apostle's sustained appeal to the antithesis between faith and works of law (cf. vss. 13,14,16,22,23,24) and to the fact that Abraham is the father of all who believe (cf. vss. 16-18). The *new* element introduced at verse 13, however, is the antithesis between *law* and *promise*, and considerations incident to promise are now developed with the same degree of cogency as was manifest in the preceding verses in the argument derived from Abraham's faith in uncircumcision.[38]

---

[37] Ibid., 17.
[38] Murray, *Romans*, 4:13. Accordingly, those who are the physical descendants of Abraham are not the real partakers of the covenant of grace. Those who are elected by God are the true possessors of the covenant of grace, and they are the true Israel who are the children of promise: "In verses 6-13 Paul's argument is that God's faithfulness to his covenant is not to be judged by the extent to which those physically descended from Abraham are partakers of salvation. God's faithfulness is vindicated by the fact that the covenant promise contemplates those who had been sovereignly chosen by God to be possessors and heirs of his covenant grace. The purpose of God according to election stands firm and this insures that the covenant promise has not come to nought." Ibid., 9:14-16. The Abrahamic covenantal promise will be realized to those who are "the true Israel" which includes Jews and Gentiles. God's electing grace will be actualized in those who have faith in Christ. To be sure,

Paul's argument in Romans 4:13, Murray states, is that the Abrahamic Covenant is completely gracious. That is why Paul utilizes the hermeneutical principle of the antithesis between law and promise to maximize the operating principle of *promise* in the Abrahamic Covenant. In other words, Murray uses the hermeneutical principle of the antithesis between Law and Grace not only for justification by faith alone apart from good works but also for the promissory character of the Abrahamic Covenant:

> And what the apostle is asserting is the complete contrast between 'law' and 'promise.' Law commands and it produces wrath when it is violated (cf. vs. 15); it knows no grace. Promise is the assurance of gracious bestowment; it is a free gift. Assuming this antithesis between the provisions of law and the provisions of promise, Paul asserts categorically that not through law was the promise to Abraham. That it was a promise was an unquestionable fact. Therefore, by reason of the implied contrast, it was not through law. This is in line with the whole development of Paul's argument from 3:20 onwards.[39]

---

the promissory aspect of the Abrahamic Covenant as over against the principle of the law, the outworking of God's electing grace and justification by faith alone in opposition to works, understood in the light of the antithesis between Law and Grace, are closely interrelated: "The covenant promise has not failed but comes to effect in the *true* Israel, the *true* children, the *true* seed (cf. vss. 6-9, 27, 29; 11:5,7). This is expressed in the words 'not from the Jews only.' The form, however, signifies that the covenant promise and the electing grace of God have broader scope than Jewry. So 'but also from the Gentiles' is added. In 4:12-17 the interest of the apostle differs from that of the present passage. There the polemic is focused upon justification by faith in opposition to works; here the interest is the fulfillment of the covenant promise. But there is a close relationship between the two passages, as may be seen particularly from 4:16. Basic in Paul's thought is the promise given to Abraham that in his seed *all the families of the earth* would be blessed." Ibid., 9:22-24.

[39] Ibid., 4:13. From the principle of the antithesis between Law and Grace, asserts Murray, we may understand the Abrahamic Covenant more clearly. The principle of promise in the Abrahamic Covenant is maximized by the Pauline principle of the antithesis between law and promise: "Since law works wrath in view of transgression, law knows no grace. Therefore the inheritance cannot be of law and those who are of law cannot be the heirs. The only alternative is the principle of faith and so the inheritance is of faith in order that it might be by grace. Faith and grace cohere; law and the promised inheritance are contradictory." Ibid., 4:16.

The heart of the Abrahamic Covenant, asserts Murray, is that the Lord will be the God of Abraham and of his descendants, as demonstrated from the passage of "I will be your God, and you shall be my people." This characterizes "union and communion with the Lord."[40] Union and communion with God is "the spirituality of the Abrahamic covenant" in contrast with the Noahic Covenant, and this spirituality signifies the "religious relationship on the highest level." Murray characteristically derives the spirituality of the Abrahamic Covenant from its *unilateral* character. He writes:

> Where there is religious relationship there is mutuality and where we have religious relationship on the highest conceivable level there mutuality on the highest plane of spirituality must obtain. This is just saying that there must be response on the part of the beneficiary and response on the highest level of religious devotion. The keeping of the covenant, therefore, so far from being incompatible with the nature of the covenant as an administration of grace, divine in its initiation, confirmation, and fulfillment, is a necessity arising from the intimacy and spirituality of the religious relation involved. The more enhanced our conception of the sovereign grace bestowed the more we are required to posit reciprocal faithfulness on the part of the recipient.[41]

The Abrahamic Covenant is solemnly *unilateral*. Obedience to the Lord is our covenantal response to the unilateral administration of divine grace and is not based on the concept of mutual agreement. Murray insists that the Abrahamic Covenant intensifies the emphasis of divine grace more than previous covenants so that it accentuates the sovereignty of divine administration. He goes on to say that "the necessity of keeping the covenant on the part of men does not interfere with the divine monergism of dispensation. The necessity of keeping is but the expression of the magnitude of the grace bestowed and the spirituality of the relation constituted. Even in this case the notion of compact or agreement is alien to the nature of the covenant constitution."[42]

In the case of Genesis 17:14, covenant breaking, states Murray, does not interfere with the perpetuity of the covenant. Rather, the covenant blessings must be maintained through the fulfillment of the

---

[40] Murray, *The Covenant of Grace*, 17.
[41] Ibid., 17-8.
[42] Ibid.

conditions by the covenant people. And "I will be your God, and you shall be my people" is the case of "mutuality in the highest sense."

> It may plausibly be objected, however, that the breaking of the covenant envisaged in this case interferes with the perpetuity of the covenant. For does not the possibility of breaking the covenant imply conditional perpetuity? 'The uncircumcised male ... shall be cut off from his people; he hath broken my covenant' (Gn. 17:14, R.V.). Without question the blessings of the covenant and the relation which the covenant entails cannot be enjoyed or maintained apart from the fulfillment of certain conditions on the part of the beneficiaries. For when we think of the promise which is the central element of the covenant, 'I will be your God, and ye shall be my people, there is necessarily involved, as we have seen, mutuality in the highest sense. Fellowship is always mutual and when mutuality ceases fellowship ceases. Hence the reciprocal response of faith and obedience arises from the nature of the relationship which the covenant contemplates (cf. Gn. 18:17-19; 22:16-18). The obedience of Abraham is represented as the condition upon which the fulfillment of the promise given to him was contingent and the obedience of Abraham's seed is represented as the means through which the promise given to Abraham would be accomplished. There is undoubtedly the fulfillment of certain conditions and these are summed up in obeying the Lord's voice and keeping His covenant.[43]

Murray argues, however, that although the promise fulfillment was contingent on the obedience of Abraham and his descendants, "it is not congruous, however, to speak of these conditions as conditions of the covenant."[44] Therefore, Murray once again comes back to his principle that "the covenant is a sovereign dispensation of God's grace. It is grace bestowed and a relation established."[45] Murray interprets the covenant breaking from a sovereign perspective: "It is not the failure to meet the terms of a pact nor failure to respond to the offer of favorable terms of contractual agreement. It is unfaithfulness to a relation constituted and to grace dispensed. By breaking the covenant what is broken is not the condition of bestowal but the

---

[43] Ibid., 18-9.
[44] Ibid., 19.
[45] Ibid.

condition of consummated fruition."[46] Thus, covenant breaking is related to covenant blessings.

Interpreting Romans 2:25, Murray maintains that because circumcision is the sign and seal of the covenant of grace, it has to be understood in the light of obedience to the covenant of grace. As such, the practice of circumcision cannot be interpreted as a practice of law in opposition to grace. In other words, circumcision is the practice of covenant obedience in the context of grace and in opposition to law:

> 'For circumcision indeed profiteth, if thou be a doer of the law.' The doing or, more accurately, the practicing of the law contemplated in this case cannot have in view the perfect fulfillment of the law on the basis of legalism. Circumcision was the sign and seal of the covenant dispensed to Abraham which was a covenant of promise and of grace. Hence it had relevance only in the context of grace and not at all in the context of law and works in opposition to grace. The practicing of the law, therefore, which makes circumcision profitable is the fulfillment of the conditions of faith and obedience apart from which the claim to the promises and grace and privileges of the covenant was presumption and mockery. The practicing of the law is thus equivalent to the keeping of the covenant. In like manner the transgression of the law which makes circumcision uncircumcision is the unfaithfulness to covenant obligations which in Old Testament terms is called the breaking of the covenant. In other words, the apostle in this passage is not enunciating the stipulations of a legalistic system but the obligations of that covenant of grace in reference to which circumcision had meaning.[47]

It is important to see that there is no difference *between the Law and Gospel, and the letter and Spirit distinction*. In this sense, Murray argues that the antithesis between letter and Spirit has the same quality as the antithesis between law and Holy Spirit. Here, Murray uses the term "mere law," which condemns human sin and ultimately leads us to Christ through the power of the Holy Spirit. In other words, without the actual involvement of the life giving power of the Holy Spirit, circumcision becomes the practice of mere law without the possession of the Gospel, and is a mistake that is fatal to the Jewish

---

[46] Ibid.
[47] Murray, *Romans*, 2:25.

religion. In this regard, Paul emphasizes the circumcision of the heart by the Holy Spirit over against that of *mere law* in Romans 2:28-29:

> Much more cogent is the consideration that the contrast between letter and Spirit in Paul is not along this line of thought (cf. 7:6; 2 Cor. 3:6,7,8; cf. vss. 17,18). The contrast is that between the Holy Spirit and the law as externally administered, a contrast between the life-giving power which the Holy Spirit imparts and the impotence which belongs to law as mere law. We shall have to adopt this contrast here. Hence what the apostle says is that the circumcision which is of the heart is by the Holy Spirit and not by the law. He is again exposing the folly of Jewish presumption and of confidence in the mere possession of the law as embodied in the Scripture.[48]

Accordingly, Murray asserts that circumcision, as the sign and seal of the Abrahamic Covenant, is truly meaningful when we presuppose justification by faith alone. As a result, people may enjoy covenantal blessings from God:

> In Genesis 17:10-14 circumcision is clearly stated to be the sign of the covenant. There is no incompatibility. As the sign and seal of the covenant it was also the seal of that faith and of the justification by faith apart from which the covenant is meaningless ... We must regard Genesis 12:1-3; 15:4-6, 18-21; 17:1-21 as the unified though progressive unfolding to Abraham of God's covenant grace and purpose, and the faith of Abraham registered in all these instances is the same faith responding with enlarged understanding and devotion to the progressive disclosures of God's purpose.[49]

3. The Mosaic Covenant

Murray gives special attention to the inauguration of the Sinaitic Covenant and evaluating its *apparent conditionality* as revealed in Exodus 19:5-6 and 24:7-8. However, these specific passages, Murray argues, do not support the idea that "the making of the covenant had to wait for the voluntary acceptance on the part of the people and their promise to obey and keep it" because the conditionality of the covenant is related to "the enjoyment of the blessing which the covenant contemplates." The Mosaic Covenant, Murray accents, has to be

---

[48] Ibid., 2:28-29.
[49] Ibid., 4:11-12.

understood exclusively in the light of the unilateral covenant of grace as the continuing outworking of the preceding Abrahamic Covenant:

> The covenant had already been established and the blood was simply the confirmation or seal of the covenant established and of the relation constituted. This gives a different perspective to our interpretation of the Mosaic covenant, and we find that the Mosaic covenant also is a sovereign administration of grace, divinely initiated, established, confirmed, and fulfilled. Later references in the Pentateuch confirm this interpretation of sovereign appointment or dispensation (Ex. 34:27,28; Lv. 24:8; Nu. 18:19, 25:13; cf. Ne. 13:29).[50]

We will discuss Murray's view of the Mosaic Covenant fully in section "C."

4. The Davidic Covenant

If the Mosaic Covenant discloses that "it is a sovereign dispensation, divine in its origin, establishment, confirmation, and fulfillment," Murray insists that "subsequent covenant administrations" should definitely be understood in the light of the redemptive historical continuity, explained in the comparison between the Abrahamic and Mosaic Covenants. Hence, the Davidic Covenant must be seen as thoroughly *unilateral*. Passages such as 2 Samuel 7:12-17 and Psalms 89:3-4 show us "the security, the determinateness, and immutability of the divine promise." The security and certainty of the Davidic unilateral covenant are clearly demonstrated by the parallelism in Psalm 89:3: 'I have made a covenant with my chosen, I have sworn unto David my servant.' Therefore, Murray concludes that "no example of covenant in the Old Testament more clearly supports the thesis that covenant is sovereign promise, promise solemnized by the sanctity of an oath, immutable in its security and divinely confirmed as respects the certainty of its fulfillment."[51]

The Davidic Covenant, Murray emphasizes, is distinctively messianic in character. The seed of David has an everlasting establishment and David's throne is foundational to all generations. In this regard, we cannot neglect the close relation between the Davidic Covenant and Isaiah' messianic prophecy about "the servant

---

[50] Murray, *The Covenant of Grace*, 21-2.
[51] Ibid., 22-3.

of the Lord" given for the covenant people (Isa. 42:1,6; 49:8; 55:3,4). As such, Murray asserts the unilateral character of the Davidic Covenant: "Nothing less than sovereign dispensation and unilateral bestowment will comport with the donation of the servant as a covenant of the people. Any notion of agreement or compact would ruthlessly violate the sovereignty of the grace involved and the divine monergism of the action entailed."[52] In these Isaianic passages, the security of the Davidic Covenant related to the people is based "in the security of the donation of the servant as a covenant of the people."

> Furthermore, in these Isaianic passages the inference is inevitable that the everlasting covenant which the Lord makes with the people is correlative with the fact that He has given the servant as a covenant of the people. The security of the covenant with the people is grounded in the security of the donation of the servant as a covenant of the people. And when Malachi calls the messenger 'the messenger of the covenant' (Mal. 3:1), there is the implication that not only is the Messiah given for a covenant of the people but that when He is sent forth to discharge His office it is in terms of the covenant that He does this. He is the angel of the covenant because He comes in pursuance of the covenant promise and purpose, and He is Himself the covenant because the blessings and provisions of the covenant are to such an extent bound up with Him that He is Himself the embodiment of these blessings and of the presence of the Lord with His people which the covenant insures.[53]

According to Isaiah 9:6, the Davidic Covenant is above all "a sovereign donation" of the Messiah. Hence, there is no contractual meaning in the declaration (Isa. 49:8) and promise (Isa. 55:3) of the Davidic Covenant.[54]

5. The New Covenant

Murray indicates that the contrast between the Old and New Covenants is accidental but not substantial. Rather, it is "the contrast within the ambit of covenant." Thus, Murray depicts the Mosaic Covenant exclusively in the light of continuity with the Abrahamic and New Covenants. As such, the New Covenant is the fulfillment of

---

[52] Ibid., 23-4.
[53] Ibid., 24.
[54] Ibid., 24-5.

the Abrahamic Covenant according to Luke 1:72 and Galatians 3:15. The New Covenant is the continuation of "a sovereign administration of grace, divine in its inception, establishment, confirmation, and fulfillment."[55]

In the New Covenant, Christ institutes the Eucharistic cup (Matt. 26:28; Mark 14:24; Luke 22:20; 1 Cor. 11:25). Murray describes it as "a designation of the sum-total of grace, blessing, truth, and relationship comprised in that redemption which His blood has secured ... It is the fullness of grace purchased by His blood and conveyed by it."[56]

The nature of the New Covenant consists in "the ministration of the Spirit as the Spirit of life", "righteousness", "liberty" and "transfiguration" in 2 Cor. 3:6-17. The epistle to the Hebrews attests to the fact that the New Covenant is the realization of the promise *par excellence*. The spiritual relationship at the heart of the covenant of grace in the Abrahamic and Mosaic Covenants is highlighted in the New Covenant (Heb. 8:6,10) and the promises are much better in the New Covenant. The New Covenant is the administration of the forgiveness of sins and the universal diffusion of knowledge (Heb. 8:11,12). The New Covenant, Murray concludes, is "a sovereign administration of grace and promise, constituting the relation of communion with God, coming to its richest and fullest expression."[57] God's glorious presence among the people of God is the core principle of the blessings of the covenant of grace in the entire history of redemption. This covenant blessing is highlighted and consummated in the New Covenant:

> The tabernacle was the focus of the assembly and of the worship. Exod. 29:42-46 is the one passage that enunciates more than any other what the tabernacle signified, and epitomizes what were the central features of the covenant relation. God meets with his people and speaks to them. He dwells among his people. Both are signified and certified by the Shekinah glory. God is their God. We cannot but see the expression here of what is central in the covenant blessing throughout its whole history, and coming to its consummation in the

---

[55] Ibid., 27.
[56] Ibid.
[57] Ibid., 28-9.

new covenant, 'I will be your God, and ye shall be my people' (cf. Rev. 21:3).[58]

διαθήκη in Hebrews 9:16-17, points out Murray, is not a covenant but a testament, as Geerhardus Vos previously suggests. This testamentary concept of a last will illustrates the transcendental power and effectiveness of Christ's death in securing the benefits of the covenant of grace, and this testamentary notion signifies *the unilateral nature* and finality of the New Covenant. Therefore, Murray writes:

> One thing is apparent that a testament is a unilateral disposition of possession. How totally foreign to the notion of compact, contract, or agreement is the disposition or dispensation which can be illustrated in respect of its effective operation by a last will! This occasional use of διαθήκη as testament cannot comport with a concept of covenant which in any way derives its definition from the idea of mutual agreement.[59]

Murray's thesis is that the testamentary notion of διαθήκη strengthens the unilateral character of the divine covenants by excluding the concept of mutual agreement and compact. This unilateral nature of the covenant is consistently applied in his sacramental theology. The Lord's Supper is the sign and seal of the New Covenant blessing in the blood of Christ Jesus. The administration of the sovereign grace of God is highlighted in the New Covenant because Christ is bestowed as the guarantee and surety of the covenant of grace.[60]

---

[58] Murray, *Collected Writings*, 2:322.

[59] Murray, *The Covenant of Grace*, 29-30.

[60] Murray, *Collected Writings*, 3:280: "The Lord's Supper is the seal of the new covenant and of the forgiveness of sins, and of both in Jesus' blood. Covenant is oath-bound certification of sovereign grace, grace that insures 'I will be your God and ye shall be my people.' It is the new covenant because it brings covenant grace to the apex of its realization, and for that reason it is the everlasting covenant. It will never give place to another. How could it? Christ is given for a covenant of the people and he himself is the guarantee, the surety, the embodiment of all covenant grace. If Christ is ours he is ours in all the completeness that is his, and in him all things are yours. 'Ye are complete in him.' All this in his blood." For Murray's extensive and comprehensive discussion of the covenant idea in sacramental theology, see his *Collected Writings*, 2:366-84; idem, *Christian Baptism* (Phillipsburg: Presbyterian and Reformed Publishing Company, 1980).

C. The Mosaic Covenant

Murray indicates that there is more plausible support for the idea of a compact in the Mosaic Covenant than any other covenant, and the function of conditions would support this notion in the Old Covenant. These considerations have been the main reason to treat the Mosaic Covenant in radical contrast both to the Abrahamic and New Covenants. Murray asserts, however, that "the idea of conditional fulfillment" is not unique to the Mosaic covenant. The bottom line is the continuity between the Abrahamic and Mosaic Covenants.[61] As such, the fulfillment of the Mosaic Covenant is basically the fulfillment of the Abrahamic Covenant:

> Another preliminary observation is that the deliverance of the children of Israel from Egypt is stated expressly to be in pursuance of the Abrahamic covenant. With reference to the Egyptian bondage we read: 'And God heard their groaning, and God remembered his covenant with Abraham, with Isaac, and with Jacob' (Ex. 2: 24). The only interpretation of this is that the deliverance of Israel from Egypt and the bringing of them into the land of promise is in fulfillment of the covenant promise to Abraham respecting the possession of the land of Canaan (Ex. 3: 16, 17, 6: 4-8; Pss. cv. 8-12, 42-45, cvi. 45). A third observation is that the spirituality of relationship which is the center of the Abrahamic covenant is also at the center of the Mosaic. 'And I will take you to me for a people and I will be to you a God ' (Ex. vi. 7; cf. Dt. xxix. 13). This fact links the Mosaic very closely with the Abrahamic and shows that religious relationship on the highest level is contemplated in both, namely, union and communion with God. We must not, therefore, suppress or discount these important considerations that the Mosaic covenant was made with Israel as the *sequel* to their deliverance from Egypt, a deliverance wrought in pursuance of the gracious promises given by covenant to Abraham.[62]

Murray's thesis lies in his argument that the inheritance of the promised land and the earthly kingdom of Israel was based upon the fulfillment of the Abrahamic Covenant. As such, the Mosaic Covenant is a *continuation* of the Abrahamic Covenant. The Sinaitic Covenant, Murray indicates, is to be interpreted from the vantage point of careful analysis of Exodus 19:5-6 and 24:7-8. Interpreting these passages, he views the Old Covenant from the perspective of *unilateral covenant*.

---

[61] Murray, *The Covenant of Grace*, 20.
[62] Ibid., 20-1.

Murray writes: "the Mosaic covenant also is a sovereign administration of grace, divinely initiated, established, confirmed, and fulfilled. Later references in the Pentateuch confirm this interpretation of sovereign appointment or dispensation (Ex. 34:27-28; Lev. 24:8; Num. 18:19, 25:13; cf. Neh. 13:29)."[63] His major theological insight is to recognize that the Abrahamic and Mosaic Covenants are similar and continuous in respect to keeping them and obeying them despite the apparent difference in the covenant-making process. Thus Murray concludes that "in reality there is nothing that is principally different in the necessity of keeping the covenant and of obedience to God's voice, which proceeds from the Mosaic covenant, from that which is involved in the keeping required in the Abrahamic. In both cases the keynotes are obeying God's voice and keeping the covenant (cf. Gen. 18:17-19; Ex. 19:5-6)."[64]

There is one constant theme in the Old and New Testaments, the theme of *eschatological salvation* in the *foedus gratiae*. Thus, the unity of both Testaments may be highlighted in the principle of one covenant of grace dealing with the individual application of salvation even though God dealt collectively with the Nation of Israel in the Old Covenant. At this point, Murray refers to the Westminster Confession, which compares the Old and New Covenants by depicting one covenant of grace as the means of eschatological salvation and justification:

> As on many other topics, the greater part of the evidence is derived from the New Testament, but because of the unity of revelation and the unity of what we call both Testaments, what is patent in the New is latent in the Old. The need is one, the covenant of grace and the way of salvation is one, the faith that saves is one. As our Confession says, 'This covenant was differently administered in the time of the law, and in the time of the gospel: under the law it was administered by promises, prophecies, sacrifices, circumcision, the paschal lamb, and other types and ordinances delivered to the people of the Jews, all foresignifying Christ to come, which were for that time sufficient and efficacious.
>
> 'Under the gospel, when Christ the substance was exhibited, the ordinances in which this covenant is dispensed are the preaching of the word, and the administration of the sacraments of Baptism and the

---

[63] Ibid., 22.
[64] Ibid.

Lord's Supper ... There are not therefore two covenants of grace differing in substance, but one and the same under various dispensations.[65]

Mentioning the New Covenant passage of Jeremiah 31:33, Murray argues that the difference between the New and Old Covenants is *not substantial* because the principle of grace of the New Covenant as in the Old Covenant, is the principle of individual regeneration and salvation: "The difference is not absolute but relative. It is the specialty of the measure of grace under the New Covenant that is stressed; it is not a denial of regenerating or forgiving grace existing in the Old."[66] An important background for understanding Murray's interpretation of the Mosaic Covenant is his criticism of the dispensational interpretation of the Mosaic Covenant. Murray explains how dispensational hermeneutics misinterprets the Sinai Covenant, and that this is the substantial problem in the dispensational understanding of the law:

> A good deal of the misconception pertaining to the relation of the law to the believer springs from a biblico-theological error of much broader proportions than a misinterpretation of Paul's statement in Romans 6:14. It is the misinterpretation of the Mosaic economy and covenant in relation to the new covenant. It has been thought that in the Mosaic covenant there is a sharp antithesis to the principle of promise embodied in the Abrahamic covenant and also to the principle of grace which comes to its efflorescence in the new covenant, and that this antithetical principle which governs the Mosaic covenant and dispensation is that of law in contradistinction from both promise and grace.[67]

---

[65] Murray, *Collected Writings*, 2:172-73.
[66] Ibid., 2:173.
[67] John Murray, *Principles of Conduct: Aspects of Biblical Ethics* (Grand Rapids, Michigan: Eerdmans Publishing Company, 1957; reprint, 1987), 195. An example of classical dispensational hermeneutics of the antithesis between the Mosaic and New Covenants in reference to John 1:17 can be seen in C.I Scofield's *The Scofield Study Bible*, 1115: "It is, therefore, constantly set in contrast to law, under which God demands righteousness from man, as, under grace, he gives righteousness to man (Rom.3:21,22; 8:4; Phil. 3:9). Law is connected with Moses and works; grace with Christ and faith (John 1:17; Rom. 10:4-10). Law blesses the good; grace saves the bad (Ex.19:5; Eph.2:1-9). Law demands that blessings be earned; grace is a free gift (Deut. 28:1-6;

Dispensational hermeneutics, Murray claims, rightly applies the absolute antithesis between Law and Gospel to the doctrine of justification and salvation. However, dispensational hermeneutics erroneously applies this antithesis to the Mosaic and New Covenants (Rom. 6:14; 7:1-4) and infers that the governing principle to achieve

---

Eph.2:8; Rom.4:4-5). (2) As a dispensation, grace begins with the death and resurrection of Christ (Rom.3:24-26; 4:24-25). The point of testing is no longer legal obedience as the condition of salvation, but acceptance or rejection of Christ, with good works as a fruit of salvation." Commenting on Romans 10:4, Murray complains that classic dispensational hermeneutics makes a radical distinction between the Old and New Covenants in relation to the governing principle of justification and salvation, saying that some commentators enunciated that "the Mosaic law had propounded law as the means of procuring righteousness." idem, *Romans*, 10:4. Meyer argues in a way that is similar to dispensational hermeneutics: "Herewith Paul, for the further confirmation of what was said in ver. 3, lays down the great principle of salvation, from the non-knowledge of which among the Jews that blinded and perverted striving after righteousness flowed. - *telos nomou*, which is placed first with great emphasis, is applied to Christ, in so far as, by virtue of His redemptive death (Gal. 3:13,4:5), the divine dispensation of salvation has been introduced, in which the basis of the procuring of salvation is no longer, as in the old theocracy, the Mosaic *nomos*, but faith, whereby the law has therefore ceased to be the regulative principle for the attainment of righteousness. Only this view of *telos, end, conclusion* ... is conformable to what follows, where the essentially *different* principles of the old and new *dikaiosune* are stated." H. A. W. Meyer, *Critical and Exegetical Hand-Book to the Epistle to the Romans*, trans. John C. Moore and Edwin Johnson (New York & London: Funk & Wagnalls Company, 1884), 404-05. In opposition to classic dispensational hermeneutics, Murray affirms that the Pauline argument does not suggest that there is an antithetical principle between the Old and New Covenants as the means of obtaining righteousness and salvation. Instead, the Pauline theology confirms that we have to verify the antithesis between the principle of the Law and Gospel to support justification by grace through faith alone: "It is strange that this notion should be entertained in the face of Paul's frequent appeal to the Old Testament and even to Moses and the Mosaic law in support of the doctrine of justification by grace through faith (cf. 3:21,22; 4:6-8,13; 9:15,16; 10:6-8; 15:8,9; Gal. 3:10,11,17-22; 4:21-31). There is no suggestion to the effect that in the theocracy works of law had been represented as the basis of salvation and that now by virtue of Christ's death this method had been displaced by the righteousness of faith." Murray, *Romans*, 10:4.

righteousness in the Mosaic Covenant was *law* and the governing principle to achieve righteousness in the New Covenant is *grace*:

> It is thought, therefore, that the Mosaic covenant is the outstanding example of works of law as opposed to the provisions of promise and grace. It is easy to see how such an interpretation of the Mosaic economy would radically affect our construction not only of the Mosaic economy itself but also of the Abrahamic covenant, on the one hand, and of the new covenant, on the other; the Mosaic would stand in sharp antithesis to both in respect of constitutive and governing principle. And the contrast between law and grace which we find in the New Testament would naturally be interpreted as a contrast between the Mosaic economy and the gospel dispensation of grace. In other words, the real contrast between 'under law' and 'under grace,' as it appears in Romans 6:14 and Romans 7:1-4, would be exemplified in the realm of the historical unfolding of covenant revelation in the contrast between the Mosaic covenant and the new covenant. This interpretation has exercised a profound influence upon the history of interpretation and has cast its shadow over the exegesis of particular passages.[68]

In other words, dispensational hermeneutics fails to make the distinction between the Law and Gospel antithesis as it correlates the doctrine of justification in the *ordo salutis* and as it correlates the relationship between the Mosaic and New Covenants in the progressive unfolding of the *historia salutis*. The failure of dispensational hermeneutics lies in the fact that it assumes that the antithesis between Law and Gospel in the doctrine of justification is identical to the antithesis between the Mosaic and New Covenant dispensations. The Mosaic Covenant was governed by the principle of law as the means of justification and salvation, whereas the New Covenant was governed by the principle of grace over against law. As such, Murray does not criticize the dispensationalist's use of the antithesis between Law and Gospel as a hermeneutical principle. His critique lies in the wrong application of the antithesis between Law and Gospel to the *historia salutis*.

Pauline theology supports, asserts Murray, *the antithesis between law and promise* in Romans 4:13. This antithesis maximizes the principle of promise in the Abrahamic Covenant as over against the

---

[68] Murray, *Principles of Conduct*, 196.

principle of law. Accordingly, there is no antithesis between the Abrahamic and Mosaic Covenants in respect to the principle of promise because the Mosaic Covenant does not cancel the promise operative in the Abrahamic Covenant:

> The word 'law' should be regarded as referring to law as commandment demanding obedience and applies to all law which falls into this category. It is true, of course, that the Mosaic law gave the most articulate and impressive revelation of the law of God in this respect and the ten commandments were the most summary and concentrated expression of what law as commandment is. But it does not provide us with the antithesis between 'law' and 'promise' in terms of the argument here to suppose that what Paul means is the contrast between the Abrahamic dispensation of promise and the Mosaic dispensation. The Mosaic administration (as Paul shows in Galatians 3:17-22) did not abrogate or suspend the promise given to Abraham–the promise was valid and fully in operation when the Mosaic covenant was given 430 years after; and it remained in operation. Hence it is misleading and indefensible to say summarily that the 'law,' referred to here in verse 13, means the law of Moses and interpret it in the sense of the Mosaic economy.[69]

Murray admits that a cursory investigation of the Sinaitic Covenant seems to support dispensational hermeneutics which sharply contrasts the *dispensations* of the Mosaic and New Covenants in terms of the distinction between the covenant of law and the covenant of grace:

> There is a plausible case that could be made out for this construction of the Mosaic covenant. The first express reference to the covenant made with Israel at Sinai is framed in terms of obedience to the commandments of God and of keeping the covenant. 'Now therefore if ye will obey my voice indeed, and keep my covenant, then ye shall be a peculiar treasure unto me above all people: for all the earth is mine. And ye shall be unto me a kingdom of priests and a holy nation' (Exodus 19:5,6). And the engagement of the people is in similar terms: 'All that the Lord hath spoken will we do and be obedient' (Exodus 24:7). Surely, we might say, these are not the terms of a covenant of grace but the terms of a covenant of legal and contractual stipulations. How, we might ask, does the condition of obedience comport with the provisions of an administration of grace? If grace is contingent upon the fulfillment of certain conditions by us, then surely it is no more

---

[69] Murray, *Romans*, 4:13.

grace. Hence, it may well be argued, this conditional feature of the Mosaic covenant requires that it be placed in a different category.[70]

To this crucial question, Murray answers that the condition of obedience in the Mosaic Covenant is not different from that in the Abrahamic Covenant:

> The Mosaic covenant in respect of this condition of obedience is not in a different category from the Abrahamic. 'And God said unto Abraham, Thou shalt keep my covenant therefore, thou, and thy seed after thee in their generations' (Genesis 17:9) ... There is nothing principally different in the necessity of keeping the covenant and of obeying God's voice, characteristic of the Mosaic covenant, from what is involved in the keeping of the covenant required in the Abrahamic.[71]

The intimate covenant relationship between God and man is required in the Mosaic Covenant to the same degree as the Abrahamic Covenant: "The Mosaic Covenant, no less than the Abrahamic, contemplates a relation of intimacy and fellowship with God epitomized in the promise 'I will be your God and ye shall be my people' (cf. Exodus 6:7; 18:1; 19:5,6; 20:2; Deuteronomy 29:13). Religious relationship on the highest level is in view."[72]

---

[70] Murray, *Principles of Conduct*, 196-97.

[71] Ibid. Murray's focal point is that there is no foundational difference respecting the covenant obligation and obedience between the Abrahamic and Mosaic Covenant. An identical argument appears in his *The Covenant of Grace*, 22: "What needs to be emphasized now is that the Mosaic covenant in respect of the condition of obedience is not in a different category from the Abrahamic. It is too frequently assumed that the conditions prescribed in connection with the Mosaic covenant place the Mosaic dispensation in a totally different category as respects grace, on the one hand, and demand or obligation, on the other. In reality there is nothing that is principally different in the necessity of keeping the covenant and of obedience to God's voice, which proceeds from the Mosaic covenant, from that which is involved in the keeping required in the Abrahamic. In both cases the keynotes are obeying God's voice and keeping the covenant (cf. Gn. 18:17-19; Ex. 19:5,6)."

[72] Murray, *Principles of Conduct*, 197. Thus, Murray interprets the Mosaic Covenant exclusively in the light of *continuity* with the Abrahamic Covenant. As a result, the spiritual relationship between God and his people is almost identical, summarized in terms of "union and communion with God.": "A third observation is that the spirituality of relationship which is the centre of

Therefore, the Israelites' obedience to the law, asserts Murray, is fundamentally the same as the believers' obedience in the Abrahamic Covenant. In the final analysis, the two covenants are to be understood exclusively in the light of the continuity of the covenant of grace:

> We may therefore sum up the matter by saying that the holiness of God demanded conformity to his holiness, that holiness was of the essence of the covenant privilege, that holiness was the condition of continuance in the enjoyment of the covenant blessings and the medium through which the covenant privilege realized its fruition. Holiness is exemplified in obedience to the commandments of God. Obedience is therefore entirely congruous with, and disobedience entirely contradictory of, the nature of God's covenant with Israel as one of union and communion with God.[73]

At the same time, the demand of covenantal obedience in the Mosaic Covenant, Murray asserts, is fundamentally identical with the requirement of the covenantal obedience in the New Covenant.[74]

The Israelites' obedience in the Mosaic economy, emphasizes Murray, is no different from Christian obedience in the New Covenant. What is paramount in Murray's thought at this point is that he does not want to draw a contrast between the Old and New Covenants in terms of the administration of the theocratic nation of Israel by *general* obedience to the law as expounded in Reformed tradition which we have seen in chapter one. Emphatically, Murray does not want to apply the principle of the law in the Mosaic Covenant

---

the Abrahamic covenant is also at the centre of the Mosaic. 'And I will take you to me for a people, and I will be to you a God' (Ex.6:7; cf. Dt. 29:13). This fact links the Mosaic very closely with the Abrahamic and shows that religious relationship on the highest level is contemplated in both, namely, union and communion with God. We must not, therefore, suppress or discount these important considerations that the Mosaic covenant was made with Israel as the *sequel* to their deliverance from Egypt, a deliverance wrought in pursuance of the gracious promises given by covenant to Abraham." idem, *The Covenant of Grace*, 20-21.

[73] Murray, *Principles of Conduct*, 199.

[74] Ibid.: "In all of this the demand of obedience in the Mosaic covenant is principally identical with the same demand in the new covenant of the gospel economy. The new covenant also finds its centre in the promise, 'I will be your God and ye shall be my people.'"

over against the principle of promise or grace in the light of the antithesis between Law and Grace:

> The disposition to construe the demand for obedience in the Mosaic economy as having affinity with works rather than grace arises from failure to recognize that the demand for obedience in the Mosaic covenant is principally identical with the same demand under the gospel. When we re-examine the demand for obedience in the Mosaic covenant (cf. Exodus 19:5, 6; 24:7) in the light of the relations of law and grace in the gospel, we shall discover that the complex of ideas is totally alien to a construction in terms of works as opposed to grace. Obedience belongs here no more 'to the legal sphere of merit' than in the new covenant.[75]

It is very interesting that Murray supports his idea by quoting Geerhardus Vos' *Biblical Theology*. It is true that Vos denies that 'law-keeping' in the Mosaic Covenant was "the meritorious ground of life inheritance." In that sense, salvation in the Old Covenant was based upon *sola gratia*. Nevertheless, Vos argues that we cannot deny that the theocratic Kingdom *continuity* was closely related to "law-observance." The Judaizers misunderstood, however, that this connection was "meritorious." What is vital to Vos' thought, unlike Murray's, is that we must understand observance to law in the light of the *typical* aspect of the nation of Israel whose temporal blessings and curses point to the eschatological heavenly blessing and eschatological curse. In other words, the category of *eschatology* is vital for contrasting the Old and New Covenants.[76] To be fair to Murray, we

---

[75] Ibid., 200.

[76] Vos, *Biblical Theology*, 127-28. In this respect, we need to quote here what Vos really wants to say in the immediate literal context of Murray's reference to Vos. It is pertinent to notice, however, that Vos develops the *eschatological* significance of the Mosaic Covenant administration in the light of the analogy between the Typological Kingdom and antitypical eschatological heavenly Kingdom according to blessing or curse on the nation based on the general principle of the people's obedience or disobedience: "As stated above, the abode of Israel in Canaan typified the heavenly, perfected state of God's people. Under these circumstances the ideal of absolute conformity to God's law of legal holiness had to be upheld. Even though they were not able to keep this law in the Pauline, spiritual sense, yea, even though they were unable to keep it externally and ritually, the requirement could not be lowered. When apostasy on a general scale took place, they could not

must recognize that he contrasts the Old and New Covenants when he interprets the tutelary or pedagogical function of the Mosaic economy as crucial to depicting justification by faith alone that God has shown us through the unfolding history of redemption:

> The people of God under the Old Testament were children of God by the divine adoption of grace. But they were as children under age, under tutors and governors until the time appointed of the father (cf. Gal. 4:2). Of this tutelary, pedagogical discipline the Mosaic economy was the minister (cf. Gal. 3:23,24). Paul is contrasting this period of tutelage under the Mosaic law with the full liberty bestowed upon all believers, whether Jews or Gentiles, under the gospel.[77]

---

remain in the promised land. When they disqualified themselves for typifying the state of holiness, they *ipso facto* disqualified themselves for typifying that of blessedness, and had to go into captivity. This did not mean every individual Israelite, in every detail of his life, had to be perfect, and that on this was suspended the continuance of God's favour. Jehovah dealt primarily with the nation and through the nation with the individual, as even now in the covenant of grace He deals with believers and their children in the continuity of generations. There is solidarity among the members of the people of God, but this same principle also works for the neutralizing of the effect of individual sin, so long as the nation remains faithful. The attitude observed by the nation and its representative leaders was the decisive factor. Although the demands of the law were at various times imperfectly complied with, nevertheless for a long time Israel remained in possession of the favour of God. And, even when the people as a whole become apostate, and go into exile, Jehovah does not on that account suffer the בְּרִית to fail. After due chastisement and repentance He takes Israel back into favour."

[77] John Murray, *Redemption: Accomplished and Applied* (Grand Rapids, Michigan: Eerdmans Publishing Company, 1955; reprint, 1989), 44-5. Thus, Murray overlooks eschatology and typology as a basis for contrasting the Old and New Covenants. He fails to note that temporal blessings and curses are contingent on Israelites' corporate obedience to law and that this typifies eschatological blessing and curse under the New Covenant: He does, however, make a contrast between the two covenants arguing that the former was "preparatory," and the latter "consummatory." Murray simply does not employ the concept of the *foedus legale* or the *foedus operum* in respect to the Mosaic Covenant *in a limited sense* which was characteristically articulated by prominent Reformed scholars: "This is apparent from Galatians 4:5, for here the adoption is contrasted with the tutelary discipline of the Mosaic economy. Israel under the Old Testament were indeed children of God but they were as children under age (cf. Gal. 3:23; 4:1-3). The adoption secured by Christ in

On another occasion, referring to Hebrews 7:20-22, Murray makes a further comparison between the Old and New Covenants. He argues that the New Covenant is better than the Old Covenant because Jesus Christ is the mediator of the New Covenant which is a far better covenant:

> It is the fact that Jesus as high priest is the surety and mediator of the new and better covenant. The new covenant is contrasted with the Mosaic. Just as the high priest of our profession is counted worthy of more glory than Moses because he is the Son over his own house, so his pre-eminence over Moses consists also in the fact that he is the surety of a new and better covenant. 'And inasmuch as not without an oath ... by so much the more did Jesus become the surety of a better covenant' (Heb. 7:20,22). And the oath was, 'thou art a priest forever' (vs. 21; cf. 9:15). The new covenant brings to its consummation the communion which is at the heart of all covenant disclosure from Abraham onwards, 'I will be your God, and ye shall be my people.' Redemptive grace reaches its zenith in the full and final realization of this promise. And if Christ as priest after the order of Melchizedek is the mediator and surety of the new covenant as the everlasting covenant, this means that his priestly function is operative in the consummating action which will bring to final and perfect fruition the redemptive counsel of God.[78]

It is, however, Murray's overall contention that there is in reality no contrast between the Old and New Covenants. Having this in mind, Murray reinterprets Leviticus 18:5 to be consistent with his understanding of the Mosaic Covenant. We have seen, however, that the Reformed tradition has generally interpreted Leviticus 18:5 to highlight the antithesis between the principle of the law and grace. As such, it is a decisive manifestation of the principle of the *foedus*

---

the fullness of the time (Gal. 4:4) is the mature, full-fledged sonship in contrast with the pupilage of Israel under the ceremonial institution. This difference comports with the distinction between the Old Testament and the New. The Old was preparatory, the New is consummatory. The adoption of the Old was propaedeutic. The grace of the New appears in this, that by redemption accomplished and by faith in Christ (cf. Gal. 3:26) all without distinction (cf. Gal. 3:28) are instated in the full blessing of sonship without having to undergo tutelary preparation corresponding to the pedagogical discipline of the Mosaic economy." idem, *Romans*, 9:4-5.

[78] Murray, *Collected Writings*, 1:47-8.

operum. Although believers in the Old Covenant were justified by faith alone according to the principle of the covenant of grace as over against the principle of the covenant of works to emphasize the redemptive historical continuity between the two covenants, God blessed and cursed the Nation of Israel according to the principle of the law, which ultimately points to the eschatological heavenly blessings or curses. In this sense, Reformed tradition has developed the idea that the principle of the law was operative in the administration of the Theocratic Nation of Israel, although it was long ago canceled as the means of salvation and justification in the postlapsarian state. Precisely at this point, Murray disagrees with the Reformed tradition. In other words, Reformed theology in general has argued that both Leviticus 18:5 and Romans 10:5 demonstrate the antithesis between the principles of the law and grace. While Murray admits that Romans 10:5 argues for this antithesis in relation to the doctrine of justification, he argues that in its context, Leviticus 18:5 argues for something completely different - Israel's covenantal obligation to obey God in response to his grace:

> There does not need to be any question but Paul in Rom. 10:5 makes allusion to Lev. 18:5 more directly than to any other Old Testament passage. He places the principle stated in Lev. 18:5 in opposition to the righteousness which is of faith and calls it 'the righteousness which is of the law.' The problem that arises from this use of Lev. 18:5 is that the latter text does not appear in a context that deals with legal righteousness as opposed to that of faith. Lev. 18:5 is in a context in which the claims of God upon his redeemed and covenant people are being asserted and urged upon Israel ... The whole passage is no more 'legalistic' than are the ten commandments. Hence the words 'which if a man do, he shall live in them' (vs. 5) refers not to the life accruing from doing in a legalistic framework but to the blessing attendant upon obedience in a redemptive and covenant relationship to God.[79]

---

[79] Murray, *Romans*, II:249. Murray makes a distinction between the implication of 'Do this and you will live' in Leviticus 18:5 and in Romans 10:5. The former has reference to the third use of law (*tertius usus legis*) in relation to the covenant people's life while the latter is applied to the second use of law (*usus elenchticus sive paedagogicus*) to summarize the antithesis between Law and Grace in relation to justification: "The difficulty with the first (Lev. 18:5) is that in the original setting it does not appear to have any reference to legal righteousness as opposed to that of grace. Suffice it to say now that the formal statement Paul appropriates as one suited to express the

principle of law-righteousness. It cannot be doubted but the proposition, 'The man that doeth the righteousness of the law shall live thereby,' is, of itself, an adequate and watertight definition of the principle of legalism." Murray, *Romans*, 10:5.

Daniel Fuller in his provocative study on *Gospel and Law: Contrast or Continuum?*, argues from the vantage point of biblical theology that the hermeneutical reference point of the antithesis between Law and Gospel cannot stand: "I realized that if the law is, indeed, a law of faith, enjoining only the obedience of faith and the works that proceed therefrom (I Thess. 1:3; II Thess. 1:11), then there could no longer be any antithesis in biblical theology between the law and the gospel. I then had to accept the drastic conclusion that the antithesis between law and gospel established by Luther, Calvin, and the covenant theologians could no longer stand up under the scrutiny of biblical theology." Daniel Fuller, *Gospel and Law: Contrast or Continuum?: The Hermeneutics of Dispensationalism and Covenant Theology* (Grand Rapids, Michigan: Eerdmans Publishing Company, 1980), xi. Based upon his thesis, Fuller agrees with Murray's exegesis of Leviticus 18:5 affirming that it does not manifest the antithesis between Law and Gospel, but Israel's covenantal obligation to the law as the people of God. Fuller, however, vigorously critiques Murray's use of the antithesis between Law and Gospel in his interpretation of Romans 10:5-6. According to Fuller's thesis, there is no hermeneutical principle of the antithesis between Law and Gospel, so that from the vantage point of biblical theology we cannot apply that principle *even* in the doctrine of justification: "From what has been said earlier in this chapter it is apparent that we regard Murray as wrong in thinking of 'the righteousness of the law' (Rom. 10:5) as standing in contrast with the 'righteousness of faith' (Rom. 10:6ff.). In drawing such a contrast, Murray reveals the deep impression that covenant theology has made on him. Yet he believes that it is due for a major overhaul." Ibid., 79.

Having this in mind, it is correct to say that we cannot equate Fuller's analysis of the Mosaic Covenant with Murray, although both show that the Mosaic Covenant is exclusively continuously related to the Abrahamic and New Covenants. Thomas Schreiner's analysis equating Daniel Fuller and John Murray on the Mosaic Covenant is not conclusive because the former rejects the antithesis between Law and Gospel as it applies even to the doctrine of justification, where the latter vigorously defends the hermeneutical principle of the antithesis between Law and Gospel faithfully applying it to justification by faith alone apart from good works: "It seems to me that Daniel P. Fuller and John Murray correctly see a fundamental problem here with typical Reformed theology. It seems more reasonable to see the covenant with Moses as wholly gracious and to conclude that Paul responds, at least in part, to a misinterpretation of the nature of the Mosaic covenant. This is not to say that the answers of Murray and Fuller are themselves completely satisfactory, but

As such, God required the Israelites' covenantal obedience, and this is the precise meaning of Leviticus 18:5: "The witness of Scripture to the necessity and actuality of this in the redeemed, covenant life of believers is pervasive. It is this principle that appears in Lev. 18:5 and in the other passages from the Old Testament cited above."[80]

D. Justification

More than anything else, Murray emphasizes an accurate understanding of the antithesis between Law and Gospel[81] because he strongly believes that it and the doctrine of justification stand or fall together. Paul's treatment of Law and Gospel is carefully manifested especially in his epistles to the Romans and Galatians. According to Paul, the antithesis between Law and Gospel is the foundational hermeneutical principle upon which justification by faith alone is built. Meanwhile, progressive sanctification may be understood as a positive use of the law in the believers' life. The genius of Murray's thought lies in his insistence on an essential balance between the Law and Gospel antithesis in relation to justification and the believers' covenantal obligation to obey the law through the power of the Spirit in relation to the doctrine of progressive sanctification:

> No subject is more intimately bound up with the nature of the gospel than that of law and grace. In the degree to which error is entertained at this point, in the same degree is our conception of the gospel

---

Karlberg's solution to the relationship between the testaments differs from Fuller's because he thinks the misunderstanding consists in applying the works principle of the Mosaic covenant to the sphere of salvation." Thomas R. Schreiner, *The Law and Its Fulfillment: A Pauline Theology of Law* (Grand Rapids, Michigan: Baker Book House, 1993), 249.

[80] Murray, *Romans*, II:251.

[81] An equivalent Pauline motif to the antithesis between Law and Gospel, asserts Murray, is *the contrast between the letter and Spirit* in Romans 7:6 and 2 Corinthians 3:6. To be sure, there is no qualitative difference in Pauline theology between *the Law and Gospel antithesis and the letter and Spirit antithesis* in depicting the gracious character of the doctrine of justification: "The contrast there between the letter and the Spirit is the contrast between the law and the gospel, and when Paul says 'the letter kills, but the Spirit makes alive,' the letter is shown by the context to refer to that which was engraven on stones, the law delivered by Moses, and the Spirit is the Spirit of the Lord (vs. 17)." Ibid., 7:6.

perverted. An erroneous conception of the function of law can be of such a character that it completely vitiates our view of the gospel; and an erroneous conception of the antithesis between law and grace can be of such a character that it demolishes both the substructure and the superstructure of grace.[82]

The true meaning of the Gospel, Murray affirms, entails the logical order of Law and Gospel in man's conversion experience. As such, Law and Gospel is not only the historical order of the governing principles as the means of *eschatological glory*, covering creation, fall and redemption but also a logical order in personal conversion experience. In other words, an antithesis between Law and Gospel is prerequisite to the experience of faith and repentance. Thus, the antithesis between Law and Gospel hermeneutics is vital for the purity and dignity of the Gospel itself.[83]

1. The Antithesis between Law and Gospel in Relation to Justification by Faith Alone

Murray asserts that the fundamental theological problem with so called *antinomianism* arises from the misconception of the Pauline usage of *nomos*, a failure to see the balance between the implications of the law for *justification* on the one hand and *progressive sanctification* on the other hand: "We are all only too painfully aware that the apostasy of our day within professed Christianity is not only from the basic tenets of the faith once delivered to the saints but also from the fundamental norms of the Christian ethic."[84]

When Paul discusses the doctrine of justification and salvation in his epistles, such as Romans and Galatians, argues Murray, the antithesis between Law and Gospel must be a decisive hermeneutical

---

[82] Murray, *Principles of Conduct*, 181.

[83] Murray, *Collected Writings*, 2:115: "Furthermore, when we come to the point of actual conversion, the faith and repentance involved in conversion do not receive their genesis apart from the knowledge of the truth of the gospel. There must be conveyed to the mind of man who believes and repents to the saving of his soul the truth-content of law and gospel, law as convicting him of sin and gospel as conveying the information which becomes the material of faith. To some extent at least there must be the cognition and apprehension of the import of law and gospel prior to the exercise of saving faith and repentance."

[84] Murray, *Collected Writings*, 4:133.

reference point: "In a word it was the relation of law and gospel. 'I do not make void the grace of God: for if righteousness is through the law, then Christ died in vain' (Galatians 2:21). 'For if a law had been given which could make alive, verily from the law righteousness would have been' (Galatians 3:21); 'By the works of the law shall no flesh be justified in his sight' (Romans 3:20)."[85] The law applied in the soteric principle of justification, therefore, cannot be confounded with grace or Gospel for if we mix Law and Gospel in the expounding of justification, we do it at the expense of the Gospel itself:

> The simple truth is that if law is conceived of as contributing in the least degree towards our acceptance with God and our justification by him, then the gospel of grace is a nullity. And the issue is so sharply and incisively drawn that, if we rely in any respect upon compliance with law for our acceptance with God, then Christ will profit us nothing. 'Ye have been discharged from Christ whosoever of you are justified by law; ye have fallen away from grace"(Galatians 5:4).[86]

---

[85] Murray, *Principles of Conduct*, 181. Murray, in his discussion on *Paul's Use of 'Nomos,'* asserts that the fulcrum of the Pauline thesis lies in the absolute antithesis between Law and Grace as the foundation for a right understanding of the Gospel according to the passages of Romans 3:19-20; 8:3 and Galatians 3:21: "The law as demand and command can do nothing to relieve the liability, the condemnation, the bondage of sin. It has no redemptive provision and therefore no redemptive potency or efficacy. It is here that the divinity of the law, the inviolable sanctity and sanction derived from this divinity, become significant for the implications of ὑπὸ νόμον. Sin does not suspend ὑπὸ νόμον any more than does law suspend or negate sin. Again Paul's own statement is eloquent: 'Whatever the law says it says to those who are under the law' - 'ἐν τῷ νόμῳ (Rom. 3:19) and that all are ἐν τῷ νόμῳ is involved in the clauses that follow: 'that every mouth may be stopped and that all the world may be guilty before God' (Rom. 3:19b). It is because the law is God's law that by divine constitution all are 'under law' and therefore under the sanctions that the law possesses, consigned to the condemnation and bondage it pronounces, and shut up to the impotence that characterizes the law. *This is why in the state and condition of sin* ὑπὸ νόμον *is the antithesis of grace* [emphasis mine]." idem, *Collected Writings*, 4:136.

[86] Murray, *Principles of Conduct*, 182. Murray emphasizes that apart from the hermeneutical reference point of the antithesis between Law and Gospel in the doctrine of justification, the Gospel itself is in jeopardy. *Works and faith are antithetically* applied to the doctrine of justification, just like the antithesis between Law and Gospel: "If we were to be justified by works, in

John Murray's Response to Federal Theology

The heart of the Protestant Reformation in opposition to Romish theology was the discovery of the Gospel of grace which could be summarized as "the doctrine of justification by faith alone and of grace alone." Furthermore, Paul identified justification by faith alone with the Gospel itself in Galatians 1:8-9. Thus, based upon Galatians 5:3-4, Murray asserts, there is an absolute antithesis between Law and Grace in the doctrine of justification. Thus, human works are completely excluded in its doctrine:

> The thought is not that of falling away from a state of grace but rather that, if, to any extent, we look to our own works for justification, then we have abandoned grace altogether. Grace does not comport with any human contribution. If grace is in operation, if it has any place, it must have the whole place, it must be exclusively operative. If we are justified to any degree by works of law, we are debtors to do the whole law (cf. Gal. 5:3) and justification must be wholly of law.[87]

---

any degree or to any extent, then there would be no gospel at all. For what works of righteousness can a condemned, guilty, and depraved sinner offer to God? That we are justified by faith advertises the grand article of the gospel of grace that we are not justified by works of law. Faith stands in antithesis to works; there can be no amalgam of these two (cf. Gal. 5:4)." idem, *Redemption*, 130. Accordingly, Murray asserts that Paul anathematizes the Galatian heresy which mixes Law and Gospel in the doctrine of justification in Galatians 1:8-9: "When Paul wrote to the Galatians thus, he was impassioned by the love of Christ and of Christ's gospel. He was persuaded to the core of his being that the heresy that crept into the Galatian churches was aimed at the destruction of the gospel. It took the crown from the Redeemer's head and was pointed to the damnation of souls. So he invoked the curse of God upon any who would pervert the pure gospel of Christ as the gospel of grace. 'Christ is become of no effect unto you, whosoever of you are justified by the law: ye have fallen away from grace' (Gal. 5:4)." idem, *Collected Writings*, 3:222-23.

[87] Ibid., 1:121-22. Of chief importance to Murray is the identification of salvation with justification by grace through faith alone apart from good works. The faith which is freely given by God in the application of redemption, is the fruit of divine electing grace: "If salvation at any point is contingent upon some contribution which man himself makes, then at that point it is *of ourselves*, and to that extent it is not of grace ... Besides, it is *salvation by grace through faith* that is the gift of God and so faith itself is of grace and not something that resides in human autonomy. The faith which God foresees is the fruit and not the root of electing grace." Ibid., 1:120-21.

The extreme example of mixing Law and Gospel in the doctrine of justification, Murray indicates, is Romish theology:

> Justification is not by the righteousness of performance on our part; it is not of works (Rom. 3:20;4:2;10:3;Gal.2:16;3:11;5:4;Phil.3:9). The Scripture is so insistent upon this that it is only by spiritual blindness and distortion of the most aggravated type that justification by works could ever be entertained or proposed in any form or to any degree. The Romish doctrine bears the patent hall-marks of such distortion. 3. We are justified by grace. It is not the reward of anything in us or wrought by us but proceeds from God's free and unmerited favour (Rom. 3:24ff.; 5:15-21).[88]

The Galatian heresy presented by the Judaizers was far better than modernist theology because the Judaizers were at least professed Christians. Nevertheless, Paul *anathematized* the Judaizers because they perverted the grand article of the Gospel, namely justification by

---

For example, C. I. Scofield notices that justification by faith alone is depicted in the light of the antithesis between works and faith when he exposits Romans 3:28. This is Murray's theological rationale for designating classic dispensationalism as *evangelical* despite its great theological inconsistency and problems: "Justification and righteousness are inseparably united in Scripture by the fact that the same (*dikaios*, 'righteous'; *dikaioo*, 'to justify') is used for both. The believing sinner is justified because Christ, having borne his sins on the cross, has been 'made unto him righteousness' (1 Cor. 1:30). Justification originates in grace (Rom. 3:24; Tit. 3:4,5); is through the redemptive and propitiatory work of Christ, who has vindicated the law (Rom. 3:24,25; 5:9); is by faith, not works ... and may be defined as the judicial act of God whereby He justly declares righteous one who believes on Jesus Christ. It is the Judge Himself (Rom. 8:31-34) who thus declares." Scofield, *The Scofield Study Bible*, 1195. Furthermore, Scofield affirms that "salvation is by grace through faith, is a free gift, and wholly without works." Ibid., 1192. Although Scofield adopts the Reformation doctrine of justification by faith alone apart from good works by applying the antithesis between Law and Gospel, he rejects the third use of law as the means of progressive sanctification, which is typical of *antinomianism*: "The test of the Gospel is grace. If the message excludes grace, or mingles law with grace as the means either of justification or sanctification (Gal. 2:21; 3:1-3), or denies the fact or guilt of sin which alone gives grace its occasion and opportunity, it is 'another' gospel, and the preacher of it is under the anathema of God." Ibid., 1241.

[88] Murray, *Redemption*, 126.

faith alone. That is Paul's argument in Galatians 1:7-9 and 5:4. As such, we cannot co-operate with modernists in evangelism whose thought is much worse than the perversion of the Gospel:

> We have good reason to believe that the heresy which disturbed the churches of Galatia was far from being characterized by many of the errors which distinguish present-day modernism. The Judaisers were undoubtedly professed Christians. And the evidence would indicate that they did not controvert Paul's gospel on many of its most precious tenets. For Paul did not find occasion in his epistle to defend many of the articles of the Christian faith which he propounds elsewhere. But because the Judaisers had perverted the grand article of justification by grace through faith he pronounced his *anathema*. He called this perversion 'another gospel, which is not another.' ... No imprecation could be stronger than that of *anathema*. Are we to suppose that Paul would have co-operated with these perverters of the gospel of Christ in promoting evangelism? The suggestion is inconceivable ... The Judaising heresy struck at the heart of the gospel. Consequently Paul's intolerance. Modernism gives us a new version of Christianity and that is worse than perversion.[89]

The major thesis of Paul in the Galatians, argues Murray, does not oppose paganism of the first century, but the extreme form of legalism presented by Judaizers who mixed Law and Gospel as the means of justification and salvation:

> The issue in the Galatian churches was not a lapse into crass paganism but an insistence on the part of Judaizers that observance of Mosaic rites was necessary to justification. The heresy was that of the synthesis of grace and observance of rites in order to acceptance with God, and turning again to weak and beggarly elements would have to be regarded in that light. Furthermore, the observance of days and months and seasons and years can most suitably be given this complexion.[90]

---

[89] Murray, *Collected Writings*, 1:158.

[90] Ibid., 4:138. Thus, Paul's polemic in opposition to the Judaizers was focused and centralized on the antithesis between Law and Gospel to depict justification by faith alone against the background of an extreme legalism in which the gospel was perverted: "In Galatians Paul is dealing with the Judaizers who were perverting the gospel at its centre. They were the propagandists of a legalism which maintained that the observance of days and seasons was necessary to justification and acceptance with God. This meant a

The Galatians did not understand the pedagogical function of the Mosaic economy in redemptive history, so they failed to grasp that the highlight of redemptive history lies in the Gospel of Christ. Thus Murray insists that we cannot go back to the Old Covenant. Rather we must interpret the Mosaic law (*lex Mosaica*) in the light of the New Covenant Gospel of Christ:

> The Galatians were lapsing into pre-Christian Judaism and therefore abandoning the maturity of the fullness of the time in favour of the tutelage of the Mosaic, and the full liberty of the gospel for the relative bondage of the old economy. What folly! But, much more serious what iniquity! It is the iniquity that is uppermost in Paul's assessment. It meant failure to understand the movement of redemptive history. It meant even the failure to understand the purpose of the Mosaic institution. In a word, it is the rejection of Christ and of the gospel, the rejection of all that is involved in Galatians 4:4-6.[91]

Paul himself was the master of the Pharisaic religion in which law functioned as the center of religion and which propagated salvation by the principle of law. Jesus Christ, however, broke through this legalism by encountering Paul on the road to Damascus and revealing the Gospel to him. Before the Damascus Road experience, Paul pursued the principle of "law-righteousness" in opposition to "God's righteousness." It was the Damascus Road Christophany which revealed to Paul, the antithesis between Law and Gospel that became so crucial for his doctrine of justification by grace through faith alone apart from good works:

> Behind this opposition was religious zeal for a way of acceptance with God that was the antithesis of grace and of justification by faith ... Pharisaism was a religion of law. Its religious horizon was defined and circumscribed by the resources of law and therefore by works of law. It was the spell of that religion that was decisively broken by Paul's encounter with Jesus on the road to Damascus (cf. Acts 9:3-6; 26:12-18). And so Paul writes: 'And the commandment, which was unto life, this I found to be unto death'(Rom. 7:10); 'For I through law died to law, that I might live to God' (Gal. 2:19); 'From works of law no flesh

---

turning back again 'to the weak and beggarly rudiments' (Gal. 4:9); it was 'a different gospel which is not another,' and worthy of the apostle's anathemas (cf. Gal. 1:8,9)." idem, *Romans*, II:172-73.

[91] Murray, *Collected Writings*, 4:138.

will be justified' before God: 'for through the law is the knowledge of sin' (Rom. 3:20). When Paul unfolds the antithesis between grace and law, faith and works, he writes of an antithesis which had been reflected in the contrast between the two periods in his own life history, periods divided by the experience of the Damascus road. And this contrast is all the more significant in his case because the zeal that marked Paul in both periods was unsurpassed in its fervour and intensity. No one knew better and perhaps none comparably the self-complacency of law-righteousness, on the one hand, and the glory of God's righteousness, on the other.[92]

Murray contends that the antithesis between Law and Gospel is a concrete hermeneutical reference point for opposing *legalism* and expounding the doctrine of justification and salvation, but this antithesis does not void the necessity of the law in the Christian life. The third use of the law (*tertius usus legis*) in the process of sanctification signifies the Christian use of the law (*usus didacticus sive normativus*) in opposition to *antinomianism* as represented by classic dispensational hermeneutics. Murray emphasizes that we should recognize the second and third uses of the law (*usus elenchticus sive paedagogicus et usus didacticus sive normativus*) in the *ordo salutis*:

> But lest we should think that the whole question of the relation of law and grace is thereby resolved, we must be reminded that Paul says also in this polemic, 'Do we then make void the law through faith? God forbid, yea we establish the law' (Romans 3:31). We are compelled therefore to recognize that the subject of law and grace is not simply concerned with the antithesis that there is between law and grace, but also with law as that which makes grace necessary and with grace as establishing and confirming law. It is not only the doctrine of grace that must be jealously guarded against distortion by the works of law, but it is also the doctrine of law that must be preserved against the distortions of a spurious concept of grace. This is just saying that we are but echoing the total witness of the apostle of the Gentiles as the champion of the gospel of grace when we say that we must guard grace from the adulteration of legalism and we must guard law from the depredations of antinomianism.[93]

---

[92] Murray, *Romans*, I: xiii-xiv.
[93] Murray, *Principles of Conduct*, 182.

One of the central issues of the Protestant Reformation, states Murray, was the doctrine of justification by faith alone. To Martin Luther it was "the article of a standing or falling Church" (*articulus stantis et cadentis ecclesiae*). It is one of Murray's greatest hopes that the Church may continue to proclaim the doctrine of justification by faith alone, expounded in the light of forensic declaration. At this point, it is fair to say that Murray does not criticize Luther's understanding of justification. He recognizes that Luther could derive justification by faith alone apart from good works from the antithesis between Law and Gospel which has been a common denominator even in the Reformed tradition. In other words, Murray does not reject the Law and Gospel antithesis developed by Luther, who articulated justification by faith alone by means of the contrast between Law and Gospel. Indeed, this reflects the traditional Reformed covenant thought.[94] Accordingly, from the vantage point of historical theology, Murray asserts that Luther and the Reformed share the antithesis between Law and Gospel in the biblical understanding of justification. Referring to Romans 3:27-28, Murray confirms justification by faith alone apart from good works:

> We are required to ask how the principle of faith is so rigidly exclusive of and antithetical to works of law in the matter of justification. The only answer is the specific quality of faith as opposed to that of works.

---

[94] Murray, *Collected Writings*, 2:203: "It may be safe to say that the greatest event for Christendom in the last 1500 years was the Protestant Reformation. What was the spark that lit the flame of evangelical passion? It was, by the grace of God, the discovery on the part of Luther, stricken with a sense of his estrangement from God and feeling in his inmost soul the stings of his wrath and the remorse of a terrified conscience, of the true and only way whereby a man can be just with God. To him the truth of justification by free grace through faith lifted him from the depths of the forebodings of hell to the ecstasy of peace with God and the hope of glory. If there is one thing the Church needs today it is the republication with faith and passion of the presuppositions of the doctrine of justification and the reapplication of this, the article of a standing or falling Church. 'Being justified freely by his grace through the redemption that is in Christ Jesus: Whom God hath set forth to be a propitiation through faith in his blood, to declare his righteousness for the remission of sins that are past, through the forbearance of God; To declare, I say, at this time his righteousness: that he might be just, and the justifier of him which believeth in Jesus' (Romans 3:24-26)."

Justification by works always finds its ground in that which the person is and does; it is always oriented to that consideration of virtue attaching to the person justified. The specific quality of faith is trust and commitment to another; it is essentially extraspective and in that respect is the diametric opposite of works. Faith is *self*-renouncing; works are *self*-congratulatory. Faith looks to what God does; works have respect to what we are. It is this antithesis of principle that enables the apostle to base the complete exclusion of works upon the principle of faith. Only faith has relevance within that gospel delineated in verses 21-26. And, if faith, then it is 'without works of law.' It follows therefore that 'by faith alone' is implicit in the apostle's argument. Luther added nothing to the *sense* of the passage when he said 'by faith alone.'[95]

Thus, there is no conflict on the issue of the doctrine of justification between Luther and Calvin because justification by faith alone apart from good works was the Protestant consensus as over against the Romish doctrine of justification in which Law and Gospel are mixed, ultimately setting forth the meritorious concept of justification and salvation. As a result of Rome's doctrine, there is no distinction between justification and sanctification. Although Romish theology purports to accept the forensic nature of justification, it cannot sustain justification by faith alone because of its mixture of Law and Gospel. In other words, the forensic nature of justification and the mixture of Law and Gospel in the doctrine of justification are mutually exclusive and cannot stand together:

> It is on this doctrine of justification as consisting in sanctification and renewal, the infusion of righteousness and sanctifying grace, that the polemic of Rome turns, and it is preeminently at this point that the issue between the Romish and Protestant positions must be joined ... For even if Rome admitted that justification as to its *nature* is forensic, she could still retain what belongs to the essence of her position, namely, that the ground upon which this favourable judgment of God rests is not the righteousness and obedience of Christ but righteousness infused, inwrought, and outwrought in the works which are the fruit of *fides formata*, namely faith informed with charity. This admission would reorient, of course, the terms of Rome's polemic as also of the anti-Romish Protestant polemic.[96]

---

[95] Murray, *Romans*, 3:27-8.
[96] Ibid., I:360.

Christ through his once for all atonement satisfied God's justice respecting the requirements of the law: "In Romans 3:25,26 we read that God set forth Christ a propitiation, to demonstrate his righteousness, 'that he might be just and the justifier of him who is of the faith of Jesus.' This states that which is satisfied or provided for in the propitiation, the justice of God. So we have a biblical basis for the concept."[97] Justification, Murray emphasizes, is exclusively forensic or judicial. We observe here, however, that Murray's understanding of the forensic perspective is possible only in terms of the antithesis between Law and Gospel. Thus, "justification affects the judicial relation to law and justice. In our relation to God it must mean that we are reckoned in his judgment as free from guilt and sustaining an upright relation in terms of the criterion of his judgment, that is to say, we are reckoned as sustaining a relation which meets the requirements of law and justice, and pronounced to be such."[98] The forensic aspect of justification revealed in Romans 8:33 and 34, Murray asserts, precludes a subjective change within us from the doctrine of justification because God declares that we are righteous on the basis of Christ's obedience:

> Romans 8:33, 34 conclusively shows that the meaning is that which is contrasted with the word 'condemn' and that which is related to the rebuttal of a judicial charge. The meaning of the word 'justify,' therefore, in the epistle to the Romans, and therefore in the epistle which more than any other book in Scripture unfolds the doctrine, is to declare to be righteous. Its meaning is entirely removed from the thought of making upright or holy or good or righteous. This is what is meant when we insist that justification is forensic. It has to do with a judgment given, declared, pronounced; it is judicial or juridical or forensic.[99]

---

[97] Murray, *Collected Writings*, 2:142-43. As such, Murray does not deviate from Luther and Calvin on the doctrine of justification by faith alone because both shared "the grand article of a standing or falling Church": "How can man *become* right with God? This was Luther's burning question. He found the answer in Paul's Epistles to the Romans and the Galatians, that we are justified by faith alone, through grace alone–'justified freely by his grace through the redemption that is in Christ Jesus' (Rom. 3:24); and 'being justified by faith we have peace with God' (Rom. 5:1)." Ibid., 1:302-03.
[98] Ibid., 2:205.
[99] Murray, *Redemption*, 121.

Murray comprehends the doctrine of justification from the *forensic or legal point of view* involved in God's once for all declaration that results from Christ fulfilling the requirements of the law: "Justification means to declare to be righteous–it is a judgment based upon the recognition that a person stands in a right relation to law and justice. Or it is a pronouncement based upon the judgment that a person is free from guilt and stands approved in relation to the standard in law relevant to the case."[100] As a result of the pronouncement or declaration of God, one is recognized in the sight of God "as free from guilt and sustains to law and justice a relation or status whereby he is accepted as righteous."[101] The forensic nature of justification, Murray argues, guarantees that the one who is justified, stands "in an unimpeachable relation to the law." Furthermore, the imputation of righteousness in justification is absolutely linked to the forensic character of justification. In other words, we must not talk about the imputation of righteousness if we do not see the doctrine of justification from *a forensic or legal point of view*. The forensic view point is closely related with the antithesis between Law and Gospel:

> When this is applied to soteric justification it means that God declares the ungodly to be free from condemnation and to be reckoned in his sight as standing in an upright relation to the demands of law and justice. Since God justifies those who are ungodly and therefore under the sentence of condemnation, the declarative act of God in justification presupposes a constitutive act on the part of God whereby he constitutes a new and upright relation to his law and to his righteousness. We found that the Scripture expressly indicates this constitutive act in such phrases as 'constitute righteous' (Romans 5:19) and 'impute righteousness' or 'impute for righteousness' (*passim* in Romans 4 etc.). So we might say that justification finds its specific character or at least finds its necessary presupposition in the imputation of righteousness (This is indeed required if the judgment of God is to be according to truth. If God declares that the demands of law and justice are reckoned by him as satisfied, this must involve

---

[100] Murray, *Collected Writings*, 2:206. Without an antithesis between Law and Gospel, Murray asserts, we may not talk about the forensic aspect of justification involved with God's once for all declaration: "In a word, justification is simply a declaration or pronouncement respecting the relation of the person to the law which he, the judge, is required to administer." idem, *Redemption*, 119.

[101] Murray, *Collected Writings*, 2:207.

righteousness as reckoned by him satisfied, this must involve righteousness as reckoned to the account of the justified).[102]

Because Murray comprehends the doctrine of justification in the light of its forensic aspect, he stresses that *the principles of works and grace are antithetical* in relation to justification. Thus the principle of the law reveals the impossibility of justification by works of the law according to Pauline passages such as Romans 3:20; 4:2; 10:3, 4; Galatians 2:16; 3:11; 5:4; Philippians 3:9; Titus 3:5. "It is not a righteousness wrought by us. It is not by our obedience to the law of God." Accordingly, Paul's argument in Romans 2:13 is hypothetical, and reveals to us the antithesis between Law and Gospel: "Paul says in Romans 2:13 that the doers of the law will be justified, but he goes on to show that there are none such, for all have sinned and come short of the glory of God." As such, Paul emphasizes that we are justified by God's grace apart from works (Rom. 3:24-26; 4:16; 5:15-21; Gal. 3:12).[103]

Paul's interpretation of Genesis 15:6 in Romans 4 proves that Abraham was justified by faith alone apart from good works. The genius of the Pauline argument is that Paul defends justification by faith alone in the light of *the antithesis between works and faith.* Accordingly, Paul reaches the brilliant conclusion that there is an absolute antithesis between justification by works and justification by faith:

---

[102] Ibid., 2:210. In Murray's thought, the declarative forensic nature of the doctrine of justification is closely tied to the once for all nature of calling, regeneration, adoption, and definitive sanctification: "We properly think of calling, regeneration, justification, and adoption as acts of God effected once for all, and not requiring or admitting of repetition. It is of their nature to be definitive. But a considerable part of New Testament teaching places sanctification in this category." Ibid., 2:277. Perhaps, one of the most distinctive contributions of Murray's theology is his dazzling insight of *definitive sanctification* in relation to the concept of union with Christ's death and resurrection based upon biblical theological outworking. See Ibid., 2:277-317; idem, *Redemption,* 141-50. For a comprehensive and constructive analysis of Murray's definitive sanctification, see David D. Cho's "The Old Princeton Presbyterian Response to the Holiness Movement" (Ph.D. diss., Westminster Theological Seminary, 1994).

[103] Ibid., 2:211-12.

One of the most significant passages in this group is Rom. 4 where Paul appeals to Gen. 15:6 in order to vindicate justification by faith in contrast with justification by works. Verses 3 and 4 indicate the crux of Paul's argument. 'Abraham believed God and it was reckoned to him for righteousness' (vs.4). It is Abraham's *believing* in God that is in the forefront as demonstrating justification by grace in contrast with one of debt on the basis of working (cf. vs.4).[104]

The 'Do this and you will live' of Romans 10:5 and Galatians 3:12, alluding to Leviticus 18:5, is not operative as the means of justification and salvation in the postlapsarian state. Therefore, the Pauline understanding of the principle of works-righteousness is only a concrete theological reference point to denote an antithesis between Law and Gospel in relation to the doctrine of justification, excluding evangelical obedience in its arena:

> The principle 'the man who does shall live' must be regarded as totally inoperative within the realm of sin. It is this truth that underlies Paul's whole polemic regarding the justification of the ungodly and the righteousness that is constitutive thereof. Justification by *doing* is the contradiction of justification by faith. *Doing* has human righteousness in view, and the only righteousness that can be operative in our sinful situation is the God-righteousness which the gospel reveals (cf. 1:17; 3:21;22; 10:3). It is this contrast that Paul institutes in Rom. 10:5,6. In alluding to Lev. 18:5 at this point he uses the formula 'the man that

---

[104] Murray, *Romans*, I:365-66. According to Murray's thesis, Paul makes an absolute antithesis between works and faith in the doctrine of justification. When this hermeneutical background is seen, then justification by faith alone becomes clear. From this concrete reference point, we may talk about the imputation of faith. In other words, justification by faith alone understood in the light of the antithesis between works and faith and the imputation of faith stands or falls together: "Paul focuses his attention on that one consideration and frames his argument accordingly, to wit, that it was faith in contrast with works that entered into God's accounting with Abraham in the matter of his justification. In terms of the formula, it was faith that was reckoned to him for the righteousness with which justification is concerned. In each case of appeal to Genesis 15:6, therefore, we must not, for dogmatic reasons, fail to recognize that it is faith that is imputed (vss. 5,9,10,11,22,23)." Ibid., 4:2-3.

According to Genesis 15:6, Abraham was a great example of justification by faith alone: "The more restricted interest of the apostle at this point must be appreciated. He is jealous to establish from the Scriptures, particularly from the Scriptures as they are concerned with Abraham, the antithesis between justification by works and that by faith." Ibid., 4:6-8.

> doeth ... shall live thereby' as a proper expression *in itself* of the principle of works-righteousness in contrast with the righteousness of faith. We have no right to contest the apostle's right to use the terms of Lev. 18:5 for this purpose since they do describe that which holds true when law-righteousness is operative unto justification and life and also express the conception entertained by the person who espouses the same as the way of acceptance with God (cf. Also Gal. 3:12).[105]

As such, 'Do this and you will live' illustrates the absolute antithesis between the principle of Law and Gospel in the doctrine of justification. To be sure, however, the law has a role in the life of believers who have already been justified. In other words, the *ordo salutis* provides a distinct place for the second use of the law in reference to justification and a distinct place for the third use of the law in reference to progressive sanctification:

> It must be understood, therefore, that the principle 'this do and thou shalt live' can have no validity in our sinful state as the way of justification and acceptance with God. To aver that it has is to deny the reality of our sin and the necessary provision of the gospel. But we must not suppose that doing the commandments as the way of life has ceased to have any validity or application. To suppose this would be as capital a mistake in its own locus as to propound works-righteousness as the way of justification. We must bear in mind that righteousness and life are never separable.[106]

Thus those who belong to Christ obey the law of God as the way of life: "In the realm of grace, therefore, obedience is the way of life. He that does the commandments of God lives in them. It could not be otherwise. The fruit of the Spirit is well-pleasing to God and the fruit of the Spirit is obedience."[107]

Interpreting Romans 10:3-4, Murray argues that there is a clear antithesis between the principle of the righteousness of the law and the righteousness of faith (*iustitia fidei*) as the way of obtaining justification. We cannot mix the Law and Gospel in the discussion of justification:

---

[105] Ibid., II:250.
[106] Ibid.
[107] Ibid., II:251.

In this epistle and in the context the antithesis is between the righteousness of the law as that of works and God's righteousness as the righteousness of faith. The next verse is the clearest demonstration of this antithesis and of the meaning we are to attach to the apostle's concept of the law as the way of attaining to righteousness ... The view most consonant with this context is, therefore, that the apostle is speaking in verse 4 of the law as a way of righteousness before God and affirming the relation that Christ sustains to this conception.[108]

The righteousness of God (δικαιοσύνη θεοῦ) revealed in Romans 1:17; 3:21, 22; 2 Corinthians 5:21, argues Murray, should be understood from the viewpoint of *the antithesis between law and faith*. Justification is founded upon *an alien righteousness* (*iustitia aliena*) apart from human righteousness, and the antithesis between Law and Gospel is the presupposition of this formulation. To be sure, "God-righteousness" is the fountain of justification, and this is logically clear when we understand it from the viewpoint of the antithesis between works and faith:

It should be noted that this righteousness is not our own, not of the law, but a righteousness of the faith of Christ. This emphasis upon the righteousness of God can perhaps be most adequately and pointedly expressed by saying that it is 'God-righteousness.' And to assess the force of this designation we may express it both negatively and positively.[109]

Christ demonstrated the righteousness of God (*iustitia Dei*) through his active and passive obedience (*obedientia activa et passiva*) to the law by satisfying the conditions of the atonement. As a result, we can talk about "the righteousness of Christ" (*iustitia Christi*) as the foundation of the doctrine of justification.[110] Furthermore, salvation and justification, Murray asserts, must be understood in the light of the

---

[108] Ibid., 10:3.

[109] Murray, *Collected Writings*, 2:212.

[110] Murray, *Redemption*, 16-7: "Now, what righteousness is equal to the justification of sinners? The only righteousness conceivable that will meet the requirements of our situation as sinners and meet the requirements of a full and irrevocable justification is the righteousness of Christ. This implies his obedience and therefore his incarnation, death, and resurrection. In a word, the necessity of the atonement is inherent in and essential to justification."

righteousness of God which is closely linked with the antithesis between Law and Faith:

> A salvation from sin divorced from justification is an impossibility and justification of sinners without the God - righteousness of the Redeemer is unthinkable. We can hardly escape the relevance of Paul's word: 'For if a law had been given which could make alive, verily righteousness would have been by the law' (Gal. 3:21). What Paul is insisting upon is that if justification could have been secured by any other method than that of faith in Christ, by that method it would have been.[111]

Sin is a violation of God's holy law and "the contradiction of God." In this respect, God demands the fulfillment of the requirements of his holy law. That is the reason why salvation must be discussed under the presupposition of "expiation and propitiation': "It is this inviolable sanctity of God's law, the immutable dictate of holiness and the unflinching demand of justice, that makes mandatory the conclusion that salvation from sin without expiation and propitiation is inconceivable."[112] The vicarious obedience of Jesus Christ, Murray states, presupposes that God's law demands the fulfillment of its penal and ethical aspects. Thus, the Redeemer's active and passive obedience fulfills the requirements of theses two aspects of the law. The vicarious obedience of Christ is required for the remission of sins and the attainment of justification:

> The real use and purpose of the formula is to emphasize the two distinct aspects of our Lord's vicarious obedience. The truth expressed rests upon the recognition that the law of God has both penal sanctions and positive demands. It demands not only the full discharge of its precepts but also the infliction of penalty for all infractions and shortcomings. It is this twofold demand of the law of God which is taken into account when we speak of the active and passive obedience of Christ. Christ as the vicar of his people came under the curse and condemnation due to sin and he also fulfilled the law of God in all its positive requirements. In other words, he took care of the guilt of sin and perfectly fulfilled the demands of righteousness. He perfectly met both the penal and the preceptive requirements of God's law. The passive obedience refers to the former and the active obedience to the

---

[111] Ibid., 17.
[112] Ibid., 18.

latter. Christ's obedience was vicarious in the bearing of the full judgment of God upon sin, and it was vicarious in the full discharge of the demands of righteousness. His obedience becomes the ground of the remission of sin and of actual justification.[113]

In this respect, the major problem of the "Pelagian, Romish, Arminian, or Liberal" doctrine of justification lies in the mixture between "God-righteousness" and "human righteousness," and the contribution of the latter "to the justifying righteousness."[114] In his review of G. C. Berkouwer's *Studies in Dogmatics: Faith and Justification*,[115] Murray emphasizes the concept of the righteousness of

---

[113] Ibid., 21-2.

[114] Murray, *Collected Writings*, 2:213.

[115] G. C. Berkouwer correctly recognizes the antithesis between work-righteousness and faith-righteousness in the Reformation doctrine of justification, which is equivalent in quality to the antithesis between Law and Gospel as a hermeneutical tool to depict justification by faith alone apart from good works: "The Reformation continually appealed to Paul only because in him the contrast between work-righteousness and faith-righteousness comes to the sharpest religious clarity ... We should pause a moment for a consideration of the sharp antithesis that Paul makes between justification by the works of the law and justification by faith. This antithesis is the heavy accent sounded in Romans and Galatians which the Reformation heard and translated in terms *sola fide-sola gratia.*" G. C. Berkouwer, *Studies in Dogmatics: Faith and Justification*, trans. Lewis B. Smedes (Grand Rapids, Michigan: Eerdmans Publishing Company, 1954), 76-7. Berkouwer expounds the forensic nature of justification, understanding it in terms of the "imputation of the righteousness of Christ," the instrumentality of faith identified as *not because of faith but through faith*, divine declaration. Ibid., 61-100.

Nevertheless, in his own understanding of the Pauline theology, Berkouwer rejects the antithesis between Law and Grace which has been a key hermeneutical principle of the Protestant Reformation and covenant hermeneutics: "In Paul all the threads of the history of revelation were drawn together. He met situations in Rome and Galatia which occasioned explicit illumination of the gospel contrast between law and grace. In this contrast the heart, the essential character of the gospel was at stake ... When Paul's eyes were first opened to the gospel, he saw against the background of his own former life that the law was fatal. This does not mean that Paul accepted an antithesis between law and grace. Paul was concerned with actual situations. Men were knocking themselves out trying to please God by their own righteousness. In respect to this situation Paul opposed grace to law, or rather

God over against human unrighteousness in the doctrine of justification. In other words, there is an antithesis between God-righteousness and human unrighteousness, and from this theological background, we affirm the righteousness of God as the basis of the doctrine of justification: "Nothing exposes the perversity of Rome and the grandeur of the gospel more than the fact that justifying righteousness is a God-righteousness and therefore contrasted not only with human unrighteousness but with human righteousness."[116] Christ's active and passive obedience respecting the requirements of the law, Murray asserts, eliminates obedience to the law as the presupposition of justification and salvation:

> Christ has redeemed us from the necessity of keeping the law *as the condition of our justification and acceptance with God*. Without such redemption there could be no justification and no salvation. It is the obedience of Christ himself that has secured this release. For it is by his obedience that many will be constituted righteous (Rom. 5:19). In other words, it is the active and passive obedience of Christ that is the price of this redemption, active and passive obedience because he was made under law, fulfilled all the requirements of righteousness and met all the sanctions of justice.[117]

---

the righteousness of faith to the righteousness of the law. This antithesis is identical with the gospel; with it the gospel stands or falls." Ibid., 69-70.

[116] Murray, *Collected Writings*, 4:291. In Murray's mind, it is clear that in the postlapsarian state because of human sinfulness, human righteousness cannot be compared with God-righteousness. Thus, there is an absolute antithesis between God-righteousness and human righteousness in the discussion of justification which is perfectly analogous to an antithesis between Law and Gospel: "It is by the righteousness of God that we are justified (Rom. 1:17; 3:21,22; 10:3; Phil. 3:9). In other words, the righteousness of our justification is a God-righteousness. Nothing more conclusively demonstrates that it is not a righteousness which is ours. Righteousness wrought in us or wrought by us, even though it be altogether of the grace of God and even though it be perfect in character, is not a God-righteousness. It is, after all, a human righteousness. But the commanding insistence of the Scripture is that in justification it is the righteousness of God which is revealed from faith to faith, and therefore a righteousness which is contrasted not only with human unrighteousness but with human righteousness. It is righteousness which is *divine* in quality." idem, *Redemption*, 127.

[117] Ibid., 45.

In line with Reformed tradition, Murray maintains that *union with Christ* (*unio cum Christo*) is the governing principle of the soteriological application of redemption, including the doctrine of justification, referring to Romans 5:17-21 and 2 Corinthians 5:21. Union with Christ does not vitiate, however, the principle of justification by faith alone apart from good works (*iustificatus fide sine operibus*), because in his detailed discussion of justification, the Law and Gospel antithesis remains a vital reference point :

> But the most significant thought of verse 21b is that we become this righteousness by union with him .... Christ is ours, and therefore all that is his is ours in union with him and we cannot think of him in his vicarious capacity or of anything that is his in this capacity except in union and communion with his people. It is the truth of 2 Corinthians 5:21 that brings to the fullest expression all that the apostle had said in Romans 5:17,18,19 in terms of justification as reception of the free gift of righteousness, as justification of life through the one righteousness of Christ, and so being constituted righteous through the obedience of the one.[118]

Murray's theological point is that if we do not make a clear antithesis between Law and Gospel in relation to the doctrine of justification, we have to bring inevitably "evangelical obedience" into it like the Remonstrants. We have already seen its extreme form in Romish theology as expounded in the light of *meritum de congruo et meritum de condigno*. In other words, it is clear that faith is the only instrument of justification when we understand the doctrine of justification in the light of an antithesis between Law and Gospel:

> In the Romish system faith as it precedes baptism is bare assent and is simply the occasional cause of first justification. Faith simply leads the person to ask for baptism. Faith that issues from baptism is *fides formata*, faith informed with love, and is that subjective condition in virtue of which we do good works well-pleasing to God. These latter

---

[118] Murray, *Collected Writings*, 2:213-14. cf. idem, *Redemption*, 161-73. It is important to notice, however, that Murray safeguards the doctrine of justification by faith alone apart from good works while he makes use of *union with Christ* as the central basis of redemption accomplished and applied: "Union with Christ is really the central truth of the whole doctrine of salvation not only in its application but also in its once-for-all accomplishment in the finished work of Christ." Ibid., 161.

have *meritum condigni* and become the ground of second justification. In either case faith is not the instrumental cause of justification. According to the Remonstrants, faith joined with evangelical obedience is the ground of justification. Though not perfect yet it is reckoned for righteousness by the grace of God.[119]

There is harmony "between faith as the instrument" of justification, "on the one hand, and the judicially constitutive and declarative nature of justification, and the righteousness of Christ as the ground of justification, on the other."[120] The presupposition of the imputation of the righteousness of Christ in our justification, Murray emphasizes, is Christ's perfect obedience to the law. In this respect, Christ's active and passive obedience to the law is the ultimate ground of our justification: "The constitutive act consists in the imputation to us of the obedience and righteousness of Christ. The obedience of Christ must therefore be regarded as the *ground* of justification."[121] Out of this specific analysis, the instrumentality of faith in justification becomes clear: "It speaks always of our being justified *by* faith, or *through* faith, or *upon* faith, but never speaks of our being justified *on account of* faith or *because of* faith."[122] Murray argues that faith as the instrument of justification (*instrumentum iustificationis*) eliminates all sorts of "the fruits of the Spirit" in its arena, having "their own specific functions in the application of redemption." As such, the instrumentality of faith in justification becomes clear when we understand it in the light of the absolute distinction between works and faith, eliminating human righteousness. Nevertheless, faith is inseparably linked with "repentance, love, and hope." Thus, a faith which is separated from these qualities is not "the faith of the contrite and therefore it is not the faith that justifies." It is, however, "faith alone that justifies" since it is founded upon the specific quality of the righteousness of Christ. The instrumental quality of faith rules out justification "*dia pistin* (on account of faith)":

> It is the stumbling-block to self-righteousness and self-righteousness is the arch-demon of antithesis to grace. It is the glory of the gospel for the contrite and brokenhearted–if we put any other exercise of the

---

[119] Murray, *Collected Writings*, 2:215-16.
[120] Ibid., 2:216.
[121] Murray, *Redemption*, 125.
[122] Ibid.

human spirit in the place of faith, then we cut the throat of the only confidence a sinner conscious of his lost and helpless condition can entertain. Justification by faith is the jubilee trumpet of the gospel because it proclaims the gospel to the poor and destitute whose only door of hope is to roll themselves in total helplessness upon the grace and power and righteousness of the Redeemer of the lost. In the words of one, 'cast out your anchor into the ocean of the Redeemer's merits.'[123]

Based on the antithesis between Law and Gospel, Murray draws out the antithesis between works and faith in the doctrine of justification. As a result, Murray argues that faith is the only instrument of justification. In other words, apart from the antithesis between works and faith, we may not talk about the instrumentality of faith in the doctrine of justification:

(1) The formula is set in contrast with justification by works of law (cf. Rom. 4:2-6,13,14,16; Gal. 3:5,6; cf. Rom. 10:5,6). In the case of justification by works it is clear that the works themselves would be the ground upon which the justification would rest (Rom. 2:13). If faith is contrasted with works, then we should expect that faith would occupy the same position as works in the event of justification by works. (2) The expression 'righteousness of faith' (cf. Rom. 4:11,13) could be interested in the sense that it is the righteousness which consists in faith, faith being an appositional or definitive genitive.[124]

---

[123] Murray, *Collected Writings*, 2:217. Faith, Murray says, is only the instrument of justification because faith as the channel of the Gospel of grace should also be understood in the light of *the antithesis between works and faith*: "It would surely seem impossible to avoid the conclusion that justification is upon the event of faith or through the instrumentality of faith. God justifies the ungodly who believe in Jesus, in a word, believers. And that is simply to say that faith is presupposed in justification, is the precondition of justification, not because we are justified on the ground of faith or for the reason that we are justified because of faith but only for the reason that faith is God's appointed instrument through which he dispenses this grace." idem, *Redemption*, 85.

[124] Murray, *Romans*, I:354. Murray's thesis is that we may not talk about the instrumentality of faith in the doctrine of justification if we mix works and faith, and it is precisely this which is the Achilles' heel of Romish theology: "Again, faith is displaced from the position which the pervasive witness of Scripture demands, namely, that it is faith, by reason of its specific character in distinction from works as well as from the other graces of the Spirit, and

In this regard, the *electing grace of God* is closely linked to justification by faith alone over against works. To be sure, the gracious element of divine election becomes solid when it is understood from the *antithetical viewpoint of works and grace*. It is essential to see that the antithesis of gracious divine election vs. human works and the antithesis of justification by faith alone vs. human works stand or fall together:

> In verse 6 the apostle adds further definition of what is implicit in the expression 'election of grace,' and he does so by setting up the antithesis between grace and human performance. If grace is conditioned in any way by human performance or by the will of man impelling to action, then grace ceases to be grace. This verse as specifying the true character of grace in contrast with works serves the same purpose at this point as does 'not of works, but of him that calleth' in 9:11 (cf. also Eph. 2:8b).[125]

---

faith alone that is brought into the instrumental relation to justification." Ibid., I:361-62.

Referring to Romans 9:30-33, Murray notices that there is an absolute antithesis between works and faith in depicting the doctrine of justification. Accordingly, faith as the instrument of justification must be understood as *faith in opposition to works*: "No further exposition is necessary other than to observe the way in which the antithesis is stated: 'not of faith but as of works.' 'As of works' indicates the conception entertained by Israel respecting the way by which justification was to be secured and the kind of righteousness constituting this justification. The misapprehension was total. Hence the failure ... It is the faith of resting upon him and in the context (cf. vss. 30,31) is viewed particularly as the faith directed to justification. The righteousness attained is that of faith in contrast with works." Ibid., 9:30-33.

[125] Ibid., 11:5-6. Thus, Murray emphasizes that *electing grace* cannot be properly understood if we do not interpret it in the light of the antithesis between works and grace. It is the vital element which depicts the gracious character of salvation. To be sure, if we do not reckon with the antithesis between Law and Grace, then we cannot defend the biblical doctrine of divine election: "The election is said to be 'of grace' (vs. 5) and the apostle in verse 6 is careful to define the true character of grace in contrast with works. When Paul emphasizes grace in this way it is the grace unto salvation that is in view (cf. 3:24; 4:16; 5:20,21; Gal. 2:21; Eph. 2:5,8; 1 Tim. 1:14; 2 Tim. 1:9). (3) 'The election' (vs. 7) is said to have obtained it and, as noted above, the thing obtained cannot be anything less than the righteousness unto eternal life (cf. 5:18,21) ... The contextual emphasis upon election as entirely of grace and therefore upon the free and sovereign will of God as the determining cause of

The failure of Romish theology, Murray asserts, is that it mixes Law and Gospel in the doctrine of justification. Because of this problem, the schoolmen state that *baptism* is the *instrument* of justification instead of faith, asserting that justification is *a process*, thereby confusing justification with progressive sanctification. In other words, Romish theology introduces good works and human merit into the doctrine of justification. Accordingly, the schoolmen cannot say that faith is the *instrument* of justification because of their rejection of the antithesis between works and faith in the understanding of justification:

> Rome's polemic is directed most vigorously against the tenet that we are justified by faith alone. This is necessitated by her conception of the nature of justification and, more particularly, by her view of the progressive character of justification and of the merits accruing to the believer from the works of faith. Here again the divergence of Rome from the sustained witness of Scripture to the effect that we are justified by faith apart from works is most patent. If anything is apparent from the evidence with which we have dealt in the commentary and in the foregoing pages of this appendix it is that 'faith' is accorded the instrumental agency in connection with justification. Nothing should serve to expose the fallacy of Rome's doctrine more effectively than the incompatibility of this sustained emphasis upon faith with the Romish emphasis upon works and the merit accruing therefrom. It is symptomatic of the total discrepancy between Rome's position and the teaching of Scripture that baptism should be conceived of as the instrumental cause. The efficiency that Scripture accords to faith Rome accords to baptism ... Justification is thus confused with regeneration, renovation, and sanctification. The effect is that the distinctiveness of the grand article of justification by grace through faith is eliminated from the gospel.[126]

The application of the antithesis between Law and Gospel in the doctrine of justification enables Murray to understand the proper relationship between man and God from a legal perspective.[127] The

---

the differentiation involved requires us to apply in this case the same doctrine stated earlier in 9:18." Ibid., 11:7-10.

[126] Ibid., I:360-61.

[127] Murray, *Collected Writings*, 2:219-20: "justification immediately and permanently changes the relation to God and to law and justice. It includes remission of the penalty of all sin, that is, it removes judicial, penal

antithesis between Law and Gospel as a concrete hermeneutical reference point is vital for understanding the biblical concept of salvation and justification by faith alone apart from good works. The message of *evangelism*, argues Murray, has to focus on the Gospel of Christ Jesus that is proclaimed in the light of Law and Gospel antithesis; it is an obligation of the evangelist: "One of the primary tasks of the evangelist, therefore, is to bring the demands of law and gospel to bear upon the consciences of men so that they may be convinced of the reality of the condemnation to which they are subject, of the reality of their separation from God, and of the certainty of eternal doom apart from the gospel of redeeming grace."[128] One of the necessary elements in preaching, argues Murray, is to proclaim the message of the Gospel in the light of an antithesis between Law and Gospel. In other words, to make intelligible the Gospel of Christ Jesus we must present the requirements of the law of God as the prerequisite of the Gospel. Otherwise, the Gospel of Jesus will be distorted and minimized. As such, we cannot think of the Gospel and salvation without the antithesis between Law and Gospel:

> When emphasis upon the demands and sanctions of God's law is neglected, there are grave consequences for the propagation of the gospel itself. And when I say 'propagation' I am thinking not merely in terms of extension but also of intention. When the proclamation of God's law is neglected, the significance of the gospel is correspondingly reduced in our presentation and in the apprehension of men. The gospel is the gospel of salvation, and salvation is, first of all, salvation from sin in its guilt, defilement, and power. If our emphasis on the judgment of God upon sin is minimal, correspondingly minimal will be our esteem of salvation and of the Saviour.[129]

---

condemnation for past, present and future sins. God is no longer a condemning Judge but a loving Father ...'I was alive without the law once: but when the commandment came, sin revived, and I died' (Rom. 7:9). When consciousness is awakened to the guilt and condemnation which sin entails, the invariable result is the death of which the apostle speaks. The only article of our faith that provides the remedy is justification by free grace through faith in Jesus' blood."

[128] Murray, *Collected Writings*, 1:129.
[129] Ibid., 1:144.

Modern theology, points out Murray, does not show respect to an antithesis between Law and Gospel in depicting the Gospel of Christ Jesus. This is fatal to the grand article of justification by faith alone. If we do not adopt an antithesis between Law and Gospel as a hermeneutical reference point, then the Gospel itself becomes a meaningless slogan. Justification by faith alone and the antithesis between Law and Gospel in relation to salvation stand or fall together.[130] Reviewing Herman N. Ridderbos' *When the Time Had Fully Come: Studies in New Testament Theology*, Murray asserts that the eschatological Kingdom of God which is properly understood in the light of *the already and not yet* in opposition to "the 'spiritual concept' of liberal theology and the eschatologism of Schweitzer," does not jeopardize the principle of justification by faith alone, as related to the *historia salutis* of Christ's once for all death and resurrection. Having said this, it is remarkable that Murray does not proceed to interpret the doctrine of justification from an already — not yet perspective:

> Ridderbos devotes a good deal of attention specifically to the teaching of the apostle Paul. This is as we might expect. One of his main concerns is the point of view from which Paul's preaching may be approached, and here we have a discriminating analysis of the question

---

[130] Ibid., 1:145: "The consciousness of guilt has suffered eclipse in the context of modern Christianity. It is easy to see, however, that when guilt is pushed into the background and the sense of guilt becomes well-nigh extinct, the grand article of the gospel becomes correspondingly meaningless. What is this grand article, the grand article of grace? If our minds do not immediately supply the answer, it is because we ourselves have become infected with the stupor so characteristic of our generation. It is, of course, the article of justification by grace through faith. The appreciation of that article, and the appreciation of the gospel as it is epitomised in that article, takes its inception from the consciousness of guilt. There is an amazing and distressing paucity of the agonizing question which is, after all, the basic religious question: how can a man be just with God? And there is likewise, and inevitably as a consequence, a paucity of the exultant joy which comes with the realization of complete and irrevocable justification by free grace through faith. The root from which all such impoverishment proceeds is the absence from our thinking and from our preaching of the divine judgment upon sin. Without the ministry of judgment and condemnation the foundation is not laid in the conviction which gives meaning and appeal to the gospel of free and sovereign grace."

as it relates to justification by faith. The latter is not, in Ridderbos' judgment, the main entrance in Paul's preaching of the gospel. Justification is of central importance. But 'the central motive of justification by faith can be understood in its real, pregnant significance' only from, what Ridderbos calls, the 'redemptive-historical viewpoint' (p.49) which is to the effect that 'in the crucified and risen Saviour the great turning-point in God's times has come' (p.48). The main theme of Paul's ministry is that what has been promised of old has *now* been fulfilled and manifested. Paul's kerygma was the '*now* of the day of salvation' (*idem*). And so 'the starting-point of Paul's preaching of justification by faith is to be found in the great turning-point in the *historia salutis*' (p.49). It is in this same connection that Ridderbos shows the significance of the identification of the believer with Christ in his death and resurrection if we are to understand the redemptive-historical character of Paul's preaching (cf. Pp. 54ff.).[131]

2. *The Antithesis Between Adam and Christ*

One of the most penetrating theological contributions of Murray is in his emphasis on the hermeneutical theological importance of the comparison and contrast of Adam and Christ in Romans 5:12-21. Murray is opposed to the dialectical hermeneutics espoused by C. H. Dodd and Emil Brunner because they destroy the biblical theological significance of the antithesis between Adam and Christ:

> The recognition of and the emphasis upon solidaric or corporate sin and guilt in our present-day theology are not to be interpreted as identical with the classic Protestant doctrine of the imputation of Adam's sin. And it does not advance the cause of theology or of exegesis to regard Paul's appeal to the fall of Adam as but the mythical form in which the fact of solidaric unity in sin is expressed.[132]

---

[131] Murray, *Collected Writings*, 4:356-57.

[132] John Murray, *The Imputation of Adam's Sin* (Grand Rapids: Eerdmans Publishing Company, 1959; reprint, Phillipsburg: Presbyterian and Reformed Publishing Company, 1987), 6. Thus, Murray shows that the neoorthodox understanding of the Adam and Christ parallel is destructive of the Gospel itself, ultimately moralizing it in the form of modern dialectical Pelagianism and rejecting original sin without which the Gospel is meaningless propaganda: "Similarly, he [Paul] says, through the moral achievement of Christ all men may rise to goodness ... If we think of Adam as a man representative of all humanity, we approach Paul's thought. But Adam is a

Over against the background of neoorthodoxy's dialectical interpretation concerning the parallel between Adam and Christ, Murray lends further support to the notion of the antithesis between Adam and Christ by referring to the Swedish scholar Anders Nygren.[133]

---

myth (though for Paul he *may* have been real); not so Jesus Christ, who certainly is a Figure of history and has determined in a unique degree the course which mankind has followed — the Representative Man in a special sense ... Thus Paul's doctrine of Christ as the 'second Adam' is not so bound up with the story of the Fall as a literal happening that it ceases to have meaning when we no longer accept the story as such. Indeed, we should not too readily assume that Paul did so accept it." C. H. Dodd, *The Epistle of Paul to the Romans* (New York / London: Harper and Brothers Publishers, 1932), 79-80; "Der seit Augustin für die christliche Anthropologie massgebend gewordene Begriff der Erbsünde ist der Bibel vollkommen fremd. Er hat aber den grossen Vorteil, die beiden Momente des biblischen Sündenverständnisses, die Sünde als herrschende Macht und die solidarische Verbundenheit aller Menschen in der Sünde durch eine anschauliche Vorstellung zu verbinden." Emil Brunner, *Die Christliche Lehre von Schöpfung und Erlösung* (Zürich: Zwingli - Verlag, 1950), 2:119; "Darum bin, dieser einzelne Mensch, beides: Adam, der von Gott geschaffene und Nachkomme "Adams." Es ist nun im höchsten Grade bedeutsam, dass die Schrift, wo sie von der Sünde spricht, nie an die Geschichte vom Sündenfall erinnert, weder im Alten noch im Neuen Testament. Die kirchliche Lehre, die ganz auf der Vorstellung von Adams Sündenfall und der Uebertragung seiner Sünde auf die folgenden Geschlechter beruht, befolgt damit einen methodus, der keineswegs der biblische ist ... Was für Augustin der Nerv des Beweises war, das *in quo omnes peccaverunt*, hat sich als falsche Uebersetzung erwiesen und ist, richtig übersetzt, gerade zum Gegenteil geworden: zur Feststellung, dass jeder durch eigene Tat zum Sünder werde." Ibid., 114.

[133] Murray, *Imputation*, 6. Nygren, as Murray points out, argues succinctly that the antithesis between Adam and Christ is a crucial theological reference point in understanding the Pauline concept of anthropology, soteriology and Christology: "But be that as it may, it is entirely clear that the meaning of his [Paul's] thought about Adam and Christ is entirely different from either Jewish or Hellenistic concepts. It is rather the direct opposite. For instance the Hellenistic concept of primeval man expected that he would reappear in the final times. But Paul does not look on Christ as an Adam redivivus. He sets up Adam and Christ in this parallel, not to affirm their identity, but contrariwise to point out the contrast between them ... Adam and Christ stand there as the respective heads of the two aeons. Adam is the head of the old aeon, the age of *death*; Christ is the head of the new aeon, the age of *life*. As

The Pelagian hermeneutical problem, Murray asserts, lies in the fact that Pelagius rejects original sin (*peccatum originale*) in his exposition of Romans 5:12. As a result, he replaces the Pauline concept of original sin with "the actual sins of men":

> In this event the thought of Paul would be that as Adam sinned and therefore died so in like manner all men die because they sin. Adam is the prototype–he sinned and brought sin and death into the world. Others in like manner sin and they also are afflicted with death. The coordination of sin and death, exemplified in Adam, applies in every case where there is sin.[134]

The Pelagian hermeneutics destroys the antithesis between Adam and Christ in Paul's analogy. It concludes that men die because of their actual sins (*peccatum actuale*), not because of Adam's original sin. At the same time, the rejection of original sin leads to the conclusion that men are justified by their own works:

> The doctrine Paul is illustrating by appeal to the analogy of the condemnation and death proceeding from Adam is the doctrine that men are justified by the free grace of God on the basis of the righteousness and obedience of Christ. What Paul has been controverting in the earlier part of the epistle is that men are justified by their own works. He is establishing the truth that men are justified and attain to life by what another has done, the one man Jesus Christ.[135]

Meanwhile, Romish polemic, Murray affirms, rejects the imputation of Adam's original sin by interpreting Romans 5:12 in the light of habitual sin inherited through each biological generation: "It is simply that in the interpretation of Romans 5:12 and of the sin in which all are implicated by reason of the sin of Adam this sin is

---

sin came into the world through one man, Adam, and death through sin, so also through one man, Christ, the righteousness of God came into the world, and through righteousness life." Anders Nygren, *Commentary on Romans*, trans. Carl C. Rasmussen (Philadelphia: Muhlenberg Press, 1949), 208- 10.

[134] Murray, *Imputation*, 9-10. The Pelagian classical form of rejection of original sin has been seen in Pelagius' *Expositions of Thirteen Epistles of St Paul* (London: Cambridge University Press, 1926), 45-8.

[135] Murray, *Imputation*, 11-12.

conceived of not as the actual sin of Adam imputed but as the habitual sin that is conveyed by natural generation."[136] The exegetical failure of Romish hermeneutics on Romans 5:12 affects their doctrine of justification which is understood as a process.[137] Meanwhile, Calvin's understanding of original sin, Murray asserts, is radically different from that of Rome: "According to Calvin the original sin which is conveyed by natural generation is itself, intrinsically, radical depravity," arguing against the Romish doctrine that "original sin consisted simply in the privation of original righteousness and integrity and that the concupiscence which resulted from the loss of integrity was not itself truly and properly sinful, and the Romish polemic was directed with equal vigour against the Protestant doctrine that original sin involved a radical corruption of our moral and spiritual nature."[138] Classic Reformed theology rightly maintains the antithetical relationship between Adam and Christ:

> The whole passage (Rom. 5:12-19) is a unit. We cannot fail to see that the central structure is the analogy that obtains between the *modus operandi* of sin, condemnation, death, on the one hand, and of righteousness, justification, life, on the other ... Hence Paul is saying that death passed on to and reigned over those who did not personally

---

[136] Ibid, 14; Referring to the work of George D. Smith, Murray argues that classical Romish hermeneutics fails to see the antithetical relationship between Adam and Christ. As a result, it conceives of transmission of original sin in Romans 5:12-21 by means of successive generations: "In Romish theology the sin referred to in the last clause of Romans 5:12 is the habitual or original sin which is transmitted to or transfused into Adam's posterity by natural generation and which as to its nature consists essentially in the privation of sanctity, a privation which can be categorised as sinful because of the logical relation it sustains to the voluntary transgression of Adam. In a word, the sin of Romans 5:12 on account of which death passed on to all is transmitted sinfulness." Ibid., 15.

[137] Ibid., 16: "Rome regards justification as consisting in regeneration and renovation wrought by the infusion of righteousness and her theologians in dealing with Romans 5:12-19 appeal to this concept of justification in support of their interpretation of verse 12, to wit, that there is an obvious parallel between the infusion of righteousness in justification and the transfusion of original sin on account of the sin of Adam."

[138] Ibid., 17.

and voluntarily transgress as Adam did, and therefore the 'all sinned' of verse 12 cannot refer to individual personal transgression.[139]

In Murray's thought, the antithesis between Adam and Christ is equivalent to the antithesis between Law and Gospel in regard to the doctrine of justification, although he rejects the antithesis between the covenants of works and grace due to his rejection of the *foedus operum*. Thus, the absolute parallel between Adam and Christ is foundational to the Pauline understanding of justification and salvation:

> When Paul writes: 'The first man Adam was made living soul' (1 Cor. 15:45) the Scripture to which appeal is made is Genesis 2:7. For Paul, Adam was the first man. But most significant in this instance of appeal to Genesis 2:7 is the way in which all that follows in the ensuing argument is built upon the truth derived from this text. What belongs to the essence of Paul's soteriology rests upon the parallel and contrast between Adam, the first man, made 'living soul,' and Christ, the second man and last Adam, made 'life-giving spirit.'[140]

By establishing the validity of imputation in comparing and contrasting Adam and Christ, Murray sets forth the question of whether it is mediate or immediate. Murray also answers the question from the vantage point of the parallel between Adam and Christ. Immediate imputation (*imputatio immediata*) is the proper way to understand the imputation of Adam's sin to his posterity and the imputation of Christ's righteousness in the believer's justification:

> The parallel instituted in Romans 5:12-19 as a whole is that between the way in which condemnation passes upon men through the sin of Adam and the way justification comes to men through the righteousness of Christ. In the case of the righteousness of Christ ... this righteousness comes to the justified through no other medium than that of union with Christ; it is not mediated through the righteousness inwrought in the believer in regeneration and sanctification. To use the language of imputation, it is not by mediate imputation that believers come into the possession of the righteousness of Christ in justification. It would be contradictory of Paul's doctrine of justification to suppose that the righteousness and obedience of Christ become ours unto

---

[139] Ibid., 19-21.
[140] Murray, *Collected Writings*, 2:11.

justification *because* holiness is conveyed to us from Christ or that the righteousness of Christ is mediated to us through the holiness generated in us by regeneration. The one ground upon which the imputation of the righteousness of Christ becomes ours is the union with Christ. In other words, the justified person is constituted righteous by the obedience of Christ because of the solidarity established between Christ and the justified person ... To put the argument in the order underlying the parallelism, immediate imputation in the case of Adam's sin provides the parallel by which to illustrate the doctrine of justification and is thus eminently germane to the governing thesis of the apostle in this part of the epistle.[141]

3. Justification and Good Works

Justification by faith alone, Murray argues, is the core principle of the Gospel and salvation, and it is rightly understood in light of the antithesis between Law and Gospel. Nevertheless, good works as the fruit of justifying faith and application of the law applying the law through the ongoing work of the Spirit are vital in the Christian life. In this sense, good works cannot be included in the doctrine of justification. One of the theological backbones of modern dispensational antinomian repugnance to the law is derived from Romans 6:14 where it says that "you are not under law, but under grace." Thus dispensationalism suggests that the law is not necessary for the Christian life. Murray explains the antinomians' hermeneutical and theological logic and antipathy toward the Christian's obligation to the law as follows:

---

[141] Murray, *Imputation*, 70. In this analysis, Murray highlights that union with Christ is the central element of soteriology embracing both justification, regeneration and sanctification. The forensic aspect of justification takes place within the category of union with Christ: "The terms 'constituted righteous' (Rom. 5:19) must be interpreted, as has been shown, within the ambit of justification and therefore forensically. We may not, however, overlook the fact that it is in union with Christ that this constitutive action takes place. It is in virtue of union with Christ that believers come to have property in Christ's righteousness unto their justification ... All the grace bestowed upon believers finds it ground or basis in union with Christ in his death and resurrection. The subjective renewal which is concomitant with justification springs from this union, for it is in virtue of solidarity with Christ in his death and resurrection that the regenerative operations of the Holy Spirit take place in the believer." Ibid., 89.

It is easy to see how an insistence that believers are under obligation to keep the law of God would seem to contradict the express statement of the apostle that believers are not under law. In like manner, when Paul says that 'before faith came we were kept in ward under law, shut up to the faith about to be revealed' (Galatians 3:23), it is obvious that the bondage implied in being kept in ward under law is terminated with the revelation of faith. Hence to speak of the believer as bound to the obedience of God's law is to bring the believer again into that bondage which it is the great burden of Paul in both Romans and Galatians to resist and controvert! 'For freedom has Christ made us free: let us stand fast therefore and not be entangled again in the yoke of bondage' (Galatians 5:1).[142]

Murray, however, points out that the main thrust of the Pauline argument lies in the fact that there is an antithetical character between the principles of the law and grace. As a result, Law and Grace are antithetical in the Pauline discussion of salvation and justification. Paul, nevertheless, does not support Christian antipathy to the law. Rather, he urges Christians to obey the law in their lives. Thus, Murray argues that Pauline theology emphasizes a great dynamic balance between the second and third uses of the law: "It must be appreciated that when Paul says in Romans 6:14, 'Ye are not under law but under grace,' there is the sharpest possible antithesis between 'under law' and 'under grace,' and that in terms of Paul's intent in this passage these are mutually exclusive. To be 'under law' is to be under the dominion of sin; to be 'under grace' is to be liberated from that dominion."[143] Law cannot be the means of justification for sinners. However, Murray argues that believers are not under the condemning function of the law because it is canceled in Christ's fulfillment of the law's requirements:

> Law can do nothing to justify the person who in any particular has violated its sanctity and come under its curse. Law, as law, has no expiatory provision; it exercises no forgiving grace; and it has no power of enablement to the fulfillment of its own demand. It knows no clemency for the remission of guilt; it provides no righteousness to meet our iniquity; it exerts no constraining power to reclaim our

---

[142] Murray, *Principles of Conduct*, 184.
[143] Ibid.

waywardness; it knows no mercy to melt our hearts in penitence and new obedience.[144]

Union with Christ, as we have seen earlier, is the governing principle of all benefits of the *ordo salutis*. Nevertheless, Murray does not want to tone down the crucial importance of the antithesis between Law and Gospel in relation to salvation and justification while he carefully notices the Christian obligation to the law. Thus, Murray's understanding of the application of redemption has to begin with the antithesis between Law and Gospel within the substructure of *unio cum Christo*[145] Therefore, Murray states that Romans 6:14 must be understood in the light of the antithesis between Law and Gospel. Out of that concrete theological reference point, we have to begin to understand the true meaning of the Gospel and Christian responsibility to the law. Without the proper antithetical reference point to the law, we cannot grasp the real meaning of grace as the core principle of the Gospel:

> And in respect of the subject with which Paul is dealing there is an absolute antithesis between the potency of law and the potency of grace, between the provisions of law and the provisions of grace. Grace is the sovereign will and power of God coming to expression, not for the regulation of thought and conduct consonant with God's holiness, but for the deliverance of men from thought and conduct that bind them to the servitude of unholiness. Grace is deliverance from the dominion of sin and therefore deliverance that which consists in transgression of the law.[146]

We cannot, Murray emphasizes, talk about the Gospel of Christ without presupposing the antithesis between Law and Gospel, for the Gospel of Christ stands or falls with this absolute antithesis.

---

[144] Ibid., 185.

[145] Ibid., 186: "It is in this light that the apostle's antithetical expression 'under grace' becomes significant. The word 'grace' sums up everything that by way of contrast with law is embraced in the provisions of redemption. In terms of Paul's teaching in this context the redemptive provision consists in our having become dead to the law by the body of Christ (Romans 7:4). Believers died with Christ and they lived again with him in his resurrection (*cf.* Romans 6:8)."

[146] Ibid.

Nevertheless, in opposition to the evangelical form of antinomianism, Murray argues that we have to strike a balance between *the antithesis of the Law and Gospel in reference to justification* and *the believers' application of the law in relation to progressive sanctification:*

> The purity and integrity of the gospel stand or fall with the absoluteness of the antithesis between the function and potency of law, on the one hand, and the function and potency of grace, on the other. But while all this is true it does not by any means follow that the antithesis eliminates all relevance of the law to the believer as a believer. The facile slogan of many a professed evangelical, when confronted with the claims of the law of God, to the effect that he is not under law but under grace, should at least be somewhat disturbed when it is remembered that the same apostle upon whose formula he relies said also that he was not without law to God but under law to Christ (1 Corinthians 9:21). This statement of the apostle demands careful examination because it bears the implication that Paul was under law to God and he expressly states that he was under law to Christ. It would seem as if he said the opposite of what he says in Romans 6:14. But in any case what Paul says to the Corinthians prohibits us from taking the formula 'not under law' as the complete account of the relation of the believer to the law of God.[147]

---

[147] Ibid., 186-87. One of the pertinent theses in Murray's mind respecting Pauline soteriology lies in that we have to strike a balance between Law and Gospel antithesis regarding the doctrine of justification and the application of the law in the life of Christian pilgrimage. Otherwise, there is no definite clue to understanding Pauline theology as a whole: "In Paul's use of νόμος it is necessary to recognize the distinct applications of the term. Grave misinterpretation of the apostle's teaching arises if we do not observe these differentiations. If, for example, we do not discern the precise import of 'under law' (ὑπὸ νόμον) in Romans 6:14, or of 'ye have been put to death to the law' in Romans 7:4, or of 'ye have been discharged from the law' in Romans 7:6, we are liable to an error that not only devastates Paul's own teaching but overthrows the whole biblical concept of law as regulative of life." idem, *Collected Writings*, 4:133. As such, Romans 6:14 does not void the guiding principle of the law in the Christian life. Rather, Paul argues that there is an antithetical principle between Law and Grace in the discussion of righteousness: "And, in terms of this passage and of the subject with which it is concerned, there is an absolute antithesis between the potency and provisions of law and the potency and provisions of grace." idem, *Romans*, 6:14.

Thus Murray suggests that the broader context of Pauline theology requires that we should understand Romans 6:14 in the light of the principle of justification. Justification by faith alone apart from works in the light of the antithesis between Law and Gospel, however, does not nullify the application of the law to believers. Paul urges emphatically that the law is spiritual for believers who are in Christ, producing good works which will be rewarded in the ultimate eschatological heavenly Kingdom:

> We have therefore abundant evidence from Paul's Epistles to elucidate what he means when he says: 'Do we then make void the law through faith? God forbid: nay, we establish the law' (Romans 3:31). This is the protestation with which Paul brings to a conclusion one of the most eloquent statements of the contrast between the function of law and the operation of grace: 'But now without the law the righteousness of God is made manifest'; 'Where then is boasting? It is excluded. Through what law? Of works? Nay, but through the law of faith. For we reckon that a man is justified by faith without the deeds of the law' (Romans 3:21,27,28). It is a protestation that Paul fully establishes and verifies

Murray reviews one of the prominent thinkers of "the Lundensian school of Swedish theological thought," Anders Nygren. Murray says that Nygren, his *Commentary on Romans* fails to achieve a dynamic balance between the function of the law in justification and sanctification. In other words, Nygren collapses his argument on the law into the antithesis between Law and Gospel in relation to justification without stating the proper function of the law as the rule of the Christian life in the arena of progressive sanctification: "This is just saying, in other words, that Nygren has not expounded for us the relation which the law of God, as the revelation of God's will for thought and conduct, sustains to the believer. He has not helped us in resolving the question how the believer who is free from the law is at the same time bound by the law as the rule of life and behaviour ... But to aver, for example, that the statement in Romans 10:4 to the effect that 'Christ is the end of the law for righteousness' and the statement in 13:10 that 'love is the fulfilling of the law' are both expressions of the same truth is to evacuate exegesis (cf. P.434). This defect is more than a hiatus. It is a deflection of thought which distorts Paul's teaching. It does prejudice to the interests of sanctification, with which Romans deals as well as with justification. We are not true to Paul nor to the whole counsel of God if, by omission or deflection, we fail to give this doctrine its proper accent and orientation. Paul, after all, is concerned with the ethical qualities of heart and mind which the grace of Christ entails and with the relation of the law to the believer as the norm and rule of life and duty." idem, *Collected Writings*, 3:354.

in the later portions of this Epistle. But, in manner characteristic of the apostle, he interjects at this early point, at the conclusion of his peroration respecting the impotence of law and the efficacy of grace, the most emphatic warning to the effect that this total impotence of law to justify the ungodly does not carry with it the inference that the law is thereby discarded or abrogated. The inferences so frequently drawn from Romans 6:14 should have been obviated by the reminder which Paul announces in Romans 3:31, and the context of Romans 6:14 advises us of the reasons why grace does not make the law of none effect. 'The law is holy, and the commandment holy and just and good' (Romans 7:12). 'The law is spiritual'(Romans 7:14). It is unqualifiedly and unreservedly good (Romans 7:13,16,19,21). And how could the unreservedly good be relieved of its relevance or deprived of its sanctity?[148]

Although Murray does not like dispensational hermeneutics in which a radical contrast is drawn between the Old and New Covenant economies without properly qualifying redemptive historical continuity, he is happy to see that it applies the antithesis between Law and Gospel in the doctrine of justification. That is the reason why he wants to designate dispensationalism as *evangelical* although it is hermeneutically inconsistent and problematic:

In modern dispensationalism a sharp antithesis in respect of governing principle is set up between the dispensation of law (Sinai to Calvary) and the dispensation of grace (Calvary to Christ's second coming), as

---

[148] Murray, *Principles of Conduct*, 194-95. Due to the spirituality of the law in the Christian life as a means of progressive sanctification, Murray logically argues that God's law is the norm of progressive sanctification. In other words, we cannot think of Christian holiness and sanctification without reference to God's moral law from which Christians identify and produce good works: "The necessity of revelation defining the respects in which likeness to God prescribes the norm of sanctification, shows how consonant with the ultimate principle are the other considerations, that the law of God, the revealed will of God, and the example of our Lord are the criteria and patterns according to which sanctification proceeds ... The Scripture speaks of the law of God as spiritual. This means that it is of divine origin and character, and more specifically, that it is derived from the Holy Spirit, is validated by his authority, and bespeaks his character ... Thus every lack of conformity to the law of God is lack of conformity to God's likeness, and all conformity to the law is but conformity to that pattern which is the primary and ultimate pattern of sanctification." idem, *Collected Writings*, 2:306-07.

also, perhaps to a lesser extent, between the kingdom dispensation (millennial reign of Christ) and the dispensation of grace. A great many of the statements of dispensationalists are perfectly correct insofar as they express the antithesis that does exist, and on which Scripture lays the greatest emphasis, between obedience to law as the way of justification and acceptance with God and the way of grace. Every evangelical must recognize and appreciate this absolute antithesis. The error of dispensationalism in this connection is two fold. First of all, it applies this sharp antithesis to the successive dispensations and interprets the Mosaic as exemplifying law in contrast with grace, and the gospel dispensation as exemplifying grace in contrast with law. Secondly, this antithesis which is applied to the successive dispensations in respect of governing principle leads dispensationalism into a false view of the place of law within the sphere of grace.[149]

It has been charged that "the doctrine of justification by free grace through faith alone is inimical to the interests of ethical living and of good works, that it tends to the lascivious and licentious principle, 'let us do evil that good may come.'" Murray, however, answers this charge from Romans 6, urging that the ultimate goal of the application of redemption is "conformity to the image of Christ." From this perspective, to be sure, we may argue that "justification is only one part or aspect of this redemptive process and must never be viewed in disjunction from its place in the context of all the other steps of the process and particularly the other aspects of the application of redemption."[150]

---

[149] Murray, *Principles of Conduct*, 264. The classical antinomian idea has been taught by Lewis Sperry Chafer: "The issue is therefore, between law and grace as governing principles in the life of Christian. Must Christians turn to the Decalogue for a basis of divine government in their daily lives? Scripture answers this question with a positive assertion: 'Ye are not under the law, but under grace.' If this be true, are the great moral values of the Decalogue discarded? By no means; for it will be seen that every moral precept of the Decalogue, but one, has been restated with increased emphasis in the teaching of grace. These precepts do not appear under grace in the character and coloring of the Law, but, rather, in the character and coloring of pure grace." Lewis Schafer, *Systematic Theology*, vol. 4, *Ecclesiology - Eschatology* (Dallas: Dallas Seminary Press, 1948), 209.

[150] Murray, *Collected Writings*, 2:219-20.

Mentioning James 2:18, "faith," Murray indicates, "works itself out by love," because the faith which does not bear good works is "not the faith that justifies." Here, we need to qualify Murray's concrete theological point that justification is to be expounded in the light of the antithesis between Law and Grace while good works in the process of sanctification are required as the concrete criterion for *eschatological heavenly reward*. Identifying himself with the Scottish theologian, James Buchanan of the nineteenth century, Murray asserts the importance of "a present justification by grace, through faith alone - and a future Judgment according to works," a remarkable theological balance between the two extremes of *antinomianism* on the one hand and *legalism* on the other hand:

> While it makes void the gospel to introduce works in connection with justification, nevertheless works done in faith, from the motive of love to God, in obedience to the revealed will of God and to the end of his glory are intrinsically good and acceptable to God. As such they will be the criterion of reward in the life to come. This is apparent from such passages as Matthew 10:41; 1 Corinthians 3:8-9,11-15;4:5; 2 Corinthians 5:10; 2 Timothy 4:7. We must maintain therefore, justification complete and irrevocable by grace through faith and apart from works, and at the same time, future reward according to works.[151]

Accordingly, Murray remarks that the *future reward* is not "justification and contributes nothing to that which constitutes justification." Therefore, "future reward is not salvation" because "salvation is by grace and it is not as a reward for works that we are saved." So Murray confirms that there are the gradations of the heavenly eschatological reward according to good works, performed by believers through the grace of God. Murray, however, argues that the heavenly reward is *a gracious reward* in opposition to the Romish concept of the meritorious concept of salvation and reward:

---

[151] Ibid., 2:221. As such, Murray reiterates that justifying faith inevitably produces good works. Thus, good works are the fruits of justification: "Faith alone justifies but a justified person with faith alone would be a monstrosity which never exists in the kingdom of grace. Faith works itself out through love (cf. Gal. 5:6). And faith without works is dead (cf. James 2:17-20). It is living faith that justifies and living faith unites to Christ both in the virtue of his death and in the power of his resurrection." idem, *Redemption*, 131.

While the reward is of grace yet the standard or criterion of judgment by which the degree of reward is to be determined is good works. (iv) This reward is not administered because good works earn or merit reward, but because God is graciously pleased to reward them. That is to say it is a reward of grace. In the Romish scheme good works have real merit and constitute the ground of the title to everlasting life. The good works are rewarded because they are intrinsically good and well-pleasing to God. They are not rewarded because they earn reward but they are rewarded only as labour, work or service that is the fruit of God's grace, confirmed to his will and therefore intrinsically good and well-pleasing to him. They could not even be rewarded of grace if they were principally and intrinsically evil.[152]

Murray interprets progressive sanctification in relation to good works as a positive application of the law in the believers' life. Murray's emphasis, however, lies in the fact that good works are the fruits of the grace of God. They are the powerful works of God within us in contrast to the meritorious concept of salvation by good works:

> Sanctification is also progressive until it is completed in glorification. It might appear that in this process there is the convergence of grace and works. We are to work out our own salvation with fear and trembling (Phil. 2:12). This activity on the part of believers must not be denied. Our whole personality in its diverse aspects and activities is enlisted in the doing of God's good pleasure. But this doing means no

---

[152] Murray, *Collected Writings*, 2:222. Thus, Murray argues that we are saved and justified by faith alone in Christ radically excluding good works while good works done in the grace of God are necessary for the eschatological heavenly Kingdom reward at the day of the final judgment. In other words, the necessity of good works does not jeopardize the principle of justification by faith alone because justification by faith alone is a matter of salvation and glory whereas good works are related to the gradation of ultimate eschatological heavenly rewards and glory: "Judgment according to works does not contravene salvation by grace. Salvation is by grace through faith. But the faith that is saving bears fruit in good works, and faith without works is dead. Good works are therefore the index to a state of salvation. The good works of believers will be rewarded (cf. Matt. 10:41,42; 1 Cor. 3:8, 12-15). This reward does not consist in salvation nor in the eternal life inherited in the world to come. It consists in the degree of glory bestowed in the state of bliss. Glory itself is the gift of grace and secured by the righteousness of Christ (cf. Rom. 5:18-21). But the degrees of glory are proportioned to the faithfulness and labour of the saints." Ibid., 2:416-17.

suspension of grace. The apostle goes on to say, 'for it is God which worketh in you both to will and to do of his good pleasure' (Phil. 2:13). Our willing and doing are altogether of God's working and therefore of grace. And this operative grace of God is not only the cause but also the urge and incentive to our activity for his good pleasure.[153]

Dispensational hermeneutics confuses the classical concept of *antinomianism* and *legalism*. Contrary to classical dispensational hermeneutics, asserts Murray, we cannot call Christian obedience to the law *legalism*. Rather, the Bible requires believers to keep the law.[154] In this respect, Murray argues that in the Pauline understanding of νομος, there is no antipathy between law and love in the Christian life as classical dispensational hermeneutics propounds. Rather, there is a close link *between law and love* in the application of Christian ethics. In other words, law and love are not antithetical for those who have faith in Christ:

> I am quite convinced, however, that no factor bears more of the onus than the failure on the part of well-intentioned proponents of Christian ethics to recognize and maintain the uncurtailed sanctity of law in the Christian institution, and along with this the failure to appreciate the correlativity of law and love in the life of faith. Whenever an antithesis is set up between love and law, and love is regarded as self-directive and self-instructing, then the basis is laid for all that today confronts us in what is called the 'new morality.' Hence it is, for that reason alone, appropriate to discuss Paul's use of *nomos*.[155]

---

[153] Ibid., 1:122-23.

[154] Murray, *Principles of Conduct*, 182-83: "It is symptomatic of a pattern of thought current in many evangelical circles that the idea of keeping the commandments of God is not consonant with the liberty and spontaneity of the Christian man, that *keeping* the law has its affinities with legalism and with the principle of works rather than with the principle of grace. It is strange indeed that this kind of antipathy to the notion of keeping commandments should be entertained by any believer who is a serious student of the New Testament. Did not our Lord say, 'If ye love me, ye will keep my commandments' (John 14:15)? And did he not say, 'If ye keep my commandments, ye shall abide in my love, even as I have kept my Father's commandments and abide in his love' (John 15:10)?"

[155] Murray, *Collected Writings*, 4:133.

Believers in the New Covenant, Murray indicates, are required to obey God's law because God bestows the covenant blessings on those who are faithful to the requirements of the covenant of grace. Furthermore, fully realized eschatological blessings will be bestowed upon those who are obedient to their covenant God through faith: "Believers under the gospel continue in the covenant and in the enjoyment of its privileges because they continue in the fulfillment of the conditions; they continue in faith, love, hope, and obedience. True believers are kept unto the end, unto the eschatological salvation; but they are kept by the power of God *through faith* (cf. 1 Peter 1:5)."[156] The ultimate goal of Christian progressive sanctification according to Pauline theology as manifested in Philippians 3:10-14 and 20-21, Murray emphasizes, is eschatological heavenly glorification and prize. Christians are moving toward that great goal because they are united and energized with "all the resources of Christ's resurrection power." It is a great mystery and dynamic of the Gospel because the eschatological consummation of covenant blessing will be attained through the perseverance of saints (*perseverantia sanctorum*) according to passages from the law of God. Murray, however, observes that the eschatological heavenly prize does not depend upon human merit as Roman Catholics have insisted. Rather, it is based upon the covenant of grace in Christ Jesus:

> This is just to say that the goal is not achieved in some automatic fashion but through a process that engages to the utmost the concentrated devotion of the apostle himself. It is not reached irrespective of perseverance, but through perseverance. And this means nothing if it does not mean concentrated obedience to the will of Christ as expressed in his commandments. We readily see, however, that the attainment of the goal is not on the meritorious ground of perseverance and obedience, but through the divinely appointed means of perseverance. Obedience as the appropriate and necessary expression of devotion to Christ does not find its place in a covenant of works or of merit but in a covenant that has its inception and end in pure grace.[157]

---

[156] Murray, *Principles of Conduct*, 199.
[157] Ibid., 200-01.

E. Summary

As we have observed, Murray styles himself *a revisionist* in the light of classic Reformed covenant theology. He rejects the *foedus operum* and identifies his view with Calvin's, and from the vantage point of his own biblico-theological understanding, he replaces the term *foedus operum* with the term "Adamic administration." Nevertheless, in the final analysis, Murray's theology is, in general, compatible with the antithesis between the covenants of works and grace because he carefully adopts all the theological insights established by means of the bi-polar covenant distinction.

Murray proposes that obedience to the law was the means of *eschatological justification and life* in the prelapsarian state. He adopts the eschatological outlook of classical covenant theology even though he rejects the concept of the *foedus operum*. If Adam had successfully passed the probation period by obeying the law, he would have been glorified in the state of *eschatological heavenly life* which is the transformation from *"posse peccare* and *posse non peccare* to *non posse peccare."* The ultimate goal of eschatological justification and life upon the completion of the probation period, however, was not *meritorious* because it was in a sense "a promise of grace." It is for this reason that Murray interprets the definition of sin as "the transgression of the law." It is precisely at this point, it has been suggested, that Murray acknowledges that creation, fall and redemption were introduced into the Adamic administration from the vantage point of the historical order of *law and grace*.

Murray understands the covenant exclusively in the light of redemptive history, rejecting the so called inter-trinitarian covenant of redemption developed in covenant theology. Murray prefers "the inter-trinitarian economy of salvation." His rejection of the *foedus operum* and the inter-trinitarian covenant of redemption arises from a biblicistic approach to the biblical term 'covenant.' The pre-diluvian Noahic Covenant revealed in Genesis 6:18-22 is the first biblical account of the covenant of grace. Murray consistently evaluates and defines the covenant of grace from the Noahic to New Covenants by conceiving of it as exclusively *unilateral* in contrast to *bilateral*, which has been the traditional conception of classical covenant theology. Accordingly, every connotation of "mutuality of agreement or compact" in the covenant of grace as understood in classical covenant theology must be eliminated. As a result of his exclusively *unilateral* understanding of the covenant of grace, Murray concludes that the divine covenants with man are *God's sovereign administration of grace and promise.*

We have noticed that Murray expounds the Abrahamic Covenant by applying the antithesis between Law and Grace to articulate the *promissory nature of this covenant* as over against the principle of law. Therefore, in the final analysis, Murray regards *the antithesis between law and promise* as a synonymous hermeneutical principle to the antithesis between Law and Grace. On the other hand, he applied the antithesis between works and faith to justification by faith alone apart from good works as faithfully expounded in Pauline theology. In other words, Murray applies the concrete hermeneutical principle of the antithesis between Law and Grace not only to justification by faith alone but also to the exclusively promissory character of the Abrahamic Covenant. The heart of the Abrahamic Covenant is that "I will be your God, and you shall be my people." It characterizes "union and communion with God," which is "the spirituality of the Abrahamic Covenant." It demands human responsibility, and in it there is mutuality in religious relationship. In addition, we have observed that Murray stands in the tradition of covenant theology by arguing that *the antitheses between Law and Gospel and Letter and Spirit* are interchangeable.

Rejection of the concept of the *foedus operum* and a strong reaction to classic dispensational hermeneutics led Murray to understand the Mosaic Covenant exclusively from the perspective of *continuity* viz-a-viz the Abrahamic and New Covenants. So the inheritance of the promised land and the continuation of the earthly kingdom of Israel were basically the successive fulfillments of the Abrahamic Covenant. Therefore, the Mosaic Covenant is also a sovereign administration of God's grace and promise from initiation to fulfillment. In this regard, the difference between the Old and New Covenants is "not absolute but relative" because even in the Old Covenant the principle of God's grace and justification by faith alone were applied as in the New Covenant. On this point, we have shown that Murray does not equate the antithesis between Law and Grace with the antithesis between the Old and New Covenants *at the level of the economy or salvation* as classical dispensational hermeneutics suggests. Classic dispensational hermeneutics argues that the Old Covenant was administered by the principle of the law as the means of justification and the New

Covenant was administered by the principle of grace as over against law. Again, Murray's criticism of dispensationalist hermeneutics is not directed against its teaching of the hermeneutical principle of the antithesis between Law and Grace, but its wrong application to the economies of salvation in the Old and New Covenants.

It has been suggested, however, that the Reformed tradition in general has interpreted the "Do this and you will live" of Leviticus 18:5 as the manifestation of the *foedus operum* in the light of the antithetical principle of the law and grace, and the Pauline corpus' adaptation of Leviticus 18:5 in Romans 10:5 and Galatians 3:12 signifies that the antithesis between Law and Gospel is applied to justification by *faith alone* apart from good works. Accordingly, even though believers in the Old Covenant were saved and justified by God's grace through the covenant of grace, God blessed and cursed the earthly nation of Israel according to the principle of obedience to the law, ultimately looking toward the eschatological heavenly Kingdom blessings or hellish curses. In other words, covenant theology has reckoned that the principle of the law was active and operative in a limited sense in the continuing administration of the earthly nation of Israel in the Old Covenant. It, however, ceased to save and justify sinners in the postlapsarian state.

Murray suggests, however, that Leviticus 18:5 is not the manifestation of the principle of the *foedus operum* as Reformed covenant theology has argued, but is the manifestation of the active role of the law in the life of the Israelites. Thus, Murray separates Leviticus 18:5 from the Pauline passages of Romans 10:5 and Galatians 3:12 because he wants to apply the antithetical principle to *only* the doctrine of justification and the promissory character of the Abrahamic Covenant. As such, Leviticus 18:5 is not the revelation of the principle of the *foedus operum* as covenant theology has reckoned, and the blessings and curses of the Old Covenant do not typify their *eschatological counterparts*. Leviticus 18:5 is the practical application of the law to the life of the people of God (*usus didacticus sive normativus*), or the third use of law (*tertius usus legis*). In this way, Murray defends exclusive *continuity* of the Old Covenant with the Abrahamic and New Covenants, rejecting the application of the principle of the law or the *foedus legale* for the administration of the nation of Israel under the Old Covenant.

We have suggested in chapter one that covenant theologians have applied the antithesis between the covenants of works and grace along with that between Law and Grace to distinguish justification by faith alone from legalism or neo-nomianism. Due to his rejection of the *foedus operum*, Murray does not apply the antithesis between the covenants of works and grace to derive justification by *faith alone*. Nevertheless, Murray applies the hermeneutical tool, namely the antithesis between Law and Gospel to distinguish the doctrine of justification by faith alone apart from good works. To be sure, without this hermeneutical reference point, Murray could not talk about justification by faith alone. We have found that Murray does not set Luther against Calvin on the issue of justification because both applied the antithesis between Law and Gospel to derive the biblical doctrine of justification by faith alone. In other words, the antithesis between Law and Gospel was *a common hermeneutical denominator* between Luther and Calvin. Accordingly, justification by faith alone developed from the hermeneutical principle of the antithesis between Law and Gospel was the Protestant consensus in opposition to the Schoolmen's doctrine of justification in which Law and Gospel were greatly confounded, confusing justification and sanctification, while holding to the doctrine of *meritum de congruo et meritum de condigno*. The forensic aspect (*actus forensis sive iudicialis*), the immediate imputation (*imputatio immediata*) of "the God-righteousness of the Redeemer," and faith as "the instrumental cause" in the doctrine of justification are valid only when we exegete them by means of the hermeneutical tool of the absolute antithesis between Law and Gospel. Most of all, it is remarkable to see that Murray uses the antithetical principle between works and faith to safeguard justification by faith alone while he emphasizes that union with Christ is the undergirding principle of all redemptive blessings for believers within the category of the *ordo salutis*. In addition, the already and not yet structure of the eschatological Kingdom of God does not lead Murray to distinguish an already and not yet aspect of the doctrine of justification because he expounds justification according to the antithesis between Law and Gospel apart from good works and argues that it is a once for all declaration by God. We have observed that the antithesis between Adam and Christ parallels the antithesis between Law and Gospel in respect to the doctrine of justification by *faith alone*.

Justification by faith alone does not tone down the requirement of good works in the *ordo salutis* because Murray harmonizes the hermeneutical balance between *the Law and Grace antithesis to the forensic nature of justification* and *the believer's application of the law through the power of the Spirit with respect to progressive sanctification*. In this regard, there is no theological conflict between Paul and James. Good works done in the process of sanctification will be a concrete criterion for eschatological heavenly Kingdom rewards openly realized in the eschatological judgment. So there are *gradations* of eschatological heavenly glory bestowed according to the principle of good works which are the *fruits* of saving grace. In the last analysis, the heavenly reward is gracious as over against the Schoolmen's meritorious idea of salvation and reward. In conclusion, we have demonstrated that the antithesis between Law and Gospel in Murray's biblico-systematic theology is a concrete exegetical or theological tool for depicting the *historia salutis* and the *ordo salutis*.

Chapter Three

MEREDITH G. KLINE'S RESPONSE TO FEDERAL THEOLOGY

Kline pursues biblical theology as a prominent Old Testament scholar, and carries out the legacy of Geerhardus Vos in the contemporary controversy over covenant and justification. His foremost interest is to draw a grand picture of how the divine kingdom has unfolded in the *historia salutis* and is richly revealed in the dynamic nature of biblical history. We will observe that Kline's understanding of the idea of the kingdom is correlated with the concept of covenant. In this regard, Kline's stance on the kingdom and covenant stands or falls together. It has been suggested by Stek that Reformed systematic theology is so *overloaded* by the covenant concept that overshadows the kingdom motif.[1] Kline on the other hand argues that covenant hermeneutics must justify the kingdom motif based upon the idea of the covenant unfolded in biblical history.

Unlike his predecessor John Murray, Kline sees the modern rejection of the *foedus operum* as a serious theological deviation because it obliterates the antithetical principles of works and grace in subsequent covenants that impinge on the bestowal of the original eschatological kingdom goal:

---

[1] John H. Stek, "'Covenant' Overload in Reformed Theology," *Calvin Theological Journal* 29 (1994): 12-41.

With respect to the overall structuring of covenant theology, once grace is attributed to the original covenant with Adam, preredemptive and redemptive covenants cease to be characterized by contrasting governmental principle in the bestowal of the kingdom on mankind. Instead, some sort of continuum obtains. A combined demand-and-promise (which is thought somehow to qualify as grace but not as works) is seen as the common denominator in this alleged new unity of all covenants.[2]

In his reaction to the contemporary rejection of the *foedus operum*, Kline demonstrates that the covenantal accounts of the prelapsarian state are in agreement with classical covenant theology. Thus he confirms the stability of law as the governing principle of the covenant of creation. After the fall, grace as over against law is the principle of the bestowal of the eschatological heavenly kingdom. In doing so, Kline establishes *law and grace* as the historical sequence in creation, fall and redemption with grace being the sole operating principle in the latter. On this basis, Kline utilizes the antithesis between the covenants of works and grace as a key hermeneutical reference point for depicting the divine kingdom program in the *historia salutis*.

Having developed the motif of the antithesis between the *foedus operum* and *gratiae* in Genesis 1-3 in the light of the original eschatological kingdom goal, which is crucial to the understanding of *eschatology* in the entire scope of biblical theology, Kline develops the importance of the principle of works under the Mosaic Covenant. In this respect, he cannot accept, for example, Murray's proposal that there is only *continuity* between the Old and New Covenants. Nevertheless, we will observe that Murray and Kline are in agreement that believers under the Old Covenant were saved and justified by the principle of the covenant of grace as over against the principle of works, the latter of which is apparently applied by classic dispensational hermeneutics as the means of salvation for the Israelites. Thus, Kline's application of the principle of works under the Old Covenant is limited to the earthly *typological* kingdom of Israel. Precisely at this point, Kline urges hermeneutical balance between continuity at the level of individual salvation and discontinuity at the

---

[2] Meredith G. Kline, *Kingdom Prologue* (S. Hamilton: Gordon-Conwell Theological Seminary, 1989), 67. Kline's critique of the rejection of the classical Law and Gospel antithesis in relation to justification and salvation can be seen in his article "Works and Grace," *Presbyterion* 9 (1983): 85-92.

level of the typological kingdom administration. We will observe that Kline considers that "Do this and you will live" of Leviticus 18:5 is the principle of the *foedus operum* at the prelapsarian state as a concrete reference point of eschatological heavenly blessings. Kline, standing in the tradition of covenant hermeneutics, argues that this principle was operative under the Old Covenant in a limited way in the administration of the earthly typological kingdom and ultimately points to the eschatological heavenly kingdom in Christ Jesus.

As we proceed further in the discussion, we will interact with the accusation that Kline's hermeneutics shares some affinity with dispensational hermeneutics.[3] In the last analysis, we will attempt to refute this contention, arguing that it is not only a misrepresentation of Kline's covenant hermeneutics but also of traditional Reformed covenant hermeneutics, as we already clarified in chapters one and two. Thus, we cannot accuse Kline of being a dispensationalist simply because he utilizes the antithesis between Law and Gospel. The issue is *how* this vital hermeneutical principle is utilized.

Having portrayed Kline's understanding of covenant theology in terms of covenant and kingdom, we will examine his biblical theological insight into the doctrine of justification by faith alone. An understanding of the antithesis between the covenants of works and grace and between Law and Gospel, Kline affirms, is required for a proper understanding of the doctrine of justification. From these hermeneutical principles, Kline establishes justification by faith alone apart from good works. In other words, Kline's view of the doctrine of justification in the light of his biblical theology is in agreement with the Protestant consensus on the doctrine of justification by faith alone. Furthermore, against the error of antinomianism, Kline states that obedience to the law is vital in the Christian life. Thus, faith and obedience are inseparable in the *ordo salutis*. On the other hand, he carefully safeguards justification by *faith alone* by utilizing the antithesis between works and faith to maintain the distinction between

---

[3] See Peter A. Lillback, "Calvin's Covenantal Response to the Anabaptist View of Baptism," *Christianity and Civilization* 1 (1982), 198-9; Moisés Silva, *Explorations in Exegetical Method: Galatians as a Test Case* (Grand Rapids, Michigan: Baker Book House, 1996), 159-95; idem, "Is the Law Against the Promises? The Significance of Galatians 3:21 for Covenant Continuity," in *Theonomy: A Reformed Critique*, ed. William S. Barker & W. Robert Godfrey (Grand Rapids, Michigan: Academie Books, 1990), 153-67.

faith and evangelical obedience. In Kline's biblical covenant theology, we will observe the antithesis between Law and Grace along with the antithesis between the covenants of works and grace as controlling motifs of the *ordo salutis* and the *historia salutis*. In doing so, we will see that he seeks to apply the antithesis between Law and Grace as the fundamental hermeneutical principle to establish the role of divine grace in the doctrine of justification, the Abrahamic Covenant and the doctrine of election.

A. The Covenant of Creation[4]

Before we get into detailed analysis of Kline's understanding of covenant theology, it is necessary to briefly explain Kline's definition of covenant. In doing so, we need to pay close attention to the fact that Kline's biblical theology makes an intimate connection between covenant and kingdom: "Taking the kingdom of God as our central, organizing theme, we inevitably find ourselves fully involved with the subject of the divine covenants of Scripture; for to follow the course of the kingdom is to trace the series of the covenants by which the Lord administers his kingdom."[5] In this regard, covenants function as the instruments of administering "God's kingly rule." Through covenants, God administers his kingdom "in the sphere of common grace and in the holy realm produced by redemptive grace." Thus, covenant is "a particular administration of God's kingdom."[6] Murray's definition of covenant, according to Kline, is not sufficiently comprehensive since his definition is limited to the covenant of grace, defining it as sovereign administration of divine grace and promise. Kline's kingdom approach results in his recognition of the covenant of works, and common grace covenant, and also in his emphasis on the

---

[4] While Kline agrees with classical covenant theology in designating the covenant of works as "God's covenant with mankind in Adam" and the means of the "attainment of the eschatological kingdom and Sabbath rest," he prefers the term, *the covenant of creation*, because he wants to preserve the unique function of the first Adam in the original covenant, separating his role from that of the second Adam who fulfilled the requirement of *the covenant of works* which the first Adam failed to fulfill. Kline, *Kingdom Prologue*, 73.

[5] Ibid., 1.

[6] Ibid., 3.

distinctive features of the covenant making process of the Abrahamic and Mosaic Covenants.[7]

As we will see, Kline does not limit himself to Genesis 1-3 in arguing for the notion of the covenant of creation. Instead, he sees it in the entire scope of biblical history, based on the evidence for the traditional concept of the covenant of works. Meanwhile, John H. Stek offers an innovative critique that the Reformed tradition has been overloaded with the "covenant" concept. He concludes that biblical theology requires that covenants are not fundamental to the Creator and creature relationship, and that the creation was not founded on a covenant.[8] Against Stek's thesis, Bartholomew responds that the main

---

[7] Ibid., 3-4: "When God takes the ratificatory oath he commits himself to maintain the stipulated order of life or, in an arrangement involving a holy covenant community, God commits himself to enforce the sanctions. Depending on whether a blessing or a curse is in view, God's commitment may be either a promise (e.g., Gen.15) or a threat (e.g., the curses of the Mosaic covenant). Both divine oath-promise and divine oath-threat may be included in a given covenant transaction. When man makes the ratificatory oath commitment it will be a pledge to perform the obligations imposed by his Lord. In this connection it should also be noted that both divine and human oath-commitments may play a role in a covenant of grace or a covenant of works. Because of this variety of types of divinely sanctioned commitment found in the divine covenants, and because there are covenants of works, the definition of covenant may not be restricted by confining the basic idea of divinely sanctioned commitment to commitment of promise or grace ... However, if our definition is intended to cover all the divine covenants in Scripture, this feature of special relationship must be omitted, for there is also the common grace covenant (cf. Gen. 9) in which God commits himself to maintain a certain order of life but does not therein bestow his holy kingdom and communion on an elect people."

[8] Stek, "'Covenant' Overloaded," 12-41. Stek's article provides a good historical survey of the biblical theological aspects of the covenant concept in Reformed theology. However, he fails to see *how* the entire divine kingdom program is founded upon the notion of covenant, even the inter-trinitarian covenant of redemption. For example, Stek argues that covenants are not the instruments of "the kingdom-founding." Kingdom was not established, maintained, and ruled by covenants primarily. Accordingly, "Kingdom and covenant" are not correlated in the Bible. Moreover, he argues that covenant does not bridge the ontological distance between God and man; it just offers assurances, strengthens faith, and reinforces commitments. Thus, Stek argues that the covenant concept in the Bible is *secondary*, claiming that Reformed

themes of the Bible are "covenant and kingdom," beginning with "the creation covenant." In this way, he identifies his view with Spykman's.[9] Kline's fresh biblical theological insights may provide a concrete answer to Stek's criticism.

1. Man as *Imago Dei*

According to Kline, the fact that man is the *imago Dei* in God's creation demonstrates that Adam had a covenantal relationship with God from the beginning. This covenantal relationship was not *added-on* to a non-covenantal, natural relationship. There is no antithesis between nature and covenant in the creation account. This line of biblical covenantal thought is one of Kline's unique contributions with respect to the nature of the formulation of the covenant of works :

> In a special sense then the particular divine fiat to create man as one invested with the Glory-image of God was a covenantal fiat. Right here it is, of course, patent that the covenantal relationship of God and man had its origin in the very act of creating man. It is not the case, as some theological reconstructions would have it, that the covenant was superimposed on a temporally or logically prior non–covenantal human state. The covenantal character of the original kingdom order as a whole and of man's status in particular was given along with existence itself. For the Creator of Genesis 1 gave name and existence simultaneously in his creative fiat–and his creative fiat-names were covenantal fiat-names of divine commitment, especially so the fiat-name that called man into being in the divine image.[10]

---

theology has wrongly construed it as the primary motif. Stek concludes that "God's kingship (-dom) is the Bible's *primary* and *pervasive* theme - from Genesis 1 to Revelation 22. Let God's kingdom take the central integrating role in Reformed theology and that theology will be more truly biblical." Ibid., 39-41.

[9] Craig G. Bartholomew, "Covenant and Creation: Covenant Overload or Covenantal Deconstruction," *Calvin Theological Journal* 30 (1995): 11-33.

[10] Kline, *Kingdom Prologue*, 12. The motif that the process of the creation was a covenant- making process that anticipated eschatological consummation is significant to Kline's thought because it means that the covenant of creation was not superimposed upon nature: "Man's creation as image of God meant, as we have seen, that the creating of the world was a covenant-making process. There was no original non-covenantal order of mere nature on which the covenant was superimposed. Covenantal commitments were given by the

Characteristically, the divine act of creation was a covenantal act. As a result, Adam and Eve began their covenantal relationship with God who was the covenant Lord of creation from the very beginning. Through the act of creation the covenantal administration of the *kingdom* was manifested. God became the Lord of the covenant and Adam and Eve became the servants of the covenant:

> But it was by an act of literal creation that God brought Adam and Eve into covenant relationship to himself. The original covenantal administration of the kingdom was in this respect unique. God not only formulated a covenant order by the word of his authority, but he dictated that order into existence by the word of his power. As previously observed, the divine fiats were covenant fiats as well as creation fiats, hence, the Lord of the covenant did not simply address the covenant servant, calling him to the fulfillment of his covenant service, but he creatively called man into being in the status of covenant service.[11]

Upon the confirmation of man as the *imago Dei*, God commanded him to rule over his creation, a command that is properly designated as the cultural mandate in Genesis 1:26-30. God's sovereign decision about the relationship between man and the world can be seen in the context of God functioning as mediator in making a covenant between man and the world. Man's privilege of dominion over God's creation was bestowed by God and signifies that there was a covenantal relationship from the beginning of the world: "Accordingly, the Creator's giving of the earth and its creatures into man's hands in Eden may be viewed as the placing of the covenantal yoke of man's lordship upon the earth."[12] Characteristically, God was profoundly committed to guiding that covenant. Reflecting upon these characteristics, we may argue that God's installment of man as vicegerent over his creation "under conditions of Edenic beatitude" in Genesis 1:28 can be seen as a concrete milieu of "a covenantal relationship between God and man."

According to Kline, the fact that man is the *imago Dei* under the covenant of creation means that he had lordship over God's creation and reflected God's glorious rule in the heavenly realm. There, man

---

Creator in the very act of endowing the man-creature with the mantle of the divine likeness. And those commitments were eschatological." Ibid., 57.

[11] Ibid., 38.
[12] Ibid., 12.

anticipated *eschatological glorification* in the realm of "a transfigured glory-image of the radiant Glory-Spirit." It is a transfiguration from "the ethical glory of a state of simple righteousness" into "the greater glory of confirmed righteousness" which could be the confirmation of *the promised heavenly eschatological glorification.*[13] Ultimately, the eschatological covenantal blessings, in the consummated kingdom would have been conferred by God for faithful obedience to his law, and might have far exceeded the original covenantal blessings of God's creation:

> As Adam received God's directives for living so as to continue in the favor and blessing of his Maker, his heart already sang, 'O how love I thy law.' And the covenant sanctions proferred to man an increase in blessing far beyond all he enjoyed at the first as the original gifts of creation. The Creator had so made man that he could undergo a consummating transformation. Along with present honors and joys man was thus given the hope of advancing to new dimensions in his experience of God's presence and of his own dominion over creation.[14]

The covenantal norm of "the imitation of God" was the law written in man's heart according to Romans 1:32 and 2:14f. Man as the *imago Dei* had "a sense of deity" (*sensus divinitatis*), of knowing God, as Paul explains in Romans 1:19ff. Kline goes on to say: "The law of the imitation of God is the law of the image-bearing child of God. It is the comprehensive norm, the unifying principle for the complex of specific covenant stipulations."[15] In other words, Kline makes a distinction between law as the covenantal norm of the administration of the kingdom program and law as the principle of works in opposition to grace, the latter of which was the operating condition upon which the promise of eschatological kingdom blessing was offered under the covenant of creation.

The primary covenantal obligation, states Kline, was to sincerely worship the Lord, and to recognize "the Spirit's gift of image-sonship" by serving the Lord. Man as the servant had to carry out a stewardship of fulfilling the primary commandment:

---

[13] Ibid., 29.
[14] Ibid., 39.
[15] Ibid., 40.

Thus, from the beginning the primary obligation of covenant life has been: 'Thou shalt worship the Lord thy God and him only thou serve' (Matt. 4:10). The covenant servant-son must be what is called in Hebrew *tam*, 'perfect,' a term which, when used to express the obligation imposed by the covenant, denotes genuine, sincere religious devotion (cf., e.g., Gen. 17:1; Job. 1:1). The oath of covenant allegiance must come from the heart; the covenant servant must be truly loyal to his Lord.[16]

2. The Sabbath

Another important covenantal motif in the creation account is the Sabbath. The covenantal "blessing sanction of the Edenic arrangement," argues Kline, was observed "in the sign of the Sabbath." The Sabbath ordinance established by God in the beginning characterizes man as the *imago Dei*, as one in covenantal relationship with his Lord:

> For one thing, the setting of man's kingdom labors in a sabbatical framework imitative of the pattern of God's work of creation was an expression of man's identity as image of God and as such the sabbatical ordinance also served to identify man as a creature in covenant with God. By the Sabbath ordinance God made covenantal commitment to man that his God-like endowment would move on in the way of obedience to a consummation of rest, indeed, to the glory of God's own Sabbath.[17]

The Sabbath commandment anticipated "the reality of the archetypal Sabbath of the Creator's seventh." In the institution of the Sabbath observation, we recognize an important indicator that the order of creation was distinctively *covenantal*. By observing his Sabbath, the Creator of all things inaugurated his reign as the Lord and sustainer of all things. Therefore, by observing "the Sabbath ordinance," "all earthly kingship" concretely testifies to its "vassal kingship under the heavenly Suzerain." That that relationship was covenantal is also supported by our knowledge of ancient suzerain-vassal treaties. Accordingly, when God made covenant with the Israelites, he designated the Sabbath ordinance as *a seal of the covenant* manifested in Exodus 20:8-11 and 31:16-17 in a manner which was strikingly

---

[16] Ibid., 41.
[17] Ibid., 13.

similar to ancient political covenant treaties. As such, the Sabbath in the Theocratic Nation of Israel was a declaration that "Yahweh was covenant Lord of the kingdom of Israel." If the Sabbath observation is "a symbolic sign of God's covenantal lordship in the holy kingdom of Israel, it is surely because the original divine Sabbath represented the Creator's covenantal lordship over the world."[18]

Thus far, Kline has sought to demonstrate that the Sabbath ordinance in creation is a prominent indicator that the process of God's glorious works of creation was indeed a process of covenant-making: "In short then, the Sabbath ordinance in Eden was a sign of the covenant of God with man already in effect there. The very fact that the Genesis creation prologue is cast in sabbatical form tells us that the creation of the world was a covenant-making process."[19] The Sabbath ordinance established in God's creation reveals to us that the covenant of creation leads toward *consummated eschatology*:

> Like redemptive history, the history of the Covenant of Creation was to be characterized by an eschatological thrust and direction. It was to have a sabbatical structure. This eschatological-sabbatical nature which the history of man had from the beginning was a consequence of the very fact that man was created in the image of the sabbatarian Creator. Entering into the kingdom program as God's servant-son, man was to reflect the divine glory, advancing through his six days of work to the seventh day of completion, from kingdom development to a Sabbath of joyous shalom.[20]

A static continuity of the original level of blessing in respect to the future of man in the covenant of creation cannot be justified because God is "the consummating God of Sabbath," who makes man the *imago Dei*. The Sabbath as the creational ordinance contains the expression of the eschatological consummating promise. At this juncture, man as the *imago Dei* anticipates the glorious eschatological consummation. Therefore, to limit man to the static continuation of his original state of blessing would have been "no blessing at all, but a curse." As such, the eschatological blessing of the covenant of creation was already manifested in man as the *imago Dei* from the very beginning of his existence and looked toward consummated perfection.

---

[18] Ibid.
[19] Ibid.
[20] Ibid., 49-50.

To be sure, man in the beginning, Kline emphasizes, had already entered into covenant relationship with God and anticipated the eschatological glory upon compliance to the law. The blessing of the covenant of creation was to enter into the eschatological Sabbath rest, and perfecting of the *imago Dei*. The "eschatological aspect of the *imago Dei*" drives man to fulfill "the kingdom mandate," pursuing "the sabbatical goal" toward which man's work must press forward. The covenant blessing sanction was intrinsic to the law of the covenant, being in fact present in the general stipulations of the covenant given before the special probation commandment.[21]

Accordingly, the eschatological consummation of the *imago Dei* and the eschatological goal of the Sabbath are intimately interrelated, looking upward and forward to *consummation of the glorious heavenly kingdom*. In this respect, the promise of the eschatological covenant blessing was implied from the beginning of man's existence as the *imago Dei*.[22] Thus, the eschatological motif antedates redemptive history. In other words, the eschatological pattern goes back to creation. Kline asserts that a covenant of works was proferred to Adam as the condition for consummating the eschatological heavenly kingdom. Accordingly, the covenant of works was the only door to the eschatological consummation. In this respect, the "original covenant of creation" was an eschatologically oriented covenant.[23]

The Sabbath ordinance as a sign of the covenantal relationship between God, the Great King, and man, a vassal-king, was confirmed later in redemptive history as we see in Exodus 31:13-16. Sabbath observance confirmed man's covenantal commitment and also served as a sign of the promised glorious consummation from God:

> In giving man the Sabbath ordinance the Lord made a covenantal commitment, promising that triumphant royal rest was to crown the genealogical-cultural history of the family of Adam, in their faithful keeping of the covenant. As the garden of Eden was a space-sign, a replica of the whole cosmos as God's dwelling, so the sabbatical week was a time-sign, a replica of the total history of man's fulfillment of the cultural mandate after the pattern of God's working in creation,

---

[21] Ibid., 57-8.
[22] Ibid., 58.
[23] Meredith G. Kline, *The Structure of Biblical Authority* (S. Hamilton: Gordon-Conwell Theological Seminary, 1989), 155.

with the Sabbath at the end of that week a promissory symbol of the hope of consummation.[24]

3. The Creation Motif

For Kline, the presence of creation motifs repeatedly throughout the Scriptures, signifies "the nature of God's covenantal actin through Moses and Jesus Christ, the mediators of the old and new covenants. In interpreting these later covenants as creational, the biblical authors reflect their understanding of the creation as covenantal."[25] Accordingly, the Mosaic economy was, in a sense, "a reproduction of the creational order as a whole" within the limitations of redemptive history, reflecting "the nature of the original Edenic order as a holy paradise-Kingdom and as a probationary-works arrangement." On the other hand, the covenantal nature of the Mosaic economy witnesses remarkably to the original covenant arrangement in God's creation.[26]

4. The Parallel between the First and Second Adams

Kline derives another covenant motif in the creation account from a comparison between the first and second Adams. The comprehensive parallel between Adam and Christ, asserts Kline, witnesses that Adam stood as the head of the covenant: "If the role of Christ as the second Adam is recognized as covenantal, this scheme provides further clear warrant for classifying the arrangement made with the first Adam as covenantal."[27] In this comparison, Adam was the representative federal head of the covenant of creation during the probationary period, while Christ as the second Adam stood as the representative federal head of the redemptive covenant, coinciding with election:

> A distinctive element in the government of the Covenant of Creation was the feature of federal representation. Adam, father of all mankind, was patriarchal head of the covenant community in the sense that he acted in a representative capacity for all in his probationary response to the Creator's claims and demands (Rom 5; 1 Cor 15). In the process of redemption the federal principle figures once again with Christ as second Adam, but in this case federal representation coincides with

---

[24] Kline, *Kingdom Prologue*, 51.
[25] Ibid., 13.
[26] Ibid.
[27] Ibid., 14.

election and is not coextensive with the holy covenant institution in its historically administered form.[28]

Jesus as the second Adam assures us that his redemptive accomplishment is resumptive of the fundamental eschatological picture that governed the covenant of creation. In fact, the work of Christ is shown by the Scriptures as "a re-creation and perfecting of the *imago Dei*." He leads God's people to their eschatological Sabbath rest in the glorious land where they have access to the tree of life. Based on this analogy, the believers' eschatological glorification is properly assured.[29]

5. The Presence of the Glory-Spirit

Kline avers that the awesome presence of the Glory-Spirit in the creation account is another good indicator of the covenant-making process. The Spirit of God hovers over the waters, proclaiming God's sovereign covenantal lordship over his creation and covering both the visible world and invisible heavenly realm :

> As the signature of the Creator-Author, the Glory-Spirit[30] of Genesis 1:2 was the sign of God's sovereign to ownership of all the world. At the beginning the creation existed under the insignia of God's covenant lordship. The Glory-Spirit of Genesis 1:2 is thus another evidence that the creation record of the Genesis prologue is at the same time the record of the making of a covenant of the Lord with man.[31]

Elohim as "the cosmic builder," after all, enjoyed the Sabbath day rest, which identifies him as the "Great King of the world," as everlasting Judge over "the cosmic temple and as sovereign Lord over the

---

[28] Ibid., 46.

[29] Ibid., 61.

[30] The motif of the Glory-Spirit in Genesis 1:2 is important to Kline's biblical covenant theology because the presence of the Glory-Spirit in the creation account signifies the goal of creation, *the consummation of the eschatological kingdom*: "The Glory-Spirit was present at the beginning of creation as a sign of the *telos* of creation, as the Alpha-archetype of the Omega-Sabbath that was the goal of creation history." Meredith G. Kline, *Images of the Spirit* (S. Hamilton: Gordon-Conwell Theological Seminary, 1986), 20.

[31] Kline, *Kingdom Prologue*, 21.

covenant community."³² The Glory-Spirit manifested "the creative Archetype of man's ectypal glory-likeness" and was present as a crown, shelter and "canopy over man" in the Garden of Eden. The Scriptural analogy of God covering his people with the Glory-Spirit is an act of covenantal engagement.³³

6. The Marriage Motif

Another concrete motif to support the covenantal arrangement in the creation account is that of marriage. Kline affirms that covenant administration from the beginning had "a community structure" in the "comprehensive societal bond of family." Furthermore, mankind began as a family, created male and female, husband and wife. Accordingly, Genesis 2:21-23 describes Adam's union with the woman by God was "a nuptial presentation." The marriage ordinance as explained in Genesis 2:24 was ordained from the origin of mankind. It is covenantal, having "the legal-institutional nature of the union in which the man and woman were joined together." Upon the institution of the family, the cultural mandate given in the Garden of Eden represents performance of the duties of the covenantal kingdom. Later, the prophet Malachi's expression, "wife of thy covenant" in Malachi 2:14f. signifies that marriage was a covenant from the beginning. In addition, Proverbs 2:17 describes marriage as a covenant. Thus, "the marriage parable" illustrates the covenant although it is not a sign of the covenant in the same sense as the Sabbath. In this regard, the marriage ordinance of Genesis 2:24 signifies the covenantal union between husband and wife. Therefore, the cultural mandate is oriented to the family structure.³⁴

Furthermore, the marriage covenant presented in Genesis 2 explicitly reflects mankind's covenantal relationship with the Lord according to social analogy. The marriage relationship between Adam and Eve instituted by creation ordinance manifests the constructive insight that man from the beginning was in a covenant relationship with God. Thus Adam received Eve, "his image, in a covenant of marriage" as we observe in Genesis 2:22-24. Later, human marriage

---

³² Ibid., 24.
³³ Kline, *Images of the Spirit*, 55.
³⁴ Kline, *Kingdom Prologue*, 45.

from the perspective of the covenantal concept was fully illustrated "in the revelation of redemptive re-creation and covenant."[35]

7. The Eschatological Sanctions

The forward-looking direction of the covenant of creation was manifested in the covenantal sanctions. Eschatological blessing or curse was set before man. The dual sanctions signify "the condition of probation" in the beginning phase of the covenant of creation.[36]

We may recognize the divine sanctions as an essential element of covenants. The original relationship between God and man, according to Kline, was covenantal because the dual sanctions of blessing or curse were conditions of the covenant:

> The paired divine sanctions of life and death, the curse of death threatened against any breach of fealty and the blessing of life promised for loyal obedience ... Thus, in pointing to the notable role of dual sanctions in Eden, we are also adducing further evidence of the presence there of the feature of commitment, which is the hallmark of covenants.[37]

As "a sovereign administration of God's lordship,"[38] the covenant of creation was sovereignly ordained and administered by the suzereign Lord. In fact, Kline's definition of the covenant of creation stems from his understanding of the creation account as the administration of the covenant and kingdom. Whatever the vassal had was "a gift of creation" expressing the highest goodness of the Creator. The covenantal obligation commanded by God, therefore expressed

---

[35] Kline, *Images of the Spirit*, 56.
[36] Kline, *Kingdom Prologue*, 57.
[37] Ibid., 12-3.
[38] This definition is crucial for understanding of Kline's biblical covenant theology. Kline conceives the divine covenant in the light of dual sanctions such as promises or threats, which administer God's sovereign lordship. As such the divine covenants are "sovereign administrations not of blessing exclusively but of curse and blessing according to the vassal's deserts." The redemptive covenants, however, are informed by the divine sovereign grace principle infallibly effected by the redemption of Christ; "they are accompanied by divine guarantees assuring a realization of the blessing sanctions of the covenant." Kline, *Structure of Biblical Authority*, 126.

"the love of a Creator" and the absolute divine right of the Lord over his creature.[39]

The message of the dual sanctions of the covenant of creation, Kline argues, may be properly paraphrased from Leviticus 18:5 as 'Do this and live–fail to do this and die.' Upon man's successful obedience to the probationary obligation, he would have entered "the Sabbath rest," attaining "the kingdom glory promised in the blessing sanction of the covenant."[40]

a. The Sacramental Tree

For Kline, the tree of life in Genesis 2:9 and 3:22 was the "arboreal sign of the promised blessing of the covenant" in which God manifested the sign of the consummated eschatological kingdom blessing to be bestowed upon the successful completion of the divine probation. As such, the tree of life was the earthly demonstration of the heavenly immortal Glory in the heavenly paradise of God and was intended as *a seal of eternal life*. Thus, it reappears in the restored eschatological kingdom of God at the consummation of *heilsgeschichte*:

> This tree is introduced in the narrative in conjunction with the tree of probationary testing, whose location in the midst of the garden it shared (Gen. 2:9); it is mentioned again in connection with the consequences of the probation in Genesis 3:22, where it is regarded as a seal of everlasting life; and subsequently in revelation in the course of redemptive history it reappears in the context of the consummated glory of the restored paradise of God (Rev 2:7; cf. Ezek 47:7,12; Rev 22:2) ... Eternal life properly so called, the life signified by the tree of

---

[39] Kline, *Kingdom Prologue*, 38-9. Covenant and kingdom, according to Kline, are closely integrated. In this respect, Kline embraces the covenants of creation and redemption as *the covenant of kingdom*, defining covenant as the sovereign administration of the kingdom of God: "The overall unity of the covenants will be provided by the concept of the kingdom of God, of which they are so many manifestations. If a general unifying term were desired it might then be Covenant of the Kingdom. For the two major divisions of the Covenant of the Kingdom our suggestions would be Covenant of Creation and Covenant of Redemption. Since the terms 'creation' and 'redemption' call attention to God's position in relation to his covenant people as their Maker and Owner-Possessor, they effectively unfold the concept of God's lordship." Kline, *By Oath Consigned*, 36-7.

[40] Kline, *Kingdom Prologue*, 67.

life, is life as confirmed and ultimately perfected in man's glory-likeness to God, life in the fellowship of God's presence. Access to the tree of life and its fruit is only in the holy place where the Glory-Spirit dwells; to be driven from there is to be placed under judgment of death. Here again it is relevant to recall the identity of the tree of life as an earthly symbolic replica of the immortal Glory. Consummation of man's life and God-likeness, like their creation, is of God, the Alpha and Omega Glory-Spirit.[41]

The blessing aspect of the covenant of creation, Kline affirms, would have come *gradually* over a long period of history, introducing the semi-eschatological kingdom before the inauguration of the fully realized eschatological kingdom. The semi-eschatological kingdom would begin with "a divine work of justification-confirmation," culminating in God's action of consummation. This is the overall flow of "the primal pattern of eschatology." Obedience to the tree of knowledge of good and evil revealed in Genesis 2:9 would have bestowed upon man "the Logos-Life to partake of the sacramental tree of life." Through his participation in sacramental communion he would have had concrete confirmation "in the beatitude of the covenant," a seal of the promise of glorified heavenly life, and an experience of Sabbath rest beyond "the onus of probation." The Spirit would have confirmed "indefectible righteousness and holiness," terminating the possibility of "a fall into sin and exposure to the covenant curse." When the covenant was fulfilled by the obedience of man, "it would be as a covenant of peace in a fellowship of life with God, confirming man as the heir of the full-orbed, luminous glory of the *imago Dei*." Kline indicates that upon successful obedience before the probational tree, the covenant of creation would have become "a covenant of peace" or "the covenant of confirmation" which would be *the inauguration of the semi-eschatological kingdom, anticipating the guaranteed consummation of the eschatological kingdom*. What is significant in Kline's primal eschatology is the onset of the eschatological kingdom which is gradual instead of all at once, moving from the semi-eschatological kingdom to the consummated eschatological kingdom in which the cultural mandate would be fulfilled on a global scale. "The ethical glory of the *imago Dei*" would be affirmed upon the fulfillment of the probation period, while the

---

[41] Ibid., 59.

heavenly glory of dominion and transformation of "the physical glory" would be realized after the completion of the global cultural mandate. In other words, although the ultimate heavenly glory, signified "by the covenantal signs of the Sabbath and the tree of life" would have been secured, the consummation would await man's historical task of building the kingdom by carrying out the cultural mandate "through a semi-eschatological stage of history." To be sure, though, that semi-eschatological journey would not have been a "wilderness trek" as we experience it in the fallen situation. In sum, "It would be a history of the development of the holy kingdom from its original focus at the mountain of God in Eden to the global fullness mandated in the cultural commission of the covenant."[42]

b. The Probation Tree

The covenant of creation anticipated an eschatological consummation "in kingdom glory," which was conditioned on the obedience of man. The probational test, Kline argues, was not a "permanent conditionality," but had a temporal limitation and its goal was to direct man to the eschatological kingdom consummation. The first Adam represented mankind as a federal head in probation. A specific proscription revealed in Genesis 2:16-17 was added to general covenantal obligations. In doing so, we do not want to reduce "man's covenantal obligations and testing" to the probation tree. Nevertheless, the probationary stipulation had a unique function in bringing the probation into a definite focus. Furthermore, the probation involved the exposure of man to "a direct Satanic solicitation." In this way, the proscription of the special probation was distinctive in "the law of the covenant." The positive stipulations demanded of man the performance of his cultural-cultic duty, while the negative special stipulation warned man not to transgress. The special probationary tree revealed God's absolute lordship, demanding of man a concrete confession of "his sovereign Lord," and bringing "man's covenantal loyalty" into "an immediate crisis." By means of the probation tree, man would be destined to "the proposed grant of the kingdom," and fight God's battle against the power of Satan. The probation tree represented "the sum and total substance of the Covenant of Creation," although we cannot reduce all the covenant

---

[42] Ibid., 60.

obligations to this probation tree because there were other covenantal requirements to carry out.[43]

During the semi-eschatological earthly history, the weekly Sabbath observation anticipated the eventual termination of "the six days of genealogical-cultural work" and man would begin to realize "the eternal seventh day of the Creator's Sabbath." The everlasting state, when it was realized, would not become the "perpetuation of man's original beatitude." Kline says it this way:

> In fact, the latter would, as we have noted, be no blessing at all in view of the eschatological hope instilled in man's heart as image of God and in view of the kingdom-program assigned to man with its ultimate objective of constructing the cosmic-human temple-city. In its ultimate form the covenant blessing must comprise the full actualization of the dominion that belonged to man as image of the Glory-Spirit, the dominion formulated as the objective of man's royal cultural commission.[44]

God's kingdom in Eden before the fall was a theocracy and a thoroughly "cultic kingdom." Accordingly, covenant breaking by disobedience to "the God of the sanctuary" resulted in expulsion from the kingdom because "God is the King of the kingdom." After the fall, it was the "sanctuary identity of the theocratic kingdom" which separated it from the other kingdoms. In the theocratic kingdom, the "great king is the Lord," who performs activities "in the name of the God-King enthroned, confessed, and worshipped in the cultic epicenter, whence theocratic holiness radiates outward, permeating all, so that the whole realm, land and people, is a sanctuary of the Creator-Lord."[45] In other words, the covenant of creation was governed by a theocratic kingdom principle in which cult and culture were dynamically integrated together:

> The polity of the covenant community was theocratic. God was in truth the ruler and protector of the family-kingdom of mankind. He was their ultimate father and they bore his surname, for he had created them his image-sons. Because this universal family kingdom was theocratic and culture and cult are institutionally integrated in a theocracy, cult and

---

[43] Ibid., 65-7.
[44] Ibid., 61.
[45] Ibid., 33-4.

culture alike were functions of this family, which was accordingly a holy cultic-cultural structure. It was the original 'kingdom of priests and holy nation' (Exod 19:6). All members of the covenant community had priestly as well as royal office.[46]

While the eschatological consummation was the proper goal of the covenant of creation, "a threat of curse" arose in Genesis 2:17. The curse resulting from disobedience would be antithetical to the blessing sanction. In this respect, death was the cancellation of the realization of "the eschatological potential of the *imago Dei* and the loss of all the glory of the divine likeness, ethical and legal, already bestowed in the creation of man." In the final analysis, "It was frustration of the hope of completion of man's historical mission beaconed by the covenant sign of the Sabbath. It was the denial of the consummation of life that was proferred in the tree of life. It was the loss of all these things, and it was their opposite."[47] As the covenant blessing motif points to the eschatological heavenly concept, the covenant curse motif delineates the eschatological nature of hell.[48]

The encounter with Satan during the probation of Genesis 3 has been characterized as "a religious allegory" justifying "a symbolic interpretation of the serpent." Modern critical scholarship rejects all supernatural aspects in the account. Against the background of this critical scholarship, Kline affirms that the serpent in Genesis 3 was "one of the real animals to be found in Eden." Satan entered the garden of Eden "through the intermediary agency of the serpent." When God placed the tree of the knowledge of good and evil in the garden of Eden, he was already setting the stage for the drama of judgment. Satan's deceptive question in Genesis 3:1 was a radical challenge to "the stipulations of God's covenant law" and the sovereign authority of God. By appealing to Eve and ignoring the headship of Adam, Satan proposed a distorted understanding of "the social structure" bestowed in the law of God's covenant. Thus, Satan proposed himself "as a rival lord" as over against the suzereign Lord, challenging "God's law-order for the world with a different order of his own." Satan tried to cancel the basic principle of "covenant law," blurring the distinction between the Creator and creature "in his

---

[46] Ibid., 47.
[47] Ibid., 63.
[48] Ibid., 64.

monistic blender" and ignoring "the unique and absolute sovereignty of the Creator-Lord, which was the foundation of the entire covenantal arrangement." In the heart of Eve, Satan replaced "Yahweh-Elohim as covenant overlord." She grasped "a covenant with death" in the place of "the covenant of life" by hearkening to the voice of "the prince of death." In effect, Eve could be described as falling into polytheism. Adam and Eve's partaking of the tree of the knowledge of good and evil was the result of "Satan's reconstruction of the situation." At the end, the sacramental tree of Satan's covenant replaced "God's sacramental tree of life." Eve's new theology embraced "the devil's concept of this tree as a special tree." Confessing anti-faith and rejecting the Lord's table, Eve participated in "the sacramental tree of the prince of demons, so ratifying her pact with him."[49] Kline points out that Adam's transgression as described by Paul in Romans 5:14b was not just a simple violation of "a precept but more specifically Adam's breaking of the death-sanctioned covenant of creation." The same covenantal framework is revealed in Isaiah 24:5. It may also be the case that the expression: "They like Adam have transgressed the covenant" of Hosea 6:7 is an explicit indication that Adam's transgression took place within the covenantal context, although this text is a controversial one.[50]

8. The Eschatological Judgment After the Fall

Correcting the traditional translation of "in the cool of the day" (לרוח היום) with "as the Spirit of the day" in Genesis 3:8, Kline suggests that "Spirit" indicates "the theophanic Glory" which had appeared in Genesis 1:2. Immediately, the Lord intervened as a judge at "the judgment site in the awesome glory of his theophanic Presence." The account of Genesis 3:8 revealed "the Glory-Spirit" depicting "the primal parousia." Thus "on the original day of the Lord in Eden, God's parousia-advent was in the theophanic mode of 'the Spirit (Presence) of the day (of judgment)." In this judgment, Adam and Eve lost the privilege of "the ethical glory of God-likeness" by which they stood before the presence of God and reflected the *gloria Dei*. As a result of disobedience to God's law, they lost "their original endowment with the image of God and had instead taken on a likeness

---

[49] Ibid., 74-9.
[50] Meredith G. Kline, "Gospel Until the Law: Rom 5:13 and the Old Covenant," *Journal of Evangelical Theological Society* 34/4 (1991): 440.

to the devil." Thus, from the beginning, Satan has been "a contra-covenantal being, the antithesis of the covenantal Lord God, holy and true."[51] Therefore, Genesis 3:8 may be seen to signify "a primal *parousia*," which would later be described "as the day of the Lord." God came to administer the covenant lawsuit against the covenant-breakers, and to condemn Satan. As such, the Shekinah-Glory was present in Genesis 3:8 as the Glory-Spirit who was also involved in man's creation as the *imago Dei* in Genesis 1:26 and 2:7.[52]

The tragic history of "covenant-breaking" revealed in Genesis 3 is followed by the Lord's covenant lawsuit and the implementation of the covenant curse in the expelling of man from God's "sanctuary-paradise" into exile to the east of Eden. Nevertheless, in the midst of the covenant curse, there was God's revelation about "grace and promise" opening up the gracious future beyond the covenant curse. Therefore, in a sense the epilogue of the covenant of creation was "an epilogue about a new covenant." Kline goes on to argue: "This new Covenant of Redemption occupies such a commanding position in the actual historical-eschatological unfolding of the kingdom of God that rather than speaking of it as epilogue to the Covenant of Creation, it would be more appropriate to speak of the latter as its prologue."[53]

Although Adam and Eve broke the original covenant, they were predestined to be the covenant people of God once again through redemptive grace. The Lord's curse on Satan contained the redemptive promise. However, God's revelation in Genesis 3:16-19 was also a

---

[51] Kline, *Kingdom Prologue*, 80-2.

[52] Kline, *Images of the Spirit*, 97-8. Kline's *primal parousia* motif is derived from "the day of the Spirit" or "the Spirit of the day" of Genesis 3:8 in conjunction with Genesis 1:2, which he defines as the presence of "the Shekinah-Glory." This motif is important for understanding his biblical theological conception of the kingdom of God, covenant and eschatology. Kline suggests that "the Glory-Spirit" was reflected in God's creation of man as the *imago Dei* and the "divine Presence" in the holy garden of Eden. This motif of primal eschatological judgment anticipates "the day of the Lord," which signifies the consummate eschatological administration of "the covenant lawsuit." The eschatological judgment revealed in Genesis 3:8 will be consummated when Christ comes "in the day of the Lord as the Spirit of the day." idem, "Primal Parousia," *Westminster Theological Journal* (1977/78): 245-80.

[53] Kline, *Kingdom Prologue*, 74.

common curse to mankind. This common curse on both the elect and the reprobate will continue until the eschatological parousia.[54]

B. The Covenant of Redemption[55]

1. The Intratrinitarian Covenant[56]

Geerhardus Vos adopts and develops the crucial importance of the inter-trinitarian counsel in his exposition on the *Pactum Salutis* following the pattern of classic covenant hermeneutics. If the prelapsarian state was governed by the *foedus operum*, contends Vos, then the covenant idea must dominate redemptive history. In this respect, the covenant of redemption as "the task of the Mediator" is the other side of the covenant of works. Accordingly, the rejection of the covenant of works goes together with a rejection of the inter-trinitarian covenant of redemption. In redemption, the triune God acts communally, although economically the origin of redemption is attributed to the Father in predestination. There is, however, judicial

---

[54] Ibid., 83-4.

[55] Kline prefers the term 'covenant of redemption' instead of the traditional term 'covenant of grace' because he understands the covenant concept in the light of "a sovereign administration of the kingdom lordship of God, the Creator and Redeemer." Furthermore, the second Adam stood under the same principle of the covenant of works as the first Adam in order to establish the foundation of the gospel. In this respect the program of redemption as well as the order of the original kingdom in Eden was founded upon the principle of works. Ibid., 86.

[56] Kline prefers to use the term *intratrinitarian covenant* for the eternal covenant among the Trinity, which is usually designated as the covenant of redemption or the inter-trinitarian covenant: "The covenantal origins of the royal grant to Christ go back before the making of the covenant with David to the intratrinitarian counsels before the world was, back to a primal divine pact. Though the covenants made between God and man in the course of human history were determined upon in eternity in the all-embracive divine decrees, the actual covenanting between the parties does not occur until the creature party is on the scene. However, since all parties of the intratrinitarian covenant are present at the determination of the eternal decrees, that decretive predestinating is at the same time an actual covenanting of the persons of the Godhead with each other with respect to their relationships in all that they decree concerning creation and redemption." Meredith G. Kline, "The Exaltation of Christ," *Kerux* 12/3 (1997): 7.

relationship to one another in the covenant of redemption.[57] As we indicated in chapter two, Vos' statement anticipates Murray's rejection of the inter-trinitarian counsel as *a covenant* and the *foedus operum*. Kline, in agreement with classical covenant theology, interprets the eternal intratrinitarian counsel as a covenant and he offers biblical theological evidence for this interpretation: "In eternal covenant with the Son, the Father in heaven had decreed that a new mankind should be redeemed out of fallen mankind and emerge at the consummation of redemptive history as God's holy temple, New Jerusalem."[58] Jesus' mission on earth was "a covenantal mission with covenantal oath-commitments from his Father" as we see in John 6:38. The Messianic passages in Psalm 2:6-9 indicate that there was a covenant between God the Father and Christ the Son in eternity. In Luke 22:28-29, Kline contends that we find a covenantal arrangement between "the Father and the Son" because the verb of διατίθεμαι "appointed" is closely related to διαθήκη "covenant." Thus, Jesus' affirmation of the intratrinitarian covenant stands in the context of his proclamation on "the sacramental seal of the new covenant" — "This is my blood of the new covenant" in Matthew 26:28; Mark 14:24; Luke 22:20; 1 Corinthians 11:25. The Father's heavenly commitments to the Son are manifested in the covenantal promise "by God to man." God's covenantal commitment, bestowed in promise and oath, was directed to Christ, who was the surety of the covenant. This concrete motif was portrayed in the divine redemptive covenants such as the Abrahamic Covenant, the Davidic Covenant in 2 Samuel 7 and Psalms 89, and the New Covenant in Galatians 3:16 and 19. Accordingly, biblical covenant theology establishes the "eternal commitments between the Father and Son as a covenant." Moreover, the goal of the intratrinitarian covenant was the reward of *kingdom* which will be granted as the result of Christ's perfect obedience to the covenant of works.[59] Consistent with his covenant and kingdom link, Kline's understanding of the intratrinitarian covenant is *a kingdom oriented covenant*:

> It was that eternal covenant that the cosmic kingdom of glory was granted to the Son as the reward for his faithful execution of the work

---

[57] Vos, *Redemptive History*, 245-46.
[58] Kline, *Kingdom Prologue*, 80.
[59] Ibid., 87.

the Father gave him to do (cf. Luke 22:29; John 17:4,5). This covenantal commitment to the Son was renewed in the course of the historical administration of the Covenant of Grace.[60]

2. The Inauguration of the Covenant of Redemption

Having argued for the intratrinitarian counsel as *covenant*, Kline suggests that the redemptive covenant inaugurated after the fall was based upon the *eternal intratrinitarian covenant*. It is the presupposition behind the redemptive covenant for "the covenantal community on earth" and restores "God's covenant with men." This indicates that Kline stands within covenant theology in its understanding of election, creation and redemption. God's eternal redemptive purpose was disclosed following the broken covenant of works. A glimmer of the redemptive plan was revealed "in the curse on Satan" in Genesis 3:15 and in the divine judgment on mankind in Genesis 3:16-19. The symbolic sign and seal of the redemptive covenant was manifested to Adam and Eve "before the sentence of exile" in Genesis 3:21. Thus the termination of the covenant of creation in Genesis 3 was at the same time the inauguration of the covenant of redemption. In Genesis 3:15, Kline sees the coming of the Son of Man as "the second federal head" undergoing "probation in another covenant of works." "The covenantal commitments made in eternity" by the Triune God must be carried out "on earth in historical time." As a result, the covenantal kingdom reward must be bestowed on the generations of Adam based on the Son of Man's obedience to "the earthly probation phase of his eternal covenant of works." Indeed, through the suffering of "the champion of the woman's seed," the New Covenant would be ratified, thereby opening the way "for the Covenant of Conferment."[61]

---

[60] Kline, "Exaltation of Christ," 8.

[61] Ibid., 89-90. The first Adam represented "all the predestined mankind" in the original *foedus operum*. He would have received the covenant of conferment if he had fulfilled the requirement of the covenant of works. The second Adam, however, did not represent all mankind but only the elect in his mission fulfillment of the *foedus operum*. To point out this specific quality of the covenant of redemption, Kline uses the term, "the Covenant of Conferment" which is applicable to the elect in Christ "by the sovereign election of divine grace." After all, Christ was "the mediator of the Covenant of Conferment between God and the community formed under this covenant." Ibid., 88.

Kline uses here the term "the Covenant of Conferment," to signify that the second Adam's fulfillment of the covenant of works confers the covenant of grace to the elect. In other words, the covenant of redemption in Christ guarantees eschatological heavenly kingdom blessings for the elect. In this sense, Kline uses *the covenant of conferment* within the umbrella of the covenant of redemption. Thus the covenant of conferment offers the eschatological kingdom goal that is guaranteed by the second Adam. We recall that *a covenant of confirmation* of entering into the semi-eschatological kingdom had been visualized in the covenant of creation if the first Adam had successfully passed the probation period by obeying the covenant of works. In the final analysis, the new redemptive covenant is *antithetical* to the covenant of works because it administers divine grace as over against works in bestowing "the kingdom of God." The goal of the eschatological heavenly kingdom is absolutely assured in the covenant of conferment because God's grace is operative as over against works. The eschatological struggle between "the woman's seed and the serpent" was "a promise of reconciliation and of the restoration of the covenant between the Lord and man."[62] Enoch's deathless translation into heavenly glory in Genesis 5:22-24 is, for Kline, "a prophetic sign of the eschatological victory of the promised seed of the woman over death."[63]

Affirming Genesis 3 as the concrete account of the redemptive covenant-making process, Kline argues that Genesis 3:21 shows the seal of the inauguration of the redemptive covenant. Interpreting and adapting the covenant motif of clothing from Ezekiel 16:8, Kline argues:

> at the level of the God-man covenant, God's covering the human covenanting party with a garment would ... itself symbolize directly God's renewal of his covenant with man ... At the human level, the covering of Adam and Eve with garments of skin would then serve, irrespective of the divorce background, as a marriage ratification ceremony.[64]

---

[62] Ibid., 89-91.
[63] Kline, "Gospel Until the Law," 437.
[64] Kline, *Kingdom Prologue*, 94.

In relation to this, Kline understands Adam's naming of Eve in Genesis 3:20 as a confession of Adam's faith interpreting it "at the level of God's covenant with man." Kline goes on to argue:

> Summing up, several lines of exegesis have converged on the interpretation of the act of clothing in Genesis 3:21 as a divine pledge answering to the faith-commitment of man described in verse 20. This symbolic ritual of mutual divine-human avowal of covenantal relationship was a ratifying of the Covenant of Redemption, or specifically, the Covenant of Conferment.[65]

Furthermore, Kline finds a sacrificial motif "at the mention of the skin used for the clothing" in Genesis 3:21 which is foundational for the redemptive covenant ratification. Thus, Kline suggests that in the postlapsarian state, if God enters into covenant with his people to bestow the heavenly eschatological kingdom, then sacrifice is necessary. Ultimately, the sacrifices would point to the fact that Christ's sacrificial death was required for atonement and for the covenant of conferment. Thus Kline affirms:

> accordingly, the new covenant, the ultimate administration of the Covenant of Conferment, was ratified in the blood of Christ (Matt. 26:28; Heb. 10:29; 13:20) and it is the prerequisite role of Christ's atonement in the establishment of the new covenant that is prototypically expressed in the symbolic sacrifices by which the premessianic administrations of the Covenant of Conferment were inaugurated from Genesis 3 onward.[66]

At the same time, the common grace[67] principle that applies to elect and non-elect, controls "the divine government of the

---

[65] Ibid., 94.
[66] Ibid., 95.
[67] Kline's biblical theological explorations of common grace are particularly important for understanding how he integrates the concept of the kingdom with the covenant idea. In striking fashion he exhibits the importance of the covenant of common grace as the background for the covenant of special grace in redemptive history. In doing so, Kline distinguishes sharply between the two covenants. In other words, the covenant of common grace provides the continuity of history in which the covenant of redemption is applied to the elect. This is a concrete indication that Kline follows the footsteps of Van Tillian presuppositional apologetics in which common grace plays a crucial

postlapsarian world." Paradoxically, God's pronouncement of common curse in Genesis 3:16-19 was indeed the beginning of common grace. As such, Kline states that the inauguration of the covenant of redemption in Genesis 3:15 was in a sense the inauguration of common grace, making possible "an interim historical environment as the theater for a program of redemption" that immediately followed in Genesis 3:16-19. The common grace principle was introduced as the historical setting for the salvation of the elect in God's plan of redemption until the eschatological parousia. In other words, common grace serves and sustains "a general history," opening the mysterious road "for holy redemptive history." Common grace provides mankind's genealogical history. It must be continued until "all the seed of woman had been born, and in particular the messianic seed." Accordingly, "common grace contributes to the purposes of the kingdom program of God's special saving grace." Therefore, in the present world, "the holy and common" coexist, but when the cosmic theocratic kingdom arrives, upon the "consummation of the holy redemptive program," common grace will be terminated along with "the antithesis between the holy and the common."[68]

---

role. Van Til, who pioneered presuppositional apologetics, articulates and applies common grace as the concrete background for the gospel in history. Common grace functions as a "point of contact" that is so crucial in presuppositional apologetics. Cornelius Van Til, *Common Grace and the Gospel* (Phillipsburg: Presbyterian and Reformed Publishing Company, 1972); idem, *The Defense of the Faith* (Phillipsburg: Presbyterian and Reformed Publishing Company, 1967), 151-78. For a comprehensive and critical analysis on Van Til's thought, see John M. Frame, *Cornelius Van Til: An Analysis of His Thought* (Phillipsburg: Presbyterian and Reformed Publishing Company, 1995). The *distinction* between saving grace and common grace has played a key role towards a proper understanding of *heilsgeschichte* and its implication to systematic theology in the Reformed tradition. For a comprehensive discussion of common grace, see Calvin, *Institutes*, 2.2.1-2.3.14; Jonathan Edwards, *Treatise on Grace and Other Posthumously Published Writings*. ed. Paul Helm (Cambridge & London: James Clarke & Co. Ltd., 1971); idem, *The Works of Jonathan Edwards: Religious Affections*. vol. 2, ed. Perry Miller (New Haven: Yale University Press, 1959); Hodge, *Systematic Theology*, 2:654-675; Murray, *Collected Writings*, 2:93-119.

[68] Kline, *Kingdom Prologue*, 95-97.

Furthermore, Kline suggests that the delay of eschatological judgment and common grace are coterminous. Thus, common grace makes a vital contribution to the new redemptive eschatological program. It provides the backdrop for redemptive history.[69]

3. The Prediluvian Noahic Covenant

The prediluvian covenant of Genesis 6:18 with Noah, Kline affirms, was "a covenant of salvation" in which its promise was fulfilled within the historical reality of the flood episode. It was made "with the holy covenant community" and promised the "kingdom of salvation." The "God remembered Noah" of Genesis 8:1 is a confirmation that the prediluvian Noahic Covenant was fulfilled "in the course of the Flood." God's remembering in Genesis 8:1 corresponds to God's covenanting of Genesis 6:18 as the fulfillment corresponds to covenantal promise. The בְּרִית revealed in Genesis 6:18 does not point to "the promises of kingdom blessings" seen in the prior revelation of the covenant of redemption; nevertheless, the prediluvian Noahic Covenant provided for a fulfillment of the previous promises. In a sense, the concrete experience of the Noahic remnant was a typological sign of "the ultimate kingdom reality" which had been anticipated from the beginning of the covenant of redemption as the ultimate goal of the eschatological kingdom. We see a concrete example of this in postdiluvian human history in the relationship of Moses' mission to the Abrahamic Covenant. Through Moses, God brought Israel into the promised kingdom—not the eschatological heavenly kingdom but the typological mode of the ultimate heavenly kingdom. Expressing his "sovereign lordship," "God calls his kingdom-covenant to Noah 'my covenant'" in Genesis 6:18. As such the grant of the holy kingdom was the purpose of the prediluvian Noahic Covenant of Genesis 6:18.[70]

The covenant made with Noah in Genesis 6:18, states Kline, was in a sense "a covenant of grant" which was "the kind of covenant that ancient rulers gave to meritorious individuals for faithful service to the crown." Noah, after all, demonstrated his fidelity to God. Thus he received "not just the proposal of a grant but the actual reward." God through the ark bestowed "the means of salvation and kingdom realization." Noah's inheritance of "the kingdom grant" resulted from

---

[69] Kline, *Structure of Biblical Authority*, 155.
[70] Kline, *Kingdom Prologue*, 159-61.

his covenantal obedience. In Genesis 7:1, God pronounced, "I have found you to be righteous before me in this generation." Of course, in the final analysis, the covenantal grant to Noah was bestowed "under the Covenant of Redemption whose administration to fallen men deserving only the curse of the broken Covenant of Creation—and Noah too was one of these fallen sons of Adam—was an act of God's pure mercy in Christ." What is crucial in Kline's analysis, however, is that *the kingdom grant* in the ark by the principle of works did not jeopardize the principle of grace for inheriting the eternal heavenly kingdom because the kingdom in the ark was pointing to the eternal heavenly kingdom as shadow and type. In other words, there was an inheritance of a typological kingdom on account of works, which must be understood in the context of *eschatology*. Thus Kline argues that when the principle of works over against grace is operative, the typological kingdom points to "the messianic king and kingdom." He goes on to suggest:

> Since, then, the introduction of the works principle in such covenantal arrangements affects only the typological overlay and not the underlying stratum of ultimate redemptive-eschatological reality, these works-grants assume their ancillary place harmoniously within the administrations of the Covenant of Redemption. And grace thus remains at all times the constant principle of eternal salvation.[71]

In this regard, Kline holds that the covenantal grant of the kingdom in the ark to Noah did not conflict with the principle of grace in the covenant of redemption because the kingdom grant to Noah subserved the gospel of grace. Indeed, Noah was a type of the Messiah, whose perfect obedience lays the ground work for the redemption of God's people. Because he was only a type, perfect obedience or the absolute standard applied to "the righteousness of Christ" was not required "in the suretyship of Noah." Noah's case was similar to "God's judging of Israel's covenantal obedience as the ground of their kingdom tenure under the old covenant." With this careful clarification, Kline notices that "Noah's exemplary righteousness" was a *type* of the messianic King's perfect righteousness in his obedience to the *foedus operum*. The righteousness of Noah provided "the ground of the covenant of grant," the guarantee of the kingdom grant in the

---

[71] Ibid., 161-63.

ark. Thus Noah was "a type of Christ as the surety who guaranteed the accomplishment of the promises of the new covenant."[72]

4. The Postdiluvian Noahic Common Grace Covenant

Unlike the covenant that God made before the Flood, the postdiluvian covenant in Genesis 8:20-9:17, according to Kline, is a common grace covenant. As a result, it is not "an administration of redemptive grace but of common grace," so it did not bestow the kingdom of God upon the elect. The bestowal of a common grace covenant with Noah and his family is similar to the original common grace covenant to Adam and Eve in Genesis 3:16-19. Moreover, the Noahic common grace covenant includes "the other living creatures of the earth" as suggested in Genesis 9:10,12,15-17. In fact, it is described as a covenant between "God and the earth" in Genesis 9:13. Thus the rainbow as the sign of this common grace covenant is different from circumcision or baptism which is the sign of the covenant of redemption, "performed by and upon a peculiar people set aside from the rest of mankind." Meanwhile, God effects the sign of the common grace covenant "in the natural world," defining "a provisional world order" in God's sovereign control. Obviously, the postdiluvian covenant of common grace was a substantial reconfirmation of "the prediluvian interim order." The וַהֲקִמֹתִי אֶת־בְּרִיתִי of Genesis 9:11 (par. vv 9 and 17) directly indicates that the postdiluvian common grace was covenantal. The rainbow as the sign of the covenant manifests the distinctive characteristics of the postdiluvian common grace order which will not be interrupted until the parousia. The covenantal commitments to common grace were *unilateral* because the בְּרִית in Genesis 9:11 and 15 denotes the promise of God by which the flood shall not destroy mankind again. As with the other divine covenants, it was "a sovereign administration of God's heavenly reign."[73] This common grace covenant motif is crucial to Kline's biblical covenant theology because common grace must be the background of *heilsgeschichte*, the latter which provides the ultimate meaning of history. In other words, the covenant of redemption and of common grace stand or fall together. At the heart of Kline's biblical theology, the distinction between the common grace covenant and the

---

[72] Ibid., 164-65.
[73] Ibid., 168-70.

redemptive covenant is crucial to depict the kingdom of God progressively unfolding in biblical history.

We do not find, argues Kline, the eschatological heavenly kingdom motif as the goal of the covenant in Genesis 8:20-9:27, because it is limited to common grace and curses on nature. In addition, the sign of the Sabbath as the prophetic sign of the eschatological cosmic kingdom is not present here because the common grace covenant will not culminate "in the new heaven and earth." Rather, it will be terminated "by the final cosmic cataclysm, which it only for a while postpones." With this in mind, Kline carefully distinguishes between the prediluvian covenant of redemption administered in Genesis 6:18 and the postdiluvian covenant of common grace in Genesis 8:20-9:17. Until the parousia, a covenant of common grace will temper the devastating impact of the common curse, assuring the general stability of the natural order and the procreation process.[74]

The postdiluvian covenant did not have a direct relationship to "the kingdom of God as holy realm." Rather, it served "the divine purpose and program of redemptive covenant and thereby, indirectly, the coming of the holy kingdom." In the final analysis, the common grace covenant narrated in Genesis 8:20-9:17 provided "the historical order" offering a legitimate ground for *heilsgeschichte* and the renewed covenant of redemption, particularly pointing to and providing the possibility of the future Abrahamic Covenant in Genesis 12ff.[75]

5. The Abrahamic Covenant

The Abrahamic Covenant signifies a distinctive stage of divine redemptive history while it demonstrates redemptive historical continuity and illustrates *the covenant of conferment*. The covenant of redemption revealed in Genesis 3 and consummated in the New Covenant, argues Kline, flowered and matured in the Abrahamic Covenant, particularly in its depiction of the goals of salvation and the ultimate eschatological kingdom. Accordingly, God's covenant with Abraham signifies redemptive historical continuity with the pre-Abrahamic covenant and the messianic New Covenant of the future. The terms of the Abrahamic Covenant were in accord with the undergirding principle of the covenant of conferment which would be

---

[74] Ibid., 170-71.
[75] Ibid., 178.

actualized in Christ and would lead to the ultimate goal of the eschatological kingdom.

Concretely, the Abrahamic Covenant was a bridge "between the past and future of the one unified Covenant of Redemption." The Abrahamic Covenant, affirms Kline, in a sense formed a contrast to the Noahic Covenant because the latter manifested "the terminal episode in the history of the world that then was," while the Abrahamic Covenant signified all subsequent redemptive covenants "in the world that now is." Thus, the Abrahamic Covenant embraced and bridged the covenantal kingdom of God of the future as revealed in the Old and New Covenants. The Abrahamic Covenant was the manifestation of the great fruit of the covenant revelation in Shem's line in the postdiluvian stage, picturing the whole redemptive covenantal harvest to come. In agreement, Paul, "as apostle to the Gentiles" in Galatians 3:8, interprets the New Covenant, "the final administration of redemptive history," in the light of the Abrahamic Covenant, proclaiming that the promise of God in the gospel revealed to Abraham would result in the blessing of all the nations.[76]

As we have seen in chapter two, Murray argues that the Abrahamic Covenant was promissory as over against the principle of works or law. He utilizes the antithesis between Law and Grace to depict the gracious character of the Abrahamic Covenant. Kline too applies the antithesis between Law and Grace to draw out the principle of grace in the Abrahamic Covenant as over against the principle of works. In this regard, Kline asserts that God's promise in the redemptive covenantal context denotes "the principle of grace, the opposite of works." Consequently, Paul analyzes the Abrahamic Covenant as promise in Galatians 3:17, setting it over against "the principle of works" in verse 18, which was active and operative in the Mosaic Covenant. Furthermore, God's promissory covenant with Abraham was synonymous with "the gospel of grace."[77]

Here, once again, we do not want to confuse Kline's analysis of the Old Covenant with classical dispensationalism, for when Kline argues that the principle of works was operative in the Mosaic Covenant, it is applied only at the level of the typological kingdom administration looking forward to the eschatological heavenly kingdom centered on the eschatological Lamb, Christ. Kline, like Murray, does not want us

---

[76] Ibid., 197.
[77] Ibid., 198.

to forget that grace was the fundamental principle for salvation under the Mosaic Covenant.

Pauline theology, Kline argues, shows that we must understand the promissory character of the Abrahamic Covenant in the light of the antithesis between Law and Grace. For example, Paul in Romans 4 derives the antithesis between the works principle of the law and gospel of grace from the Abrahamic promise. In Romans 4:16, Paul emphasizes the faith by which Abraham embraced God's promise as over against works. According to verse 13, inheritance was not based on the works of the law because that would be antithetical "to the promise-grace-faith-forgiveness principle" in verses 14-15 and 4-8. Based on verses 3 and 13, Kline emphasizes that the promise of the kingdom was inherited by "the righteousness of faith." In other words, in the Abrahamic Covenant, "justification was by faith's 'Amen'[78] to God's promises" (Gen. 15:6; Rom. 4:3). In the final analysis, the Abrahamic Covenant was subservient to the grand picture of *the covenant of conferment* which was mediated by Christ who fulfills the eternal intratrinitarian covenant, "the foundation of the entire Covenant of Redemption."[79]

The divine commitments in the Abrahamic Covenant were decisively revealed and highlighted in Genesis 15 where the concrete covenantal word בְּרִית was first applied to the Abrahamic promissory covenant. As such, Genesis 15 was "the formal ratification of the covenant by oath ceremony." The transition from Genesis 12 to 15 is echoed in Genesis 24:7. Abraham, according to Genesis 15:4-5, was reassured by God that he would be the "father of a line of heirs" to God's promises. In addition, God renewed the land promise in Genesis 15:7. In the end, God sealed the covenantal promise with a solemn oath in Genesis 15:9ff. That is the concrete meaning of the ritual passage "through the midst of the slain and divided animals." In fact, "the ratification of covenant commitments" by animal rituals was common, as Jeremiah 34:8ff. and 18f. shows. "The terrible self-malediction was conditional: *if* God failed to fulfill his promise." Kline transfers this motif to the principle of the Gospel, arguing that "according to the revelation of the gospel of grace, the glory of the re-creation victory over the dragon involves necessarily the bruising of

---

[78] See Meredith G. Kline's "Abram's Amen," *Westminster Theological Journal* 31 (1968/69): 1-11.

[79] Kline, *Kingdom Prologue*, 198-99.

the heel of the champion-seed of the woman" revealed in Genesis 3:15. Paradoxically, the glory of the eschatological kingdom fulfillment will be realized "only through the suffering of the seed of Abraham." Of course, the suffering Savior would be none other than the Lord of Glory. As such, Kline effectively links the covenant oath in Genesis 15 to the suffering motif of Christ. Indeed, our Lord would not experience "the curse of the Genesis 15 oath-ritual as a covenant-breaker." He kept the covenant by fulfilling the eschatological curse through suffering as the Lamb of God. In this sense, the oath-passage of God was "a commitment to the death-passage of Jesus in the gloom of Golgotha." In the final analysis, "it was a covenant to walk the way of the cross." The sacrificial cutting motif in Genesis 15 reappears in "a later divine oath to Abraham" in Genesis 22. Once again, the story reveals that God's commitment is "to the way of the Cross." Abraham obeyed God's directions, prepared "the altar on the Mount of Moriah," and proceeded to slay and offer Isaac, "his only and beloved son" in Genesis 22:1ff., but the Lord graciously provided a ram "as a substitute offering" in the place of Isaac. In doing so, God swore *unilaterally* by a solemn oath that he would certainly fulfill the covenant promises, that would culminate "in the gospel promise of the blessing of the nations through Abraham's seed" (Gen. 22:15-18). Thus, the confirmatory oath to Abraham in Genesis 22 was a divine commitment "not to spare his own Son but to deliver him up as our sacrificial substitute." Kline convincingly argues that Hebrews 6:13ff refers to Genesis 22 and signifies that God's oath was added to the Abrahamic Covenant promises to re-establish and strengthen the promissory-faith aspect over against the principle of works.[80]

Kline correlates Abraham's covenantal obedience in Genesis 22:16-18 to both the *historia salutis* and the *ordo salutis*. For example, James from the perspective of the *ordo salutis* interpreted Abraham's obedience as a vivid manifestation of the principle that we are justified by faith alone but the faith which justifies is never alone. Redemptive history in the promissory program of the Abrahamic Covenant would, Kline argues, continue "to unfold because Abraham had done this."

---

[80] Ibid., 199-202. Thus, Kline suggests that Genesis 15 is a good example of a covenant sealed by God's solemn oath. "God invoked the curse of the oath upon himself should he prove false to it." God himself swears in the covenant ratification ceremony, and it signifies the Abrahamic Covenant as "one of promise." Kline, *By Oath Consigned*, 16-17.

The redemptive historical significance of Abraham's obedience as the foundation of "God's favorable action towards his descendants" is reflected in the Lord's oracle to Isaac in Genesis 26:2-5. In this context, we cannot limit the works of Abraham to the realm of the *ordo salutis* because his covenantal obedience was applied to maintain "a causal relationship to the blessing of Isaac and Israel." Thus Abraham's obedience had "a meritorious character that procured a reward enjoyed by others." "The term עֵקֶב, 'because,' used in Genesis 26:5" and 22:18 signifies Abraham's obedience "as a matter of merit." As a result, "an Abrahamite kingdom of God" would be shaped by the obedience of Abraham, providing the foundation for the typological earthly kingdom of Israel. Although Abraham's obedience was not the ground of the heavenly inheritance, it was the ground for Israel's inheritance of the promised land. Consequently, John's gospel does not demonstrate that Abraham's obedience was the ground of eschatological salvation., but that eschatological salvation would come from "the Abrahamites, the Jews," *because of* Abraham's obedience (John 4:22).[81] Kline summarizes the perspective of *heilsgeschichte* in relation to Abraham's obedience as follows:

> In Genesis 15 it was the oath-passage of the Lord through the way of death. In Genesis 22 it was the provision of the ram as the sacrificial substitute for Isaac. Placing the disclosure concerning the meritorious role of Abraham's obedience in the context of these powerful pointers to Christ and his obedience, which was the meritorious ground of the antitypical blessings of the covenant, was a safeguard against misconstruing the significance of Abraham's work as extending to the antitypical level. It was limited to the prototypal sphere.[82]

---

[81] Kline, *Kingdom Prologue*, 216-17.

[82] Ibid., 217. For the view point of the *historia salutis*, we agree with Kline's observation that Abraham's obedience provided the ground of the Israelites' inheritance of the promised land, but we do not think that his obedience was *meritorious* since it was a wonderful fruit of *the covenant of grace*. We agree with Calvin, who pointed out that Abraham's obedience became the basis of *earthly reward* in the promised land to Abraham's descendants. In other words, we suggest distinguishing *reward and merit* to avoid confusion in respect to the concept of merit: "What is it [Gen. 22:16-18] that we hear? Did Abraham merit by his obedience the blessing whose promise he had received before the commandment was given? Here, surely, we have shown without ambiguity that the Lord rewards the work of believers with the same benefits as he had given them before they contemplated any

Kline suggests that kingdom program in the Abrahamic Covenant resumes the prophecies of the *heilsgeschichte* kingdom presented in Genesis 3:15 and 9:25-27, further explicating the expectation of the eschatological kingdom in the covenant of creation. The eschatological kingdom visualized as "the goal of the process," was the same eschatological creational kingdom "symbolically portrayed from the beginning by the Sabbath and tree of life in the garden of God." The continuity of the eschatological expectation of the covenant of redemption is also revealed "in the reappearance of various features of the sanctuary kingdom of Eden in redemptive prophecy, notably so in the book of Revelation." Thus the theme of *heilsgeschichte* was carried forward leading into "the New Jerusalem." As God gave "the kingdom mandate" to Adam and Eve, so the Abrahamic Covenant kingdom promise would focus on "multiplying and filling the contemplated domain." Therefore, "the promised kingdom included the two components of people and territory." The progressive unfolding of the kingdom promise in the Abrahamic Covenant was manifested "from Genesis 12 to Genesis 13,15,17,22,26 and 28." The kingdom promise in the Abrahamic Covenant was ultimately an eschatological paradise "flowing with milk and honey, a new heaven and earth with river and trees of life," having the glory of God's "Shekinah Presence" like the eschatological goal of the garden of Eden. As Kline has consistently suggested, the covenant of creation required the realization of the kingdom. This kingdom fullness would come through "the multiplying of Abraham's seed and their filling-subduing the allotted land" as indicated in Genesis 35:11. As such, the covenantal nation blessing promised in Genesis 12:2a pointed to the redemptive restoration and consummation of "the creation kingdom."[83]

Kline sees the land promise fulfillment in the Abrahamic Covenant in terms of *typology*. It points to the *antitypical* reality of

---

works, as he does not yet have any reason to benefit them except his own mercy." Calvin, *Institutes*, 3:18:2. As we explained in chapter one, we limit meritorious obedience to Adam and Christ since merit according to our definition is possible only in the case of *perfect obedience*, which is impossible in the postlapsarian state for anyone except Christ. To be sure, Kline limits Abraham's obedience to the typological blessing. Nevertheless, it is not proper to see Abraham's obedience as *meritorious* since it was not perfect obedience.

[83] Ibid., 218-21.

eschatological fulfillment. The inheritance and fulfillment of this promise is to be understood as "an anticipatory portrayal of the consummated kingdom-land, the Metapolis kingdom-city of the new heavens and earth which the Creator covenanted to man from the beginning." Having said this, Kline indicates that Canaan as the promised land fulfillment was a *typological* land, being "a limited land," not the cosmic-eschatological goal of "the creation kingdom." In addition, Canaan was not the eschatological Sabbath experience as Hebrews 4 manifests because even the New Covenant believers are still waiting for that eschatological rest. Accordingly, the first level fulfillment of the promised land in Canaan served a pedagogical purpose, looking upward and forward "to the second level fulfillment;" the possession of everlasting heavenly rest.[84]

Here, Kline clarifies the confusion on the geophysical dimension of the second level kingdom. It is commonly alleged that covenantal hermeneutics spiritualizes while classical dispensational hermeneutics does not. Kline argues that the basic issue is that how to relate the two levels of the promised kingdom in the Abrahamic Covenant to another. He clarifies "the relationship of the old covenant with Israel to the new covenant with the church" by *typology*. In the final analysis, dispensational hermeneutics fails to acknowledge *typology* in this crucial matter. It fails to reckon "the Bible's identification of the new covenant (or second level) realization of the kingdom promise as standing in continuity with the old covenant (or first level) realization as antitypical fulfillment to typal promise."[85] In other words, the kingdom of Israel in the Old Covenant was a fulfillment of the Abrahamic Covenant promise, but this covenant also contained a "prophetic promise" pointing to "the second level fulfillment under the new covenant." Covenantal hermeneutics, argues Kline, rightly understands the typological nature of the kingdom of Israel under the Old Covenant and "the antitypal, perfective, permanent nature of the second level kingdom." According to Kline, classical dispensationalism employs an exclusively literalistic hermenetuic, therefore it rejects a typological hermeneutic as a means to "depict the second level kingdom in the typological idiom of the first level

---

[84] Ibid., 225.
[85] Ibid., 226.

model."[86] Thus it rejects the typological nature of the kingdom of Israel in the Old Covenant.

Having established the promissory character of the Abrahamic Covenant as over against the principle of works, Kline depicts the concept of divine election in the context of the Abrahamic Covenant. Indeed, Paul asserts double predestination by explaining God's preference for Jacob rather than Esau in Romans 9. In the context of Romans 9, argues Kline, Paul deals with a problem of how the identity of God as the covenant keeper can be explained "in the face of the failure of the Israelite community as a whole to enter into the blessings of the new covenant." Paul resolves this problem by asserting "a two-level structure of the meaning and realization of the promises of the Abrahamic Covenant." The first level was "the level of the typological kingdom of Israel under Moses in the Old Covenant." Kline argues that in this typological level "all the Israelites were the promised seed" and their inheritance of Canaan fulfilled the land promise (1 Kings 4:20-21). The second level of the promises covered spiritual areas, tasted even in "the patriarchal period, as well as in the old covenant era ... and which under the new covenant comes to fulfillment in every respect in the antitypical, eternal kingdom of righteousness and peace in the Spirit." Understanding the promises on the spiritual level, Paul teaches in Romans 9:6-8 that Abraham's natural descendants were not all "the intended seed of promise." Abraham's believing seed, Kline argues, was "only a remnant within Israel, a remnant according to the election of grace" in Romans 11:5, "an individual election within the national election" in Romans 11:2 and 28. As such, the benefits of Christ's spiritual kingdom accrue to Abraham's *spiritual* seed "as the promised seed." Abraham's spiritual seed continued throughout the history of Israel, "an elect remnant from within the total covenant community, sovereignly produced" by God.[87]

The election of Jacob and reprobation of Esau is clearly manifested in biblical history. Under the Old Covenant, the Israelite theocracy consisted of an elect nation descended from Jacob which dwelled in the promised land. It was opposed by the Edomites who were a reprobate nation descended from Esau. Paul affirms that the national election of Israel rested upon Jacob's individual election (Rom. 9:13, citing Mal. 1:2-3). The patriarchs' election by God highlights and

---

[86] Ibid.
[87] Ibid., 203-204.

strengthens the sovereign aspect of divine grace concretely manifested in the promises of the Abrahamic Covenant. The sovereignty of grace revealed in God's election of Jacob in Romans 9:11-12 is the concrete basis for blessings bestowed by covenant promise. Kline affirms that the Abrahamic Covenant was a direct reflection of the intratrinitarian covenant in eternity, where Christ became the Surety for the elect. The realization of salvation and the heavenly kingdom was "a simple matter of pure sovereign grace." However, the typological level is not that simple. Here a proper understanding of Kline's position requires our careful observation and analysis. God's sovereign promise constituted "the Abrahamic-Isaac-Jacob line into the people Israel who should experience the national election to become the holy kingdom in the promised land and so continue until Christ." Kline, however, argues that the *continuity* of national election was contingent on "national fidelity to the Lord." In this limited sense, Kline affirms that the works principle was *operative* under the Old Covenant.[88]

Kline, like Murray, sets forth the antithesis between Law and Grace as the key to understanding the concept of sovereign grace in divine election. Paul taught that the promise and the Spirit principle as over against the works principle was operative in Isaac's birth in Galatians 4:23 and 29, while Ishmael was born under the principle of flesh in verse 28. This is a Pauline parallel to show that there is a contrast "between the grace of the gospel of freedom in Christ and the works principle that brings into bondage" in verses 21ff. This dynamic historical-covenantal context highlights the Abrahamic Covenant as "one of promise," manifesting God's sovereign saving grace in opposition to the principle of works.[89]

Kline suggests that the "Walk before me and be perfect" of Genesis 17:1 was a concrete manifestation of "a conditionality of human responsibility" which entered into "the stipulated terms" of the Abrahamic Covenant promise. Kline, however, carefully emphasizes that the conditionality of the covenant does not jeopardize "the guarantee of kingdom fulfillment" and "the pure principle of grace" which grant eschatological heavenly kingdom blessings. The covenantal context of Genesis 17 includes "the observation of circumcision as a sign" of the Abrahamic Covenant in verses 9-14. Circumcision as a covenantal oath was a human response to God's

---

[88] Ibid., 205.
[89] Ibid., 206-07.

comprehensive demand "for covenantal devotion and service" which we observe in Genesis 17:1-2. In the light of redemptive history, circumcision signifies *unio cum Christo* "in his crucifixion-circumcision as a satisfaction of divine justice and it thus means safe passage through the death-judgment to the resurrection unto justification" according to Colossians 2:11ff. and Romans 4:11. Furthermore, circumcision in Christ signifies that we die to sin and put off the old man.[90]

6. The Mosaic Covenant

Although Kline shows a deep appreciation for Murray's insightful analysis of the Sinaitic Covenant, presented in *The Covenant of Grace*, 20-22, he is not convinced by Murray's exclusive emphasis on *continuity* between the Abrahamic, Mosaic and and New Covenants.[91]

First of all, Kline points out that in the covenant ratification ceremony of Exodus 24 "the oath was sworn by the people of Israel, not by the Lord." The Israelites responded together, "We will do everything the Lord has said; we will obey" (Exod. 24:7). This is a clear manifestation that "the solemn commitment by which this covenant was ratified was not made by the Lord but by Israel," and

---

[90] Ibid., 209-212. Kline suggests that New Covenant baptism as the sign of the covenant signifies the eschatological judgment in which the covenant Lord brings his servants to account, whereas the traditional understanding of baptism emphasizes God's grace and blessing as its primary significance. For a comprehensive and incisive explanation of the redemptive historical significance of circumcision and baptism in relation to the covenantal and kingdom motifs, see Kline's *By Oath Consigned: A Reinterpretation of the Covenant Signs of Circumcision and Baptism* (Grand Rapids, Michigan: Eerdmans Publishing Company, 1968). A brief discussion of Kline's positive contribution to the theology of circumcision and Christian baptism can be seen in John H. Stek's review of *A New Theology of Baptism? Baptism: A Sign of Grace or of Judgment?*, by Meredith G. Kline, *Calvin Theological Journal* (1966): 69-73.

[91] Kline, *By Oath Consigned*, 18. Reflecting on Murray's thoughts on the Mosaic Covenant, Kline stresses the need to expound its *distinctiveness*: "The systematic theologian must beware lest his proper concern for the unity and continuity of the divine covenants or for the sovereignty of God in the covenant relationship blur or even virtually obliterate in his thought the distinct identity of the Sinaitic Covenant as a particular administration with its own historical beginning in a concrete occasion of covenant making." Ibid.

marks a sharp *discontinuity* from the ratification of the Abrahamic Covenant in Genesis 15. Meanwhile, Kline observes *the continuity of the covenant of redemption* within the covenant making process of Exodus 19-24. For example, Exodus 19:5 and 6 signify the continuity of the blessings of the covenant of redemption, and the sacrificial motif of Exodus 24:5ff. by which the covenant was ratified indicates God's promise of salvation according to the principle of the covenant of redemption as it is interpreted in Hebrews 9:18ff. Nevertheless, the distinctive aspect of the covenant making process at Mount Sinai is evident in the Israelites' "act of sworn commitment." Accordingly, the covenant formula of Exodus 19-24 is not to be identified as "a unilateral promissory commitment from the divine side" in the manner of the Abrahamic Covenant ratification of Genesis 15. In contrast to the promissory character of the Abrahamic Covenant, the Sinaitic Covenant was "a law covenant" since it was founded on "Israel's formal pledging obedience to God's law."[92]

The Mosaic Covenant, according to Kline, is *continuous* with the Abrahamic Covenant of promise in terms of its individual application of redemption and initial fulfillment of the kingdom promise in the promised land. Nevertheless, it is in *contrast* to the Abrahamic and New Covenants since it was governed by "a principle of works." Paul's discussion in Galatians 3:10 ff. and Romans 10:4 ff. signifies that both *continuity* and *discontinuity* exist between the Old and the New Covenants. The Pauline thesis substantiates that "the works

---

[92] Kline, *By Oath Consigned*, 17-18. The significance of Israel's corporate oath in the covenant ratification between Jehovah and Israel was recognized by Geerhardus Vos, and Kline expands this motif for the purpose of identifying the nature of the Sinaitic Covenant. The corporate response of the Israelites, described as "We will do everything the Lord has said" of Exodus 19:8 and 24, affirms Vos, manifests the peculiarity of the Mosaic Covenant: "It should be noticed, that here the בְּרִית appears for the first time as a two sided arrangement, although that is by no means the reason of its being called a בְּרִית. This reason lies entirely in the ceremony of ratification. As to the arrangement itself, great emphasis is placed on the *voluntary acceptance of the* בְּרִית *by the people* [my emphasis]. It is true, the initiative in designing the terms is strictly vindicated for Jehovah. No parleying, no co-operation between God and man in determining the nature and content are from the standpoint of the narrative conceivable. It is Jehovah's covenant exclusively in that respect. Still, the בְּרִית is placed before the people, and their assent required [Ex. 19.5, 8; 24:3]." Vos, *Biblical Theology*, 121-22.

principle" was operative in the Mosaic Covenant, while "the promise-grace-faith principle of the gospel" was continually serving for individual believers' salvation in the light of the continuity of *the covenant of redemption*. The Israelites must obey the law to continue "the blessings of the typological kingdom community" as epitomized in Leviticus 18:5. Accordingly, the continuance of the typological national election depended upon the Israelites' corporate obedience. In other words, theocratic kingdom blessings were not guaranteed by *the covenant of redemption* in Christ. Rather, it was to be "merited by the Israelites' works of obedience to the law." Jeremiah identifies the Old Covenant as a breakable one, which is a concrete indication that it was based on "the principle of works" in respect to the typological kingdom maintenance (Jer. 31:32).[93] We will discuss Kline's detailed biblical theological outworkings on the Mosaic Covenant in section "C."

7. The Davidic Covenant

Completing the conquest of the promised land through David, Yahweh arranged for the building of the temple on the holy mount through the provision of *a covenant* in 2 Samuel 7. Moreover, the Davidic kingdom was established, and permanently guaranteed in this Davidic Covenant. "Nathan's covenant oracle to David" parallels the Israelites's victory song of Exodus 15 in its application of "the victory hymn genre." The integrity of verse 13 of 2 Samuel 7 has been questioned by some critical scholars, arguing that it is "a harmonizing addition by a later editor." But the originality of verse 13, argues Kline, is supported by "the lyric reflection of the 2 Samuel 7 episode in Psalm 132," and its centrality in 2 Samuel 7. In fact, the Psalmist proclaims that the king's temple-building for Yahweh is a central motif in the establishment of the Davidic kingdom by the covenant oath. In the future, the Davidic Covenant will be consummated in the divine descendant, Christ Jesus. In the New Covenant age, Christ as the son of David builds God's eternal house. Moreover, Christ himself is "the true temple of God." As Peter explains in 1 Peter 2:5, believers are mysteriously united with Christ. Thus, the believers' union with Christ and the incarnation of the Son of God manifest "God's holy dwelling," signifying the ultimate transmutation of God's temple. Finally, the eschatological re-creation will be "a divine house

---

[93] Kline, *Kingdom Prologue*, 214-15.

building" of the new heaven and new earth after the final judgment, fully-establishing the eternal rest secured by the son of David. Kline understands the Davidic Covenant *Christocentrically* because it is fulfilled in the redemptive work of Christ as the son of David.[94]

For Kline, the Davidic Covenant, like the Abrahamic Covenant, is under the umbrella of the redemptive covenants, and focuses sharply on divine sovereignty "in the promises of blessing to which absolute guarantees are attached, while human responsibility is presupposed in the covenant stipulations, pointedly so in the accompanying threats of curse," as it is strikingly portrayed in 2 Samuel 7:14.[95]

8. The New Covenant

The prophecy of the New Covenant in Jeremiah 31:31-34, argues Kline, indicates that the typological kingdom administered in the Old Covenant was not a permanent stage, but *a temporary and probationary stage* governed by the principle of works. Thus it was a breakable covenant which would be eventually terminated. Paul observes that, by this means, all people including Jews and Gentiles "were shut up together under the sentence of having failed to attain the kingdom on the ground of obedience to the law." As a result, all were put into the position of having to depend solely upon the grace and mercy of God as is clearly manifested in the Gospel as recorded in Romans 11:32.[96]

Indeed, Paul implicitly links the discontinuity between the Old and New Covenants to Jeremiah's contrast in Jeremiah 31:31-34. As such, the New Covenant cannot be broken like the Old Covenant because the everlasting antitypical kingdom of the New Covenant is established on the basis of Christ's meritorious obedience, and its accomplishment is guaranteed to the people of God in Christ, while the earthly kingdom of Israel was terminated by God's covenantal curse due to *corporate disobedience* by the Israelites. In this respect, Kline argues that "between the old and new covenant there is contrast as well as continuum." At the level of individual salvation, the principle of redemptive grace was operative in the Old Covenant economy and demonstrates *continuity*. Nevertheless, at the level of the typological kingdom, the principle of works over against "the grace-promise-faith

---

[94] Kline, *Structure of Biblical Authority*, 82-6.
[95] Ibid., 146.
[96] Kline, *Kingdom Prologue*, 229.

principle" was operative and demonstrates *discontinuity*. "By reason of the presence of this different principle of works, the old covenant was breakable–and in that respect stood in contrast to the new covenant, not in continuum with it."[97]

The Pentecost of the New Testament, affirms Kline, signifies the coming of the Glory-Spirit sealing the New Covenant "as divine Witness." This event recapitulated the glorious descent of the Spirit on Mount Sinai "as the Glory-Witness to the old covenant." Striking connection between the two covenants is the appearance of fire and sound signifying the presence of the Glory-Spirit. The Glory theophany of the Old Covenant reappeared at the time of the New Covenant Pentecost after the incarnation and glorification of Christ Jesus. Above all, "the mighty voice" from heaven was the primary phenomenon or "insignia of the Presence."[98]

C. The Mosaic Covenant

The theocratic kingdom of Israel under the Old Covenant, argues Kline, was "a redemptive renewal of the paradise-sanctuary of Eden and a prototypal preview of the eternal theocratic sanctuary" of the eschatological kingdom consummation. Accordingly, "the Glory-Presence" reappeared as "the Edenic cultus" was reconstituted in relation to "the mountain of God as cultic focus for a kingdom fullness." In this respect, the theophany and cultus of the patriarchal period had "a pre-Glory character, which evidenced the pre-kingdom nature of that age." When the kingdom as a type of the eternal kingdom was established under the Old Covenant, theophanic glory manifested itself in "the form of the fiery cloud of the Glory-Spirit," guiding the Israelites from Egypt to the promised land and bringing catastrophic judgment on the Amorites. Kline affirms that this points ultimately to the antitypical messianic judgment at the parousia by the Son of Man who introduces the eschatological fiery judgment "on the clouds of heaven in the Glory of the Father," and brings the eschatological consummated kingdom-temple "in the Spirit." The final judgment day and the realization of "the kingdom-temple" will be accompanied by revelation of the "Glory-Spirit." The absence of the "Shekinah-Presence in glory" in the patriarchal age from Abraham to

---

[97] Meredith G. Kline, "Of Works and Grace," *Presbyterion* 9 (1983): 86-7.
[98] Kline, *Images of the Spirit*, 99-100.

Jacob shows that the patriarchal age was "a pre-kingdom stage" in redemptive history.[99]

Along with the covenant community kingdomization and the Edenic theocratic renewal in the promised land, "there was a typological restoration of the mountain of God as the sanctuary focus of the kingdom." The altar located at the holy mountain "in the royal tabernacle court of the Glory-Presence," was "the typological expression of the promised restoration of the cultic focus of the kingdom of God."[100]

The Glory-Spirit, argues Kline, who created "the cosmic temple in the beginning" was the major builder of the tabernacle. In Exodus 25-40 "the building of the tabernacle" was an immediate result of the covenant-making process initiated by the Glory-Spirit's revelation at Mount Sinai "as Lord and divine covenant Witness." At the same time, the creation account of Genesis was marked as a covenantal event by the presence of the same Glory-Spirit hovering over the waters as was cited in Genesis 1:2. A holy cosmic kingdom order under the covenant of creation focused on "the microcosmic Edenic sanctuary." In a similar way, the Sinaitic Covenant installed "a holy kingdom-order" focused on "the Mosaic tabernacle." In this respect, the building of "the Mosaic tabernacle was a replica of the Glory-Spirit, the archetypal temple itself." "The Glory theophany" presence in creation and in the midst of Israel was "the invisible heavenly temple" manifested as "a veiled pre-consummation form of visibility." Accordingly, the Mosaic tabernacle was a copy of heavenly things and "an antitype of the greater archetypal tabernacle," as the author of Hebrews explains in Hebrews 9:11,23 and 24. Upon its completion, "the Glory theophany" entered and filled the Mosaic tabernacle, thus identifying himself with it. This is concrete biblico-theological evidence that the tabernacle was designed to be "a symbolic reproduction of the reality of the heavenly temple, where the God of Glory is enthroned in the midst of the angelic divine council."[101]

The historical allegory revealed in Ezekiel 16:8, according to Kline, alludes to nuptial imagery manifesting God's covenantal protection of Israel "under the Glory-cloud." Furthermore, the Psalmist in Psalm 105:39 uses the verb פרש, which occurs in Ezekiel

---

[99] Kline, *Kingdom Prologue*, 243-44.
[100] Ibid., 245.
[101] Kline, *Images of the Spirit*, 38-9.

16:8, to portray "the spreading of the theophanic cloud-canopy" as "God's extending the edge of his robe." As such, "Ezekiel's allegorical transcription of the Sinaitic covenant-making" signifies that Israel's covering by the theophanic Glory Presence was "a divine plighting of troth." Thus, the awesome presence of "the Glory-Spirit on Mount Sinai was an oath stance, signifying covenant ratification."[102]

In this respect, under the Old Covenant, a comprehensive manifestation of the heavenly-eschatological kingdom was projected into world history in the form of the theocratic kingdom: "Heaven came to earth in supernatural realism in the phenomenon of the Glory-Spirit revealed in the sanctuary in Israel's midst." Kline argues here that the typological kingdom manifestation in Israel that pointed to the kingdom of heaven was "an intrusive phenomenon in the common grace order." This kingdom-intrusion of the Old Covenant was typological of cosmic eschatological restoration and redemptive blessing. One can also observe typological patterns in "the political life of Israel, notably in the deliverance from Egypt, the conquest of Canaan, and the restoration from exile, though also throughout the governmental-judicial provisions of the Mosaic law."[103]

As we proceed in our discussion, we will recognize that Kline's view is not fundamentally different from that of classical covenant hermeneutics in the Reformed tradition. For Kline, the Old Covenant was governed by the principle of grace in relation to justification and salvation, in agreement with classical covenant theology, but in disagreement with classical dispensational hermeneutics. Nevertheless, Kline mentions that the principle of works was also operative in the Old Covenant for the administration of the typological kingdom of Israel. We see this as the *flowering* of covenant theology, in which the principle of corporate obedience to the law was the basis for *the continuation of the theocratic earthly kingdom of Israel*. Answering an objection to this latter aspect, Kline asserts:

> Also contradicting the contention that no divine covenants have ever been governed by the works principle is the irrefutable biblical evidence that the Mosaic economy, while an administration of grace on its fundamental level of concern with the eternal salvation of the individual, was at the same time on its temporary, typological kingdom

---

[102] Ibid., 50-1.
[103] Kline, *Kingdom Prologue*, 98.

> level informed by the principle of works. Thus, for example, the apostle Paul in Romans 10:4ff. and Galatians 3:10ff. (cf. Rom. 9:32) contrasts the old order of the law with the gospel order of grace and faith, identifying the old covenant as one of bondage, condemnation, and death (cf. 2 Cor. 3:6-9; Gal. 4:24-26). The old covenant was law, the opposite of grace-faith, and in the postlapsarian world that meant it would turn out to be an administration of condemnation as a consequence of sinful Israel's failure to maintain the necessary meritorious obedience. Had the old typological kingdom been secured by sovereign grace in Christ, Israel would not have lost her national election.[104]

If we carefully observe the substance of Kline's thesis, then we cannot identify Kline with a Lutheran or dispensationalist position because Kline adopts and builds on classic covenant theology in his understanding of the Old Covenant. As we have consistently argued, covenant theology bases individual justification and salvation on the principle of the covenant of grace in Christ in the Mosaic economy. Nevertheless, in a limited sense, the Old Covenant was the *foedus legale* because it entailed the principle of the obedience to the law in the typological or earthly kingdom of Israel as a condition of blessing or curse, ultimately looking forward and upward to the eschatological heavenly blessing or eternal curse. In summary, Kline develops the eschatological kingdom motif of covenant hermeneutics in the administration of the typological kingdom according to the principle of works, as over against the principle of grace by which believers are saved and justified. Most importantly, Kline consistently applies the principle of works at the level of the typological kingdom of Israel without undermining the continuing principle of the covenant of grace operating throughout *heilsgeschichte*. This principle of works looks back to the covenant of works operating in the Garden of Eden. In this regard, the Mosaic Covenant was "also a re-enactment (with necessary adjustment) of mankind's primal probation - and fall." This helps us to understand how Christ, as the true Israel who came under the law, was the second Adam. This also signifies that "the covenant with the first Adam, like the typological Israel re-enactment of it, would have been a covenant of law in the sense of works, the antithesis of the grace-promise-faith principle."[105] Exegeting Romans 5:13b and

---

[104] Ibid., 68.
[105] Ibid., 69.

14b, Kline suggests that the prelapsarian state and the Old Covenant were governed by the principle of works, the former being a covenant of works, while the latter applied works only to the earthly typological kingdom, pointing to the ultimate heavenly eschatological kingdom fulfillment. Because of all of this, Kline stresses that the recognition of the covenant of works in the prelapsarian state in covenant hermeneutics and the application of the principle of works under the Old Covenant are equally important hermeneutical tools.[106]

Covenant theology recognizes *the Christocentric motif* as the unifying principle of the covenant of redemption both in the Old and New Covenant economies, while also recognizing some significant *discontinuity* between the two economies. Kline argues that the form of government administered in the Old Covenant is not "the community polity" which the New Covenant Church has adopted, while the ritual legislation of the Old Covenant is not guidance for the cultic practice of the Church. Furthermore, the conquest program prescribed in the Old Covenant cannot be equated with the evangelistic Church mission in the New Covenant economy.[107]

The administration of "the external typological kingdom" in the Mosaic Covenant was governed by the principle of the law or works, which is the antithesis of "the gospel principle of promise." Precisely this motif is revealed in Deuteronomy which is "the treaty record of the subsequent renewal of the Sinaitic Covenant" before the Israelites entered the promised land. At the highlight of the covenant renewal ceremony, the Israelites confirmed the covenant oath to their covenant Lord in Deuteronomy 29. However, Israel broke this covenant oath soon after they entered the promised land in the days of the judges and the kings. Indeed, the covenant curses which warned against unfaithfulness "in the Deuteronomic treaty" were concretely applied to the Israelites, driving them out of the holy typological kingdom and into exile. Exile from the holy promised land was the result of "a protracted legal process" in which the covenant Lord prosecuted "a covenant lawsuit" against Israel through the prophets. Nevertheless, Israel refused to heed the prophets' messages until they finally were cut off from the place of God's sanctuary and blessing. The administration of an "ancient international treaty" had a similar kind of covenantal legal process in which a suzerain-king prosecuted "his

---

[106] Kline, "Gospel Until the Law," 439.

[107] Kline, *Structure of Biblical Authority*, 99.

lawsuit against rebellious vassals through the agency of special messengers."[108]

Kline does not criticize classical dispensationalism for using the antithesis between Law and Grace. Rather, he criticizes it for applying this antithesis at the level of the means of the eschatological kingdom blessings to contrast the Old and New Covenants. As such, Kline argues that classical dispensational hermeneutics fails to grasp that the principle of works was limited to the typological kingdom under the Old Covenant economy, while the individual's justification and inheritance of the everlasting heavenly kingdom were governed by the principle of grace. As indicated earlier, classical dispensational hermeneutics lacks an *typology* and its *eschatological fulfillment*. As a result, the classical dispensational hermeneutics applies the principle of works even in the dispensation of the future millennial kingdom. Consistent with this, classical dispensationalism has characteristically understood the present church age as the dispensation of grace, seeing it as a *parenthesis* between "the two kingdom dispensations of the law and the millennium." According to Kline, this is fatal because it suggests two antithetical means of eschatological kingdom inheritance and salvation in the fallen world, *law* under the Old Covenant and *grace* under the New Covenant. Thus, classical dispensational hermeneutics mistakenly argues that Israel's promised kingdom in the future millennial dispensation would depend on their meritorious obedience to the requirements of the law "apart from the gospel of grace" in Christ. The major problem of classical dispensational hermeneutics is that it is contradictory to the proclamation of the gospel of Jesus Christ as the only means of eschatological salvation in the fallen world. Precisely, at this point, it stands with Judaism against "Christianity's witness to Jesus as the Christ." As a result, dispensational hermeneutics fails to challenge non-Christian Zionists who appeal to the promises of the Abrahamic Covenant for the right to inherit the earthly kingdom in Palestine without faith in Christ Jesus. "Zionist ideology," however, is a truncated understanding of the kingdom of God - "a land without the temple, an earthly fullness without a heavenly focus."[109]

---

[108] Kline, *Kingdom Prologue*, 74.

[109] Ibid., 229-30. For example, Chafer, in contrast to the covenant theologian Charles Hodge, gives the *impression* that the Jews under the Mosaic Covenant were saved and justified by the principle of obedience to the

law, while believers under the New Covenant are saved by the principle of faith in Christ Jesus. Thus, Christ tells an expert in the law that obedience to the Mosaic law is the means of attaining eternal life, as we read in Luke 10:25-29: "Dr. Charles Hodge states: 'The Scriptures know nothing of any other than two methods of attaining eternal life: the one that which demands perfect obedience, and the other that which demands faith' (Systematic Theology, Vol. II, p.117). That offer of eternal life which depends on obedience is thought by Dr. Hodge and others to be hypothetical and unattainable by anyone, and therefore serves to enforce the fact that there is but one practical way to secure eternal life-by faith alone. There are two important factors often omitted from this discussion: (a) Eternal life, if offered on the ground of obedience at all, is offered only to those who are Israelites, and (b) they had the continuing animal sacrifices which, when faithfully offered, maintained for them a righteous position before God and became the ground of forgiveness for every failure. Because of this forgiveness, the standing of a Jew before God could not have been hypothetical. If any clarity is to be gained as to the difference between Israel's privileges under the Mosaic system and the present privileges of the Church, distinction must be made between the law as a *rule of life* which none were able to keep perfectly, and the law as a *system* which not only set forth the high and holy demands upon personal conduct, but also provided complete divine forgiveness through the sacrifices. The final standing of any Jew before God was not based on law observance alone, but contemplated that Jew in the light of the sacrifices he had presented in his own behalf." Lewis Sperry Chafer, "Dispensationalism," *Bibliotheca Sacra* 93 (1936): 423.

In a similar way, expositing Romans 8:2-8, Chafer nuances the two different ways of inheriting life between the Old and New Covenants: "In this context, the law stands as the representation of the merit system - that divine arrangement which, according to the New testament, is held as the antipodes of God's plan of salvation by grace. Beyond the one truth that both systems are ordained of God for application in such ages as He may elect, they set up contrasts at every point." idem, *Systematic Theology*, 3:343.

When the future millennial kingdom comes, argues Chafer, the Mosaic law will again become the means of governing principle: "The essential elements of a grace administration - faith as the sole basis of acceptance with God, unmerited acceptance through a perfect standing in Christ, the present possession of eternal life, an absolute security from all condemnation, and the enabling power of the indwelling Spirit - are not found in the kingdom administration. On the other hand, it is declared to be the fulfilling of 'the law and the prophets' (Matt. 5:17,18; 7:12), and is seen to be an extension of the Mosaic Law into realms of meritorious obligation which blast and wither as the Mosaic system could never do (Matt. 5:20-48)." Ibid., 416. This future millennial kingdom, argues Chafer, is based upon the promise of the Davidic

Kline also points out that revised dispensational hermeneutics repudiates the concept of two means of salvation, toning down the sharp discontinuity "between the kingdom dispensations on the one side and the parenthetical church age on the other" which had been advocated in classic dispensational hermeneutics. The revisionists classify the earthly Jewish kingdom of the dispensations of the law and the future millennial kingdom "as belonging to the 'salvation' received in Christ by grace" and affirm that the Israelites of the millennium can inherit the redemptive blessings of the Jewish millennial kingdom if they are in Christ Jesus. However, Kline would argue that a Jew who is in Christ Jesus is not a Jew any more, just as a Gentile who is in Christ Jesus is not a Gentile any more. This is because there is no distinction between Jew and Gentile in Christ Jesus, as Paul indicates in Galatians 3:28-29 and Colossians 3:11. As such, we cannot justify the distinction between Jew and Gentile for those who have faith in Christ Jesus under the New Covenant. The concept of Jews who are in Christ Jesus as inheritors of the Jewish millennial kingdom justifies "a continuance

---

Covenant of 2 Samuel 7:18-29 and Psalms 89:20-37, and it is not the heavenly kingdom but the earthly one when Christ returns to the earth. idem, *Dispensationalism*, 434-35; "it will be seen that all that is *demanded* under the law of the kingdom as a condition of blessing, is, under grace, divinely provided ... Under grace, the fruit of the Spirit *is*, which indicates the present possession of the blessing through pure grace; while under the kingdom, the blessing *shall be* to such as merit it by their own works." idem, *Systematic Theology*, 4:219; "A covenant purely of law-works is stated in the passage [Matt. 6:8-15; 7:7-11] in question. Such a covenant is the very foundation of all kingdom teaching; but it is wholly foreign to the teachings of grace ... In this age, God is dealing with men on the ground of His grace as it is in Christ. His dealings with men in the coming age are based on a very different relationship. At that time, the King will rule with a rod of iron. There is no word of the cross, or of grace, in the kingdom teachings." idem, *Systematic Theology*, 4:222.

Accordingly, Chafer concludes that the Old Covenant and the future millennial kingdom are governed by the principle of the law, while the present dispensation is governed by the principle of grace: "Thus it may be concluded that the teachings of the law, the teachings of grace, and the teachings of the kingdom are separate and complete systems of divine rule which are perfectly adapted to the varied conditions in three great dispensations. The teachings of Moses and the teachings of the kingdom are purely legal, while the instructions to the believer of this dispensation are in conformity with pure grace." Ibid., 225.

of the distinction" which Christ Jesus terminated. The author of Hebrews in Hebrews 11 and 12 argues that all those who are in Christ Jesus will inherit the same eschatological heavenly kingdom, and participate in "the one heavenly Zion" which covers all believers throughout *heilsgeschichte*. Scripture does not support the revisionist dispensational position that there will be "a separate salvation-kingdom" for the Jews in a future millennium. Another problem of revised dispensationalism is its abandonment of the correct principle of classical dispensationalism that the principle of works was operating in the Old Covenant economy although the latter applied it in a wrong way. As a result, it too fails to find the balance between *continuity* and *discontinuity*. Revised dispensationalists reject the aspect of *discontinuity* in which the earthly typological kingdom was governed by the principle of works in an effort to maintain redemptive historical continuity with respect to eschatological salvation. This, Kline concludes, is the result of the hermeneutical failure to apply "the type-antitype relationship of the old and new covenants."[110]

---

[110] Kline, *Kingdom Prologue*, 230-31. The editors of *The New Scofield Reference Bible* (1967) try to clarify the means of salvation. They acknowledge that there has always been one way of salvation by grace through faith while still maintaining seven different dispensations, correcting the apparent mistake of *The Scofield Reference Bible* which teaches two ways of salvation, *law and grace*: "Although not all Bible students agree in every detail of the dispensational system presented in this Reference Bible, it is generally recognized that the distinction between law and grace is basic to the understanding of the Scriptures. As a further aid to comprehending the divine economy of ages, a recognition of the dispensations is of highest value, so long as it is clearly understood that throughout all the Scriptures there is only one basis of salvation, i.e. by grace through faith." E. Schuyler English, ed., *The New Scofield Reference Bible* (New York: Oxford University Press, 1967), vii. Expounding Genesis 1:28, the editors emphasize only one way of salvation by grace in different dispensations in the postlapsarian state: "These different dispensations are not separate ways of salvation. During each of them man is reconciled to God in only one way, i.e. by God's grace through the work of Christ that was accomplished on the cross and vindicated in His resurrection ... But salvation has been and will continue to be available to him by God's grace through faith." Ibid., 3.

Ryrie, for example, asserts that in all ages believers have been saved by grace through faith. Nevertheless, he rejects the notion that salvation by grace through faith was based upon *the covenant of grace* because it is anachronistic and reductionistic. In other words, although Ryrie corrects the classic dispensational hermeneutics problem in which two ways of salvation are proposed, he is not ready to accept the covenant hermeneutics idea that in the postlapsarian state salvation has been founded upon the principle of *the covenant of grace*: "Although both dispensational and covenant theologies teach salvation by grace, the way each explains it is entirely different. The dispensationalist sees grace in the context of the tests of the various dispensations, whereas the covenant theologian grounds it in the covenant of grace ... Salvation, according to this [WCF, 7:3], was both provided and mediated through the covenant of grace, which is in effect throughout all ages ... Dispensationalists reply that this covenant of grace is an a priori approach which yields artificial results ... In other words, for them the covenant view point is a historically impossible anachronism ... The primacy of faith in salvation in all ages is agreeable to dispensational and covenant theologians alike. Thus the condition of salvation, by faith, was the same in the Old Testament as today."" Charles C. Ryrie, *The Grace of God* (Chicago: The Moody Bible Institute, 1963; reprint, Moody Press, 1975), 112-13.

Nevertheless, modified dispensationalism makes a sharp distinction between the dispensations of the Mosaic Law, the future millennial kingdom and the present church dispensation, making a radical distinction between Jews and Gentiles despite its recognition of the one way of salvation by grace through faith: "The dispensation of the Mosaic Law, the present dispensation of grace, and the future dispensation of the millennial kingdom. We believe that these are distinct and are not to be intermingled or confused, as they are chronologically successive. We believe that the dispensations are not ways of salvation nor different methods of administering the so-called Covenant of Grace. They are not in themselves dependent on covenant relationships but are ways of life and responsibility to God which test the submission of man to His revealed will during a particular time ... We believe that according to the 'eternal purpose' of God (Eph. 3:11) salvation in the divine reckoning is always 'by grace, through faith,' and rest upon the shed blood of Christ." Dallas Theological Seminary, *Doctrinal Statement* (Dallas: Dallas Theological Seminary, 1952), Article V. "The distinction between Israel and the church" is still the essence of the modified dispensationalism grown from "literal/historical/grammatical interpretation" although it does not exclude the application of "types, illustrations, apocalypses" within the basic structure of literal hermeneutics. Charles C. Ryrie, *Dispensationalism* (Chicago: Moody Bible Institute, 1966; revised and expanded, Moody Press, 1995), 38-41. In this respect, the entire divine program will be culminated "not in eternity but in history, in the millennial kingdom of the Lord Christ," which is "the climax of history and the great goal of God's program for the ages." Ibid., 95.

In doing so, Ryrie provides an innovative critique of covenant hermeneutics, to justify dispensational hermeneutics' seven dispensations. He does not accept the distinction between the covenants of works and grace

Finally, half-way or progressive dispensationalists identify themselves as covenantalists instead of dispensationalists and reject the position of earlier dispensationalists who saw the church age as a parenthesis in redemptive history. They still recognize, however, the Jewish millennial kingdom. To some extent, they recognize that "the typological, first level realization of the promises was provisional and has been replaced by the antitypical realities of the messianic order. Inconsistently, however, they adopt the dispensational hermeneutic in their interpretation of the land promise."[111]

While progressive dispensationalists regard participation in the other promises as "the common experience of all, Jew or Gentile" in the New Covenant church, they separate "the land promise from the others, attributing to it a continuing first level, Palestinian application on into the second level stage of kingdom eschatology in the messianic age." They argue that Jewish Christians will participate in this specific form of land promise-blessing. Kline repudiates half-way dispensational hermeneutics based upon its inconsistent hermeneutics. In the realm of the kingdom of God "the people and the land," Kline suggests, are closely tied together representing "the twin cultural task of filling the earth with people and subduing the kingdom realm as that creational program gets taken up into redemptive history." Therefore, the promises of land and people *must* go together both in

---

developed by covenant hermeneutics because they contradict the distinctive dispensations of dispensational hermeneutics, and because he cannot find those terms in the Bible. In this respect, Ryrie's understanding of the covenant is limited and biblicistic brought about by his literal interpretation. Ibid., 183-95.

To be sure, Ryrie recognizes the theological motifs and concepts of the covenants of works and grace although he refuses to use the terminology: "The ideas and concepts contained in the covenant of works and grace are not unscriptural. But they are ideas that are not systematized, formalized, and stated by Scripture as covenants ... The covenant theologian *never* finds in the Bible the terms *covenant of works* and *covenant of grace* ... The dispensationalist has more inductive evidence for the existence of the specific dispensations than does the covenant theologian for his covenant of works and grace ... What the covenant theologian does to make up for the lack of specific scriptural support for the covenant of works and grace is to project the general idea of covenant in the Bible and the specific covenants (like the covenant with Abraham) into these covenants of works and grace." Ibid., 189-90.

[111] Kline, *Kingdom Prologue*, 231.

the typical stage of the cultural program under the Old Covenant theocratic kingdom and its antitypical stage under the New Covenant. The awkward progressive dispensational combination of "old covenant land and new covenant people" vitiates "the conceptual unity of these two cultural components of the kingdom," ignoring the discontinuity between the typological and antitypical kingdoms. In addition to this, there is another problem; half-way dispensational hermeneutics violates a consistent theme of the Bible that there is no distinction between Jew and Gentile for those who are in Christ Jesus, specifically with respect to the inheritance of the kingdom.[112]

---

[112] Ibid., 231-32. The extensive discussion of a half-way dispensationalism or progressive dispensationalism can be seen in Craig A. Blaising, and Darrell L. Bock, eds., *Dispensationalism, Israel and the Church* (Grand Rapids, Michigan: Zondervan Publishing House, 1992); idem, *Progressive Dispensationalism* (Wheaton, Illinois: A Bridge Point Book, 1993); Robert L. Saucy, *The Case for Progressive Dispensationalism: The Interface Between Dispensational & Non-Dispensational Theology* (Grand Rapids, Michigan: Zondervan Publishing House, 1993). The progressive dispensationalists do not understand the church age to be a parenthesis in the *historia salutis* like the classic and revised dispensationalists. In this regard, the eschatological kingdom which anticipates the millennial and eternal kingdom as the complete fulfillment of the Abrahamic and Davidic Covenants is already present in the church in Christ. In other words, progressive dispensationalists do not make a sharp distinction between the church and kingdom. Blaising, and Bock, *Progressive Dispensationalism*, 49-56.

Accordingly, the future millennial kingdom will be "a worldwide political and religious" kingdom, established on earth and centered in the city of Jerusalem. Ibid., 228-230. The Messianic millennial kingdom will "fulfill and surpass the ideal typology of the Davidic and Solomonic kingdoms." The important thought of progressive dispensationalists is that they understand the eschatological kingdom in the light of the already / not yet through successive historical stages and dispensations. Therefore, in the present eschatological kingdom, the Spirit of God works in Jews and Gentiles without distinction because both of them are "citizens of the kingdom" composing the church. Nevertheless, the future millennial kingdom will be established in the promised land as the final fulfillment of the Abrahamic and Davidic Covenants. Ibid., 278-83.

Walter C. Kaiser, Jr. may belong to this category. He tries to find a mediating hermeneutical position between covenant theology and dispensationalism, identifying it as "Epangelicalism or Promise Theology." Walter C. Kaiser, Jr., "The Eschatological Hermeneutics of 'Epangelicalism':

Having traced out Kline's biblical theological critique of three kinds of dispensational hermeneutics, we need to clarify some confusion concerning Kline's position. Commenting on with Galatians 3:12-21, Silva states that Kline's hermeneutics has affinity with Lutheran or dispensationalist hermeneutics, which we believe is a puzzling thought:

> As is well known, the Reformers' concern with the doctrine of justification by faith alone led some groups to emphasize the differences between the two covenants. The Lutheran tradition in particular has consistently held up the law-grace contrast as one of its most distinctive teachings. From a different perspective, modern dispensationalism too has been zealous to stress the antithesis between the Mosaic administration and the 'age of grace.'
>
> The Reformed tradition, in contrast, has been concerned to minimize the antithetical elements, to assert the coherence of God's gracious provisions in both dispensations, and to stress the continuing validity of God's law for the Christian. Some writers, such as John Murray, have sought to highlight the unity among the various covenants beyond what one finds in the standard Reformed formulations ...
>
> To be sure, one very important strand in the Reformed tradition has sought to guard carefully the distinctions between law and promise.

Promise Theology," *Journal of Evangelical Theological Society* 13 (1970): 91-100.

His hermeneutical approach emphasizes the continuity of redemptive history between the Old and New Covenants which he believes is a solution to the problems of dispensational hermeneutics. On the other hand, the Jewish millennial kingdom fulfillment in the promised land, which distinguishes between Israel and the Church, is his hermeneutical answer in opposition to covenant hermeneutics: "While covenant theology has stressed the continuity of God's redemptive program for the people of God and thereby faithfully exegeted that aspect of the promise which related Abraham's seed to the gospel to be proclaimed to all nations, it has failed to include the other aspect of that eternal promise where that same seed in the nation Israel is the 'pledge,' symbol or 'earnest' of God's presence in man's history and its conclusion. God will conclude history with that same people who were the first to be the 'pledge' of his presence in the complete soteriological and eschatological triumph. On the other hand, dispensationalism stresses the different times, methods, growth and progressive revelation too strongly while legitimately sensing an element of discontinuity between Israel and the Church." Ibid., 98-9.

Meredith G. Kline, for example, focuses on Galatians 3 and states, 'Paul found the difference between two of the Old Testament covenants to be so radical that he felt obliged to defend the thesis that the one did not annul the other (Gal 3:15ff.).'[113]

---

[113] Silva, *Is the Law Against the Promises?* 153-54. We, however, need to clarify Silva's critique from the vantage point of historical theology. As we have observed, the antithesis between Law and Gospel has been a key hermeneutical reference point, depicting the gracious aspect of salvation and justification. In this respect, we cannot label someone as a Lutheran or dispensationalist based upon their application of the hermeneutical tool of the antithesis between Law and Grace. The issue is *how* they apply this antithesis between Law and Grace. As we have observed, Kline has never argued that believers under the Old Covenant were justified and saved by the principle of law, which is the apparent pattern of classical dispensational hermeneutics. Instead, Kline's application of the principle of works in the Old Covenant is operative only at the level of the earthly *typological* kingdom, where individual believers were saved and justified by the principle of the *covenant of grace*.

Having said this, if we regard Kline as dispensationalist, then we must put the whole Reformed covenant tradition into the category of dispensationalism. This is the reason why we have a problem with Silva's analysis: "Over against orthodox Lutheranism and classic dispensationalism, the Reformed tradition has understood clearly that the Pauline critique of the law has reference only to its soteriological function: in this respect it was preparatory, not life-giving. If so, we may argue that Galatians 3– that is, the Pauline passage that most directly addresses the question of covenant continuity–gives no support to recent attempts among Reformed scholars to redefine the relationship between the old and new covenants." Ibid., 166-67; "If my understanding of Paul's argument is correct, the theological implications are significant. Chapter 3 of Galatians has often been used as evidence that Paul saw the law and the promise as opposed to each other. This approach is common in the Lutheran tradition and in other circles (such as dispensationalism) that stress the discontinuity between law and gospel, but it is also found among Reformed theologians. Meredith Kline, for example, appeals to 3:18 in support of the contention that Paul sees a 'radical opposition of the law covenant of Sinai to the principle of inheritance.' In fact, it can be plausibly argued that the very burden of the passage is to deny any such opposition. Kline's reading of Galatians 3 appears to be that *Paul's own view* of the opposition between law and promise raised 'the urgent question' whether the one annulled the other. But here we must inquire into the historical context that called forth the Epistle to the Galatians, since the polemic tone of the passage suggests strongly that Paul is responding to accusations from his Judaizing opponents." idem, *Explorations in Exegetical Method*, 190. A similar charge against Kline is made by Peter Lillback: "An interesting departure from historic Reformed covenant theology is that viewpoint articulated by Meredith G. Kline, *By Oath Consigned* (Grand Rapids: W. B. Eerdmans, 1968), pp. 16-25. Kline in essence accepts the view point of dispensationalism in asserting that there is a fundamental opposition of the covenant made at Sinai with that made with Abraham and renewed by Christ. Hence, Kline articulates the law-gospel distinction as portrayed by Lincoln as the difference between the 'law-covenant' and the 'promise covenant.'" Lillback, "Calvin's Covenantal Response," 198. Again, Lillback's charge against Kline fails to distinguish Kline's hermeneutical difference with classic dispensationalism. Perhaps, this failure rises from the confusion of his own historical theological reading. Once, he properly argued that Calvin together with Luther and Melanchthon maintained the Law and Gospel contrast which influenced Ursinus' development of the *foedus creationis*: "While it is true that Ursinus was long a student of Melanchthon, it is equally certain that Ursinus identified his theology with that of the Reformed. While Melanchthon taught three crucial ideas necessary for the exposition of the covenant of works, namely, the natural law idea of an innate knowledge of the Decalogue, the law / gospel distinction, and the covenant of baptism, nevertheless, it must be remembered that these ideas preceded Melanchthon in Luther and were forcefully maintained by Calvin." idem, "Ursinus' Development," 287. Later, however, he contradicted himself by asserting that Calvin's covenant theology was undergirded by the principle of the Letter and Spirit hermeneutic and so did not use the Law and Gospel distinction: "And precisely because works righteousness can stand with faith righteousness before God at the same time in Calvin's system, he has ceased to use the law / gospel hermeneutic of Luther. This is rather the letter / spirit hermeneutic that grows out of the covenantal system." idem, *Binding of God*, 306. Furthermore, Lillback argues that Calvin did not apply the Law and Gospel distinction even in the doctrine of justification as over against Luther: "This was the explanation that Calvin gave as to how the promises of the law are put into effect by the gospel. In this idea one finds the real difference between Lutheran and Reformed views of good works and justification. Calvin's approach to the covenant was not to consist of a law / gospel distinction in an absolute sense, but rather, in a letter – spirit hermeneutic." Ibid., 339. We, however, in chapter one demonstrated that Calvin's covenantal mutuality and conditionality do not tone down *justification by faith alone* understood in the light of both the Law / Gospel and Letter / Spirit distinctions. In other words, the antithesis between Law and Gospel is a synonymous hermeneutical tool with the Letter and Spirit distinction when Calvin expounds the doctrine of justification. Once again, the issue is *how* to apply the Law and Gospel distinction. Lillback's historical theological misreading led him to conclude that Calvin's understanding of justification stands between Luther and medieval sophists because Calvin's

Our problem with Silva's analysis is that he does not fully elaborate Kline's position. As we have already noticed, Kline has carefully distinguished between his covenantal hermeneutics and dispensational hermeneutics. To be fair, Kline does not apply the principle of law under the Old Covenant economy, understood in the light of the contrast between Law and Grace at the level of individual justification and salvation. This he vigorously objects to as the fundamental hermeneutical problem of classical dispensationalism. To be sure, if our historical theological analysis stands on objective ground, as we have traced in chapters one and two, the Reformed, dispensational and Lutheran traditions have all utilized the antithesis between Law and Gospel to clarify the doctrine of justification *by faith alone* apart from good works. Furthermore, the covenant hermeneutics developed in the Reformed tradition has recognized that the principle of law was operative in the Old Covenant, designating it as the *foedus legale* in a limited sense, and pointing out the *eschatological* motif present in the administration of the earthly nation of Israel in the promised land. Believers under the Old Covenant were saved and justified by the principle of the covenant of grace that continuous throughout the Abrahamic / New Covenants and Old Covenant.

For example, Silva cites Kline's *By Oath Consigned*, 22 to support his critique: "The Sinaitic administration, called 'covenant' in the Old Testament, Paul interpreted as *in itself* a dispensation of the kingdom inheritance quite opposite in principle to inheritance by guaranteed promise: 'For if the inheritance is by law, it is no longer by promise' and 'the law is not of faith; but, he that doeth them shall live in them' (Gal 3:18a, *RSV*, and v. 12, *ARV*; cf. Lev. 18:5)."[114] If we paraphrase this quotation, Galatians 3:12; 18 and Leviticus 18:5 contrast the principles of works and faith and teach that the former was *operative* in the Old Covenant economy. Immediately, we may ask a question: Does this mean that Kline argues that individual salvation and justification under the Old Covenant economy were by the principle of works? Our answer is emphatically No! The immediate literary

---

Letter and Spirit distinction separates him from Luther's Law and Gospel distinction. However, we have already observed that for Calvin the antitheses between Law and Gospel and Letter and Spirit are synonymous hermeneutical categories that he uses to interpret justification *by faith alone* apart from good works. cf. Ibid., 287-339.

[114] Silva, *Is the Law Against the Promises?* 154.

context of Kline's work refutes this contention: "The promise of God to Abraham and his seed (cf. Gen. 13:15; 17:8) was not annulled by the law which came later (Gal. 3:17). The chronological details show that Paul was contrasting the promise covenant not to some general law principle but to the particular historical administration of law mediated through Moses at Sinai after Israel's 430 years in Egypt."[115] In this respect, Kline clarifies his position more clearly on the next page:

> How did the apostle arrive at so radical an assessment of the nature of the Sinaitic Covenant as something opposite to promise and faith, an assessment that might seem to jeopardize his great theme of justification by faith alone? He obviously knew that the demands made by God's covenant upon the individual could be construed in a way consistent with the promise principle. For in the theology of Paul the demands of covenant law both as stipulations and sanctions are met and satisfied for men in their faith-identification with the Christ of promise.[116]

Over all, Kline's hermeneutics is thoroughly based upon covenant hermeneutics. Even John Murray analyzes the Abrahamic Covenant by carefully utilizing the antithesis between Law and Grace to depict its promissory and gracious administration as over against law and to elucidate the doctrine of justification *by faith alone*. To be sure, although Murray emphasizes exclusively the unity of the various covenants, he does not blur the principle of works and law in the prefall "Adamic Administration." Having said this, we need to observe Kline's response to Silva's criticism. Silva's rejection of the principle of works in the Old Covenant economy, argues Kline, fails to grasp the *eschatological* motif derived from the earthly typological kingdom of Israel which was governed by the principle of works and ultimately pointing to the eschatological heavenly kingdom:

> Thus, according to Moisés Silva, the law, though 'leading to life,' could not be and was not in the divine purpose intended to be a 'source of righteousness and life.' To this extent he agrees with classic covenantalism. But because the Murray position followed by Silva so minimizes the significance of the typological stratum as virtually to

---

[115] Kline, *By Oath Consigned*, 22.
[116] Ibid., 23.

reduce the old covenant to the one level of its continuity with other administrations of grace, his suggestion leaves the law principle functioning merely as a hypothetical proposal of salvation by works and in no other way.[117]

Having evaluated the contention that Kline has hermeneutical affinity with dispensationalism, we now proceed to discuss Kline's debate with Daniel P. Fuller. Kline argues that a *radical continuity* between the Old and New Covenant economies, which is the opposite feature of classic dispensational hermeneutics, can be seen in Daniel P. Fuller's hermeneutics as presented in his *The Unity of the Bible* (Zondervan, 1992) and *Gospel and Law: Contrast or Continuum?* (Eerdmans, 1980). According to Kline, Fuller rejects the contrast between the principle of works and grace developed by covenant hermeneutics, and the notion of works "governing Israel's retention of the kingdom in Canaan." The antithetical understanding presented by covenant hermeneutics is in agreement with Pauline theology as seen in Acts 13:39; Romans 5:13-14, 10:5-10; 2 Corinthians 3:6-9 and Galatians 3:11-18, 4:21-26. Covenant theology, Kline states, recognizes that the everlasting salvation of the elect is based on God's grace alone in Christ and covers the *heilsgeschichte* "from the Fall to the Consummation." Therefore, the Old Covenant is included in the overarching covenant of grace. Fuller's radical continuity thesis lacks the proper balance between *discontinuity* and *continuity*. In opposition to Fuller, Kline suggests that covenant hermeneutics reckons that the typological earthly kingdom was governed by the principle of works in the Old Covenant, while Old Covenant believers were saved by the principle of the covenant of grace, as seen in Charles Hodge's theology. Fuller rejects the discontinuity between the Old and New Covenants in respect to the typological earthly kingdom of the Old Covenant in order to emphasize that no works principle is operative in the relationship between God and humankind. Thus he rejects the principle of works in the Old Covenant economy as reckoned by covenant hermeneutics. He logically denies the covenant of works in the original relationship between God and Adam because he claims "a continuum of divine 'grace' throughout all God's dealings with man,

---

[117] Kline, "Gospel Until the Law," 434-35.

pre-Fall as well as redemptive."[118] As a result, Fuller rejects any possibility of "human merit" even in the prelapsarian state. Kline argues that Fuller's proposal fails to resolve a major hermeneutical problem in classic dispensational hermeneutics because he rejects a concrete hermeneutical principle, the antithesis between Law and Grace as carefully applied by covenant hermeneutics, along with the understanding of the Old Covenant in the light of "works-inheritance." Fuller fails to grasp that the principles of works and grace were operative in the Old Covenant economy, which covenant hermeneutics has recognized. In other words, covenant hermeneutics has rightly understood that believers under the Old Covenant attained the everlasting heavenly kingdom by the principle of redemptive grace as under all other redemptive covenants. However, the administration of the typological earthly kingdom was governed "by the principle of works in that the Israelites' compliance with the covenant stipulations was made the ground of tenure with respect to the kingdom blessings."[119]

---

[118] Meredith G. Kline, "Covenant Theology under Attack," *New Horizons* 15/2 (1994): 3. Against Daniel Fuller's hermeneutics in which the antithesis between Law and Grace is nullified, Kline refers to Charles Hodge as an example of covenant hermeneutics, who establishes the principle of works based on Leviticus 18:5 for the administration of the earthly kingdom of Israel: "Besides this evangelical character which unquestionably belongs to the Mosaic covenant, it is presented in two other aspects in the Word of God. First, it was a national covenant with the Hebrew people. In this view the parties were God and the people of Israel; the promise was national security and prosperity; the condition was the obedience of the people as a nation to the Mosaic law; and the mediator was Moses. In this aspect it was a legal covenant. It said, 'Do this and live.' Secondly, it contained, as does also the New Testament, a renewed proclamation of the original covenant of works. It is as true now as in the days of Adam, it always has been and always must be true, that rational creatures who perfectly obey the law of God are blessed in the enjoyment of his favour; and that those who sin are subject to his wrath and curse. Our Lord assured the young man who came to Him for instruction that if he kept the commandments he should live." Hodge, *Systematic Theology*, 2:375.

[119] Kline, "Of Works and Grace," 85-6. According to Fuller, the law given by God on Mount Sinai, as Paul demonstrates in Galatians 3:21-23, was "a law of faith," making the Israelites righteous as does the gospel. In other words, Fuller's systematic destruction of the discontinuity between Law and Gospel makes the path of obedience to the law the road to salvation and

Fuller's revision of covenant hermeneutics by rejection of the antithesis between Law and Gospel unifies "all covenants, not just the old and new redemptive covenants but the preredemptive and redemptive covenants." Fuller's proposal appears to be the most concrete hermeneutical answer to classical dispensational hermeneutics. In the final analysis, however, his *radical revision* fails to correct dispensational hermeneutics because it jeopardizes the doctrine of justification by *faith alone* and introduces a *new legalism*.[120] At this point, Kline identifies himself with traditional covenant hermeneutics, and we believe that he is correct in doing so.

---

justification. In addition, the author of Hebrews in Hebrews 4:2 affirms that there is an ultimate similarity between the law and the gospel: "Paul was necessarily implying that the law itself, both in its content and its thought structure, was as capable of making people righteous as was the gospel ... This comparison of law and gospel necessarily implies that the law presented at Sinai was one of faith, with essentially the same content needed for salvation as the message people received in New Testament times." Fuller, *The Unity of the Bible: Unfolding God's Plan for Humanity* (Grand Rapids, Michigan: Zondervan Publishing House, 1992), 346, 350.

[120] Kline, "Of Works and Grace," 92. To be sure, Murray is *a revisionist* in his understanding of the Old Covenant. Nevertheless, when Kline deals Romans 5:13-14, he does not do justice to Murray by placing him in "the revisionist tradition," or "the Murray tradition" without distinguishing his view for that of Daniel P. Fuller. As we have suggested in chapter two, Murray understands the covenant of grace in the light of the antithesis between Law and Grace. Furthermore, he carefully utilizes the antithesis between Law and Gospel to derive the doctrine of justification by faith alone apart from good works. For this reason, we do not think that it is fair to place Murray, Daniel P. Fuller and others in the common category of *revisionists*. Granted, both explain the Old Covenant economy in the light of continuity with the Abrahamic and New Covenants, explaining the means of eschatological salvation. Fuller, however, unlike Murray, does not explain the covenant of grace in the light of the antithesis between Law and Grace. Furthermore, he does not utilize the antithesis between Law and Gospel to exposit the doctrine of justification, and Kline properly recognizes that this leads him into a new legalism. In this sense, Murray must be separated from others who reject the antithesis between Law and Grace: "My immediate interest here is the intriguing exegetical puzzle posed by this parenthesis, but I am also using it as an entrance into the question of the nature of the old covenant, particularly as debated within the Reformed camp by proponents of classic covenant theology and *the revisionist tradition represented by John Murray* [emphasis mine]. The basic question is obviously of wider evangelical

Opposing Fuller's hermeneutics, Kline suggests that Paul establishes that the principle of works was operative in the Mosaic Covenant economy in respect to the administration of the typological earthly kingdom, but the inheritance of the eternal, heavenly, spiritual kingdom was administered by the principle of grace. Thus the law did not annul the promise of the Abrahamic Covenant or the continuity of the covenant of grace.[121]

---

and indeed ecumenical interest, as witnessed in the burgeoning literature on the Pauline view of the law." idem, "Gospel Until the Law," 433; "Necessary to make sense of Rom 5:13-14 (and thus taught there by clear implication) is the presence of the works principle in the law covenant in contrast to the covenants that preceded and followed it. The rather bizarre explanation of v. 14b that *the Murray tradition* [emphasis mine] finds itself forced into should trigger reappraisals of its rejection of this view of the law and prompt a return to the classic covenantal analysis of the law-gospel contrast mandated by Rom 5:13-14." Ibid., 444.

[121] Kline, "Of Works and Grace," 86. Fuller correctly points out that Calvin developed the contrast between Law and Gospel from the exegesis of the Pauline corpus such as Romans 10:5-8 and Galatians 3:10-12, 15-24, including Leviticus 18:5. However, contrary to Calvin's thought, Fuller argues that there is no contrast between Law and Gospel but a continuum. For example, the Judaizers, argues Fuller, considered the Mosaic Covenant as a "law of works," as Paul demonstrates in Romans 3:27 and 9:32. In this regard, Paul's contrast between the Abrahamic promissory blessing and the law reflects Paul's critique of the Judaizers' misinterpretation of *the law* as a "law of works." When Galatians 3:17-18 is viewed from this perspective, Calvin's analysis that "Paul regarded the Mosaic covenant as something opposite to the gracious promises of the Abrahamic covenant and the gospel," cannot be maintained. Accordingly, the law given to the Israelites was "a law of faith," requiring "obedience that comes from faith" as Paul shows in Romans 1:5. It then produces "works of faith" according to 1 Thessalonians 1:3 and 2 Thessalonians 1:11. Therefore, the conditional promises of the Mosaic Covenant are not different from the Abrahamic covenant promise, but because of the perversion of the heart of Israel, the Judaizers misinterpreted the law of Galatians 3:21 as "a 'law of works' instead of a 'law of faith.'" Furthermore, Romans 10:5-8, argues Fuller, signifies "not a contrast but a continuum between what Paul meant by the righteousness of the law and the righteousness of faith." As such, "the righteousness of the law" that Paul cites from Leviticus 18:5 is the same as "the very righteousness of faith described in Deuteronomy 30:12-14." Finally, the law in Galatians 3:10-12 reflects Paul's critique against the Judaizers' legalistic understanding of the law as the "works of the law." In conclusion, Fuller affirms that there is no antithesis

Against the background of the revisionist tradition, Kline suggests that Paul makes the concrete antithesis between Law and Gospel a decisive hermeneutical tool in Romans 10:5-8. Paul "juxtaposed quotations, both from the Torah: Lev 18:5 as expressive of works, Deut 30:12-14 as proclaimimg the way of faith in Christ." In other words, Paul signifies that it is important to notice that there is an absolute antithesis between the principle of works and faith in reference to eschatological kingdom blessings and justification. In this respect, classical covenant hermeneutics, affirms Kline, has rightly believed that believers under the Old Covenant were saved by the principle of faith in Christ and by the logic of the *continuity* of the covenant of grace, whereas the typological earthly kingdom of Israel was governed by the principle of works. The principle of works proposed in Leviticus 18:5 was indeed *operative* in the Old Covenant economy at the level of the typological kingdom. Some scholars, however, have wrongly suggested that Paul does not conceive of an antithesis between the principle of the law and faith, but it is "a Judaizing misunderstanding that he is opposing." Indeed, Kline argues that Paul opposes "a Judaistic misinterpretation of the law," but what kind of misinterpretation? Not that Judaizers erroneously contended that there was a principle of law operating in the Old Covenant economy, but that they erroneously tried to apply the principle of law in the realm of eternal salvation and justification, failing to restrict it to the administration of the earthly typological kingdom of Israel.[122]

Kline suggests that in Romans 5:13-14 Paul does not provide a pattern of general world history but "the history of the covenant community," selecting Adam and Moses as decisive turning points in redemptive, covenantal history. Furthermore, Paul analyzes "the nature and interrelationships of the covenant promise to Abraham, the law covenant mediated by Moses, and the new covenant with its gospel of justification by faith." In this respect, the parenthesis of Romans 5:13-14 signifies covenant history "from the covenant of creation to the new covenant in the fullness of time." "From Adam" points out that there is "a contrast between the patriarchal/Abrahamic order and the prelapsarian covenant of creation." From this exegetical, biblical

---

between the law and faith/promise as Calvin suggested because the law signifies a "law of faith" according to Exodus 20:6 and Romans 9:32. Fuller, *The Unity of the Bible*, 459-80.

[122] Kline, "Gospel Until the Law," 434.

theological understanding, Kline concludes that "the exegetical demands inherent in the terminus indicators in this passage cannot be satisfied except with the recognition that while grace was the principle of kingdom blessing in the Abrahamic covenant (and new covenant), in the covenant of creation and in the old covenant (at that typological level in terms of which Paul here and elsewhere identifies it) the operating principle was works."[123] Kline suggests that Paul personifies the Old Covenant community "in autobiographical style" using the first person singular, *ego* in Romans 7:7-12, and asserts that there is not relative but radical discontinuity between the Abrahamic and Old Covenants because it is a contrast "between life and death," a motif revealed in Deuteronomy 30:15. This is in a basic agreement with the Pauline argument of Romans 5:13-14.[124]

D. Justification

Kline, as we have already observed, is primarily a biblical covenant theologian who develops the progressive nature of the biblical motif of the kingdom of God in relation to the covenantal theme. Consequently, Kline does not extensively discuss the doctrine of justification as does a systematic theologian like John Murray. Nevertheless, he discusses the important theological theme of the doctrine of justification in relation to the antithesis between Law and Gospel, along with the antithesis between the *foedus operum* and *foedus gratiae*. We will briefly trace out Kline's thought on the doctrine of justification.

1. The antithesis between Law and Gospel in relation to Justification by Faith Alone

Upon confirming the covenant of works based upon biblico-covenantal theology, Kline equates the antithesis between the covenants of works and grace as the hermeneutical reference point as being equivalent to the antithesis between Law and Gospel. This hermeneutic yields the biblical doctrine of justification:

> The principle of works forms the foundation of the gospel of grace. If meritorious works could not be predicated of Jesus Christ as second

---

[123] Ibid., 436-38.
[124] Ibid., 444. cf. Douglas J. Moo, "Israel and Paul in Romans 7:7-12," *New Testament Studies* 32 (1986): 122-35.

Adam, then obviously there would be no meritorious achievement to be imputed to his people as the ground of their justification. The gospel invitation would turn out to be a mirage. We who have believed on Christ would still be under condemnation. The gospel truth, however, is that Christ has performed the one act of righteousness and by this obedience of the one the many are made righteous (Rom. 5:18-19). In his probationary obedience the Redeemer gained the merit which is transferred to the account of the elect. Underlying Christ's mediatorship of a covenant of grace to the salvation of believers is his earthly fulfillment, through meritorious obedience, of his heavenly covenant of works with the Father.[125]

This recognition of the principle of works is required, Kline suggests, to lay the foundation for the principle of the gospel. Thus, the rejection of "the possibility of meritorious works" is subversive to the gospel itself, damaging the biblical principle of saving grace.[126]

Following this comprehensive analysis of the Abrahamic Covenant, Kline confirms that Abraham, referred to in Genesis 15:6, was justified by faith alone excluding good works. Kline explains Abraham's justification in the light of the antithetical hermeneutical principle between works and faith which Paul employs in Romans 4:2-16. For this reason, the human obedience required in the Abrahamic Covenant cannot have a role in justification but is the *evidence* of justifying faith:

> Such indispensability of obedience did not, however, amount to the works principle. For in the Abrahamic Covenant, human obedience, though indispensable, did not function as the meritorious ground of blessing. That ground of the promised blessings was rather the obedience of Christ, in fulfillment of his eternal covenant with the Father. And man's appropriation of salvation's blessing was by faith. Paul took as his text for this point Genesis 15:6, the record of Abraham's faith-Amen to the covenantal promises and the Lord's answering declaration that Abraham was righteous ... This showed that Abraham was not justified by works (Rom. 4:3). If justified on the ground of his own works, Abraham would be able to glory in himself (v.2). He would have earned his reward (v.4). But Abraham had in fact found justification through faith in the promising God, by believing in him who justifies the ungodly (vv.3,5). And because he was justified

---

[125] Kline, *Kingdom Prologue*, 68.
[126] Ibid.

and became heir of the world through faith, it was a matter of grace not works (vv.13,16).[127]

Observing the distinctive character of Genesis 15:6, Kline objects to von Rad's conclusion that the text is a statement of *existential mental occurrence* between Abraham and Yahweh. Von Rad maintains that verse 16 is the result of the revisionist's theological reflection on "old narrative materials," which causes him to insert a theological significance. Contrary to von Rad's *dehistorization* of Genesis 15:6, Kline claims that this verse described "an actual moment in the particular historical episode." Von Rad's psycho - religious dialectical approach which abstracts the passage from historical reality is unacceptable to Kline because it is "too artificial a reconstruction of the course of the inspired recording of the history." Having refuted von Rad's contention, Kline proceeds to disclose that "Genesis 15 is the account of a solemn covenant ritual and an 'Amen' response by the covenant vassal in such ceremonies is attested in the records of both biblical and extra-biblical covenants." Here, Kline asserts that the delocutive verb of הֶאֱמִן indicates that "Abram's Amen" is "a confessional act." Kline goes on to contend:

> Also indicative of the external - procedural rather than internal - psychological level of Genesis 15:6 is the terminology of its second clause. The verb חשב, 'reckon,' is employed for the rendering of decisions in cultic - judicial process (cf. Lev. 7:18; 17:4; Num. 18:27). And the substance of the divine reckoning, 'righteousness,' points to the judicial locution, 'You are in the right.' Thus, in the case of Yahweh's act, too, intimations of an outward occurrence are present in Genesis 15:6 itself.[128]

---

[127] Ibid., 213.

[128] Meredith G. Kline, "Abram's Amen," *Westminster Theological Journal* (1968/69): 1-3. As Kline argues, von Rad rejects Genesis 15:1-6 as historical account and considers it only from psycho - cultic and theological perspectives in which the narrator signifies a concrete existential encounter between Abraham and Yahweh that culminates in an existential-faith *relationship* between the two: "The narrative- which is lacking in events-is essentially built up from forms of discourse which unquestionably derive from the sphere of the cult (God's presentation of himself, the oracle of salvation, the declaration of righteousness). But whether it was the Elohist who composed an Abraham narrative in so unusual a way is very questionable ... The narrator leaves the stargazing man, so to speak, and turns to the reader, to whom he

Kline summarizes that הֶאֱמִן בַּיהוָה of Genesis 15:6 signifies that Abram pronounced "'Amen' in the name of Yahweh." Furthermore, his pronouncement was "primarily a confession of faith" in God's promises, witnessing to God's lordship. Kline goes on to say:

> The covenant servant who offers such a confessional witness in sincerity, not deceitfully, shall receive blessing from Yahweh, even righteousness from the God of his salvation. This judicial consequence comes to expression in the sequel to Abram's 'Amen.' For Genesis 15:6b records the Lord's verdict of justification pronounced in Abram's hearing during the course of the covenant ceremony.[129]

In the final analysis, to view Genesis 15:6 as a theological insertion from the later prophetic period, argues Kline, is a fundamental misreading of the *historical narrative* as an existential occurrence. Through the "delocutive interpretation of הֶאֱמִן in Genesis 15:6" Kline traces out the unfolding nature of the truth of justification by faith alone in progressive biblical revelation. The teaching of Paul and James is compatible with "the confessional nature of justifying faith," since both refer to Genesis 15:6 in their arguments. As such, "the confessional aspect of faith" is Paul's argument against *legalism*, while James corrects the distortion of *antinomianism*. As James indicates in James 2:23, the confessional nature of faith is a "godly

---

communicates theological opinions of great theological compactness, without describing the actual occurrence upon which these opinions are founded, either in the case of Abraham or in the case of Yahweh. When one attempts to comprehend in any way - psychologically, for example - what the narrator designates in sum as perfect 'faith,' the text refuses any concrete possibility. It appears to concern something that cannot be described ... Even though ancient narrative material forms the basis of this paragraph, it can no longer be considered as 'saga' in view of its unusual theological reflectiveness. Its climax in v. 6 almost has the quality of a general theological tenet." Gerhard von Rad, *Genesis: A Commentary*, ed. G. Ernest Wright and others, trans. John H. Marks (Philadelphia: The Westminster Press, 1972), 182-85. At the same time, James Barr rejects the idea that *heemin* has the historical background for the confessional connotation of 'Amen': "Certainly no one is likely to believe that *heemin* in fact developed from the practice of saying 'Amen,' and probably Weiser does not mean this." James Barr, *The Semantics of Biblical Language* (London: Oxford University Press, 1961; reprint, 1967), 179

[129] Kline, "Abram's Amen," 9.

expression which distinguishes it from, for example, the shuddering belief of demons." Nevertheless, the confessional nature of justifying faith cannot blur the absolute antithesis between works and faith in the Pauline discussion of justification by faith alone, as we observe in Romans 4:3,17 and Galatians 3:6. In this respect, the Pauline antithesis between works and faith in the doctrine of justification has "nothing to do with the distinction between inward and outward, between heart and lips (or hands) ... More than that, Paul explicitly correlates believing in the heart and confessing with the lips as twin aspects of saving-justifying faith." Thus, Paul affirms that "the word of faith which he preached was at once on the lips and in the heart," as he shows in Romans 10:5-10.[130]

Paul, affirms Kline, treats "a righteousness of God" (*iustitia Dei*) manifested χωρὶς νόμου(v.21) as the central idea behind the doctrine of justification in Romans 3:21-28. Here, the apostle suggests that "the law" is not just "commandments but a (covenant governed by a) juridical principle antithetical to the grace operating in the gospel." In this respect, Paul continues to argue that justification under the covenant of grace is by faith alone χωρὶς ἔργων νόμου (v.28). In other words, "a righteousness of God" cannot be properly understood without a hermeneutical reference point, namely the antithesis between Law and Grace. Furthermore, Paul, by utilizing the contrast between Law and Grace to interpret the Abrahamic Covenant, concludes that the covenant blessing of justification and eschatological heavenly kingdom was bestowed "not through the law (Οὐ γὰρ διὰ νόμου) but through the righteousness of faith" (Rom. 4:13,14).[131]

2. The Antithesis between Adam and Christ

The covenant of works with Adam involves a very important theological concept in respect to the doctrine of justification. If Adam had obeyed the covenant stipulations successfully, he would have been justified by his Lord. To be sure, Kline indicates that the declaration of *forensic justification* would not have been "an autonomous accomplishment" in the light of the Creator and creature distinction. Adam's justification, however, would have been based upon his obedience to the law. God's declaration of Adam's justification would

---

[130] Ibid., 9-11.
[131] Kline, "Gospel Until the Law," 441.

have been "an act of justice, pure and simple." Thus, Kline does not want to mix Law and Grace in the arena of Adam's justification because Adam's justification was based upon his obedience to the law as over against the principle of grace: "There is absolutely no warrant for introducing the idea of grace into the theological analysis of such an achievement of justification and thereby clouding and indeed contradicting its meritorious character and the works-justice nature of this covenant."[132]

Because of the possible confusion of Law and Grace in respect to Adam's justification, Kline does not want to introduce the concept of grace into the account of the covenant of works. At the same time, he makes a careful distinction between the Creator and creature. Precisely, at this point, we give credit to Kline for his ability to penetrate to the heart of the covenant of works without blurring the Creator and creature distinction. If we introduce and radicalize the concept of grace within the prelapsarian state, the covenant of works, suggests Kline, cannot be maintained "for works is the opposite of grace." Thus, Kline perceives that "God's creational manifestation of goodness was an act of divine love, but not of grace."[133] If we can make a complete parallel and antithesis between the first and second Adams, then the way of justification must be antithetical too. Thus, in the covenant of works, justification would have been secured by works, while in the covenant of grace justification is by grace through faith alone.[134]

Kline maintains that recognizing the prelapsarian principle of works is not a departure from classical covenant theology. Conversely, if we fail to grasp this principle in the covenant of works, we inevitably revise the fundamental theological motif of "federal representative probation and forensic imputation." At this point, Kline suggests that successful completion of probation by a federal representative head (either the first or second Adam) becomes "meritorious ground for justification and inheritance of the consummate kingdom." Their righteousness become the basis for imputing righteousness to others (Rom. 5:18). Furthermore, Kline indicates that we must look at the two Adams from the vantage point of the antithesis between Law and Grace. If we reject Christ's

---

[132] Kline, *Kingdom Prologue*, 69.
[133] Ibid., 71.
[134] Ibid., 72.

"meritorious achievement of active obedience," then we must also abandon the doctrine of justification proclaimed in the historical orthodox Church. The anti-forensic understanding of justification that results from mixing Law and Grace is symptomatic "influence of the theology of Rome and Neo-orthodoxy."[135]

J. Gresham Machen's farewell testimony, affirms Kline, penetrates to the heart of the Gospel: "I'm so thankful for the active obedience of Christ. No hope without it." Christ's active obedience is the fulfillment of the requirements of "the covenant probation." Furthermore, Christ guarantees our forgiveness of sins through "the passive obedience" of his atoning death. The second Adam fulfills the probationary mission of overcoming the power of Satan. God imputes the righteousness of Christ obtained through "the victory of his active obedience in his probationary battle against Satan." Thus, Christ earns "God's promised reward" and merits salvation through one decisive act of righteousness for the elect. This truth is the fruit of the hermeneutics of covenant theology. It grows from the idea of "federal representation" and is based on the antithesis between the first and second Adams.[136]

Kline contends that covenant hermeneutics recognizes the *sharp antithesis* between "the pre-Fall covenant and the subsequent covenant of grace" which Daniel Fuller rejects. Because of the theological problem posed by Fuller's hermeneutic, Kline suggests not using the term *grace* in the original covenant of works because "*grace* is of course the term we use for the principle operative in the gospel that was missing from the pre-Fall covenant." Kline states:

> Properly defined, grace is not merely the bestowal of unmerited blessings, but God's blessing of man in spite of his demerits, in spite of his forfeiture of divine blessings. Clearly, we ought not apply the term *grace* to the pre-Fall situation, for neither the bestowal of blessings on Adam in the very process of creation nor the proposal to grant him additional blessings contemplated him as being in a guilty state of demerit. Yet this is what Fuller and company are driven to do as they argue for a continuum between the pre-Fall and the redemptive covenants. Only by thus using the term *grace* (obviously in a different sense) for the pre-Fall covenant can they becloud the big, plain contrast that actually exists between the two covenants (cf. Rom. 4:4).

---

[135] Ibid.
[136] Kline, "Covenant Theology under Attack," 3.

> Not grace, but simple justice, was the governing principle in the pre-Fall covenant; hence, it is traditionally called the covenant of works.[137]

Kline's effort to keep *grace* out of the covenant of works is intended to strengthen the covenantal hermeneutics' distinction between the *foedus operum* and *foedus gratiae* that successful completion of probation by a federal representative head (either the first or second Adam) would *merit* justification.

Christ the Son of God earned a reward because "there was no grace in the Father's reward to the Son. It was a case of simple justice." Christ was under a covenant of works, and his active and passive obedience (*obedientia activa et obedientia passiva*) were *meritorious.* Kline maintains that the first Adam was a type of the second Adam in respect to the role of federal representative head (Rom. 5:14). This parallelism, argues Kline, reinforces the sharp antithesis between the covenants of works and grace. Thus he concludes:

> Accordingly, the pre-Fall covenant was also a covenant of works, and there, too, Adam would have fully deserved the blessings promised in the covenant, had he obediently performed the duty stipulated in it. Great as the blessings were to which the good Lord committed himself, the granting of them would not have involved a gram of grace. Judged by the stipulated terms of the covenant, they would have been merited in simple justice.[138]

According to Kline, Daniel Fuller's rejection of the antitheses between Law and Gospel,[139] and between the covenants of works and

---

[137] Ibid.

[138] Ibid., 4.

[139] Fuller rejects the antithesis between Law and Gospel expounded by Calvin and derived by classical covenantal hermeneutics from the classic Pauline passages such as Romans 10:5-8 and Galatians 3:10-12. Mixing Law and Gospel together, Fuller inevitably introduces "the obedience of faith" into the arena of the gospel as the condition of salvation: "In light of this conclusion, Calvin can no longer say that Galatians 3:10-12 is, along with Romans 10:5-8, a passage which 'most clearly' affirms an antithesis between the conditional promises of the law and the supposedly unconditional ones of the gospel. To the contrary, Galatians 3:10-12 affirms that the law and the gospel are one and the same, and the antithesis stated in Galatians 3:12 represents the Jewish *mis*representation of the law. We also conclude that the

grace, inevitably obscures the fundamental theological doctrine of "forensic-representative probation and forensic imputation." Biblical theology, Kline affirms, requires us to recognize the first and second Adams' probationary role. The two Adams were representative federal heads of "those they represented, serving as ground for justification and inheritance" of the eschatologically consummated kingdom of God. Federal representation signifies that one act of righteousness is a decisive clue to "the judicial imputation to the many of a specific accomplishment of righteousness by the federal representative." Paul argues that the probationary obedience is the decisive point of contact between the covenants of works and grace, thus he characterizes it as "one act of righteousness" in Romans 5:18. Indeed, the second Adam's "one act of righteousness" includes both active and passive obedience. Christ's righteousness (*iustitia Christi*) is imputed to believers "as their act of righteousness and as their claim on the grant of the kingdom proferred in the kingdom." As such, Kline asserts that without recognizing the antithesis between Law and Grace the biblical doctrine of probation and imputation must be abandoned. Unlike covenant hermeneutics, Fuller argues that "a declaration of justification and the bestowal of the promised eschatological blessings of the covenant in consequence of a successful probation, whether of Adam or of Christ, would not have been a matter of simple justice ... but a matter of grace."[140]

This discrepancy in Fuller's thought, according to Kline, leads to the conclusion that "there would then be no meritorious achievement of active obedience on the part of Christ to be imputed to the elect as the ground of their justification and inheritance of the kingdom." Thus, Christ's active obedience (*obedientia activa Christi*) does not come into focus in Fuller's doctrine of justification, while his passive obedience occupies a prominent position. This results from his unbalanced emphasis on union with Christ in the doctrine of

---

two passages (Galatians 3:10-12 and Romans 10:5-8) indicate that all God's soteric promises are fulfilled on the basis of satisfying the condition which the Scripture calls 'the obedience of faith' (Rom. 1:5; 16:26). Therefore all talk of distinguishing between conditional 'law' promises and unconditional 'gospel' promises will have to cease. We will have to modify Calvin's most fundamental statement of this in *Institutes* III, 2, 29." Fuller, *Gospel and Law*, 103.

[140] Kline, "Of Works and Grace," 90-1.

justification. In this regard, Kline properly suggests that both the motif of union with Christ and the forensic nature of justification, implied from the antithesis between works and grace, must be harmoniously maintained in the doctrine of justification by faith alone, without excluding each other.[141]

---

[141] Ibid., 90-1. Because Fuller rejects the antithesis between Law and Gospel, he argues that faith and works are the instrumental cause of justification, which is a revolt against the Reformation insight that faith resting on Christ's righteousness alone is the instrument of justification. In other words, Fuller's rejection of the antithesis between works and faith inevitably makes him combine works and faith as the instrument of justification, which is a classic example of neo - nomianism: "I find it impossible to abstract Moses' work of faith, consisting in his journeying from Pharaoh's palace to Goshen, from his conviction about the surpassing worth of Christ's eternal treasures, so I would say that Moses was justified by the work, or obedience, of faith. If Robertson were to agree with this, then he could handle the many passages in Scripture in which good works are made the instrumental cause of justification." Daniel P. Fuller, "A Response on the Subjects of Works and Grace," *Presbyterion* 9/1-2 (1983): 79.

Consequently, Fuller makes "the obedience of faith" as the instrument of justification a notion that was vigorously repudiated by the Protestant Reformation. In this respect, Fuller argues that Abraham's justification in Genesis 15:6, which is a classic passage for demonstrating justification by faith alone apart from good works, was actually *by faith and works*. Thus Fuller rejects the proposition that the imputation of Christ's righteousness is sufficient for justification. In other words, he repudiates *the forensic nature of justification*, arguing that the condition of justification is "the obedience of faith" and "persevering faith" : "But Abraham was as completely justified as anyone today (Gen. 15:6). It should, however, also be noted that his justification depended on persevering faith, for Genesis 15:6 is quoted to prove his justification after laughing the laugh of faith that Sarah would conceive Isaac (Rom. 4:22) and after offering up Isaac (James 2:21). That works were involved in these last two acts of faith which led to justification by no means makes justification depend on good works in which men can boast. Rather, these acts of faith were instances of faith producing works complying with God's will." Ibid., 78; "Theses two facts from Abraham's life thus lead to the thesis that *the condition for justification is persevering faith.*" idem, *The Unity of the Bible*, 310. John Piper has popularized Fuller's hermeneutics, rejecting the antithesis between Law and Gospel in the discussion of the doctrines of justification and covenant. See John Piper, *The Justification of God: An Exegetical and Theological Study of Romans 9:1-23* (Grand Rapids, Michigan: Baker Book House, 1983); idem, *Love Your*

Kline argues that Fuller's hermeneutical rejection of the antithesis between the covenants of works and grace in reference to the parallel between the first and second Adams ultimately undermines "the gospel of grace" because the fact that "Adam could not do anything meritorious would apply equally to the case of Jesus, the Second Adam." The biblical parallel between Adam and Christ requires that if Adam could not merit anything, neither could Christ. If Christ's obedience does not have "meritorious value," then the foundation of the gospel collapses. If his active and passive obedience does not have merit, "there is then no justification-glorification for us to receive as a

---

Enemies: Jesus' Love Command in the Synoptic Gospels & the Early Christian Paraenesis (Grand Rapids, Michigan: Baker Book House, 1991). For a comprehensive, critical and excellent analysis of Fuller's doctrines of covenant and justification from the vantage point of covenant hermeneutics, see W. Robert Godfrey's "Back to Basics: A Response to the Robertson-Fuller Dialogue," *Presbyterion* 9/1-2 (1983): 80-4; O. Palmer Robertson, review of *Gospel and Law: Contrast or Continuum*, by Daniel P. Fuller, *Presbyterion* 8 (1982): 84-91. Robertson's critique of Fuller is excellent from the vantage point of covenant hermenutics as far as it goes. Nevertheless, he makes a historical theological mistake when he says, "Covenant theology has maintained consistently a continuum in the relationship between 'law' and 'gospel' for men since the fall. The good news of the gospel is that Christ does it all *for* us as well as *in* us." Ibid., 91.

As we have consistently elaborated in chapters one and two, the covenant hermeneutics expounded in the Reformed tradition has maintained the antithesis between Law and Gospel. The burning issue is *how* to apply this hermeneutical tool in the arenas of biblical and systematic theology. Wilber Wallis is sympathetic to Fuller's revisions of the doctrines of covenant and justification, evaluating them in the light of covenantal and premillennial hermeneutics. His analysis, however, is ambiguous, failing to do justice to covenant hermeneutics: "Fuller's argument that the Abrahamic Covenant is conditional, is acceptable to the covenant theologian, since he understands that the Abrahamic Covenant is simply the gospel offer, conditioned on acceptance by faith ... I regret the lack of theological perspective which leads Fuller to reject what he supposes is covenant theology, because of the supposed legalism of the 'covenant of works.' Let it be understood as a 'covenant of life,' and it can be seen as a gracious covenant ... Fuller, in his able demonstration of the unity of the plan of redemption, and affirmation of *soli deo gloria*, may not be as far from covenant theology as he thinks." Wilber Wallis, review of *Gospel and Law: Contrast or Continuum?*, by Daniel P. Fuller, *Presbyterion* 8 (1982): 81-2.

gift of grace by faith alone." Because Fuller mishandles Christ's active obedience, there is no room "for a divine justice functioning positively in reward of obedience, no room for an accomplishment of righteousness by anybody that might be imputed to somebody else." This misstep inevitably leads to Fuller's mixture of justification and sanctification into a *new legalism* that introduces good works into the realm of the doctrine of justification. At the heart of Fuller's hermeneutical problem is the irony that "a continuum of 'grace' everywhere ends up with no genuine gospel grace anywhere. An approach that starts out by claiming that a works principle operates nowhere ends up with a kind of works principle everywhere."[142] His rejection of the antithesis between Law and Gospel leads him into a new legalism, which is really a relapse from the Reformation to Rome.[143]

Fuller argues that "law as something in polar contrast to gospel has *never* existed in God's kingdom transactions with man." Furthermore, he denies "the Covenant of Works with Adam" as developed in covenant hermeneutics and this rejection leads him to void "the meritorious nature of the work of Christ, the second Adam." Contrary to Fuller's hermeneutics in which the traditional Law and Gospel contrast is rejected, Kline argues that we must employ the antithesis between Law and Gospel to denote the doctrine of justification "in God's covenantal dealings with Adam and Christ." In the prelapsarian state, if the first Adam had accomplished God's covenant stipulations, then he would have been declared righteous by God. Adam's justification would have been on the basis of obedience to the law. The forensic nature of Adam's righteousness signifies that the righteousness of Adam would have been "an act of justice, pure and simple." Kline suggests that the forensic nature of Adam's righteousness rules out the concept of grace because it was based upon the principle of works in contrast to grace. Therefore, the principle of works must be stressed in the pre-fall covenant of works by applying the antithesis between Law and Gospel. According to Kline, Fuller's rejection of the antithesis between Law and Gospel inevitably requires that the second Adam's justification was not based on "the principle of works in contrast to grace," but finds on "the operation of a principle

---

[142] Kline, "Covenant Theology under Attack," 5.
[143] Ibid.

involving some sort of grace – a grace required because of the inadequacy of Christ's works to satisfy the claims of justice." Any inadequacy in Christ's meritorious work devastates the doctrines of the atonement, and justification by faith alone "through the imputation of Christ's righteousness to believers." The repudiation of the antithesis between the covenants of works and grace developed in covenant heremeneutics leads to the conclusion that "the justification of believers under the gospel is also by their works." All of this theological damage comes about from Fuller's rejection of "the justification of the first and second Adams by works."[144]

According to Kline, the biblical understanding of justice states that "if man does good, not evil, in terms of the covenant stipulations, it will be a matter of justice that he receives from God good, not evil, in terms of the covenant's eschatological sanctions." Biblical theology, articulates Kline, identifies "such a covenantal transaction as one of works, not grace." In the light of the goal of God's creation, it is a necessary process that "whom he justified, he also glorified," as Paul makes clear in Romans 8:30. This paradigm is applicable to both the covenants of works and grace. Thus, the antithesis between works and

---

[144] Kline, "Of Works and Grace," 87-9. Fuller's rejection of the antithesis between the *foedus operum* and *gratiae*, elaborated in covenant hermeneutics, inevitably leads him into legalism, ultimately denying the unconditional character of the covenant of grace in which believers are justified by faith alone apart from good works and saved by the principle of *sola gratia* over against the principle of human works. Perhaps it is a logical dilemma when someone refutes a concrete biblical hermeneutical principle, namely the antithesis between the covenants of works and grace along with the discontinuity between Law and Gospel: "So he [Calvin] and his followers, who down to the present advocate what is often called covenant theology, have regarded Adam and Eve as under what is called a 'covenant of works.' According to this system, when Jesus came to earth, he fulfilled the covenant of meritorious works that Adam and Eve broke. Consequently, the gospel by which we are saved is then a 'covenant of grace,' made such by Jesus' having merited it for us by his perfect fulfillment of the covenant of works. Reformed theology declares that the covenant of grace is thus 'unconditional,' though I have yet to find anywhere in Scripture a gospel promise that is unconditional. Sometimes repentance, but always faith, is the explicit condition a person must meet in order to receive the forgiveness of sins made possible by Jesus' finished work in his incarnation and death on the cross." Fuller, *The Unity of the Bible*, 181-82.

grace must be consistently applied to depict the doctrine of justification both in the preredemptive and redemptive covenants. Kline goes on to say:

> If justification is secured on the ground of works and as a matter of simple justice (as in the preredemptive covenant), glorification will not be by grace. And if justification is by grace through faith (as it is under the gospel), glorification will not be by works. Therefore, with respect to God's total dealings with the first Adam and (in the eternal covenant of Father and Son) with the second Adam, the operative principle is works not grace and God's response to obedience is one of justice, no more, no less. To suggest that God's reward might have been something less than was proferred is to suggest that God might have acted unjustly.[145]

3. Justification and Good Works

Against antinomians, Kline argues that faith and obedience are indispensable twin blessings of the saving grace of God and twin fruits of the Holy Spirit. This twin motif was readily apparent in the Abrahamic Covenant. Because of the inevitable connection between faith and obedience, "obedience functions with respect to the acquisition of the promises as a criterion of the validity of confessed faith." In this regard, human obedience is a confirmation of "the genuine faith which appropriates the promised gift of grace." James' argument in James 2:14 emphasizes the importance of obedience in opposition to *antinomianism*. Furthermore, Paul, in condemning the popular notion of *antinomianism* in Romans 6:15-23, teaches that "the believer's obedience" is the evidence that one is "the servant of righteousness and of God."[146]

Accordingly, the good works of the believer function "as a confirmation of saving faith," wonderfully supporting "the grace-promise-faith principle of salvation." The good works performed by believers arise from God's renewing grace and do not jeopardize the guarantee of the eschatological kingdom blessings by the principle of faith as over against the principle of works. In other words, the necessity of obedience to the law in the Christian life does not void the principle of the gospel, namely justification by faith alone excluding good works. In this sense, Kline argues that "attainment of the

---

[145] Kline, "Of Works and Grace," 90.
[146] Kline, *Kingdom Prologue*, 213.

covenant blessings is unthinkable apart from this obedient devotion to covenant law" reflected in the Abrahamic Covenant. In fact, "the acme of the redemptive blessings provided in Christ is the restoration of man, the image of God, to conformity to the glory of such godliness (Rom. 8:29,30; Eph. 2:10)."[147]

In the patriarchal age, "the Spirit as Glory-theophany," states Kline, was not present, nevertheless, the Spirit was working within the heart's of God's people's as the re-creating Spirit. He was working within the patriarchs' hearts to replicate the *imago Dei*. Restoration of "the ethical dimension of the glory-image in man" by the Spirit is one of the theses presented in the Genesis 12-50. This is the difference between "the pre-kingdom age" governed by "re-creation in the divine image" and "the Mosaic age" which shifted to "the dimensions of the physical and the judicial glory." Thus, the Genesis history develops the theme of the progressive sanctification of the patriarchs and of Jacob's covenant family-community. Representatively, Jacob's life shows us that "spiritual conversion and sanctification" were important aspects of God's covenant with his people. Jacob, indeed, experienced a radical conversion "in an arresting 'Damascus road' encounter with the Lord of hosts at Bethel." In this radical experience, Jacob received a new impetus to seek the kingdom by depending on the God of the gracious covenant promises. Through Jacob's family history, we grasp "a premessianic anticipation of the mission of the Spirit of Pentecost."[148]

On the one hand, the inner spiritual transformation of Jacob's family in Genesis 37-50 anticipates the powerful eschatological working of the Spirit in the hearts of the people of God in the New Covenant Church family. Under the New Covenant, this eschatology is realized by the Spirit who recreates the covenant people in the *imago Dei*. On the other hand, the patriarchal age enjoyed a measure of realized eschatology through the blessings of the Spirit. Kline comments: "It was a pre-kingdom age for it was not yet time for the Glory-Spirit-Parousia and the inheritance of the kingdom realm. But the kingdom was already present in the reign of God through the re-creating Spirit within."[149]

---

[147] Ibid., 214.
[148] Ibid., 248-50.
[149] Ibid., 250.

E. Summary

As we have seen, Kline establishes the *covenantal* character of Genesis 1-3 as well as the antithesis between the covenants of works and grace, integrating covenant and kingdom motifs together, while the eschatological kingdom goal is anticipated in this original *covenant of creation*. Thus, the covenant of creation is a crucial hermeneutical reference point in Kline's biblical covenant theology. This covenant is synonymous with the covenant of works long recognized in the covenant theology of the Reformed tradition. Kline also lays out several important motifs in the Bible which verify this classical concept of the covenant of works.

Furthermore, in Kline's federal theology, the fact that man is the *imago Dei* signifies that God's creating act was *a covenant-making process*. As a result, man had a religious covenantal relationship with the Lord in the Garden of Eden, that anticipated the eschatological promises of consummation. Here, obedience to the *law* was the path to the eschatological heavenly blessing; grace was not. In addition, through the Sabbath ordinance, God made a covenantal commitment to man that he would enjoy the consummation of eschatological rest upon his completion of probation. Furthermore, the Sabbath was the sign and seal of God's covenantal lordship over the world. The comprehensive parallel between the first and second Adams, states Kline, implies that Adam was the representative head of the covenant of creation, whereas Christ is the representative head of the covenant of redemption. Kline also asserts that the awesome presence of the Glory-Spirit in Genesis 1:2 is evidence that the creation account was a covenant making process between the Lord and man. Moreover, the presence of the Glory-Spirit in the beginning of the world was a sign of the eschatological kingdom goal of creation. The marriage ordinance instituted in Genesis 2:24 is later described as covenantal in Proverbs 2:17 and Malachi 2:14f. This indicates that the account of creation is covenantal, subservient to the purpose of carrying out the cultural mandate and duties in the Edenic covenantal kingdom. The tree of life of Genesis 2:9 and 3:22 was the sign of the covenantal blessing in which the Lord provided a sign and seal of the eschatological heavenly kingdom blessings. Kline's distinctive contribution to covenant hermeneutics is his extensive development of the original eschatology of the Garden in which man would have entered into a "covenant of peace" or "covenant of confirmation" upon his completion of probation. Man then would have entered a semi-eschatological stage, in which he would have carried out the cultural mandate on a global scale in "the ethical glory of the *imago Dei*" while waiting for the consummation of the eschatological kingdom. Kline also points out that threatened curse in Genesis 2:17 was a covenantal curse. As such, the covenantal curse motif signifies eschatological hell. God comes after the fall to prosecute and signify the covenant lawsuit against the covenant violators in Genesis 3:8. Furthermore, the presence of the Glory-Spirit in Genesis 3:8 indicates that the Edenic judgment based on the covenant lawsuit foreshadows the eschatological judgment to come at the parousia of Christ.

Unlike Murray, Kline conceives the inter-trinitarian counsel *covenantally*. In this respect, the covenant of redemption inaugurated after the fall was founded upon the intra-trinitarian covenant. Accordingly, Kline understands election, creation and redemption in the light of the covenant concept. In a sense, the epilogue of the covenant of works in Genesis 3 was the inauguration of the covenant of redemption. Christ as the Son of Man, contends Kline, undergoes probation as the second Adam to fulfill the covenant of works that was broken by the first Adam. Kline also coins the term "Covenant of Conferment" to describe the blessings of the covenant of redemption that are guaranteed and bestowed on the elect by the second Adam because he fulfilled the covenant of works on their behalf. Furthermore, the covenant of redemption is *antithetical* to the covenant of creation because it bestows God's grace and guarantees the goal of the eschatological heavenly kingdom in the covenant of conferment. By clothing Adam and Eve in Genesis 3:21, God seals the newly inaugurated covenant of redemption. This amounts to a divine pledge in response to Adam's faith-commitment in Genesis 3:20, where he names his wife Eve. Furthermore, Genesis 3:21 points to the sacrificial motif which is required for ratification of the covenant of redemption. Kline also argues that the inauguration of the covenant of redemption is at the same time the beginning of common grace, which provides the historical stage for the drama of divine redemption until the parousia.

The prediluvian Noahic Covenant, according to Kline, belongs to the covenant of redemption because its promise was realized in the history of the flood episode. The divine remembrance of Genesis 8:1 is a good indication that the covenant promise of Genesis 6:18 was fulfilled within the diluvian history. The *kingdom* in the ark was a type of the everlasting heavenly kingdom which had been granted to Noah on the basis of works. Nevertheless, the covenantal grant of a typological kingdom in the ark did not jeopardize the principle of grace in the redemptive covenant because the grant of a typological kingdom was subservient to the purpose of the gospel of grace. Thus Noah's righteousness was the basis of the covenantal grant of a kingdom and served as a type of the work of Christ.

On the other hand, the post-diluvian Noahic Covenant of Genesis 8:20-9:17, according to Kline, was not a redemptive covenant but a common grace covenant. The rainbow was the seal of the covenant and pointed to the *commonness* of the postdiluvian covenant. Furthermore, the idea of the eschatological kingdom is absent from Genesis 8:20-9:27. Thus, the postdiluvian Noahic Covenant was an administration of common grace and sets the stage for a renewal of the *historia salutis* and the covenant of redemption.

The Abrahamic Covenant, asserts Kline, was strictly promissory and not based on the principle of works. In this respect it is antithetical to what came before it (the covenant of creation) and what came after it (the Mosaic Covenant). Kline makes this assertion by utilizing the antithesis between Law and Grace. As a promissory covenant, the Abrahamic anticipated the gospel of grace. Pauline theology requires that we should interpret the promissory aspect of the Abrahamic Covenant in the light of the antithesis between Law and Grace. In the last analysis, the Abrahamic Covenant anticipates the great covenant of conferment, fulfilled and guaranteed by Christ. God himself sealed the covenantal promise with a solemn oath, as seen in Genesis 15:9ff. Paradoxically, eschatological kingdom glory will be realized by the suffering of Abraham's seed. In this respect, the divine oath here points to the atoning work of Jesus at Golgotha. In addition, the divine oath in Genesis 22:15-18 reasserts the promissory aspect of the Abrahamic Covenant as over against the principle of works. Abraham's covenantal obedience in Genesis 22:16-18 has two important aspects. From the vantage point of the *ordo salutis*, his obedience is the evidence of justifying faith. Justification itself is by faith alone apart from good works. From the vantage point of the *historia salutis*, his obedience provided the concrete foundation for the typological kingdom of Israel in the promised land, as we see in Genesis 26:2-5 although Christ's obedience is the concrete foundation for the antitypical eschatological kingdom. The Abrahamic Covenant re-introduces the goal of this eschatological kingdom from the covenant of creation, now under the covenant of redemption. Here, it is crucial to recognize the function of *typology*. The fulfillment of the land promise of the Abrahamic Covenant points to the *antitypical* realization of the eschatological kingdom in Christ. The national election of Israel constituted the theocratic kingdom of Israel in the promised land and was the fulfillment of the Abrahamic Covenant, and the continuation of national election was contingent on the Israelites' obedience to the Lord. Individual election, however, was always governed by the principle of sovereign grace, as seen in the election of Jacob in Romans 9:11-12.

Kline points out that the prophecy of Jeremiah 31:31-34 indicates that the New Covenant is unbreakable. This is possible only because the everlasting kingdom is guaranteed by the principle of grace bestowed in Christ. By way of contrast, the earthly kingdom of Israel was terminated because of Israel's corporate disobedience and the subsequent covenant lawsuit.

According to Kline, *the presence of the Glory-Spirit* in the form of the fiery cloud under the Old Covenant demonstrates its fundamental nature in the *historia salutis*. It signified that the formation of the nation of Israel in Canaan as a *kingdom* was a type of the eternal heavenly kingdom. Furthermore, this theophanic Glory-presence anticipates the ultimate antitypical Messianic judgment at the parousia and the spiritual nature of the fulfillment of the eschatological *kingdom*.

After identifying the nation of Israel under the Sinaitic Covenant as a *typological kingdom*, Kline proceeds to discuss *how* the theocratic kingdom was governed and administered. Kline affirms that individual believers under the Old Covenant were justified and saved on the basis of the covenant of grace, whereas the *continuance* of the typological kingdom of Israel was dependent upon the Israelites' corporate obedience to the law. In this regard, Kline stresses the need to recognize *typology* in order to achieve a comprehensive understanding of the complicated nature of the Old Covenant. The typological kingdom of Israel instituted in the promised land was a recasting of the original covenant of creation with those modifications suitable to the specific requirements of redemptive history in the fallen world. In a limited sense, the *foedus operum* was applied to the nation of Israel in that the typological kingdom was governed according to the principle of works and not grace, that it administered blessing or curse, and ultimately looked forward and upward to the eschatological kingdom blessing or eternal curse. In other words, Kline applies the antithesis between Law and Grace to expound the specific nature of the typological kingdom of Israel, which was governed by the principle of the law. We have argued that Kline's understanding of the typological kingdom of Israel as administered by the principle of works *cannot* be identified with dispensational hermeneutics because he applies the principle of works only at the level of the typological kingdom, while he carefully depicts individual salvation in accordance with the principle of the covenant of grace in Christ under the Old Covenant as well as the New. In other words, Kline consistently applies the principle of works at the level of the typological kingdom without jeopardizing the underlying principle of the covenant of grace for individual justification and salvation. Recognizing the importance of the principle of works in hermeneutics, Kline states that the application of the *foedus operum* in the prelapsarian state and the principle of works under the Sinaitic Covenant are required in biblical hermeneutics. As such, the principle of works as over against grace revealed in Leviticus 18:5 was *operative* and *active* under the Mosaic Covenant, administering the typological kingdom of Israel. As we have already shown in chapter one, the application of the principle of works to the Old Covenant has, among covenant theologians, historically denoted the theocratic kingdom of Israel from the vantage point of *eschatology* and *typology*, but this is lacking in Murray's thought. In this respect, we conclude that Kline's biblical covenant theology reestablishes and advances the further development of classical covenant hermeneutics in the Reformed tradition. Furthermore, Kline is highly critical of *radical revisionists* such as Daniel P. Fuller, who in effect rejects the antithesis between Law and Gospel by seeking to unify all covenants without distinction, including the preredemptive and redemptive covenants. This radical revision, however, fails to correct the dispensational hermeneutical problem, jeopardizes justification by faith alone, and inevitably leads to a new legalism. In the final analysis, Kline's understanding of the Old Covenant maintains the biblical balance between *continuity* and *discontinuity* in accord with classical covenant hermeneutics.

As a biblical covenant theologian, Kline correlates the antithesis between the covenants of works and grace and the antithesis between Law and Grace into the doctrine of justification by *faith alone*. For example, Abraham was justified by faith alone apart from good works, as asserted in Genesis 15:6. Furthermore, Kline applies the antithesis between works and faith as a hermeneutical background to elucidate Abraham's justification as Paul expounds it in Romans 4:2-16. Under the original covenant of works, Kline argues that Adam's eschatological justification would have been based on the principle of works, in compliance with the requirements of the law. Kline does not want to introduce the idea of grace into the original covenant of works in respect to Adam's justification, although he grants that there was divine condescension owing to the distinction between the Creator and creature. Under the covenant of works, justification would have been declared by the principle of works rather than grace, whereas believers are justified by faith alone apart from good works in the covenant of grace in the postlapsarian state. In short, the forensic understanding of justification and the antithesis between Law and Grace stand or fall together. There is *no continuity* between the covenants of works and grace in regard to the means of justification. The Pauline parallelism in Romans 5:12-21 signifies that the first and second Adams, as representative covenantal heads, would merit justification upon the fulfillment of probation. The covenantal or federal representative idea provides the basis for the forensic imputation of Christ's righteousness to those who are in him. Thus, Kline emphasizes that both the doctrines of probation and of imputation cannot be maintained without a consistent recognition of the antithesis Law and Grace as the fundamental hermeneutical principle.

Nevertheless, Kline, in opposition to *antinomianism*, asserts that faith and obedience are inseparable blessings in the economy of grace. The evangelical obedience of believers evinces saving faith and such obedience does not contradict justification by grace through faith alone apart from good works.

In conclusion, we have seen that Kline's biblical covenant theology applies the antithesis between Law and Gospel along with the antithesis between the *foedus operum* and *foedus gratiae* as the key hermeneutical principles for interpreting the *historia salutis* and *ordo salutis*. He urges us to apply the antithesis between Law and Grace and the antithesis between the covenants of works and grace to undergird justification by faith alone and to understand the progressive unfolding of biblical history in terms of covenant and kingdom, applying typology and eschatology. Now we move on to our final chapter to critically assess Murray and Kline with respect to historical and biblical theology.

Chapter Four

CRITICAL ASSESSMENT

As we come to our final chapter, we want to focus our discussion on Murray's and Kline's thought in the specific areas of 1) the reaffirmation of the distinction between the covenants of works and grace, 2) the Mosaic Covenant and 3) the doctrine of justification in the light of the antithesis between Law and Gospel and the antithesis between the *foedus operum* and *foedus gratiae*.

In our assessment, we will see that Murray's revision of covenant theology, in respect to the *foedus operum* and the Mosaic Covenant, fails in general as we have already discussed. His revision, nevertheless, does not mitigate the importance of the doctrine of justification by faith alone apart from evangelical obedience, because he carefully preserves the hermeneutical principle of the antithesis between Law and Gospel in his discussion. Kline, meanwhile, being Murray's student and colleague at Westminster, has the advantage of evaluating Murray's revision of covenant theology. As a result, Kline's biblical covenant theology brings to maturity classic covenant theology while maintaining the validity of the antithesis between the covenants of works and grace.

Both of them, however, agree in the important doctrine of justification by faith alone apart from good works. In doing so, they consistently apply the antithesis between Law and Gospel as a decisive hermeneutical scheme. Moreover, Kline applies the antithesis between the covenants of works and grace to develop justification by faith alone. For these reasons, we will reaffirm that the antithesis between the covenants of works and grace and the antithesis between Law and Gospel are necessary hermeneutical principles in the proper understanding of the *ordo salutis* and *historia salutis*.

A. The Reaffirmation of the Antithesis between the Covenants of Works and Grace: The Adamic Administration versus The Covenant of Creation

Murray defines the divine covenant as a "sovereign administration of grace and promise." His definition of the covenant concept is a distinctive contribution in terms of his emphasis on *divine sovereignty*, eliminating the traditional understanding of the contractual idea which depicts the concept of a mutual agreement or compact between God and man. Nevertheless, his definition is deficient because it only includes *the covenant of grace* within its purview and excludes the covenant of works.[1] Meanwhile, Kline defines the divine covenant much more comprehensively, incorporating covenant and kingdom. In doing so, Kline observes that Murray's exclusively *unilateral*

---

[1] Murray, *The Covenant of Grace*, 31. Edward J. Young brilliantly portrays the necessity of the hermeteutical antithesis between the covenants of works and grace in the adequate exposition of the biblical history in doing biblical theology over against modern blurring of it: "Modern interpretations of the early chapters of Genesis often overlook the fact that God approached man first as an unfallen being, and that He also approached him as a fallen being ... If the historicity of the work of Adam is to be discarded, it follows that the analogy which Paul draws between the work of the first Adam and that of the second Adam has no weight. There is one interpretation only which does justice to the Scriptural data, and that is the one which takes seriously the claims of the Bible that God truly entered into covenant with unfallen Adam, and that He again entered into covenant with fallen Adam. This fact is basic to a proper understanding of all Old Testament revelation." Edward J. Young, *The Study of Old Testament Theology Today* (Westwood, New Jersey: Fleming H. Revell Company, 1959), 68-9. However, inconsistently Young adopts Murray's definition of the covenant which is *exclusively* the reflection of the covenant of grace eliminating the covenant of works: "In Scripture, the language of the covenants which men are wont to make is employed, but a careful study of the Scriptural phenomena makes it clear that the biblical concept of a covenant is not that of a binding compact or agreement among equals. Nor are conditions necessarily laid down in the making of a covenant. My colleague, Professor John Murray, has defined a divine covenant as 'a sovereign administration of grace and of promise. It is not compact or contract or agreement that provides the constitutive or governing idea but that of dispensation in the sense of disposition.' If this definition does justice to the Scriptural data, and I believe that it does, we may expect to find the elements of a covenant present, even when there is no express usage of the word itself. Such is, indeed, so." Ibid., 63.

understanding of the divine covenant is not comprehensive enough even though he properly recognizes "the responsibility of the covenant recipients."[2] Nevertheless, Kline acknowledges Murray's emphasis on *the sovereign aspect* as a distinctive contribution to covenant theology.[3] Thus, Kline defines the divine covenant by adopting Murray's emphasis on *divine sovereignty* even though he modifies it by incorporating it with the kingdom motif: "God's covenant with man may be defined as an administration of God's lordship, consecrating a people to himself under the sanctions of divine law. In more general terms, it is *a sovereign administration of the kingdom of God* [my emphasis]. Covenant administration is kingdom administration."[4]

After a careful evaluation of Murray's and Kline's definition of the covenant, Robertson provides some insight into the concept of the divine covenants, again by emphasizing the significance of divine *sovereignty*. He defines a covenant as a "bond in blood sovereignly administered" which is a mediating view between Murray and Kline. His mediating view tries to incorporate *grace and law* under the rubric of the divine sovereignty because he thinks that Murray emphasizes grace while Kline highlights the law in the definition of covenant.[5] Here, we think that Robertson misreads Murray's and Kline's discussion on the concept of the covenant. Again, Murray's definition of the covenant is controlled by the motif *of the covenant of grace*, whereas Kline's definition embraces the covenants of works and grace and the covenant of common grace incorporated with the kingdom motif. Therefore, if we can establish the important biblico-theological fact that covenant and kingdom are closely interrelated, then the definition of a covenant as a "sovereign administration of the kingdom of God" is the best kind of analysis of the divine covenant in biblical history, and under this definition we may provide a comprehensive analysis of creation, fall and redemption from the perspective of covenant and kingdom.

---

[2] Kline, *By Oath Consigned*, 15.
[3] Ibid., 18: "Though venturing to differ from Prof. John Murray in this regard, I would like to acknowledge with appreciation indebtedness to him for illumination of the things of most import in our relationship to our covenant Lord."
[4] Ibid., 36.
[5] Robertson, "Divine Covenants," 66-70.

In previous chapters, we have already positively evaluated the biblical-theological justification for the covenant of works that is extensively elaborated and developed in the Reformed tradition. For this reason, we will limit our discussion here to those areas contributing to the biblical-theological affirmation of the prelapsarian covenant of works.

According to Murray, the *foedus operum* is not a proper designation for the prelapsarian state of Adam. Thus, it is important to fully unpack Murray's biblical and historical theological rationale for rejecting the covenant of works.

The Adamic administration, argues Murray, is not designated as a covenant by Scripture. Moreover, Hosea 6:7, according to Murray, does not justify a covenantal interpretation for the Adamic administration. Kline himself does not appeal to this passage to justify the prelapsarian covenant of works. We believe it is disputable whether this passage confirms the original covenant of works. Therefore, we do not want to rely on it as *definitive evidence* for the affirming of the *foedus operum*. Scholarly opinions are widely divergent in its interpretation. Some suggest that כְּאָדָם refers to a geographical site while translating it as *in Adam or at Adam*[6]; others

---

[6] For example, RSV translates כְּאָדָם as *at Adam*, giving it a geographical connotation. G. I. Davies provides the reason *why* he interprets כְּאָדָם as a geographical sight: "MT reads 'like Adam' or 'like a man' (cf. Vss.), but the following *there* requires a reference to a place, and it is characteristic of Hosea to specify the places where evils were committed (cf. vv. 8-9, and 5:1) ... Adam was in the Jordan valley (Jos. 3:16), perhaps at Tell ed-Damiye near the modern bridge, which is *on the way to Shechem* from *Gilead* (cf. vv. 8-9)." G. I. Davies, *The New Century Bible Commentary: Hosea* (Grand Rapids, Michigan: Eerdmans Publishing Company, 1992), 171. For the scholars who follow this line of argument, see Francis I. Anderson and David Noel Freedman, *The Anchor Bible: Hosea*, vol. 24 (Garden City, New York: Doubleday & Company, Inc., 1980), 435-7; S. L. Brown, *The Book of Hosea*, Westminster Commentaries (London: Methuen & Co. Ltd., 1932), 6:7; W. J. Dumbrell, *Covenant and Creation: A Theology of Old Testament Covenants* (Nashville, Tennessee: Thomas Nelson Publishers, 1984), 45; David Allan Hubbard, *Hosea: An Introduction & Commentary* (Downers Grove, Illinois / Leicester, England: InterVarsity Press, 1989), 128-9; James Luther Mays, *Hosea: A Commentary* (Philadelphia, Pennsylvania: The Westminster Press, 1969), 100-1; Lloyd J. Ogilvie, *Hosea, Joel, Amos, Obadiah, Jonah*. The Communicator's Commentary. vol. 20 (Dallas, Texas: Word Books Publisher,

interpret it as *like man* or *like mankind*[7]; some read it as *like dirt*[8]; and others read it as *like Adam*[9], which we believe the most suitable

---

1990), 102-3; Hans Walter Wolff, *Hosea*, trans. Gary Stansell & ed. Paul D. Hanson (Philadelphia: Fortress Press, 1974), 121-2.

[7] The Septuagint translates it as ὡς ἄνθρωπος which nuances *like man* or *like mankind*. A similar pattern of translation was adopted by KJV, NKJV and John Calvin, who interprets it *as men*, which indicates that the Israelites *themselves* manifest the sinfulness of mankind by violating the covenant: "'They *as men* [emphasis mine] have transgressed the covenant.' I therefore interpret the words more simply, as meaning, that they showed themselves to be men in violating the covenant. And there is here an implied contrast or comparison between God and the Israelites; as though he said, 'I have in good faith made a covenant with them, when I instituted a fixed worship; but they have been men toward me; there has been in them nothing but levity and inconsistency ... We then see in what sense the Prophet says that they had transgressed the covenant of God as men." Calvin, *Hosea*, 6:7. In his further discussion, Calvin refuses to exposit the Israelites' violation of the covenant in relation to Adam's disobedience toward the law or the covenant: "Others explain the words thus, 'They have transgressed as Adam the covenant.' But the word, Adam, we know, is taken indefinitely for men. This exposition is frigid and diluted, 'They have transgressed as Adam the covenant;' that is, they have followed or imitated the example of their father Adam, who had immediately at the beginning transgressed God's commandment. I do not stop to refute this comment; for we see that it is in itself vapid." Ibid. For further discussion interpreting כְּאָדָם as *like men*, see: Ebenezer Henderson, *The Twelve Minor Prophets*. Thornapple Commentaries (Grand Rapids, Michigan: Baker Book House, 1980), 36-7; Knight, G. A. F., *Hosea: God's Love*, Torch Bible Commentaries (London: SCM Press, 1960), 79-80.

[8] Douglas Stuart, for example, translates כְּאָדָם עָבְרוּ בְרִית as "they have walked on my covenant like it was dirt." Douglas Stuart, *Hosea-Jonah*. vol. 31. Word Biblical Commentary. eds. David A. Hubbard and Glenn W. Barker (Waco, Texas: Word Books Publishers, 1987), 98.

Although Stuart does not relate the Israelites' covenant infidelity to Adam's violation of the *foedus operum*, he correctly recognizes that the Israelites' disobedience to the covenant resulted in covenant lawsuit: "*Adam* is far more likely a variant of אדמה 'dirt' than the E. Jordan city of Adam (Josh. 3:16); עבר probably means 'walk on' rather than the more abstract 'transgress' ... The concern of this statement is not how the covenant was broken 'there at Adam,' but that by treating the covenant 'like dirt,' the nation has betrayed ... Yahweh himself. Here in Hosea בְרִית 'covenant' appears only for the second time. In 2:20 [18] the term denoted the future universal covenant. In the present passage the Mosaic covenant is clearly at issue. Its stipulations were

translation, which recognizes the covenantal context of the prelapsarian state.

Thomas McComisky, who acutely critiques the geographical interpretation, rightly argues that *like Adam* points to the first man who violated the divine covenant established in the Garden of Eden:

> If we understand 'Adam' to refer to the first man, the application of the analogy to the whole nation becomes clear. As Adam violated covenant strictures imposed on him, so the people of Hosea's day had violated the covenant made with them at Sinai. The strictures placed on the man Adam fall into the category of בְּרִית (covenant), even though the term בְּרִית (covenant) does not appear in the context that describes the nature of Adam's probation (Gen. 2:17).[10]

Israel's law; when broken wholesale, the covenant was negated and Israel brought under its curses (cf. 4:1-2; 4:6; 8:12). The people were guilty of treason." Ibid., 111.

[9] Keil and Delitzsch interprets this verse from the vantage point of the *covenantal context* of the prelapsarian state: "כְּאָדָם, not 'after the manner of men,' or 'like ordinary men,' ... but 'like Adam,' who transgressed the commandment of God, that he should not eat of the tree of knowledge. This command was actually a covenant, which God made with him, since the object of it was the preservation of Adam in vital fellowship with the Lord, as was the case with the covenant that God made with Israel." C. F. Keil & F. Delitzsch, *Biblical Commentary on the Old Testament: The Twelve Minor Prophets*, vol. 1 (Edinburgh: T. & T. Clark, 1868), 99-100. For scholars who follow this line of argument, see Henry Cowles, *The Minor Prophets* (New York: D. Appleton and Company, 1867), 6:7; Theo. Laetsch, *The Minor Prophets*. Bible Commentary (Saint Louis, Missouri: Concordia Publishing House, 1956), 60-1; C. Von Orelli, *The Twelve Minor Prophets*. tr. J. S. Banks. (Minneapolis, Minnesota: Klock & Klock Christian Publisher, 1977), 38-9; E. B. Pusey, *The Minor Prophets: A Commentary*, vol. 1 (Grand Rapids, Michigan: Baker Book House, 1979), 6:7.

[10] Thomas Edward McComiskey, *The Minor Prophets: An Exegetical and Expository Commentary: Hosea, Joel, and Amos*. vol. 1 (Grand Rapids, Michigan: Baker Book House, 1992), 95. Although McComiskey understands the prelapsarian state *covenantally* designating it as the covenant of works or the covenant of creation, he fails to interpret the covenant of works in the light of *eschatology* which is rightly developed by covenant theologians, and this is a result of a failure to examine the covenants of works and grace *antithetically*: "An examination of the conditions of the covenant of works in Genesis 2:15-17 shows that the prospect of death, not life, was set before Adam. It says, 'In the day that you eat of it you shall die' (v. 17, RSV). The

Moreover, Wayne Grudem's interpretation of Hosea 6:7 is worthy of citation: "Hosea 6:7, in referring to the sins of Israel, says, 'But *like Adam* they transgressed *the covenant*' (RSV mg.; so NIV, NASB). This passage views Adam as existing in a covenant relationship that

---

conclusion that life was offered to Adam is, at best, an inference. We may understand the condition of the covenant of works, taken at face value, to offer only one thing, that is death–the cessation of the relationship that Adam enjoyed with God ... It was not a covenant of promise, for Adam was not promised life; he was promised death if he disobeyed. Life flowed to Adam from his privilege as a created being, placed in an environment in which he had direct access to God. The viability of that gracious privilege depended on his obedience. *It is difficult to see its promise as the offer of eternal life* [emphasis mine]. We thus may draw the conclusion that God always acted on the basis of grace. Mankind was never offered eternal life solely on the basis of legal obedience. The admixture of law and grace that may result from too formal a structuring of the theological construct called the covenant of works may even impinge on the clarity of the gospel." idem, *The Covenants of Promise: A Theology of the Old Testament Covenants* (Grand Rapids, Michigan: Baker Book House, 1985), 218-9.

Herman Hoeksema provides a similar argument preferring כְּאָדָם as *like Adam* which is an indicative of the covenantal context of Adamic administration: "However, even though the first three chapters of the book of Genesis do not mention the covenant, there can be no doubt that the relation between God and Adam was such a covenant relation. This truth does not have to be based upon a single text, such as Hosea 6:7, although this passage certainly may be quoted with reference to this truth. The Lord in that passage accuses His apostatizing people that they have transgressed the covenant 'like Adam.'" Herman Hoeksema, *Reformed Dogmatics* (Grand Rapids, Michigan: Reformed Free Publishing Association, 1985), 220. Nevertheless, evaluating the classical covenant of works developed in covenant hermeneutics, Hoeksema rejects its *eschatological* direction. This approach results from his failure to interpret *antithetically* the covenants of works and grace, and Adam and Christ: "Many and serious objections may be raised against this rather generally accepted doctrine of the covenant of works. That the relation between God and Adam in the state of righteousness was a covenant relation we readily admit. But that this covenant should be an established agreement between Adam and his Creator, consisting of a condition, a promise, and a penalty, and that it was essentially a means whereby Adam might work himself up to the highest state of eternal life and heavenly glory that is now attained by the believers in Christ, we deny ... Hence, we cannot accept the theory of the covenant of works, but must condemn it as unscriptural." Ibid., 217, 220.

he then transgressed in the Garden of Eden."[11] O. Palmer Robertson, reviewing the different interpretations of Hosea 6:7, provides insightful biblical- theological reasoning that Hosea 6:7 is one of the key passages for a *covenantal* understanding of biblical history prior to the Noahic Covenant: "The more traditional interpretation has seen in the phrase 'like Adam' an explicit reference to the sin of the first man. This interpretation is the most straightforward, and offers the fewest difficulties. As Adam transgressed the covenant arrangement established by creation, so Israel has transgressed the covenant appointed at Sinai."[12] This passage requires more elucidation in relation to the function of the *foedus legale* in the prelapasarian state and Mosaic economy. Adam broke the *foedus legale* or *foedus operum*, which was the condition of *eschatological blessings in the heavenly kingdom*. As a result, Adam and Eve lost access to paradise in the garden of Eden. Later, the Israelites broke the *foedus legale* instituted on Mount Sinai in Exodus 19-24, which was the condition of continued typological national blessings in the promised land even though believers under this economy were saved by the principle of the *foedus gratiae*. This agrees with Hosea 8:1, where God prosecutes the covenant lawsuit against rebellious Israelites *because* they have broken the *foedus legale* which was sworn by their ancestors on Mount Sinai. This lawsuit brought condemnation upon the nation of Israel, which led to the exile, and culminated in the total destruction of the nation in AD 70.

Murray limits the covenant concept to redemptive contexts, defining it as a sovereign administration of divine grace and promise. His covenantal theological logic is biblicistic in that it causes him to overlook the rich biblical-theological evidence for the covenant of works such as man as the *imago Dei*, the Sabbath motif and others as we have already observed in the previous chapters. For example, we do not find the term Trinity in Scripture. Nevertheless, we have rich biblical-theological evidence for the doctrine of the Trinity throughout the Bible. By a similar procedure, covenant hermeneutics has inferred

---

[11] Wayne Grudem, *Systematic Theology: An Introduction to Biblical Doctrine* (Grand Rapids, Michigan: Zondervan Publishing House, 1994), 516.

[12] O. Palmer Robertson, *The Christ of the Covenants* (Phillipsburg, New Jersey: Presbyterian and Reformed Publishing Company, 1980), 22-3.

the covenant of works from biblical-theological evidence in Scripture even though the term is not found in Genesis 1-3. Kline's development of several biblical-theological motifs in the prelapsarian state serves to support and mature covenant hermeneutics' understanding of the covenant of works.

Murray asserts that the term *foedus operum* is not proper since "the elements of grace" were present entering into the prefall Adamic Administration.[13] The term "works," according to Murray, undermines the gracious aspect of the prelapsarian state. Here, Kline's approach is helpful since he eliminates the concept of grace in the prelapsarain state, asserting that God's blessings through his creational acts were "an act of divine love, but not of grace."[14]

The pre-redemptive covenant established by God in Genesis 1-2, was strictly controlled by the administration of law. This provides the logical foundation for Kline to place the law covenant into historical priority. The definition of covenant drawn from the *foedus gratiae* cannot comprehensively embrace the pre-redemptive covenant of law. The covenant of law lays the foundation for the covenant of grace because it is effective through the Mediator's perfect obedience to the covenant of law. This is one of the reasons why Kline broadens his definition of the covenant to embrace the kingdom motif.[15]

Meanwhile, Robertson offers a suggestive criticism concerning Kline's thesis that historical priority lies with the law covenant administered in the prelapsarian state. Robertson writes, "If elements of 'law' and 'promise' are found in each covenantal administration, an effort to establish the priority of a law-type covenant over a promise-type covenant becomes a moot question ... This representation of God's relation to man as being one purely of law appears unconvincing."[16] While Kline suggests that in the prelapsarian state, ultimate eschatological blessings were contingent on obedience to law, he nevertheless recognizes that the elements of grace were present in that economy from the perspective of the distinction between the Creator and creature. However, it is important to notice that Kline later moved away from this formulation and does not use the term *grace* for the prelapsarian state:

---

[13] Murray, *Collected Writings*, 2:49.
[14] Kline, *Kingdom Prologue*, 71.
[15] Kline, *By Oath Consigned*, 29-30.
[16] Robertson, "Divine Covenants," 73.

> Grace, in the specific sense that it effects restoration to the forfeited blessing of God, is of course found only in redemptive revelation. But in another sense grace is present in the pre-redemptive covenant. For the offer of a consummation of man's original beatitude, or rather the entire honor and glory with which God crowned man from the beginning, was *a display of the graciousness and goodness of God* [my emphasis] to this claimless creature of the dust.[17]

Reflecting on the above quotation, Robertson argues that the priority of law cannot be sustained even in the thought of Kline himself since it is a vivid manifestation of the priority of grace/promise over law:

> On such a background, it could be argued that grace was prior to law in the creational relationship. Clearly the whole of man's circumstance arose out of the graciousness of the Creator-God. Man did not have to look forward to the possibility of a state of blessedness; he began his existence in a condition of blessedness. Thus it could be argued that historically grace was prior to law. However, it seems that the whole law/grace or law/promise scheme as presented by Kline is a false one. Law simply cannot be set over against grace or promise. The revelation of God's law to his people represents a most gracious provision. The law of God itself embodies the grace of God.[18]

Robertson's argument misdirects the discussion of law and grace. When Kline prioritizes law over grace in the prelapsarian state, Kline refers to the means of eschatological justification and life. In other words, perfect obedience to law was the condition of eschatological blessing in the prelapsarian state. On the other hand, grace in Christ is the only means of justification and eschatological blessing in the postlapsarian state. This is Kline's reason for viewing law as historically prior to grace, affirming *law and grace* as the historical order covering creation, fall and redemption. If we put this another way, the historical order of *law and grace* becomes clear when we understand it in the light of the antithesis between the covenants of works and grace in which the two the means of justification and salvation are manifested as works and faith. Kline argues that if we validate the covenants of works and grace as the two antithetical means of *ultimate eschatological blessings*, covering creation, fall and

---

[17] Kline, *By Oath Consigned*, 36.
[18] Robertson, "Divine Covenants," 74.

redemption, then the historical order of *law and grace* must be affirmed. In his later writings, Kline, observing the possibility of confusion or misunderstanding in respect to the covenant of works, does not introduce *the concept of grace* into the prelapsarian state in order to safeguard the principle of works over against grace in the covenant of works, while he makes a careful distinction between the Creator and creature. In other words, if the antithesis between the covenants of works and grace is validated in respect to the condition of justification and eschatological blessings, then works and grace are two antithetical means of inheritance of divine blessing:

> Turning directly now to God's covenant with Adam, we can bring out its identity as a covenant of works-justice by concentrating on the subject of justification. If Adam had obediently fulfilled the covenant stipulations, then assuredly he would have been worthy of being declared righteous by his Lord. Though, since he was a creature, his achievement of righteousness would not be an autonomous accomplishment, nevertheless Adam's justification would have been on the grounds of his works and would have been precisely what those good works deserved. It is unthinkable that God might have declared evil what was good. His approbation of Adam as righteous would have been *an act of justice pure and simple* [emphasis mine]. There is *absolutely no warrant for introducing the idea of grace* [emphasis mine] into the theological analysis of such an achievement of justification and thereby clouding and indeed contradicting its meritorious character and the works-justice nature of this covenant.[19]

Kline argues that it is confusing to use the terms *grace* and *unmerited* or *demerit* to describe God's goodness in providing the blessings of creation as well as the eschatological blessing of confirmation in righteousness. He says we must strictly speak in terms of merit when describing the prelapsarian state of the covenant of works. By passing or failing probation, Adam would either *merit* or *demerit* eschatological blessing. Kline infers this from the antithetical parallel between Adam and Christ in which Christ strictly merited eschatological blessing as representative head of covenant. Adam's *demerit* resulted from his failure to pass probation and to *merit* eschatological blessing as representative head of the covenant. *Unmerited*, however, is not an appropriate term to describe

---

[19] Kline, *Kingdom Prologue*, 69.

eschatological blessing under the covenant of works. It is only appropriate to describe the imputation of Christ's merit under the covenant of grace. As a result of Kline's biblical-theological logic, the historical order of *law and grace, the covenants of works and grace, and merit and demerit,* stand or fall together:

> We might speak of this creational act of love as unmerited, but it would be better to avoid that term. It is an abstraction whose use, whether for God's creational goodness or redemptive mercy is liable to considerable theological confusion. In the only situation where merit enters the picture (that is, in connection with human response to divine demand) there is either merit or demerit. In this situation of accountable response to covenant duty obedience brings merit and failure to perform the probationary task incurs demerit. There is either merit or demerit, but no 'unmerit.' Unmerited is not, therefore, a proper description of the blessings bestowed against an historical background of (unsatisfactory) exercise of covenant responsibility. And to speak of the goodness of God shown in the act of creation as unmerited is not apropos since there can be no thought of merit at all in that context.[20]

Accordingly, Kline expresses God's goodness in his creation as "an act of divine love" and avoids the term grace: "We will perceive that God's creational manifestation of goodness was an act of divine love, but not of grace. And we have seen that the presence of paternal love in a covenantal arrangement is no impediment to its being a covenant of works."[21] The principle of works is an important window for a proper understanding of the role of the first and second Adams, who stood as the representative covenantal heads:

> The function of probationer that Christ assumed as the true Israel-Servant was more basically his in terms of his identity as second Adam (Rom. 5:14; 1 Cor. 15:45-47). The covenant with the first Adam was a works-probation arrangement. Hence, for the Son to covenant with the

---

[20] Ibid., 70.

[21] Ibid., 71. Since the condition of eschatological blessing in the covenant of works was *works as over against grace*, Kline uses the term divine love in stead of the term grace in the preredemptive covenant because the former does not obscure the principle of works: "Bestowal of the reward contemplated in the Covenant of Creation was a matter of works; it was an aspect of God's creational love, but it was not a matter of grace." Ibid., 72

Father to become a second Adam means he must win the promised messianic exaltation (which he shares with his own) as the reward for a victory of obedience in a probationary mission.[22]

Kline's biblical-theological reasoning requires that if we introduce the element or concept of *grace* into the original covenant of works, we make it impossible for Adam to have ever merited eschatological blessing, and the antithetical parallel between Adam and Christ, requires us to conclude that it was also impossible for Christ to have ever merited eschatological blessing for his own. But the core of the intratrinitarian covenant was the Son's purpose to merit this blessing by perfectly obeying the broken covenant of works. For this reason, Christ is the mediator of the covenant of grace:

> As advertised by his birth under the Torah covenant of works (Gal. 4:4), Christ came to earth as one under the intratrinitarian covenant of works. It was by fulfilling the probation of that supernal works covenant that he became the mediator of the Covenant of Grace, the covenant in which his people become by faith joint-heirs with their Lord of the eternal kingdom of glory. Law is thus foundational to gospel; gospel-grace honors the demands of divine justice as definitively expressed in law covenant.[23]

Once again, the principle of works was the door into the eschatological kingdom and its blessings in the original covenant of works; whereas the principle of faith is the only door into that kingdom and its blessings in the covenant of grace. Although God manifests divine goodness to his creatures in the prelapsarian covenant of works, Kline does not see this covenant as *gracious*. He believes that as soon as we employ the idea of grace in that administration, we obscure or confuse the real quality of the covenant of works. We see this as Kline's *contribution* to covenant hermeneutics. He reaffirms and strengthens the antithesis between the covenants of works and grace, while carefully qualifying divine justice and merit in the prelapsarian state:

> Though the covenant produced by creation displayed God's goodness and love, it was not a grace transaction, for none of its benefits, whether original or proferred, had been or would have been bestowed

---

[22] Kline, "Exaltation of Christ," 27.
[23] Ibid., 27-28.

on people who had forfeited them by sin. The divine benevolence *complemented* the principle of simple justice governing this works covenant; it did *not qualify* that justice.[24]

According to Kline,, the concept of grace in the prelapsarian state may cause damage to the real meaning of the covenant of works, the concept of merit, and divine justice, which are all closely related to each other. In other words, the antithesis between the covenants of works and grace, the contrast between Law and Gospel, and the historical order of *law and grace* are *coterminous*, and stand or fall together:

> It is God's covenantal word that defines divine justice. Analysis of God's covenant with Adam has been plagued with a tendency to judge the terms stipulated in this covenant by some extraneous standard and to pronounce the value of the award offered disproportionate to the value of the service. Thereby any 'merit' still attributed to the performance of the stipulated duty in this arrangement (confusingly dubbed 'gracious') is radically qualified, the law-gospel contrast is changed into a continuum, the absoluteness of God's justice is relativized, and the foundation of the gospel is destroyed.[25]

Although Robertson is confused in respect to the historical priority of *law and grace*, he affirms the antithesis between the covenants of works and grace. Thus, we would argue that Robertson's rejection of the historical order of *law and grace* is simply an inconsistency in his thought.[26] Here is some evidence that Robertson views the covenants of works and grace *antithetically*:

---

[24] Ibid., 27.

[25] Ibid.

[26] Robertson, "Divine Covenants," 74-5. Robertson properly affirms faith as the means of justification in the covenant of grace. He recognizes the absolute antithesis between works and faith in the discussion of justification in the fallen world. We suggest that since Robertson uses the antithesis between works and faith as a hermeneutical tool to demonstrate justification by faith alone and he recognizes the antithesis between the covenants of works and grace, then the historical order of *law and grace* must be valid. This is why we argue that Robertson is inconsistent: "Faith must be registered for actual participation in the ultimate benefits of Christ's righteousness. In this connection, 'faith' must be understood as generically opposed to 'works,' representing the abandonment of personal law-keeping as a way to

Man as graciously created possessed broad obligations in relation to the creation as well as specific obligations respecting the test of probation. A legal relationship was involved, as Kline indicates. But the whole was conceived graciously, as Kline affirms ... Every man, since the fall, stands condemned under the obligations of the creation covenant. Yet he is maintained in life by the grace of God.[27]

As Robertson properly recognizes, Adam's probation was based on "a legal relationship;" eschatological blessings were contingent on perfect obedience. Because of this, Kline urges that law or works was the governing principle of the covenant of creation. Therefore, Robertson's statement that "the whole was conceived graciously, as Kline also affirms" does not do justice to Kline's position. Kline would argue that the governing motif in the covenant of creation was law as over against grace. Robertson continues:

'Before the foundation of the world' Christ was offered in the purposes of God to fulfill the requirements of the law for his people. This legal fulfillment may be understood in the context of God's unmerited favor toward undeserving sinners. In fulfillment of covenantal promises, Christ was born under the law 'in the fullness of time' as the son of David according to the flesh. By his life and death he fulfilled graciously the demands of God's law for his people. Kline has indicated appropriately the role of law in the covenant at this point.[28]

If the second Adam fulfilled the requirement of the law that was broken by the first Adam, as Robertson properly indicates, then he validates the antithesis between the covenants of works and grace in his thought. For this reason we urge the recognition of the historical order of *law and grace* instead of *grace and law* in order to reaffirm the antithesis between Law and Gospel.

Meanwhile, Murray affirms that the principle of "works-righteousness" as over against faith-righteousness was operative in the prelapsarian state. This is echoed in Leviticus 18:5. In doing so, he

---

righteousness. Faith should not be understood as a basis on which righteousness is achieved, but as a means by which righteousness is achieved. In the strictest sense, 'faith' should not be described as a 'requirement' for righteousness, but as a 'channel' to righteousness." Ibid., 75.

[27] Ibid., 74-5.
[28] Ibid., 75.

admits that "perfect righteousness" was the condition of *eschatological justification and life* in the prefall Adamic administration but he does not consider this obedience to be *meritorious*.[29] According to his theological reasoning, the 'Do this and you will live' of Leviticus 18:5; Romans 10:5 and Galatians 3:12 was not based upon "justice," but "God's faithfulness":

> In connection with the promise of life it does not appear justifiable to appeal, as frequently has been done, to the principle enunciated in certain texts (cf. Lev. 18:5; Rom. 10:5; Gal. 3:12), 'This do and thou shalt live.' The principle asserted in these texts is the principle of equity that righteousness is always followed by the corresponding award. From the promise of the Adamic administration we must dissociate all notions of meritorious reward.[30]

The Pauline antithetical parallel between Adam and Christ, according to Murray, is a concrete milieu in which to show that both Adam and Christ stood as representative heads (1 Cor. 15:22, 44-49). Thus Christ's obedience became the firm foundation of the believer's "righteousness, justification, and life." In a similar way, Adam's obedience would have been a foundation of "eternal life for all represented by him."[31]

Therefore, we believe that Murray's understanding of the Adamic administration fits into the historical order as *law and grace*. He argues that the basis of eschatological justification and blessing in the prelapsarian state was the perfect obedience of Adam, while Christ's perfect obedience is the basis for the believers' justification and eschatological life in the postlapsarian state. The fact that Murray applies this traditional hermeneutical tool of covenant theology to his own understanding of the eschatological goal of the Adamic administration indicates that his theology is compatible with the antithesis between the covenants of works and grace: "He [Adam] might pass from the status of contingency to one of confirmed and indefectible holiness and blessedness, that is, from *posse peccare* and *posse non peccare* to *non posse peccare*."[32] To be sure, Murray rejects

---

[29] Murray, *Romans*, II:249-50.
[30] Murray, *Collected Writings*, 2:55-6.
[31] Ibid., 2:49.
[32] Ibid.

the *foedus operum* in respect to the Adamic administration. Nevertheless, he uses covenantal language in regard to man's original relationship to God, saying that "between man and God there is *the ethico-religious bond* [emphasis mine], a relationship not hinted in the case of the other creatures. For man there is the cultural mandate (cf. Gen. 1:28) co-ordinated with the dominion bestowed upon him."[33] This religious bond culminated in an intensive period of probation which was patterned and shaped by the law, as revealed in Genesis 2:15-17. The probation tree, according to Murray, was law: "The purpose of law in man's original state was not to give occasion to sin but to direct and regulate man's life in the path of righteousness and, therefore, to guard and promote life."[34] Furthermore, the eschatological blessings of the Adamic administration, argues Murray, were contingent upon Adam's obedience, which he calls a "perfect legal reciprocity," a notion which is analogous to *merit*.[35]

The distortion of existentialist hermeneutics, as represented by Rudolf Bultmann, rejects the historical order of *law and gospel*. Murray's criticism proves our thesis that Murray affirms the historical order of *law and grace*: "There is the basic fallacy that men apart from the conviction created and conditioned by law and gospel are able to know what their real situation and need are."[36] In addition, Murray asserts that the definition of the law must be understood in the light of "the transgression of the law." Adam's sin resulted from the violation of the law. Murray writes, "If sin is the transgression of the law, righteousness must be conformity to the law."[37] As such, Adam's original sin was a violation of "expressly revealed law." In other words, "Adam's trespass was disobedience to expressly revealed commandment."[38] Thus far, we have seen that even though Murray disapproves the term *foedus operum* in respect to eschatological justification and blessings in the prelapsarian state, he affirms that perfect obedience to the law was the means of eschatological blessings in that state. For this reason, we reaffirm that Murray's theology is

---

[33] Ibid., 2:10.
[34] Murray, *Romans*, 7:10.
[35] Murray, *Collected Writings*, 2:47
[36] Ibid., 1:294.
[37] Murray, *Principle of Conduct*, 191.
[38] Murray, *Romans*, 5:13-14; 20-21.

fully compatible with the antithesis between the covenants of works and grace as developed in the Reformed tradition.

Kline critiques Murray's idea of "a promise of grace" in respect to the eschatological blessings of the Adamic administration, since he believes that it manifests an inconsistency and creates confusion:

> In one variation of the attack on the Covenant of Works formulation (cf. especially John Murray), a beginning (creational) stage governed by justice (conceived of as a legal reciprocity or balance of benefits) is isolated from a second (covenantal) stage, introduced by God's promises to Adam of eschatological rewards for obedience ... Then on the basis of a definition of justice as an equal balancing of such values it is concluded that since the reward would exceed all claims of equity, the governmental principle in this covenantal stage is no longer justice but grace.[39]

To validate the *foedus operum* in the prelapsarian state, Kline says we must affirm its forensic nature, otherwise we confuse the ideas of divine justice and grace and blur the distinction between the covenants of works and grace:

> To its credit this view [John Murray's] does recognize (though only abstractly) the legitimacy of the works principle in the religious relationship. But in its rejection of that principle from the second stage it too indulges in arbitrary, speculative concepts of justice and grace. If justice is to occupy the place given to it in Scripture, then, like grace, it must be defined in the forensic context of covenantal commitments. When that is done it will be recognized that reception of the promised reward by an obedient Adam would have been a matter of works-justice and not at all of grace.[40]

In other words, Kline insists that we must consistently use the language of justice and works in opposition to the language of grace and faith or we can no longer meaningfully speak of the two as antithetical paths to eschatological justification and blessing. Justice and works belong to the covenant of works, while grace and faith belong to the covenant of grace. Thus Kline says, "If our concepts of justice and grace are biblical we will not attribute the promised reward

---

[39] Kline, *Kingdom Prologue*, 71
[40] Ibid.

of the creation covenant to divine grace. We will rather regard it as a just recompense to a meritorious servant, for justice requires that man receive the promised good in return for his doing the demanded good."[41]

Although Murray recognizes Adam's perfect obedience as the means of eschatological justification and blessing in the prelapsarian state, he rejects its meritorious ground since he believes that the eschatological blessings would have been "a promise of grace": "From the promise of the Adamic administration we must dissociate all notions of meritorious reward. The promise of confirmed integrity and blessedness was one annexed to an obedience that Adam owed and, therefore, was a promise of grace."[42] In this argument, Murray highlights the theocentric aspect of the Adamic administration. Because of the distinction between the Creator and creature, he concludes that there was no merit in Adam's obedience. Adam was a mere creature, and meritorious obedience, according to the definition of Murray, is limited to Christ alone. Here we differ with Murray; we apply the concept of merit to both Adam and Christ. Murray continues, "All that Adam could have claimed on the basis of equity was justification and life as long as he perfectly obeyed, but not confirmation so as to insure indefectibility. Adam could claim the fulfillment of the promise if he stood the probation, but only on the basis of God's faithfulness, not on the basis of justice. God is debtor to his own faithfulness."[43] Although Adam's perfect obedience was a *means* of eschatological justification and life in the Adamic administration, Murray argues that it was bestowed on the *basis* of divine faithfulness, "not on the basis of justice." By disconnecting the concept of divine justice from Adam's eschatological blessing, Murray excludes the idea of merit from it.

Arthur Davies provides a puzzling comment on *grace* after reading Charles Wingard's *The Doctrines of Grace*.[44] His brief comment is worthy of citation because he supports his thought from his own understanding of Murray's notions of covenant and grace:

---

[41] Ibid.
[42] Murray, *Collected Writings*, 2:56.
[43] Ibid.
[44] Charles Wingard, "The Doctrines of Grace," *New Horizons* 18/5 (1997): 6-9. In this short article, Wingard basically expounds the so called five points of Calvinism incorporating with it, the concept of divine grace.

> The all-encompassing theme of Scripture is the sovereign grace of God. The May issue, on "The Doctrines of Grace," affirms that Reformed teaching. The relationship of God as Creator to us, his creatures, was from the beginning and always is purely a matter of grace. We cannot earn or merit what God alone can and does give, namely, life itself.
>
> That relationship between Creator and creature is called covenant in Scripture. The covenant of grace is the unifying theme from Genesis to Revelation. John Murray stresses the importance of seeing covenant as a gracious relationship, not a compact between God and man ("Covenant," *New Bible Dictionary*, Eerdmans, 1962).
>
> In his innocent state, Adam realized, just as we do, that he was completely dependent on his Creator. But he refused to submit to that gracious dispensation of God. He forfeited the promised blessing.[45]

According to Davies' understanding of Reformed theology, it "always is purely a matter of grace." Here he rejects the historical order of *law and grace* and the antithesis between the covenants of works and grace, and he radicalizes the prelapsarian state as a "gracious dispensation of God." In other words, Davies not only misrepresents Reformed theology, but also misreads Murray's theology. As we have consistently argued, Reformed theology affirms the historical order of *law and grace* although divine graciousness or benevolence was involved in the light of the distinction between the Creator and creature in the prelapsarian state, and the antithesis between the covenants of works and grace is another way to recognize the antithesis between Law and Gospel.

To the contrary, Davies argues that "the covenant of grace is the unifying theme from Genesis to Revelation." To be sure, Murray's covenant of grace begins from the prediluvian Noahic Covenant, but his Adamic administration recognizes *the stability of law* in the prelapsarian state and defines the concept of grace in the light of the distinction between the Creator and creature. Mark Karlberg responds to Arthur Davies' comment:

> In the August/September issue, Arthur Davies, responding to the May issue on 'The Doctrine of Grace,' denies the historic doctrine of the covenant of works when he asserts: 'The relationship of God as Creator to us, his creatures, was from the beginning and always is

---

[45] Arthur Davies, "Grace," *New Horizons* 18/8 (1997): 22-3.

purely a matter of grace. We cannot earn or merit what God alone can and does give, namely, life itself.'

Let's be clear: this was not the view of John Murray. Whatever the peculiarities of his interpretation of the covenants, Murray passionately upheld the classic Protestant antithesis between law and gospel, defining the former in terms of the principle of 'perfect legal reciprocity,' that is, 'merit.' Of course, traditional Reformed theology is not suggesting that man is an autonomous creature who can place demands upon our sovereign, righteous God. But denial of the legal requirement originally laid upon Adam as our federal head compromises the truth concerning the gospel of saving grace, justification by faith apart from the works of the law.[46]

We believe that in general Murray would agree with Karlberg's criticism of Arthur Davies' understanding of his view on covenant and grace. From the broader scope of Murray's theology, we can argue that he recognizes the condition of the Adamic administration as perfect obedience to the law, which forms one half of the antithesis between Law and Gospel. Because our definition of merit requires perfect obedience, it is safe to say that Murray's concept of "perfect legal reciprocity" is equivalent to *merit*.

R. C. Sproul maintains the antithesis between the covenants of works and grace in his discussion of covenant theology.[47] He,

---

[46] Mark W. Karlberg, "Works and Grace," *New Horizons* 18/9 (1997): 23.

[47] R. C. Sproul, *Grace Unknown: The Heart of Reformed Theology* (Grand Rapids, Michigan: Baker Book House, 1997), 109-14. In his discussion of covenant theology, Sproul makes a careful distinction between the covenants of works and grace. In doing so, he notices that the condition of the *foedus operum* was perfect obedience as the means of attaining eschatological heavenly blessings, while the perfect obedience of Christ in respect to the broken covenant of works provides the foundation of the *foedus gratiae*. From this theological analysis, Sproul defends the essence of the gospel, namely justification by faith alone: "The condition [of the covenant of works] is personal and perfect obedience. This is a condition of works, and this is the covenant's chief stipulation. Life is promised as a reward for obedience, for satisfying the condition of the covenant ... Law is given at the beginning, and obedience to its functions as a stipulation for covenant blessing ... Though the gracious doctrine of justification by faith is the essence of the gospel, we ought not forget that our salvation is ultimately accomplished by the fulfillment of the covenant of works. This is achieved by the second Adam, Christ himself, who by his perfect and personal obedience fulfills the

nevertheless, emphasizes inconsistently the concept of grace, understood in the light of the distinction between the Creator and creature in the prelapsarian state. Once again, this confusion weakens the antithesis between the covenants of works and grace by introducing divine grace into the arena of the covenant of works:

> The names of the two covenants, one of works and one of grace, may be misleading. The names may give the idea that the original covenant lacks any element of grace. That God creates us and gives us the gift of life is already an act of grace. God was under no obligation to create anyone. Once created, we had no claim on God to enter into a covenant with us. God's promise of life on the condition of obedience has its origin in his grace. Even in the covenant of works the reward promised for obedience is *de pactio*. The reward is given, not because the works themselves, due to their intrinsic value, impose an obligation on God to reward them, but because God in his grace offered such a reward as part of an agreement. Theoretically God could have justly and righteously imposed an obligation on his creatures to obey his law without any promise of reward whatsoever. It is the creature's intrinsic duty to obey his Creator, with or without the prospect of reward.[48]

The *Westminster Statement on Justification*, published on May 27, 1980 provides for the meritorious ground of the covenant of works while also recognizing a distinction between the Creator and creature which it calls "God's gracious goodness," and which promises everlasting heavenly blessing. The meritorious ground of the covenant of works is pertinent since it is the result of a careful exposition of the antithesis between the covenants of works and grace. While the magnitude of the promised reward dwarfs the condition for receiving it, the condition, if fulfilled, is meritorious, and is rewarded by divine justice. In other words, the statement correctly urges divine justice and the concept of merit in the original covenant of works:

> That covenant has been called the covenant of works. God promised eternal blessedness upon condition of a limited period of obedience; he threatened death for disobedience. Although *God's gracious goodness* [emphasis mine] can be seen in the disproportion between the limited requirements of the covenant of works. What is so gracious about the covenant of grace is that God accepts Christ's obedience to the covenant of works in our place." Ibid., 109,113.

[48] Ibid., 111.

requirement and the eternal reward, the covenant required the obedience of faith as its condition. By that obedience *the promised reward could be claimed as merited* [emphasis mine].[49]

G. C. Berkouwer rejects the historical order of *law and grace*, emphasizing divine love and communion in the prelapsarian state. In doing so, he even denies the antithesis between the covenants of works and grace, and this is the result of his rejection of the antithesis between Law and Grace as a hermeneutical tool. After the manner of Barth's thesis, he writes:

> Because of that fact we can never construe an antithesis between the covenant of 'works' and 'grace.' We err if we interpret this distinction as though God's original covenant had to do with *our* work or *our* achievement or *our* fulfillment of his law, while the later covenant of grace has reference to the pure gift of his *mercy* apart from all *our works*. If we assume this we are compelled to say that God's original relation to man was strictly 'legal,' or that the structure of that relation was determined by man's merit. In that case, we lose sight of the fact that man's obedience to God's command can never be different from a thankful response to God's own fellowship.[50]

---

[49] Westminster Theological Seminary, "Westminster Statement on Justification" (Philadelphia: Pennsylvania, 1980), VII. There was continuing controversy over the doctrine of justification at Westminster Theological Seminary in Pennsylvania from 1975 to the early 1980s. The *Westminster Statement on Justification*, approved by the faculty of the seminary, is a doctrinal statement on justification covering various related issues which reflect the general nature of controversy. It reflects the orthodox view in the light of historical and biblical theology, which integrates covenant and justification. Applying the antitheses between Law and Gospel and the covenants of works and grace, it affirms justification by faith alone apart from good works. It is another good indication that covenant theology, although it emphasizes covenant obligation, does not jeopardize justification by faith alone since it applies the hermeneutical principle of the antithesis between Law and Gospel. cf. Ibid., 1-17.

[50] Berkouwer, *Sin*, 206-07. Berkouwer's adaptation of Karl Barth's rejection of the antithesis between Law and Gospel and the antithesis between the covenants of works and grace in the light of Barth's *Christomonistic perspective* is also seen in Berkouwer's representative work, *The Triumph of Grace in the Theology of Karl Barth*, trans. Harry R. Boer (Grand Rapids, Michigan: Eerdmans Publishing Company, 1956). Berkouwer's *crossmonistic understanding* of divine grace is in the final analysis destructive to the

Berkouwer's rejection of the antithesis between the covenants of works and grace springs from his denial of the contrast between Law and Gospel. According to him, the antithesis between Law and Gospel as a hermeneutical tool does not exist. His rejection of the antithesis between the covenants of works and grace along with the antithesis between Law and Gospel arises from his *crossmonistic interpretation* of sin and law, which is analogous to Karl Barth's *Christomonistic*

---

sovereign grace of God as manifested in divine election, salvation and covenant. His *crossmonistic interpretation of divine grace* obscures the Christ centered theology in biblical revelation. For a critical appraisal of Berkouwer's new synthesis toward neoorthodox theology, see Cornelius Van Til, *The Sovereignty of Grace: An Appraisal of G. C. Berkouwer's View of Dordt* (New Jersey: Presbyterian and Reformed Publishing Company, 1969). Van Til carefully expresses and evaluates the gradual synthesis of Berkouwer's thought into Barthianism as follows: "Berkouwer was therefore leading us forward when, in his earlier works, he constantly pointed out that the Reformed doctrine of Scripture and the Reformed doctrine of salvation by grace alone as involved one another stand alone in their final opposition to those who start from human subject as though it were autonomous. In his later works, however, Berkouwer is making an alliance with those whose theology is, in the last analysis, based on the assumption of human autonomy. Admitting that Barth's 'revised supralapsarianism blocks the way to ascribing *decisive* significance to history,' Berkouwer none-the-less insists that his 'main concern is to speak of the all-conquering grace of God in Christ Jesus.' Barth denies, as basically destructive of the gospel of free grace, that which Berkouwer, in his earlier work, stressed as being foundational to all true theology, namely, the direct revelation of God in history through Scripture and the step-by-step redemptive work of Christ in history. Yet, Berkouwer now considers Barth as a fellow-defender of grace. Not only this. Berkouwer now advocates principles similar to those of Barth and of neo-orthodoxy as though through them alone we can defend the teaching of free grace. Yet Berkouwer appears not to be certain of himself in his advocacy of the neo-orthodox pattern of thought, as a new and better way. Committed as he is to the historic Christian position of salvation through the work of Christ in history, he halts and objects when Barth goes *too far* in rejecting this. When Reformed Christians today read Berkouwer, they should realize that there are two mutually destructive principles operative in his theology. There is the position of the historic Reformed Faith and there is the position that would go beyond the first position by means of a modern existentialist pattern of thought. The first position is now gradually being snowed under. It is now said to be formalist and determinist." Ibid., 85-6.

interpretation of the divine covenant.⁵¹ On this basis, he denies that the principle of law was operative in the prelapsarian state and proceeds to argue that *the traditional covenant of works* introduced legalism into the prelapsarian state: "If we drive a wedge between these concepts of *works* and *grace* we interpose the notion of an impersonal legalism within the original relation of God and man."⁵² Berkouwer's thesis is influenced by Karl Barth's radical reverse of the historical order *from law and gospel to gospel and law* and this reversion according to Berkouwer is the triumph of grace that escapes legalism:

> Barth contends that 'in Scripture we do not find the Law alongside the Gospel but *in* the Gospel.' Therefore he reverses the usual order of 'law and Gospel' and speaks of 'the Gospel and the law.' He recognizes that *within* this sequence there is room for reflecting on 'the law and the Gospel.' Nevertheless, the right accent is preserved only when we speak of the *Gospel first.*
>
> This reversal of the sequence has everything to do with the inner structure of Barth's theology. Negatively, we find a radical antilegalism in Barth - for Barth is against the law as a means of salvation. Positively, we find the triumph and priority of grace.⁵³

The rejection of the covenant of works and the historical order of *law and grace*, according to Berkouwer, is a concrete answer to *legalism*, and the Christomonistic approach to the divine covenant is the triumph of divine grace in Christ. We see this approach as a systematic distortion of the concept of *legalism and Christocentric theology*. We suggest that until we recognize the historical order of

---

⁵¹ Ibid., 199: "Yet the harmony of Scripture is broken as soon as we conclude from this accent a temporal sequence of law-and-Gospel. Our legitimate concern for preserving the correlation of 'guilt and forgiveness' is then reduced to an illegitimacy; furthermore, the law is then isolated from the Gospel, while the Gospel is seen as the answer to the state of dejection aroused by the law-in-itself. The only possible result in this kind of thinking is a dualism within our picture of God ... For if anything is clear in the biblical revelation it is certainly that the cross is the revelation of God's love but *also, at the same time*, of his holiness and justice. In the cross we can see how futile it is to separate these attributes of God."

⁵² Ibid., 208.

⁵³ Ibid., 204.

law and grace along with the antithesis between the covenants of works and grace, we abandon and distort a true concept of grace oriented *Christocentric theology*. Berkouwer denies that perfect obedience to the law was the condition of eschatological blessing in the prelapsarian state. In agreement with DeGraaf, Berkouwer suggests that the antithesis between the covenants of works and grace does not do justice to "God's favor, communion and love," which existed already in the beginning. Moreover, although God threatened death as a result of disobedience, according to Berkouwer, he did not promise eternal life through obedience. This clearly obscures eschatological direction and goal undertaken by the principle of obedience to the covenant of works.[54]

Barth, evaluating the antithesis between Law and Gospel in Luther's theology, asserts that it cannot be maintained in the light of biblical teaching. Barth's thesis certainly emphasizes that *law in the gospel* is the only proper window to expound the biblical concept of law. In other words, he elaborates the concept of law from the vantage point of *Christomonistic grace*: "In Scripture we do not find the Law alongside the Gospel but in the Gospel, and therefore the holiness of God is not side by side with but in His grace, and His wrath is not separate from but in His love."[55] At this juncture, Barth's *law in the gospel* becomes a hermeneutical tool that replaces covenant hermeneutics' antithesis between Law and Gospel. Barth cannot accept the antithesis between the covenants of works and grace, because in his view, the intertrinitarian covenant only validates the covenant of grace. He argues that introducing the covenant of works into biblical history is nonsense because it is foreign to biblical revelation:

> In fact it derives from anxiety lest there might be an essence in God in which, in spite of that contract, His righteousness and His mercy are secretly and at bottom two separate things. And this anxiety derives from the fact that the thought of that intertrinitarian contract obviously cannot have any binding and therefore consoling and assuring force. This anxiety and therefore this proposition of a covenant of works could obviously never have arisen if there had been a loyal hearing of

---

[54] Ibid., 207.
[55] Barth, *Church Dogmatics*, 2/1:362-63.

the Gospel and a strict looking to Jesus Christ as the full and final revelation of the being of God. In the eternal decree of God revealed in Jesus Christ the being of God would have been seen as righteous mercy and merciful righteousness from the very first. It would have been quite impossible therefore to conceive of any special plan of a God who is righteous *in abstracto*, and the whole idea of an original covenant of works would have fallen to the ground.[56]

Barth's Christomonistic approach to the divine covenant is fatal to the gospel because it destroys the antithetical parallel between the first and second Adams. This, in turn, destroys the antitheses between Law and Gospel and the covenants of works and grace. Since these are foundational to the doctrine of justification by faith alone, Barth's theological system nullifies the gospel.[57]

---

[56] Ibid., 4/1:65.

[57] In a letter to Hans Küng, Barth recognizes the consensus between the Roman Catholic doctrine of justification and his own. The decisive ecumenical point of contact between the two is their rejection of the antithesis between Law and Gospel, the Protestant evangelical hermeneutical principle to draw out justification by faith alone apart from good works: "All I can say is this: If what you have presented in Part Two of this book is actually the teaching of the Roman Catholic Church, then I must certainly admit that my view of justification agrees with the Roman Catholic view; if only for the reason that the Roman Catholic teaching would then be most strikingly in accord with mine! Of course, the problem is whether what you have presented here really represents the teaching of your Church." Karl Barth, in Hans Küng, *Justification:The Doctrine of Karl Barth and a Catholic Reflection*, trans. Edward Quinn (Philadelphia, Pennsylvania: The Westminster Press, 1981), xl. Thus Barth's *law in grace or gospel* replaces *the Reformation antithesis of Law and Gospel* and leads him into an existential and moralistic concept of justification that coalesces the imputation and infusion of the righteousness of Christ in which the final reference point and emphasis are on moral transformation. This ecumenical synthesis in Barth's thought is well summarized by the acute pen of Godfrey: "Another influential stage in the effort to balance law and gospel came in the work of Karl Barth. Barth wrote of 'gospel and law,' arguing a basic unity between the two. He agreed with the Roman Catholic Hans Küng that the Reformers had set law and gospel too much in opposition. Barth's amalgam of gospel and law led him to agree with Küng that justification was both by the imputation of Christ's righteousness and by an infusion of his righteousness resulting in moral transformation.

Dispensationalism in general is a form of *evangelical theology* that fails to grasp the antithesis between the covenants of works and grace. It rejects the historical order of *law and grace*. By rejecting the *foedus operum*, dispensational theology fails to perceive the eschatological goal and direction of the prelapsarian state. Charles Baker, for example, argues that there is no such thing as the *foedus operum* and eschatological blessings in the prelapsarian state. This state was *static* rather than *eschatological*:

> This so-called Covenant of Works, which is a basic concept in Covenant Theology, is not to be found in Scripture ... Cocceius and Turretin invented this teaching back in the seventeenth century and it has since become a dogma of the Reformed bodies. It is true that Adam's obedience was tested by the command: 'Thou shalt not eat of it,' (Genesis 2:17), but there is no suggestion that Adam had to earn eternal life. He was created with life. He was not created in a lost condition wherein he needed to obtain life. He had life as a gift from God, but his continuance in that life depended upon his obedience to God.[58]

The preceding quotation reveals several misunderstandings of covenant theology. As we already demonstrated in chapter one, the development of the *foedus operum* goes back to the sixteenth century, even back to Calvin whose theology is fully congenial with the antithesis between the covenants of works and grace even though he does not use the term *foedus operum* in respect to the prelapsarian state. Covenant theology does not suggest that Adam was created in "a lost condition" as Baker argues. Instead the main principle of the covenant of works points and directs to eschatological heavenly kingdom blessing which is the translation into the glorious stage of *non posse peccare* from the original state of *posse peccare* and *posse non peccare*. Baker's lack of eschatological understanding in respect to the prelapsarian state is a great theological mistake since it fails to make biblical theological inferences from the antithesis between the first and second Adams. Furthermore, Baker denies the antithesis

---

Barth's position self-consciously rejects the Reformation balance and moves in the direction of moralism. Yet his position has affected evangelical theologians such as Daniel Fuller." Godfrey, "Law and Gospel," 380.

[58] Charles F. Baker, *A Dispensational Theology* (Grand Rapids, Michigan: Grace Bible College Publications, 1971), 10.

between the covenants of works and grace as a hermeneutical principle developed in covenant hermeneutics to depict the *historia salutis* and *ordo salutis* because of his commitment to dispensational theology's seven *distinctive* dispensations in biblical history.[59]

B. The Mosaic Covenant

When we come to the discussion of the Mosaic Covenant, it is apparent that there is a sharp dispute between John Murray and Meredith G. Kline. In this section, we want to penetrate the difference between Murray and Kline, evaluating it in the light of historical and biblical theology. Murray seeks to revise, whereas Kline tries to mature and flower covenant theology in respect to the Mosaic Covenant. Both basically agree that believers in the Old Covenant were saved and justified by the principle of the *foedus gratiae*, the traditional view of classical covenant hermeneutics. Nevertheless, a sharp dispute arises when they discuss the specific nature of the inauguration of the Mosaic Covenant in Exodus 19-24 and the interpretation and application of the 'Do this and you will live' in Leviticus 18:5 in the Old Covenant.

Murray identifies the apparently unique nature of the inauguration of the Mosaic Covenant revealed in Exodus 19:5-6 and 24:7-8 in comparison with the preceding Abrahamic Covenant. Nevertheless, Murray argues that the condition of covenant obedience is in no way different from that of the Abrahamic Covenant.[60] At this juncture, Murray highlights the *unilateral* character of the Mosaic Covenant that is characteristic of the Abrahamic and New Covenants: "We find that the Mosaic Covenant also is a sovereign administration of grace, divinely initiated, established, confirmed, and fulfilled."[61] On this point, Murray is critical of classic covenant theology in which the conditionality of the Mosaic Covenant has been understood in the light of the *foedus legale*, even though its scope was limited to the administration of the typological earthly blessing or curse: "It is too frequently assumed that the conditions prescribed in connection with the Mosaic covenant place the Mosaic dispensation in a totally different category as respects grace, on the one hand, and demand or

---

[59] Ibid., 87-103.
[60] Murray, *Covenant of Grace*, 20-2.
[61] Ibid., 22.

obligation, on the other."[62] Murray wishes to exclusively emphasize the *continuity* between the Abrahamic and Mosaic Covenants in spite of apparent contrast in how these covenants were made. Thus, he rejects the interpretation of the Mosaic Covenant as a limited reapplication of the so-called the Adamic covenant of works, which has been the important hermeneutical milieu of covenant hermeneutics:

> The view that in the Mosaic covenant there was a repetition of the so-called covenant of works, current among covenant theologians, is a grave misconception and involves an erroneous construction of the Mosaic covenant, as well as fails to assess the uniqueness of the Adamic administration. The Mosaic covenant was distinctly redemptive in character and was continuous with and extensive of the Abrahamic covenant.[63]

Kline cannot accept Murray's exclusive emphasis on the *unilateral* character of the Mosaic Covenant and its continuity with the Abrahamic and New Covenants. Kline understands the Old Covenant in the light of both *discontinuity* and *continuity* with the Abrahamic/New Covenants. Kline finds conclusive biblical theological support for his thesis in the contrast between the covenant making processes in Genesis 15 and Exodus 19-24. God made a solemn commitment to Abraham in Genesis 15. This indicates that the Abrahamic Covenant is a promissory covenant, not a law covenant. By way of contrast, the Israelites make a solemn commitment to God in Exodus 19-24. This specific nature of the ratifying Mosaic Covenant was also observed by Geerhardus Vos as we saw in chapter three. Following the pattern of Vos' thought, Kline suggests that the "We will do everything the Lord has said; we will obey" (Exod. 19:8 ; 24:3,7) indicates that the Old Covenant is "a law covenant" as over against the Abrahamic Covenant which is promissory.[64]

Kline's biblical-theological evaluation of the Mosaic Covenant-making process actually matures the character of the *foedus legale* as interpreted and defined by covenant hermeneutics. According to Kline's biblical-theological rationale, the principle of works under the

---

[62] Ibid.
[63] Murray, *Collected Writings*, 2:50.
[64] Kline, *By Oath Consigned*, 17-18.

Old Covenant was limited to administering *the typological nation of Israel* because the principle of law cannot be used to save and justify sinners in the fallen world. On the other hand, the principle of the *foedus gratiae* is found in the Mosaic Covenant-making process (Exod. 19:5-6; 24:5-8). So Kline argues that believers under the Old Covenant were saved and justified by the principle of the *foedus gratiae*.[65] The continuation of the *foedus gratiae*, according to Kline, is well manifested by the restoration of the nation of Israel from Babylonian exile after seventy years captivity, when God remembers the Abrahamic promissory covenant despite the Israelites' failure to keep the *foedus legale* instituted on Mount Sinai. Satan, in the fourth vision of Zechariah, for example, accuses Joshua's community on the basis of the Israelites' infidelity to the *foedus legale*, but this is a grave misconception and deception of Satan since he ignores the continuing validity of the *foedus gratiae* which will culminate in the New Covenant in Christ:

> Though God had indeed cast off Israel for breaking the Mosaic covenant of works, when the appointed seventy years were completed (cf. Zech. 1:12), he had regathered a remnant from exile in remembrance of his covenant with Abraham (Lev. 26:42; cf. 2 Kgs. 13:23) and with a view to the true fulfillment of that covenant in the eventual coming of Christ from Israel as the promised seed of Abraham. This act of restoration from the Babylonian captivity was in fact a prophetic portrayal at the typological level of the promised antitypical restoration of the elect to covenant fellowship with God as a heavenly kingdom of priests and holy nation, the fruit of the redemptive accomplishment of the second Adam.[66]

The restoration of the nation of Israel from Babylonian captivity based on the Abrahamic Covenant indicates that believers under the Old Covenant were saved and justified by the principle of the *foedus gratiae*. The specific nature of the *foedus gratiae* is included in the inauguration of the Mosaic Covenant on Mount Sinai.

According to Murray, Leviticus 18:5 in the context of the Old Covenant, is not the manifestation of the *foedus legale* as covenant theologians have argued: "The problem that arises from this use of Lev. 18:5 is that the latter text does not appear in a context that deals

---

[65] Ibid.
[66] Kline, "The servant and the Serpent," *kerux* 8/1 (1993): 34.

with legal righteousness as opposed to that of faith. Lev. 18:5 is in a context in which the claims of God upon his redeemed and covenant people are being asserted and urged upon Israel."[67] In other words,

---

[67] Murray, *Romans*, II:249. Walter C. Kaiser, Jr. tries to mediate between covenant and dispensational hermeneutics. He identifies his view as *eschatological hermeneutics* which we believe similar to progressive dispensational hermeneutics. Walter C. Kaiser, Jr., "The Eschatological Hermeneutics," 91-9. His eschatological hermeneutics, however, obscures an *eschatological* understanding of the Old Covenant by arguing that the principle of the law or works was not operative under the Old Covenant. Thus, he interprets 'Do this and you shall live' of Leviticus 18:5 from the vantage point of the exclusively third use of law which is applicable to progressive sanctification. idem, "Leviticus 18:5 and Paul: Do This and You Shall Live (Eternally?)," *Journal of Evangelical Theological Society* 14 (1971), 19-28. Kaiser rightly interprets the Mosaic Covenant in the light of *continuity* with the Abrahamic and New Covenants for the believer's election and salvation: "The covenant is everlasting and conditionless when viewed from the perspective of God's promise and election. It does not depend upon merit for favoritism, but only God's grace and his election for *service*. This same covenant, with the same promises, continues into the Mosaic revelation and is no more conditional or unconditional than was the Abrahamic Covenant." Ibid., 23.

Kaiser's *promise theology*, however, undermines the Pauline hermeneutical principle of the antithesis between Law and Gospel which is vital for denoting sovereign grace in the doctrine of justification and election. In other words, Kaiser does not see the principle of works in Leviticus 18:5 which is essential for understanding the eschatological direction of the *original* covenant of works and the eschatological direction of the Old Covenant which is limited to the typological kingdom blessing or curse. In circular fashion, this leads him to obscure the Pauline hermeneutical principle of the antithesis between Law and Gospel which is manifested in Romans 10:5-8 and Galatians 3:10-12 which both allude to Leviticus 18:5; Deuteronomy 30:12 and Habakkuk 2:4: "In order to show to the Jew that this is so, Paul quotes extensively from the Old Testament from here on out starting first with two quotes from Moses in Leviticus 18:5 and Deuteronomy 30:11-14. These two quotes from Moses are *not antithetical in the Pentateuch, much less here in Paul* [emphasis mine] ... Nor can it be said that Paul is just borrowing the language of the Old Testament to capture the principle of law-righteousness, as John Murray affirms ... The alleged antithesis then is only in the misconception of Paul's generation of Jews." Ibid., 27; "The law was never intended as an alternative method of obtaining salvation or righteousness - not even hypothetically ... Clearly, then, the law never was intended to be a means by which people

Murray interprets Leviticus 18:5 *only in the light of the third use of law* (*tertius usus legis*), namely, the covenantal obligation of believers (*usus didacticus sive normativus*) in the context of the Old Covenant. Murray's critique, however, does not answer the question *why* covenant theologians designate the Mosaic Covenant as the *foedus legale* in relation to the Adamic covenant of works. In other words, when covenant theologians designate the Mosaic Covenant as the *foedus legale*, they have applied its principle only to the administration of the typological kingdom which points to the eternal heavenly kingdom that was temporarily lost when Adam failed to fulfill the original *foedus legale*.

Contrary to Murray, Kline asserts that Leviticus 18:5 reapplies the principle of the covenant of works from the prelapsarian state to the Mosaic Covenant at the level of the administration of the typological kingdom. In his interpretation of Zechariah 6:9-15, Kline says that:

> Zechariah casts his prophecy of Christ and the church in the prophetic idiom, employing the old typological order to depict the new covenant realities. And according to the covenantal constitution for the old order, corporate Israel must earn the continuing enjoyment of the typological kingdom inheritance by their obedience. This works principle is a conspicuous feature of the sanctions section of the Mosaic treaties. Expressing things in old covenant terms, Zechariah therefore says that God's kingdom of glory is the reward for the probationary obedience of the elect corporately ... As Paul's appeal to Lev. 18:5 shows (Rom. 10:5; Gal. 3:12), a legal principle of meritorious works was operating in the Torah covenant opposite to the gospel principle of grace.[68]

Divine prosecution of the covenant lawsuit and the Babylonian exile indicate that the Israelites were under the principle of works in the Old Covenant. For these reasons, Kline rightly argues that the principle of works was not just *hypothetical* but *active* in the Mosaic Covenant since it was required for the administration of the theocratic

---

could earn eternal life; thus, it never was viewed as being in opposition to the promises and grace of God." idem, "The Law as God's Gracious Guidance for the Promotion of Holiness," in *Five Views on Law and Gospel*, by Wayne G. Strickland (Grand Rapids, Michigan: Zondervan Publishing House, 1996), 178. See further, Ibid., 182-199.

[68] Kline, "Exaltation of Christ," 26

typological nation which typifies the eternal heavenly kingdom. This is why Kline argues that Leviticus 18:5 reapplies the principle of works from the covenant of creation for the limited purpose of *typological kingdom administration*.[69]

Kline, in his interpretation of Zechariah 3, the fourth vision of Zechariah, utilizes the *foedus legale* under the Mosaic Covenant, designating it as "the Torah-covenant of works," or "the Mosaic covenant of works," to distinguish it from the original Adamic covenant of works, since the Mosaic covenant of works operated at the level of the typological theocratic kingdom. He also carefully preserves the continuing validity of the *foedus gratiae*:

> The half-truth lie urged by Satan is expressed in that figurative idiom: Behold Joshua/Israel standing before the tribunal in filthy clothes, shamefully defiled transgressors of the Torah-covenant of works ... The apostle was eager to insist that the covenant of grace confirmed long before was not disannulled by the law so as to make the promise void (Gal. 3:17). Satan, on the contrary, by identifying Joshua exclusively in terms of his filthy garments (i.e., his transgression of the law) insinuated an interpretation of the Mosaic covenant of works as overriding and abrogating the Abrahamic covenant.[70]

Another important theological concern of Murray is that if we somehow recognize the idea of the *foedus legale* as covenant theology has identified it, then there will be great confusion since classic dispensationalism makes a sharp contrast between the Old and New Covenants, giving the impression that people under the Old Covenant were saved and justified by the principle of law whereas believers in the New Covenant are saved and justified by the principle of grace: "It has been thought that in the Mosaic covenant there is a sharp antithesis to the principle of promise embodied in the Abrahamic covenant and also to the principle of grace which comes to its efflorescence in the new covenant, and that this antithetical principle which governs the Mosaic covenant and dispensation is that of law in contradistinction from both promise and grace."[71]

According to Murray, classical dispensational hermeneutics utilizes the antithesis between Law and Grace to stress *total discontinuity*

---

[69] Kline, "Gospel Until the Law," 434-35.
[70] Kline, "The servant and the Serpent," 33-4.
[71] Murray, *Principles of Conduct*, 195.

between the Old and New Covenants economies: "The Mosaic would stand in sharp antithesis to both [the Abrahamic and New Covenants] in respect of constitutive and governing principle. And the contrast between law and grace which we find in the New Testament would naturally be interpreted as a contrast between the Mosaic economy and the gospel dispensation of grace."[72] Murray's biblical-theological answer to dispensational hermeneutics is that there is *only continuity* between the Old and Abrahamic / New Covenants. According to Murray, this continual aspect is the most definitive and conclusive answer to dispensational hermeneutics. Consequently he denies that the *foedus legale* was operative in the Mosaic Covenant. Murray's answer to classical dispensationalism comes at the expense of the *eschatology* richly revealed in the Old Covenant, which has been developed in covenant hermeneutics by applying the *foedus legale* in the administration of the typological kingdom. In other words, the principle of works or the *foedus legale* must be operative under the Old Covenant and the blessings or curses applied to the theocratic nation according to the *general principle of obedience of the Israelites*. All of this ultimately points to the eschatological blessings in the heavenly kingdom which come through in the New Covenant in Christ.

Kline's contribution in his analysis of the Mosaic Covenant is his great emphasis on *typology* to highlight the biblical theological nature of *eschatology* which has been a common interest in covenant hermeneutics. He also carefully combines the covenant and kingdom motifs in the Mosaic economy. We, however, suggest a minor revision to Kline's approach to the Mosaic Covenant. For example, he argues that the Israelites' corporate obedience was necessary to *merit* continuation of their national blessings and security: "The old covenant was law, the opposite of grace-faith, and in the postlapsarian world that meant it would turn out to be an administration of condemnation as a consequence of sinful Israel's failure *to maintain the necessary meritorious obedience* [emphasis mine]."[73] Obviously,

---

[72] Ibid., 196.

[73] Kline, *Kingdom Prologue*, 68. "But it also sees and takes at face value the massive biblical evidence for a peculiar discontinuity present in the old covenant in the form of a principle of meritorious works, operating not as a way of eternal salvation but as the principle governing Israel's retention of its provisional, typological inheritance." idem, "Gospel Until the Law," 434.

Kline limits the principle of works to the level of typological kingdom administration, which is a brilliant observation in the light of biblical theology. But, there is *the possibility of confusion* when we use the concept of *merit* to describe the Israelites' obedience even though it is limited to blessings in the typological kingdom. As we already argued in previous chapters, we limit the application of the concept of *merit* to *perfect obedience* which was possible only for the first and second Adams although it did not happen to the first Adam. To be sure, Kline recognizes that the Israelites' obedience at its best was never perfect. This is precisely why we suggest that the term *merit* should not be used for the Israelites' obedience. In this respect, Geerhardus Vos' approach to the Israelites' corporate obedience is more suitable than Kline's. While Vos correctly recognizes that the principle of works was operative in the administration of the typological kingdom, he does not apply *merit* to their corporate and general obedience since it has *a typological significance*, that points to believers' eschatological heavenly perfect state: "The connection is of a totally different kind. It belongs *not to the legal sphere of merit* [emphasis mine], but to the symbolico-typical sphere of *appropriateness of expression*. As stated above, the abode of Israel in Canaan typified the heavenly, perfected state of God's people."[74]

C. Justification

John Murray and Meredith G. Kline both affirm justification by faith alone since both apply an important hermeneutical principle, namely, the antithesis between Law and Gospel in matters concerning the *ordo salutis*. Kline also utilizes the antithesis between the covenants of works and grace to depict the doctrine of justification whereas Murray does not because he rejects the *foedus operum*. The bottom line, however, is their basic agreement concerning this important doctrine of the evangelical Church.

Murray, crediting the rediscovery of the gospel to Martin Luther, pays special attention to this important doctrine: "If there is one thing the Church needs today it is the republication with faith and passion of the presuppositions of the doctrine of justification and the reapplication of this, the article of a standing or falling Church."[75]

---

[74] Vos, *Biblical Theology*, 127.

[75] Murray, *Collected Writings*, 2:203. For the past two decades, E. P. Sanders has dominated the discussion of the Pauline concept of the law in

relation to *Palestine Judaism* of the first century, and his new perspective, known as "covenantal nomism," has been an overarching principle of contemporary New Testament hermeneutics. Sanders' *Paul and Palestine Judaism* (1977) gained enormous attention from other scholars. Using the method of comparative religious study, he interpreted first century Palestine Judaism, not through the traditional lens of *legalism*, but through the lens of "covenantal nomism" which allegedly was a dominant pattern of Judaism from the second century BC to the second century AD. In this regard, Sanders argues that Judaism in general was not a *legalistic religion* as Protestant scholars have traditionally argued. Rather it was religion that balanced *grace and works*, and this may be called *covenantal nomism* as over against *legalism*: "We must say that the Judaism of before 70 kept grace and works in the right perspective, did not trivialize the commandments of God and was not especially marked by hypocrisy. The frequent Christian charge against Judaism, it must be recalled, is not that some individual Jews misunderstood, misapplied and abused their religion, but that *Judaism necessarily tends* toward petty legalism, self-serving and self-deceiving casuistry, and a mixture of arrogance and lack of confidence in God. But the surviving Jewish literature is as free of these characteristics as any I have ever read. By consistently maintaining the basic framework of *covenantal nomism*, the gift and demand of God were kept in a healthy relationship with each other, the minutiae of the law were observed on the basis of the large principles of religion and because of commitment to God, and humility before the God who chose and ultimately redeemed Israel was encouraged." E. P. Sanders, *Paul and Palestine Judaism: A Comparison of Patterns of Religion* (London: SCM Press LTD, 1977), 426-7. Thus he argues that *covenantal nomism* was the general pattern of Judaism in the region of Palestine before the destruction of the Jerusalem Temple at AD 70. From this new perspective, he interprets Paul's religion and the gospel, identifying it as *new covenantal nomism*: "Thus one can see already in Paul how it is that Christianity is going to become a new form of covenantal nomism, a covenant religion which one enters by baptism, membership in which provides salvation, which has a specific set of commandments, obedience to which (or repentance for the transgression of which) keeps one in the covenantal relationship, while repeated or heinous transgression removes one from membership." Ibid., 513. Thus Judaism before AD 70, also known to Jesus and Paul was not a *legalistic religion but covenantal nomism* which is manifested and evidenced in Rabbinic literature in that period. Sanders' new approach cannot accept the Reformation principle of justification by *faith alone* understood as a forensic declaration since he interprets justification from the perspective of *a subjective change and participation instead of an objective divine declaration*. The bottom line of Sanders' new approach is his denial of the antithesis between Law and Gospel in relation to Pauline soteriology: "Luther, plagued by guilt, read Paul's passages on 'righteousness by faith' as meaning that God reckoned a Christian to be righteous even though he or she was a sinner. Luther understood 'righteousness' to be judicial, a declaration of innocence, but also fictional, ascribed to Christians 'by mere imputation,' since God was merciful. Luther's phrase for the Christian condition was not Paul's 'blameless' or 'without blemish' (for example 1 Thess. 5:23), but rather *simul justus et peccator*, 'at the same time righteous and sinner': 'righteous' in God's sight, but a 'sinner' in every day experience. Put another way, Luther saw the Christian life as summed up in Romans 7:21, 'I find it to be a law that when I want to do right, evil lies close at hand,' whereas Paul thought that this was the plight from which people were freed through Christ (Rom. 7:24; 8:1-8). 'You,' he wrote, 'are not in the Flesh, you are in the Spirit': and those in the Spirit, he thought, did not do the sinful deeds 'of the Flesh' (Rom. 8:9-17; Gal. 5:16-24). Luther's emphasis on fictional, imputed righteousness, though it has often been shown to be an incorrect interpretation of Paul, has been influential because it corresponds to the sense of sinfulness which many people feel, and which is part and parcel of Western concepts of personhood, with their emphasis on individualism and introspection. Luther sought and found relief from guilt. But Luther's problems were not Paul's, and we misunderstand him if we see him through Luther's eyes." idem, *Paul* (Oxford / New York: Oxford University Press, 1992), 49. Explaining Romans 10:1-4, Sanders offers a new understanding of the Pauline concept of God's righteousness compared to that of law righteousness. According to him, Jew pursued righteousness under the Old Covenant or the Mosaic Covenant by the law. It was not *legalism* because God instituted and accepted it as the norm and means for *staying in the covenant*. The Jews' only fault was to reject Jesus as the Christ who is the new revelation of God's righteousness which comes by faith. Therefore, Paul criticizes the Jews not for their law righteousness, but for their exclusivism in rejecting the inclusivism of Jews and Gentiles in Christ. Ironically, Sanders' new approach falls into *radical legalism* by jeopardizing the continuum of the Gospel of grace between the Old and New Covenants: "How is the right goal defined? 'God's righteousness,' which is contrasted to 'their own,' is for '*all* who have *faith*': it is available to Jew and Gentile equally on the basis of faith in Christ. This brings to an end the other righteousness, by law (Rom. 10:4). 'Their own righteousness is the righteousness peculiar to Jews as a group, not that earned by individuals. Jewish righteousness springs from loyalty to the law of Moses, which applies only to Jews, and which is thus 'their own' and is not 'for all.' Paul's focus in Romans 10:1-4 is, again, historical and communal: he is thinking of the people of Israel as a group and the relation of the Mosaic dispensation to God's plan of salvation. He is not analyzing the interior effect of the law on the individual Jew. The people of Israel posed a problem because, on the whole, they persisted in accepting the first dispensation and did not see that God had offered another." Ibid., 121. Sanders insists that Jesus, like Paul, does not criticize *covenantal nomism*. Rather he presupposed Jewish law righteousness as the foundation of the new dispensation of the Gospel mission: "We can likewise see that Jesus accepted 'covenantal nomism.' His mission was to Israel in the name of the God of Israel. He thus evidently accepted his people's special status, that is, the election and the covenant. I think that it is equally clear that he accepted obedience to the law as the norm. He did not stress or dwell on the 'nomism' part of the scheme." idem., *Jesus and Judaism* (Philadelphia: Fortress Press, 1985), 336. In this sense, Sanders' *covenantal nomism* as a hermeneutical tool is almost synonymous to the Barthian *law in grace or grace in law* since the bottom line of both hermeneutical tools is the rejection of the antithesis between Law / Gospel and works / faith as it pertains to Christology, soteriology and *heilsgeschichte*. Sanders denies the doctrine of *justification by faith alone* apart from good works arguing that it was a Reformation product that was biased by Western *individualism* that ignores communal and participatory aspects of that doctrine in the biblical revelation. Many scholars have followed and popularized Sanders' *covenantal nomism* with minor modifications in biblical and systematic theology since Sanders published his provocative work, *Paul and Palestine Judaism* (1977). Heikki Räisänen adopts *covenantal nomism* in his biblical hermeneutics and writes about the importance of Sanders' *Paul and Palestine Judaism* in contemporary biblical hermeneutics: "Another major reading experience during my struggling with Paul was E. P. Sander's magisterial *Paul and Palestine Judaism*. Sanders argues cogently and with great expertise for a view of Palestine Judaism rather different from that still prevalent in much New Testament scholarship. I had been groping in the same direction for quite some time without knowing too well just where I was or what the goal might be; the publication of Sanders's illuminating work was like a gift from heaven for my own quest." Heikki Räisänen, *Paul and the Law* (Tübingen: J. C. B. Mohr (Paul Siebeck), 1987), v. For the popularizers of Sanders' *covenantal nomism*, see: James D. G. Dunn, "The Incident at Antioch (Gal. 2:11-18),' *Journal for the Study of the New Testament* 18 (1983): 3-57; idem, "The Justice of God: A Renewed Perspective on Justification by Faith," *Journal of Theological Studies* 43 (1992): 1-22; idem, "The New Perspective on Paul," *Bulletin of the John Rylands University Library of Manchester* 65 (1983): 95-122; idem, "Works of the Law and the Curse of the Law (Galatians 3:10-14)," *New Testament Studies* 31(1985): 523-42; idem, "Yet Once More—'The Works of the Law': A Response," *Journal for the Study of the New Testament* 46 (1992): 99-117; D. B. Garlington, "The Obedience of Faith in the Letter to the Romans; Part I: The Meaning of *hupakoen pisteos* (Rom 1:5;16:26)," *Westminster Theological*

According to Murray, the doctrine of justification by grace through faith alone - the gospel itself - collapses apart from the biblical hermeneutical principle of the antithesis between Law and Gospel: "The simple truth is that if law is conceived of as contributing in the least degree towards our acceptance with God and our justification by him, then the gospel of grace is a nullity." Moreover, Paul utilizes a correlative hermeneutical principle, the antithesis between works and faith to defend the gospel against the background of the Judaizers' legalism:

> If we were to be justified by works, in any degree or to any extent, then there would be no gospel at all. For what works of righteousness can a condemned, guilty, and depraved sinner offer to God? That we are justified by faith advertises the grand article of the gospel of grace that we are not justified by works of law. Faith stands in antithesis to works.[76]

Kline, too, insists that the antitheses between Law and Gospel and works and faith are vital hermeneutical principles for understanding justification by faith alone. In this respect, Kline is in *complete agreement* with Murray:

> In Romans 4, drawing the same contrast between the works principle of the law and the gospel principle found in the promise to Abraham,

---

Journal 52 (1990): 201-24; idem, "The Obedience of Faith in the Letter to the Romans; Part II: The Obedience of Faith and Judgment by Works," *Westminster Theological Journal* 53 (1991): 47-72; idem, *'The Obedience of Faith': A Pauline Phrase in Historical Context* (Tübingen: J. C. B. Mohr (Paul Siebeck), 1991; Heikki Räisänen, "Galatians 2:16 and Paul's Break with Judaism," *New Testament Studies* 31(1985): 543-53; idem, *Jesus, Paul and Torah: Collected Essays*, trans. David E. Orton (Shefield: JSOT Press, 1992); idem, "Legalism and Salvation by the Law: Paul's Portrayal of the Jewish Religion as a Historical and Theological Problem," in *The Pauline Literature and Theology*, ed. S. Pedersen, 63-83 (Göttingen: Vandenhoeck and Ruprecht, 1980); idem, *Paul and the Law* (Tübingen: J. C. B. Mohr, 1983); idem, *The Torah and Christ* (Helsinki, 1986); N. T. Wright, *The Climax of the Covenant: Christ and the Law in Pauline Theology* (Minneapolis: Fortress, 1991); idem, "The Paul of History and the Apostle of Faith," *Tyndale Bullletin* 29 (1978): 61-88; idem, *What Saint Paul Really Said* (Grand Rapids, Michigan: Eerdmans Publishing Company, 1997).

[76] Murray, *Redemption*, 130.

Paul emphasizes the faith of Abraham by which the promise was appropriated ... 'It is of faith that it may be according to grace' (v.13). Inheritance of the promise was not through the works principle of the law (v.13), for that is contrary to the promise-grace-faith-forgiveness principle (vv.14,15; cf. vv.4-8). The promise of the kingdom was rather through the righteousness of faith (v.13; cf. v.3). If justification and kingdom inheritance are by works, the glory goes to oneself as a matter of merit and due, 'but not to God' ... But in God's covenant with Abraham justification was by faith's 'Amen' to God's promises.[77]

Paul himself discovers the gospel of grace in his personal encounter with the exalted Christ during his Damascus Road experience (Acts 9:3-6; 26:12-18). This experience, according to Murray, is the source of Paul's hermeneutical principles of the antitheses between law and grace, and works and faith: "When Paul unfolds the antithesis between grace and law, faith and works, he writes of an antithesis which had been reflected in the contrast between the two periods in his own life history, periods divided by the experience of the Damascus road."[78]

If we confound law and gospel, then according to Murray, we cannot talk about *forensic justification* since this doctrine can only be maintained by the hermeneutical principle of the antithesis between Law and Gospel. Paul, for example, views the doctrine of justification from the vantage point of forensic declaration in Romans 8:33-34: "Its meaning is entirely removed from the thought of making upright or holy or good or righteous. This is what is meant when we insist that justification is forensic. It has to do with a judgment given, declared, pronounced; it is judicial or juridical or forensic."[79] Kline also maintains that if we do not accept the hermeneutical principle of the antithesis between Law and Gospel, then the forensic view of salvation and justification is nullified. In other words, the forensic view of justification goes together with the antithesis between Law and

---

[77] Kline, *Kingdom Prologue*, 198.

[78] Murray, *Romans*, I:iv. For the further elaboration on this matter, see Dennis E. Johnson, *The Message of Acts in the History of Redemption* (Phillipsburg, New Jersey: Presbyterian and Reformed Publishing Company, 1997), 105-21; Seyoon Kim, *The Origin of Paul's Gospel* 2nd and rev. ed. (Tübingen: J. C. B. Mohr, 1984); J. Gresham Machen, *The Origin of Paul's Religion* (Grand Rapids, Michigan: Eerdmans Publishing Company, 1976), 58-68, 145-7, 205, 305.

[79] Murray, *Redemption*, 121.

Gospel: "Grace lives and moves and has its being in a legal, forensic environment. In the biblical proclamation of the gospel, grace is the antithesis of the works principle. Grace and works could thus be contrastively compared only if they were comparable, that is, only if the term grace, like works, functioned in a forensic context."[80]

Perhaps the most important contribution of Kline's biblical theology in respect to the doctrine of justification is his interpretation of justification by faith alone in the light of the *complete* antithesis between the covenants of works and grace. In other words, Kline properly interprets Adam's eschatological justification by works in the covenant of creation from forensic or legal view point. Thus it becomes a great biblical-theological anticipation of believers' justification by faith alone in the covenant of redemption, in which the second Adam fulfilled the requirements of the covenant of works that was broken by the first Adam:

> If the first Adam had obediently fulfilled the stipulations of God's covenant with him, then assuredly he would have been worthy of being declared righteous by his Lord. Adam's justification would have been on the grounds of his works and would have been precisely what those good works deserved. God's declaring Adam righteous would have been an act of justice, pure and simple.[81]

According to Murray, the imputation of Christ's righteousness is closely related to the forensic understanding of justification. They stand or fall together because they are tied together by the antithesis between Law and Gospel: "So we might say that justification finds its specific character or at least finds its necessary presupposition in the imputation of righteousness ... If God declares that the demands of law and justice are reckoned by him as satisfied, this must involve righteousness as reckoned by him satisfied."[82] Kline also interprets the imputation of righteousness in the doctrine of justification in the light of the antithesis between Law and Gospel. Furthermore, Kline strengthens the forensic nature of justification by demonstrating more sharply than before the contrast between the covenants of works and grace:

---

[80] Kline, *Kingdom Prologue*, 69-70.
[81] Kline, "Works and Grace," 88.
[82] Murray, *Collected Writings*, 2:210.

An encounter with Satan was a critical aspect of the probationary crisis for each of the two Adams. To enter into judicial combat against this enemy of God and to vanquish him in the name of God was the covenantal assignment that must be performed by the servant of the Lord as his 'one act of righteousness.' And it was the winning of this victory of righteousness by the one that would be imputed to the many as their act of righteousness and as their claim on the consummated kingdom proferred in the covenant.[83]

When Paul affirms the antithesis between works and faith in his discussion of the doctrine of justification, he is simultaneously affirms, according to Murray, the *instrumentality* of faith. Without the antithesis between Law and Gospel, we cannot verify faith as the only instrument of justification: "It is faith, by reason of its specific character in distinction from works as well as from all the other graces of the Spirit, and faith alone that is brought into the instrumental relation to justification."[84]

Murray grants that the principle of works in the "Do this and you will live" of Leviticus 18:5 was *operative in the prelapsarian state* as the means of eschatological life and justification. This use of the principle of works, however, was canceled after the fall. Therefore, Murray interprets Paul's quotation of Leviticus 18:5 in Romans 10:5 and Galatians 3:12 as a strategic use of the antithesis between Law and Gospel or works and faith to defend justification by faith alone against *legalism*: "Justification by doing is the contradiction of justification by faith ... It is this contrast that Paul institutes in Rom. 10:5,6. In alluding to Lev. 18:5 at this point he uses the formula 'the man that doeth ... shall live thereby' as a proper expression *in itself* of the principle of works-righteousness in contrast with the righteousness of faith."[85] One thing is very clear. Although Murray does not utilize the

---

[83] Kline, *Kingdom Prologue*, 73.

[84] Murray, *Romans*, I:361-62.

[85] Ibid., II:250. The *Westminster Statement on Justification* correctly states that Galatians 3:11-12, Romans 10:5 and Leviticus 18:5 are key passages for denoting the principle of law or works as over against grace or faith. Moreover, it affirms justification by faith alone from the vantage point of the antithesis between Law and Gospel or works and faith. In other words, Scripture requires the antithesis between Law and Gospel hermeneutics to identify the principle of faith or grace for our salvation and justification: "All of God's covenantal dealings after the fall are administrations of God's one

foedus legale as being operative in a limited sense under the Old Covenant with respect to the temporal blessings or curses in the typological kingdom continuity over against the Abrahamic/New Covenants as Kline properly does, he does use Romans 10:5-6 and Galatians 3:12 alluding to Leviticus 18:5 to confirm the antithesis between Law and Gospel, which is required for the biblical doctrine of justification by faith alone.

While Murray utilizes the Pauline antithesis between Law and Gospel to defend the doctrine of forensic justification against legalism, he, like Paul in Romans 3:31, affirms the need of the law for the sanctification of believers: "We are compelled therefore to recognize that the subject of law and grace is not simply concerned with the antithesis that there is between law and grace, but also with law as that which makes grace necessary and with grace as establishing and confirming law."[86] In this respect, the believer's application of the law for progressive sanctification is vital to stave off *antinomianism*, while the antithesis between Law and Gospel is foundational for depicting justification by *faith alone* against *legalism*. This reveals that Murray desires to establish a careful hermeneutical balance:

> The purity and integrity of the gospel stand or fall with the absoluteness of the antithesis between the function and potency of law, on the one hand, and the function and potency of grace, on the other.

---

master-plan of grace. There is therefore continuity in their succession (W.C. VII:v). Yet they differ in form. The promise orientation of the covenant with Abraham differs from the emphasis on law obedience in the subordinate covenant with Israel at Sinai (Gal. 3:17-22). Paul writes that the demand of the law that he who does the commandments will live in them is not of faith but of works (Gal. 3:11,12; Rom. 10:5; Lev. 18:5). No sinner can be justified by that law, for no sinner can keep it. The law is good: it states what is pleasing to God and marks the path of life. Yet it can only condemn and not justify the sinner. The law given at Sinai does not cancel out the promises, however. It was given not only to reveal sin, but to be sought and heeded by those who would live by faith, as did Abraham. Those who walked by faith realized that they could not keep the law and trusted in the forgiveness of sins through the blood of the covenant provided on God's altar; they looked for the promise of righteousness from 'the Lord our righteousness' (Jer. 23:6)." Westminster Theological Seminary, *Westminster Statement on Justification*, 9-10.

[86] Murray, *Principles of Conduct*, 182.

But while all this is true it does not by any means follow that the antithesis eliminates all relevance of the law to the believer as a believer.[87]

Murray states that classic dispensationalism correctly applies the antithesis between Law and Gospel in respect to justification by faith alone. This is the biblical-theological rationale for Murray putting classical dispensationalism into the category of *evangelicalism*. Classical dispensationalism, however, fails to see the application of the law to the believers' life, which is a typical pattern of *antinomianism*:

> A great many of the statements of dispensationalists are perfectly correct insofar as they express the antithesis that does exist, and on which Scripture lays the greatest emphasis, between obedience to law as the way of justification and acceptance with God and the way of grace. Every evangelical must recognize and appreciate this absolute antithesis.[88]

Believers' good works performed in the course of progressive sanctification in Christ are acceptable to God. Reflecting on Matthew 10:41; 1 Corinthians 3:8-9,11-15; 4:5; 2 Corinthians 5:10 and 2 Timothy 4:7, Murray notices that good works are the criterion of heavenly rewards. In other words, Murray's solution to *antinomianism* is to recognize the implication of the law in the believers' life for good works and gradations of heavenly rewards, whereas justification by faith alone from the vantage point of the antithesis between Law and Gospel hermeneutics is the definitive biblical- theological answer to *legalism*: "We must maintain therefore, justification complete and irrevocable by grace through faith and apart from good works, and at the same time, future reward according to works."[89] According to Rome, salvation and heavenly rewards are based on *meritum de congruo et meritum de condigno*. In opposition to this legalistic interpretation of salvation and justification, Murray notices that believers' good works are correlated to gradations of eschatological heavenly rewards:

---

[87] Ibid., 186.
[88] Ibid., 264.
[89] Murray, *Collected Writings*, 2:221.

> While the reward is of grace yet the standard or criterion of judgment by which the degree of reward is to be determined is good works. This reward is not administered because good works earn or merit reward, but because God is graciously pleased to reward them. That is to say it is a reward of grace. In the Romish scheme good works have real merit and constitute the ground of the title to everlasting life.[90]

Once again, Murray emphasizes that the blessing of eschatological heavenly glory itself is God's free gift in Christ. He argues, however, that *degrees* of eschatological glory will corresponds to believers' good works. In this respect, Murray agrees with the general pattern of thought in covenant hermeneutics, as we have demonstrated in chapter one. Murray writes:

---

[90] Ibid. Here, Murray follows the nineteen century Scottish theologian, James Buchanan who makes a careful distinction between justification by faith alone and the gradation of future glorification according to works: "Some have imagined that the doctrine of a free Justification now by grace, through faith alone, is inconsistent with that of a future judgment according to works ... But there is no real inconsistency between the two doctrines ... 'I would have every preacher,' said Dr. Chalmers to the author, 'insist strenuously on these two doctrines–a present justification by grace, through faith alone–and a future Judgment according to works;' and all faithful ministers have made use of both, that they might guard equally against the peril of self-righteous legalism, on the one hand, and of practical Antinomianism, on the other." James Buchanan, *The Doctrine of Justification: An Outline of Its History in the Church and of Its Exposition from Scripture* (Grand Rapids, Michigan: Baker Book House, 1955), 238-39.

The *Westminster Statement on justification* adapted the traditional view of gradation in respect to eschatological heavenly glorification while it safeguards justification by faith alone excluding good works from the vantage point of the antithesis of Law and Gospel: "We affirm that for believers the final judgment is not only a matter of assigning relative degrees of blessing or reward, but, with a view to the ultimate outcome of eternal life or eternal destruction, is an open acquittal or final reconfirmation of their justification, and that this open acquittal is 'according to works' (Rom. 2:6,7), understood as the fruit and criterion of a true, living faith; and we deny that the open acquittal at the day of judgment has any other ground than the imputed righteousness of Christ or any other instrument than faith, or that the good works of the believer in any way contribute to it." Westminster Theological Seminary, "Westminster Statement on Justification," 17.

The good works of believers will be rewarded (cf. Matt. 10:41, 42; 1 Cor. 3:8, 12-15). This reward does not consist in salvation nor in the eternal life inherited in the world to come. It consists in the degree of glory bestowed in the state of bliss. Glory itself is the gift of grace and secured by the righteousness of Christ (cf. Rom. 5:18-21). But the degrees of glory are proportioned to the faithfulness and labour of the saints.[91]

Meanwhile, Kline's approach in respect to eschatological heavenly glorification is different from Murray's. Kline's biblical theology does not permit *gradations* of eschatological heavenly glory because he believes that this may obscure the fact that Christ merited our justification and salvation. Therefore, Kline admits the application of the law to believers in opposition to *antinomianism*, but he does not allow for the gradation of eschatological heavenly rewards according to good works:

> According to God's creational ordering it is a necessary and inevitable sequence, in preredemptive covenant as well as in redemptive history, that 'whom he justified, him he also glorified' (Rom. 8:30). Within the frame work of this judicial-eschatological bonding of glorification to justification, once it has been determined on what principle justification operates under a given covenant, the principle governing the grant of eschatological blessings in that covenant has also been determined. If justification is by grace through faith, as it is under the gospel, glorification will not be by works. And if justification is secured on the grounds of works, as it clearly is in the preredemptive covenant, glorification will not be by grace.[92]

Murray and Kline agree that heavenly glorification itself is based upon God's grace alone. Kline does not allow for the *gradation* of the eschatological kingdom blessings, but Murray allows for it on the basis of believers' good works in obedience to the law during the process of sanctification. We believe however that Murray's approach *conforms* moreto the general direction and guidance of Scripture (Matt. 5:12; 2 Tim. 4:6-8; James 1:12; Rev. 22:12), while recalling that justification by faith alone apart from works is based on the antithesis between Law and Gospel.

---

[91] Murray, *Collected Writings*, 2:416-17.
[92] Kline, *Kingdom Prologue*, 71-2.

D. Summary

We have revisited John Murray's and Meredith G. Kline's interpretation of the antithesis between the *foedus operum* and *foedus gratiae*. As we affirmed the *foedus operum* in the prelapsarian state from the vantage point of historical and biblical theology, we argued that Murray's definition of covenant as a "sovereign administration of grace and promise" is inadequate because it only reflects *the covenant of grace* and excludes *the covenant of works*. Murray's weakness certainly contributed to Kline's definition of the covenant, for it combines the motifs of covenant and kingdom. Nevertheless, Kline adopts the *sovereign aspect* of Murray's definition and defines covenant as "a sovereign administration of the kingdom of God."

Although Murray does not affirm the covenant of works, he does recognize the historical order of *law and grace* in respect to eschatological justification and blessing. Nevertheless, he does not interpret the prelapsarian Adamic administration from a *forensic perspective* by means of the antithesis between the first Adam and second Adam. One of the theological reasons that Murray does not like the term *foedus operum*, is because it undermines "the elements of grace" in the prelapsarian state. While Murray highlights the distinction between the Creator and creature, this is still a weakness in his approach. Nevertheless, he affirms the principle of "works-righteousness" *operates* in the prelapsarian state as the means of eschatological justification and life, to which the 'Do this and you will live' of Leviticus 18:5 alludes. An inconsistency arises when he argues that eschatological justification and life are not based upon "justice," but "God's faithfulness." This results from Murray's failure to interpret the prelapsarian state from a *forensic* or *legal* viewpoint. Murray's interpretation, however, is over all compatible with the antithesis between the covenants of works and grace.

Kline, affirming the antithesis between the covenants of works and grace does not want to introduce *the idea of grace* into the prelapsarian state while he still makes a careful distinction between Creator and creature. He takes this approach because he believes the contrast between the first and second Adams, requires a *forensic* or *legal* interpretation of the original covenant of creation that anticipates consummate justification and kingdom blessings. In other words, Adam's perfect obedience to the law would have been the ground of eschatological forensic justification and life.

Murray does not interpret the prelapsarian state of the first Adam *forensically*. However, we suggested, according to our definition of merit, that Murray's interpretation agrees with the meritorious standing of the first Adam because he demonstrates that Adam's perfect obedience to the law was the means of the consummate blessings. Meanwhile, Kline recognizes the meritorious standing of the first Adam, which he closely integrates with the forensic aspect of the prelapsarian state. Thus, Adam's eschatological justification and kingdom blessings would have been grounded on his meritorious obedience, which is based on the antithesis between the first and second Adams.

In the Mosaic Covenant-making process of Exodus 19-24, Murray does not affirm that the *foedus legale* was somehow operative, even though he does recognize an apparently legal element in contrast to the previous Abrahamic Covenant. For this reason, Murray interprets the Mosaic Covenant exclusively in *continuity* with the Abrahamic and New Covenants. Kline, however, tries to maintain that the Mosaic Covenant was in a limited and typological sense the *foedus legale* or *foedus operum* which reflects the original covenant of works. The Israelites made a solemn commitment to God in the Mosaic Covenant-making process saying, "We will do everything the Lord has said; we will obey" (Exod. 19:8; 24:3,7). This identifies the Mosaic Covenant as "a law covenant." Moreover, *continuity* with the *foedus gratiae* is found within the covenant-making process in Exodus 19:5-6 and 24:5-8. Kline, therefore, argues that the theocratic kingdom blessings which typify the eschatological heavenly kingdom blessings were dependent on the Israelites' general obedience to the law, while individual believers under the Old Covenant were saved and justified by the principle of the *foedus gratiae*. This eschatological understanding of the Old Covenant is lacking in Murray's approach because he does not allow for the outworking of the *foedus legale* in the administration of nation of Israel. Thus, 'Do this and you will live' of Leviticus 18:5, according to Murray, does not signify the principle of the law under the Old Covenant. Rather, it indicates the believers' covenant obligation which is analogous to the third use of the law. Kline, in agreement with classical covenant theology, sees Leviticus 18:5 as the biblical theological manifestation of the principle of works under the Old Covenant for the purpose of administering the *typological kingdom of Israel*. Kline explains the Israelites' obedience under the

Old Covenant as *meritorious* but limited to the continuation of the blessings of the typological kingdom. We suggested that the concept of merit should be limited to the obedience of the first and second Adams since perfect obedience does not exist in the postlapsarian state with the single exception of Christ.

Both Murray and Kline affirm justification by faith alone apart from good works or evangelical obedience, interpreting it in the light of the antithesis between Law and Gospel. Their consensus on forensic justification is integrated with the imputation of Christ's righteousness and the instrumentality of faith. Both Murray and Kline correctly indicate that good works or evangelical obedience is the *fruit* of justifying faith. Murray argues that *degrees* of heavenly glory and reward will be assigned to believers according to their good works; this reflects both the overall view of Scripture and of covenant hermeneutics. Kline, however, does not permit the *gradation* of heavenly glory because the concept of gradation may obscure Christ's meritorious work for our justification and salvation.

CONCLUSION

Our study has endeavored to prove that the development of federal theology, centered on the antithesis between the covenants of works and grace, does not fall into *dualism* or *legalism* as critics have often claimed. Rather, covenant theology has demonstrated the biblical theological legitimacy of the antithesis between the covenants of works and grace as a necessary hermeneutical tool for interpreting biblical revelation *covenantally* and *eschatologically*.

Calvin's *bilateral* covenant of grace does not deviate from the Protestant evangelical consensus that justification is *by faith alone* apart from evangelical obedience, because it utilizes the antithesis between Law and Gospel. In other words, *law and gospel hermeneutics*, as illustrated by Pauline theology, rather than *law in gospel* controls Calvin's depiction of the doctrine of justification *by faith alone* and the principle of sovereign grace in divine election. In this respect, good works in the believer's life are the *fruit* or *evidence* of justifying faith. Moreover, the mixture of Law and Gospel, according to Calvin, inevitably leads to *legalism* as represented by the theology of medieval Schoolmen. Thus, we have proven that the antithesis between Law and Gospel and the doctrine of justification by faith alone apart from good works stand or fall together.

Meanwhile, we have paid special attention to the fact that even though Calvin does not designate the prelapsarian state as the *foedus operum*, he interprets it *eschatologically*. The prelapsarian state was governed by the principle of the law as the means of the eschatological heavenly blessing even though it was not realized due to the entrance of sin. The one covenant of grace inaugurated in Genesis 3:15 becomes the principle of justification and salvation in the postlapsarian state, including the Old Covenant. Thus there is *heilsgeshichte continuity* between the Old and New Covenants. Nevertheless, we have shown that Calvin recognizes the Old Covenant as the *foedus legale* in a limited sense for the purpose of administering the earthly nation of Israel in types and figures by blessing or curse according to the *general* principle of obedience, ultimately anticipating the eschatological heavenly blessing in Christ or everlasting curse. Calvin's eschatological interpretation of the Old Covenant by application of the *foedus legale*, provides the biblical theological background for the further development of Old Covenant *eschatology* and an *eschatological* understanding of the original covenant of works by later covenant theologians. In the final analysis, we have demonstrated that Calvin's theology is fully congruous with the later Calvinists' developments of the antithesis between the covenants of works and grace. Thus, the antithesis between the covenants of works and grace developed and elaborated by covenant theologians exposits *the Christocentric motif and theology* in the *ordo salutis* and *historia salutis*.

Evaluating the development of the antithesis between the covenants of works and grace from John Calvin to Geerhardus Vos, we dealt with the problem of *merit* in relation to the antithesis between the first and second Adams revealed in Romans 5:12-21. Along with Charles Hodge, we affirmed that the original covenant of works is to be interpreted from a *forensic* or *judicial perspective*. From this perspective, Adam's standing as the representative covenantal head was *meritorious*. Thus, the first Adam's perfect obedience would have *merited* eschatological justification and blessing, while in the covenant of grace, Christ's *meritorious* righteousness, resulting from his perfect obedience to the law, is the only ground for the believer's justification and salvation. Therefore, we provided biblical theological logic to limit *meritorious* obedience to the two Adams. In this respect, *merit and grace, letter and spirit, and Law and Grace are antithetical* in relation to the doctrine of justification by faith alone. We also found that the 'Do this and you will live' of Leviticus 18:5 reflects the principle of works in the *foedus operum* or *foedus legale*, ultimately providing the Pauline antithesis between Law and Gospel in Romans 10:5-6 and Galatians 3:10-12. On the one hand, these passages manifest a definitive hermeneutical principle for depicting justification by faith alone, and provide a biblical theological reason to contrast the Mosaic and New Covenants at the level of the typological kingdom administration. On the other hand, the principle of the covenant of grace continued to be the basis of salvation and justification under the Mosaic Covenant.

Having laid the historical theological background of the development of covenant theology, we studied John Murray, who identified himself as *a revisionist*. We argued that his revision failed since his understanding of the covenant is somewhat *biblicistic*, as evidenced by his rejection of the covenant of works. Although he rejects the antithesis between the covenants of works and grace, his biblical-systematic theology is compatible with the antithesis between the covenants of works and grace. We demonstrated that Murray recognizes the historical order of *law and grace*, and that the means of eschatological justification and life in the prelapsarian state was perfect obedience to the law.

We saw that Murray interprets the Old Covenant exclusively in the light of *continuity* with the New Covenant. This is a reaction against classical covenant theology, which identifies and interprets the Old Covenant in relation to the *foedus legale* in a limited sense, and classical dispensationalism, which contrasts the two covenants at the level of *salvation*. However, Murray does this at the expense of the rich *eschatological* motif rightly observed by other covenant theologians. The 'Do this and you will live' of Leviticus 18:5 was the principle of the law *only* in the prelapsarian state. Contrary to *classical covenant theology*, Murray argues that the 'Do this and you will live' of Leviticus 18:5 was not operative under the Old Covenant as the governing principle of the typological nation of Israel. Rather, it revealed the believer's covenant obligation under the Mosaic Covenant. Murray strongly defends this contrast of Law and Gospel in order to place justification *by faith alone* against *legalism* represented by the Schoolmen and Judaizers' of the early church. Of course, his systematic theology is controlled by the motif of *union with Christ* (*unio cum Christo*), especially in his interpretation of the *ordo salutis*, but he rightly argues that the centrality of union with Christ and the *eschatological* kingdom of God as *the already / not yet* cannot jeopardize the doctrine of justification by faith alone, since the doctrine of justification is to be understood by the hermeneutical principle of the antithesis between Law and Gospel as demonstrated by the apostle Paul. Meanwhile, in opposition to *antinomianism*, Murray affirms that the believer's application of the law in the process of progressive sanctification produces good works. In the final analysis, Murray rightly urges that we apply the antithesis between Law and Gospel as a proper hermeneutical tool to understand the *ordo salutis* and *historia salutis*.

As we have seen, Murray's revision of covenant theology is not well received by Kline although he acknowledges Murray's contribution in respect to the *sovereign* aspect of covenant. Kline demonstrates the antithesis between the covenants of works and grace from the vantage point of biblical theology. He weaves together the motifs of *covenant, kingdom* and *eschatology*, which shed light on the comprehensive interpretation of the biblical revelation. Kline interprets the original covenant of creation from a *judicial* or *forensic* perspective which is justified by the complete antithesis between Adam and Christ manifested in Romans 5:12-21. Thus, the antithesis between the covenants of works and grace correctly interprets the prelapsarian state from the perspective of divine justice and Adam's *meritorious* standing in respect to the covenant of works. Thus, Kline rightly insists on preserving the historical order of *law and grace*. In doing so, he does not introduce the idea of *grace* into the prelapsarian state, but makes a proper distinction between the Creator and creature. The goal of the *eschatological* heavenly kingdom would have been fulfilled if Adam had obeyed the requirement of the covenant of works. Accordingly, Kline develops covenant and kingdom motifs in relation to *the goal of the eschatological kingdom*, which is directed by the covenant of works in the prelapsarian state, and by the covenant of grace in the postlapsarian state.

The covenant of grace, according to Kline, is the means of eschatological salvation and justification in the postlapsarian state, even under the Old Covenant. This demonstrates covenantal *continuity*. Kline, however, argues that the *foedus legale* was operative at the level of the typological theocratic kingdom which signifies the antitypical heavenly kingdom blessing in Christ. The covenant making process of Exodus 19-24 is biblical evidence that the Mosaic Covenant is the *foedus legale*, since it was solemnly sworn by the Israelites, while the *foedus gratiae* was also present as the principle of individual justification and salvation. At this point, we refuted the contention that Kline has an affinity with dispensational hermeneutics, proving that he is a thoroughly covenant theologian since he avoids *legalism* by applying *typology*. In other words, the principle of the *foedus legale* is utilized only for the administration of the typological kingdom. The 'Do this and you will live' of Leviticus 18:5 was applied under the Old Covenant as the principle of the law which administers the typological kingdom of Israel, and we substantiated that this line of argument rightly follows from *classical covenant theology*. However, we do not want to call the Israelites' obedience under the Old Covenant *meritorious* as does Kline. Kline limits *merit* to the typological kingdom blessing, recognizing that the Israelites' obedience was never perfect, but we suggested that the concept does not to apply to the Israelites' corporate obedience, because obedience must be perfect to be *meritorious*. Hence meritorious obedience was only possible for the two Adams. We demonstrated that Kline affirms justification by faith alone against the *legalism* represented by Roman Catholics and ecumenical theology. In answer to *legalism*, he greatly urges that we apply the hermeneutical principle of the antithesis between Law and Gospel along with the antithesis between the covenants of works and grace. Moreover, this antithetical hermeneutical principle plays a crucial role in his biblical theology for expounding *biblical eschatology*, *covenant* and *kingdom*. In other words, without applying the hermeneutical principle of the antithesis between Law and Gospel, it is impossible to expound the biblical concept of justification and salvation. Good works in believers' lives that result from the application of the moral law, according to Kline, are required in the process of progressive sanctification in opposition to *antinomianism*.

In the final analysis, our thesis tried to contribute to the exposition and defense of true *grace oriented and Christocentric theology* against critics of covenant theology. In other words, *Christocentric theology* based on divine grace is abundantly fruitful when we carefully apply the hermeneutical principle of the antithesis between the covenants of works and grace along with the antithesis between Law and Gospel. D. Clair Davis insightfully states *how* evangelicals practice theology from the perspective of *Christocentric theology*, the centerpiece of biblical revelation:

> Before the entire evangelical world is the greatest religious issue of all: law and Gospel, justification and sanctification, propitiation and deliverance, cross and resurrection, the whole Jesus Christ 'in all of his offices.' Remember Luther's gratitude to Erasmus, that he had

finally placed on the agenda a question worth discussing, the question of free will and the Gospel. The church of Christ can unite in gratitude today, that in the face of a self-conscious attack on the name of Christ, it can again self-consciously address the most significant issue of all, that of Jesus Christ as both Savior and Lord.[1]

In conclusion, we suggest that *the evangelical world* utilize the antithesis between the covenants of works and grace along with the antithesis between Law and Gospel. They are necessary to expound the doctrines of sovereign grace in divine election, forensic justification and salvation against *legalism*, and to require believers to obey the law and produce good works in opposition to *antinomianism*. Moreover, by utilizing the antithesis between the covenants of works and grace, we may gain rich insights into the *ordo salutis* and *historia salutis*, which are crucial both to biblical and systematic theology.

---

[1] D. Clair Davis, "A Challenge to Theonomy," in *Theonomy: A Reformed Critique*, eds. William S. Barker & W. Robert Godfrey (Grand Rapids, Michigan: Zonderban Publishing House, 1990), 402.

BIBLIOGRAPHY

A. Primary Sources

Calvin, John. *Ioannis Calvini opera quae supersunt omnia.* 59 vols. Battles. Vol. XX and XXI In *The Library of Christian Classics.* Philadelphia, Pennsylvania: The Westminster Press, 1975.

_____. *Calvin's Commentaries.* 22 vols. Various Translators. Edinburgh: Calvin Translation Society, 1863. Reprint, Grand Rapids, Michigan: Baker Book House, 1996.

_____. *Selected Works of John Calvin: Tracts and Letters.* 7 vols. ed. Henry Beveridge, David Constable, and Marcus R. Gilchrist. Grand Rapids, Michigan: Baker Book House, 1983.

Hodge, Charles. *The Epistle to the Romans: A Commentary on Romans.* Reprint, The Banner of Truth Trust, 1975.

_____. *Systematic Theology.* 3 vols. Reprint, Grand Rapids, Michigan: Eerdsmans Publishing Company, 1995.

Kline, Meredith G. "Abram's Amen." *Westminster Theological Journal* 31 (1968/69): 1-11.

_____. "Because It Had Not Rained." *Westminster Theological Journal* 20 (1957/58): 146-57.

_____. "Bible Book of the Month: Lamentations." *Christianity Today* 5 (March 27, 1961): 567-68.

_____. "Bible Book of the Month: Zechariah." *Christianity Today* 2 (April 14, 1958): 23-24, 33.

_____. "Bible Book of the Month: Song of the Songs." *Christianity Today* 3 (April 27, 1959): 22-23, 39.

_____. *By Oath Consigned: A Reinterpretation of the Covenant Signs of Circumcision and Baptism.* Grand Rapids, Michigan: Eerdmans Publishing Company, 1968.

_____. "Canon and Covenant, I." *Westminster Theological Journal* 32 (1969/70): 49-67.

_____. "Canon and Covenant, II." *Westminster Theological Journal* 32 (1969/70): 179-200.

_____. "Canon and Covenant, III." *Westminster Theological Journal* 33 (1970/71): 45-72.

_____. "The Correlation of the Concepts Canon and Covenant." In *New Perspectives on the Old Testament,* ed. J.B. Payne, 265-79. Waco, Texas: Word Books, 1970.

_____. "The Covenant of the Seventieth Week." In *The Law and the Prophet,.* ed. John H. Skilton. Nutley, New Jersey: Presbyterian and Reformed Publishing Company, 1974.

_____. "Covenant Theology under Attack." *New Horizons* 15/2 (1994): 3-5.

_____. "Creation in the Image of the Glory-Spirit." *Westminster Theological Journal* 39 (1976/77): 250-72.

_____. "Death, Leviathan, and the Martyrs: Isaiah 24:1-27." In *A Tribute to Gleason Archer,* eds. Walter C. Kaiser Jr. and Ronald F. Youngblood, 229-49. Chicago, Illinois: Moody Press, 1986.

_____. "Deuteronomy" and "Job." In *The Wycliffe Bible Commentary,* eds. C.F. Pfeiffer and E.F. Harrison, 155-204, 459-90. Chicago, Illinois: Moody Press, 1962.

_____. "Deuteronomy" and "Job." In *The Zondervan Pictorial Bible Dictionary,* ed. M.C. Tenney, 214-15, 443-44. Grand Rapids, Michigan: Zondervan Publishing House, 1963.

_____. "Divine Kingship and Genesis 6:1-4." *Westminster Theological Journal* 24 (1961/62): 187-204.

_____. "Double Trouble." *Journal of the Evangelical Theological Society* 32/2 (1989): 171-79.

_____. "Dynastic Covenant." *Westminster Theological Journal* 23 (1960/61): 1-15.

_____. "The Exaltation of Christ." *Kerux* 12/3 (1997): 3-29.

_____. "The First Resurrection." *Westminster Theological Journal* 37 (1974/75): 366-75.

_____. "The First Resurrection: a Reaffirmation." *Westminster Theological Journal* 39 (1976/77): 110-19.

_____. "Genesis." In *The New Bible Commentary.* 3d ed. and eds. D. Guthrie and J.A. Motyer, 79-114. Grand Rapids, Michigan: Eerdmans Publishing Company, 1970.

_____. "Gospel until the Law: Romans 5:13-14 and the Old Covenant." *Journal of the Evangelical Theological Society* 34/4 (1991): 433-46.

_____. "The Ha-BI-ru." Ph.D. diss., Dropsie College, 1955.

_____. "The Ha-Bi-ru: Kin or Foe of Israel?, I." *Westminster Theological Journal* 19 (1956/57): 1-24.

_____. "The Ha-Bi-ru: Kin or Foe of Israel?, II." *Westminster Theological Journal* 19 (1956/57): 170-74.

_____. "The Ha-Bi-ru: Kin or Foe of Israel?, III." *Westminster Theological Journal* 20 (1957/58): 46-70.

_____. "Hebrews" and "Ten Commandments." In *The New Bible Dictionary*, ed. J.D. Douglas, 511-12, 1251-252. London: Inter-Varsity Press, 1962.

_____. *Images of the Spirit*. S. Hamilton, Massachussets: Gordon-Conwell Theological Seminary, 1986.

_____. "Intrusion and the Decalogue." *Westminster Theological Journal* 16 (1953/54): 1-22.

_____. "Investiture with the Image of God." *Westminster Theological Journal* 40 (1977/78): 38-62.

_____. "Is the History of the Old Testament Reliable?" In *Can I Trust My Bible?: Important Questions Often Asked About the Bible: With Some Answers by Eight Evangelical Scholars*, 135-51. Chicago, Illinois: Moody Press, 1963.

_____. *Kingdom Prologue*. S. Hamilton, Massachussets: Gordon-Conwell Theological Seminary, 1989.

_____. "Law Covenant." *Westminster Theological Journal* 27 (1964/65): 1-20.

_____. "Lex Talionis and the Human Fetus." *Evangelical Theological Society* 20 (1977): 193-201.

_____. "Oath and Ordeal Signs, I." *Westminster Theological Journal* 28 (1964/65): 115-39.

_____. "Oath and Ordeal Signs, II." *Westminster Theological Journal* 28 (1965/66): 1-37.

_____. "The Oracular Origin of the State." In *Biblical and Near Eastern Studies: Essays in Honor of William Sanford LaSor*, ed. G.A. Tuttle, 132-41. Grand Rapids, Michigan: Eerdmans Publishing Company, 1978.

_____. "The Old Testament Origins of the Gospel Genre." *Westminster Theological Journal* 38 (1975/76): 1-27.

_____. "Primal Parousia." *Westminster Theological Journal* 40 (1977/78): 245-280.

_____. "The Relevance of the Theocracy." *Presbyterian Guardian* 22 (February 16, 1953): 26-7, 36.

_____. "The Rider of the Red Horse, I." *Kerux* 5 (September 1990): 2-20.

_____. "The Rider of the Red Horse, II." *Kerux* 5 (December 1990): 9-28.

_____. "The Servant and Serpent." *Kerux* 8/1 (1993): 20-37.

_____. "The Servant and the Serpent." *Kerux* 8/2 (1993): 10-34.

_____. "Structure of the Book of Zechariah." *Journal of the Evangelical Theological Society* 34/2 (1991): 179-93.

_____. *The Structure of Biblical Authority*. Rev. ed. S. Hamilton, Massachussets: Gordon-Conwell Theological Seminary, 1989.

_____. *Treaty of the Great King: The Covenant Structure of Deuteronomy*. Grand Rapids, Michigan: Eerdmans Publishing Company, 1963.

_____. "The Two Tables of the Covenant." *Westminster Theological Journal* 22 (1959/60): 133-46.

_____. "Gospel Until the Law: Rom 5:13-14 and the Old Covenant." *Journal of the Evangelical Theological Society* 34 (1991): 433-46.

_____. "Of Works and Grace." *Presbyterion* 9 (1983): 85-92.

Murray, John. "Abounding Hope." *The Banner of Truth* 150 (March 1976): 1-5.

_____. "Abstinence," "Adoption," "Atonement." In *The Encyclopedia of Christianity*, vol.1, 37-9, 70-4, 465-80. Delaware: The National Foundation for Christian Education, 1964.

_____. "Adam," "Covenant," "Ethics," "Law (in the NT)," "Mediator," "Repentance," "Sin." In *The New Bible Dictionary*, ed. J.D. Douglas, 14, 264-68, 394-97, 721-23, 802-04, 1083-84, 1189-93. London / Grand Rapids: Tyndale Press & Eerdmans Publishing Company, 1962.

_____. "Adoption, I." *The Presbyterian Guardian* 22/10 (1953): 193-195.

_____. "Adoption, II." *The Presbyterian Guardian* 22/11 (1953): 213-214.

_____. "Adoption," "Divorce" and "Elect, Election." In *Baker's Dictionary of Theology*, ed. E.F. Harrison, 25-6, 169-71, 179-80. Grand Rapids, Michigan: Baker Book House, 1960.

_____. *The Atonement*. Grand Rapids, Michigan: Baker Book House, 1962.

_____. "The Authority of Scripture." *The Presbyterian Guardian* 9/8 (1941): 121-23.

_____. "Baptism," "Elect, Election," "The Fall," "Foreknow, Foreknowledge," "Foreordain, Foreordination," "Intercession of Christ." In *The Zondervan Pictorial Bible Dictionary*, 1:468-69, 2:270-74, 2:492-94, 2:590-93, 2:594, 3:294-95. Grand Rapids, Michigan: Zondervan Publishing House, 1969.

_____. "Christ our Sin Bearer." *The Banner of Truth* 221(February 1982): 13-15.

_____. *Christian Baptism*. Phillipsburg, New Jersey: Presbyterian and Reformed Publishing Company, 1980.

_____. "The Calling of the Westminster Assembly." *The Presbyterian Guardian* 11/2 (1942): 26-8.

_____. "The Christian Doctrine of Vicarious Atonement: The Origin of the Idea of Vicarious Atonement, II." *The Homiletic Review* 102/2 (1931): 93.

_____. *Collected Writings of John Murray: The Claims of Truth*. vol.1. The Banner of Truth Trust, 1976.

_____. *Collected Writings of John Murray: Select Lectures in Systematic Theology*. vol.2. The Banner of Truth Trust, 1977.

_____. *Collected Writings of John Murray: Life (by IainH. Murray), Sermons and Reviews*. vol.3. The Banner of Truth Trust, 1982.

_____. *Collected Writings of John Murray: Studies in Theology*. vol.4. The Banner of Truth Trust, 1983.

_____. "The Coming of the Spirit." *The Banner of Truth* 188 (May 1979): 9-11.

_____. "The Confessional Statement of the United Presbyterian Church." *Christianity Today* 2/9 (1932): 7-8.

_____. *The Covenant of Grace: A Biblico-Theological Study*. Phillipsburg, New Jersey: Presbyterian and Reformed Publishing Company, 1988.

_____. "Covenant Theology." In *The Encyclopedia of Christianity*, vol.3. ed. P.E. Hughes.

_____. "Creed Subscription in The Presbyterian Church in the U.S.A." In *The Case for Full Subscription to the Westminster Standards in the Presbyterian Church in America*. ed. Morton Howison Smith. Greenville, South Carolina: Greenville Presbyterian Theological Seminary, 1992.

_____. *Divorce*. Phillipsburg, New Jersey: Presbyterian and Reformed Publishing Company, 1961.

_____. "Divorce." In *The Encyclopedia of Christianity*. vol.3. ed. P. E. Hughes, 421-24. Delaware: The National Foundation for Christian Education, 1972.

_____. "Dr. Machen's Hope and the Active Obedience of Christ." *The Presbyterian Guardian* 3 (1937): 163.

_____. "The Epistle to the Romans." vols.1 & 2. In *The New International Commentary on the New Testament*, ed. Gordon D. Fee. Grand Rapids, Michigan: Eerdmans Publishing Company, 1968.

_____. "Faith." *The Presbyterian Guardian* 22/3 (1953): 48-9.

_____. "The Fourth Commandment." *The Calvin Forum* 6/10 (1941): 204.

_____. "Glorification, I." *The Presbyterian Guardian* 23/7 (1954): 131.

_____. "Glorification, II." *The Presbyterian Guardian* 23/8 (1954): 154-155.

_____. *The Imputation of Adam's Sin*. Phillipsburg, New Jersey: Presbyterian and Reformed Publishing Company, 1959.

_____. "The Infallibility of Scripture." *The Banner of Truth* 30 (1963): 8-13.

_____. "The Inspiration of Scripture." *The Presbyterian Guardian* 9/7 (1941): 108-110.

_____. "Is Infant Baptism Scriptural?" *The Presbyterian Guardian* 5 (1938): 227-229.

_____. "Is the Decalogue Abrogated?" *The Calvin Forum* 6/10 (1941): 236-39.

_____. "Justification, I." *The Presbyterian Guardian* 22/5 (1953):88-9.

_____. "Justification, II." *The Presbyterian Guardian* 22/6 (1953): 109.

_____. "Justification, III." *The Presbyterian Guardian* 22/7 (1953):129- 30.

_____. "Justification, IV." *The Presbyterian Guardian* 22/9 (1953): 168-69.

_____. "The Kingdom of Heaven and the Kingdom of God." *The Presbyterian Guardian* 3 (1937): 139-41.

_____. "The Light of the World." *The Presbyterian Guardian* 13/17 (1944): 263-64.

_____. "Love and Its Correlatives." *The Banner of Truth* 159 (December 1976): 13- 5.

_____. "Love to Christ: The Supreme Necessity." *The Banner of Truth* 202 (July 1980): 1-4.

_____. "Memory and Prospect." *The Banner of Truth* 172 (January 1978): 1-4.

_____. "Ministers, Members of Local Congregations." *The Presbyterian Guardian* 21/5 (1952): 85-6.

_____. "The Necessity of the Scripture." *The Presbyterian Guardian* 9/6 (1941): 90-1.

_____. *The Pattern of the Lord's Day*. London / Edinburgh: The Lord's Day Society, 1973.

_____. "Perseverance, I." *The Presbyterian Guardian* 23/2 (1954): 33-4.

_____. "Perseverance, II." *The Presbyterian Guardian* 23/3 (1954):54-6.

_____. "Pictures of Christ." *The Reformed Herald* (February 1960).

_____. *Principles of Conduct: Aspects of Biblical Ethics*. Grand Rapids, Michigan: Eerdsmans Publishing Company, 1991.

_____. "Proposed Confessional Revision in the Presbyterian Church in U.S.A." *The Presbyterian Guardian* 5 (1938): 207-10.

_____. "The Proposed Doctrinal Basis of Union." *Christianity Today* 2/10 (1932): 8-10.

_____. *Redemption: Accomplished and Applied*. Grand Rapids, Michigan: Eerdsmans Publishing Company, 1989.

_____. *Reformation Principles*. The Annual Lecture of the Evangelical Library, 1953.

_____. "The Reformed Faith and Modern Substitutes, I-IV." *The Presbyterian Guardian* 1 (1935): 88-9, 142-43, 163-64, 200-01, 211.

_____. "The Reformed Faith and Modern Substitutes, V-VII." *The Presbyterian Guardian* 2 (1936): 27-9, 77-9, 210-12.

_____. "Regeneration, I." *The Presbyterian Guardian* 22/1 (1953): 9, 16-7.

_____. "Regeneration, II." *The Presbyterian Guardian* 22/2 (1953): 28-9.

_____. "Repentance." *The Presbyterian Guardian* 22/4 (1953): 68-9.

———. "The Revision of the Form of Government." *The Presbyterian Guardian* 23/9 (1954): 171-73.

———. *The Sabbath Institution*. London / Edinburgh: The Lord's Day Observance Society, 1953.

———. "Sanctification." In *Basic Christian Doctrines*, ed. C.F. Henry, 227-33. Grand Rapids, Michigan: Baker Book House, 1962.

———. "Shall We Include the Revision of 1903 in our Creed?" *The Presbyterian Guardian* 2 (1936): 249-51.

———. "The Sabbath Symposium." *The Calvin Forum* 7/4 (1941): 70-2.

———. "Sanctification, I." *The Presbyterian Guardian* 22/12 (1953): 232-33.

———. "Sanctification, II." *The Presbyterian Guardian* 23/1 (1954): 15-6.

———. "Situation Ethics." *The Banner of Truth* 226 (July 1982):7-16.

———. *The Sovereignty of God*. Philadelphia, Pennsylvania: Great Commission Publications, 1965.

———. "Structural Strand in New Testament Eschatology." Unpublished. 1954.

———. "The Sufficiency of Scripture." *The Presbyterian Guardian* 9/9 (1941): 137-39.

———. "Systematic Theology, II." *Westminster Theological Journal* 26/1 (1963): 33-46.

———. "That They All May Be One." *The Presbyterian Guardian* 19/3 (1950): 45-6.

———. "Theology Proper: Person and Work of Christ." Unpublished Lecture Notes from John Murray Taken by Students.

———. "The Theology of the Westminster Standards." *The Calvin Forum* 9 (1944): 111-15.

———. "Tradition: Romish and Protestant, II." *The Presbyterian Guardian* 16/10 (1947): 150, 152-53.

———. "Unbelief in the Presbyterian Church in U.S.A." *The Presbyterian Guardian* 18/2 (1949): 32-5.

———. "Union with Christ, I." *The Presbyterian Guardian* 23/4 (1954): 71-2.

———. "Union with Christ, II." *The Presbyterian Guardian* 23/5 (1954): 94-6.

_____. "Union with Christ, III." *The Presbyterian Guardian* 23/6 (1954): 110-11.

_____. "The Unity of the Body of Christ." *The Banner of Truth* 231 (November 1982): 10-5.

_____. "What Is Amillennialism?" *The Presbyterian Guardian* 3 (1937): 242-44.

_____. "The Westminster Confession of Faith and the Salvation of Infants." *The Presbyterian Guardian* 3 (1936): 120-21.

_____. "Why We Baptize Infants." *The Presbyterian Guardian* 5 (1938): 143-44.

_____. "The Work of the Westminster Assembly." *The Presbyterian Guardian* 11/3 (1942): 37-8.

Olevianus, Caspar. *An Exposition of the Symbole of the Apostles.* trans. John Fielde. London, 1581.

_____. *A Firm Foundation: An Aid to Interpreting the Heidelberg Catechism.* trans. and ed. Lyle D. Bierma. Grand Rapids, Michigan: Baker Book House, 1995.

_____. *De Substantia Foederis Gratuiti inter Deum et Electos.* Geneva, 1585.

Owen, John. *Biblical Theology.* trans. Stephen P. Westcott. Pittsburg, Pennsylvania: Solideo Gloria Publications, 1994.

_____. *An Exposition of the Epistles to the Hebrews.* 7 vols. eds. William H. Goold. London, Johnstone & Hunter, 1855. Reprint, Grand Rapids, Michigan: Baker Book House, 1980.

_____. *The Works of John Owen.* 16 vols. ed. William H. Goold. The Banner of Truth Trust, 1977.

Rollock, Robert. *Select Works of Robert Rollock.* 2 vols. ed. William M. Gunn. Edinburgh: The Woodrow Society, 1844 &1849.

Turretin, Francis. *Institutes of Elenctic Theology.* 3 vols. trans. George Musgrave Giger and ed. James T. Dennison, Jr. Phillipsburg, New Jersey: Presbyterian and Reformed Publishing Company, 1992 & 1994.

Vos, Geerhardus. *Biblical Theology: Old and New Testaments.* Grand Rapids, Michigan: Eerdmans Publishing Company, 1948. Reprint, 1988.

_____. *The Pauline Eschatology.* Reprint, Phillipsburg, New Jersey: Presbyterian and Reformed Publishing Company, 1994.

_____. *Redemptive History and Biblical Interpretation*. ed. Richard B. Gaffin. Phillipsburg, New Jersey: Presbyterian and Reformed Publishing Company, 1980.

_____. *The Teaching of the Epistle to the Hebrews*. ed. Johannes G. Vos. Phillipsburg, New Jersey: Presbyterian and Reformed Publishing Company, 1956.

B. Secondary Sources

Allis, Oswald T. "The Covenant of Works." In *Basic Christian Doctrines: Contemporary Evangelical Thought*, ed. Carl F. H. Henry, 96-102. New York/Chicago/San Francisco: Holt, Rinehart & Winston, 1962.

_____. "Modern Dispensationalism and the Doctrine of the Unity of the Scripture." *The Evangelical Quarterly* 8 (January 1936): 22-35.

_____. "Modern Dispensationalism and the Law of God." *The Evangelical Quarterly* 8 (January 1936): 272-89.

_____. *Prophecy and the Church*. Phillipsburg, New Jersey: Presbyterian and Reformed Publishing Company, 1945.

Althaus, Paul. *Die Prinzipien der deutschen reformierten Dogmatik im Zeitalter der aristotelischen Scholastik*. Leipzig: Deichert, 1914. Reprint, Darmstadt: Wissenschaftliche Buchgesellschaft, 1967.

Anderson, Francis I. & Freedman, David Noel. *Hosea*. The Anchor Bible. Garden City, New York: Doubleday & Company, Inc., 1980.

Arminius, James. *The Writings of James Arminius*. 3 vols. vols. 1 and 2 trans. James Nichols. vol. 3 trans. William Nichols. Grand Rapids, Michigan: Baker Book House, 1986.

Armour, Rollin S. *Anabaptist Baptism: A Representative Study*. Scottdale, Pennsylvania: Herald Press, 1966.

Augustine. *St. Augustin's City of God and Christian Doctrine*. ed. Phillip Schaff. The Nicene and Post-Nicene Fathers, vol. 2. Edinburgh: T & T Clark / Grand Rapids, Michigan: Eerdmans Publishing Company, 1993.

_____. *St. Augustin: Anti-Pelagian Writings*. ed. Phillip Schaff. The Nicene and Post-Nicene Fathers, vol. 5. Edinburgh: T & T Clark / Grand Rapids, Michigan: Eerdmans Publishing Company, 1991.

Bahnsen, Greg L. *Theonomy in Christian Ethics: Expanded Edition with Replies to Critics.* 2d. ed. Phillipsburg, New Jersey: Presbyterian and Reformed Publishing Company, 1984.

_____. "M.G. Kline on Theonomic Politics." *Journal of Christian Reconstruction* 6 (Winter 1980): 196-221.

Baker, Charles F. *A Dispensational Theology.* Grand Rapids, Michigan: Grace Bible College Publications, 1971.

Baker, J. Wayne. *Heinrich Bullinger and the Covenant: The Other Reformed Tradition.* Athens, Ohio: Ohio University Press, 1980.

Ball, John. *A Treatise of the Covenant of Grace.* London: G. Miller, 1645.

Barker, William S. & Godfrey, Robert W. eds. *Theonomy: A Reformed Critique.* Grand Rapids, Michigan: Academie Books, 1990.

Barr, James. *The Semantics of Biblical Language.* Reprint. London: Oxford University Press, 1967.

Barth, Karl. *Church Dogmatics.* 4 vols. trans. G. W. Bromiley. Edinburgh: T.&T. Clark, 1974.

_____. "Gospel and Law," *God, Grace, and Gospel.* trans. J. S. McNab. Scottish Journal of Theology Occasional Papers No. 8 London: Oliver Boyd, 1959, 1-28.

Bartholomew, Craig G. "Covenant and Creation: Covenant Overload or Covenantal Deconstruction." *Calvin Theological Journal* 30 (1995): 11-33.

Bavinck, Herman. *Our Reasonable Faith: A Survey of Christian Doctrine.* trans. Henry Zylstra. Grand Rapids, Michigan: Baker Book House, 1977.

Berkhof, Louis. *The History of Christian Doctrines.* Reprint, The Banner of Truth Trust, 1991.

_____. *Systematic Theology.* Grand Rapids, Michigan: Eerdmans Publishing Company, 1939. Reprint, 1988.

Berkouwer, G. C. *Faith and Justification.* trans. Lewis B. Smedes. Grand Rapids, Michigan: Eerdmans Publishing Company, 1954.

_____. *Sin.* trans. Philip C. Holtrop. Grand Rapids, Michigan: Eerdmans Publishing Company, 1971.

_____. *The Triumph of Grace in the Theology of Karl Barth.* trans. Harry R. Boer. Grand Rapids, Michigan: Eerdmans Publishing Company, 1956.

Bierma, Lyle D. "Covenant or Covenants in the Theology of Olevianus?" *Calvin Theological Journal* 22 (1987): 228-50.

_____. "The Covenant Theology of Caspar Olevian." Ph.D. diss., Duke University, 1980.

Blaising, Craig A., and Bock, Darrell L. eds. *Dispensationalism, Israel and the Church: The Search for Definition.* Grand Rapids, Michigan: Zondervan Publishing House, 1992.

_____. *Progressive Dispensationalism.* Wheaton, Illinois: Victor, 1993.

Bogue, Carl W. "Jonathan Edwards on the Covenant of Grace." In *Soli Deo Gloria,* ed. R. C. Sproul. Nutley, New Jersey: Presbyterian and Reformed Publishing Company, 1976.

Bratcher, Dennis A. *The Concepts of Conditionality and Apostasy in Relation to the Covenant.* Unpublished Th.M Thesis, Westminster Theological Seminary, 1986.

Bright, John. *A History of Israel.* 3d ed. Philadelphia, Pennsylvania: The Westminster Press, 1981.

Brown, S. L. *The Book of Hosea.* Westminster Commentaries. London: Methuen & Co. Ltd., 1932.

Brown, W. Adams. "Covenant Theology." In *Hastings Encyclopedia of Religion and Ethics,.* ed. James Hastings, vol.4. New York: Charles Scribner's Sons, 1912.

Bruggink, Donald J. "Calvin and Federal Theology." *The Reformed Review* 13 (1959-60): 15-22.

Brunner, Emil. *Die Christliche Lehre von Schöpfung und Erlösung: Dogmatik.* Band 2. Zürich: Zwingli - Verlag, 1950.

Bullinger, Heinrich. *De Testamento Seu Foedere Dei Unico Et Aeterno.* Tiguri, 1534.

Bultmann, Rudolf. *Existence and Faith.* trans. Schubert M. Ogden. Cleveland, Ohio: Meridian, 1960.

_____. *Faith and Understanding.* ed. Robert W. Funk. trans. Louise Pettibone Smith. New York: Harper and Row, 1969.

_____. *Kerygma and Myth.* New York: Harper and Row, 1961.

_____. *The Presence of Eternity: History and Eschatology.* New York: Harper and Brothers, 1957.

_____. *Theology of the New Testament.* New York: Charles Scribner's Sons, 1951.

Burrage, Champlin. *The Church Covenant Idea: Its Origin and Its Development.* Philadelphia, Pennsylvania: American Baptist Publication Society, 1904.

Burrell, S. A. "The Covenant Idea as a Revolutionary Symbol: Scotland, 1596-1637." *Church History* 29 (1958): 338-50.
Campbell, Ken M., *God's Covenant*. Unpublished Th.M Thesis. Westminster Theological Seminary. Philadelphia, Pennsylvania, 1971.
Chafer, Lewis Sperry. "Dispensationalism." *Bibliotheca Sacra* 93 (1936): 390-449.
_____. *Dispensationalism*. Dallas, Texas: Dallas Seminary Press, 1951.
_____. *Systematic Theology*. 7 vols. Dallas, Texas: Dallas Seminary Press, 1948.
Cho, David D. *The Old Princeton Presbyterian Response to the Holiness Movement*. Ph.D. diss., Westminster Theological Seminary, 1994.
Clowney, Edmund P. *Preaching and Biblical Theology*. Nutley, New Jersey: Presbyterian and Reformed Publishing Company, 1975.
_____. *The Unfolding Mystery: Discovering Christ in the Old Testament*. Phillipsburg, New Jersey: Presbyterian and Reformed Publishing Company, 1988.
Cocceius, Johannes. *Summa Doctrine de Foedere et Testamento Dei*. Amsterdam, 1648.
Cooper, Karl T. "Paul and Rabbinic Soteriology: A Review Article." *Westminster Theological Journal* 44 (1972): 123-39.
Cottrell, Jack W. *Covenant and Baptism in the Theology of HuldreichZwingli*. Ph.D. diss., Princeton Theological Seminary, 1971.
Cowles, Henry. *The Minor Prophets*. New York: D. Appleton and Company, 1867.
Dabney, Robert L. *Systematic Theology*. 2d ed. Carlisle / Edinburgh: The Banner of Truth Trust, 1985.
Dallas Theological Seminary. *Doctrinal Statement*. Dallas: Dallas Theological Seminary, 1952.
Davies, Arthur. "Grace." *New Horizons* 18/8 (1997): 22-23.
Davies, G. I. *Hosea*. The New Century Bible Commentary. Grand Rapids, Michigan: Eerdmans Publishing Company, 1992.
Davis, D. Clair. "A Challenge to Theonomy." In *Theonomy: A Reformed Critique*, eds. William S. Barker & W. Robert Godfrey, 389-402. Grand Rapids, Michigan: Zondervan Publishing House, 1990.

_____. "How did the Church in Rome Become Roman Catholicism." In *Roman Catholicism: Evangelical Protestants Analyze What Divides and Unites Us*, ed. John Armstrong, 45-62. Chicago, Illinois: Moody Press, 1994.

_____. "Inerrancy and Westminster Calvinism." In *Inerrancy and Hermeneutic: A Tradition, A Challenge, A Debate*, ed. Harvie M. Conn, 35-46. Grand Rapids, Michigan: Baker Book House, 1990.

DeJong, Peter Y. *The Covenant Idea in New England Theology*. Grand Rapids, Michigan: Eerdmans Publishing Company, 1945.

Dodd, C. H. *The Epistle of Paul to the Romans*. New York / London: Harper and Brothers Publishers, 1932.

Dumbrell, William J. *Covenant and Creation: An Old Testament Covenantal Theology*. Nashville, Camden & New York: Thomas Nelson Publishers, 1984.

_____. "Law and Grace: The Nature of the Contrast in John 1:17." *Evangelical Quarterly* 58 (1986): 25-37.

Dunn, James D. G. "The Incident at Antioch (Gal. 2:11-18)." *Journal for the Study of the New Testament* 18 (1983): 3-57.

_____. *Jesus, Paul, and the Law: Studies in Mark and Galatians*. Louisville: Westminster, 1990.

_____. "The Justice of God: A Renewed Perspective on Justification by Faith." *Journal of Theological Studies* 43 (1992), 1-22.

_____. "The New Perspective on Paul." *Bulletin of the John Rylands University Library of Manchester* 65 (1983), 95-122.

_____. "Works of the Law and the Curse of the Law (Galatians 3:10-14)." *New Testament Studies* 31 (1985), 523-42.

_____. "Yet Once More — 'The Works of the Law': A Response." *Journal for the Study of the New Testament* 46 (1992): 99-117.

Edwards, Jonathan. *Treatise on Grace and Other Posthumously Published Writings*. ed. Paul Helm. Cambridge & London: James Clarke & Co. Ltd., 1971.

_____. *The Works of Jonathan Edwards* 16 vols. eds. Perry Miller, John E. Smith and Harry S. Stout. New Haven: Yale University Press, 1957-1998.

Eenigenburg, Elton M. "The Place of Covenant in Calvin's Teaching." *Reformed Review* 10 (1957): 1-22.

Eichrodt, Walther. *Theology of the Old Testament*. 2 vols. trans. J. A. Baker. Philadelphia, Pennsylvania: The Westminster Press, 1961 & 1967.

Emerson, Everett H. "Calvin and Covenant Theology." *Church History* 25 (June 1956): 136-44.
Faber, Jelle. *Essays in Reformed Doctrine*. Neerlandia / Alberta, Canada: Inheritance Publications, 1990.
Fairbairn, Patrick. *The Revelation of Law in Scripture*. Phillipsburg, New Jersey: Presbyterian and Reformed Publishing Company, 1996.
_____. *The Typology of Scripture*. Grand Rapids, Michigan: Zondervan Publishing House, 1952.
Feinberg, Charles L. *Millennialism: The Two Major Views. The Premillennial and Amillennial Systems of Biblical Interpretation Analyzed and Compared*. 3d. ed. Chicago, Illinois: Moody Press, 1980.
Ferguson, Sinclair B. *A Heart for God: If He Can Be Known, How Can We Discover Him?* Colorado Springs, Colorado: NavPress, 1987.
_____. "John Murray." In *Hand Book of Evangelical Theologians*, ed. Walter J. Elwell, 168-181. Grand Rapids, Michigan: Baker Book House, 1993.
_____. *John Owen on the Christian Life*. Carlisle / Edinburgh: The Banner of Truth Trust, 1987.
_____. "The Teaching of the Confession." In *The Westminster Confession in the Church Today*, ed. Alasdair I. C. Heron, 28-39. Edinburgh: Saint Andrews Press, 1982.
Ferguson, Sinclair B. Wright, David F. and Packer, J.I. eds. *New Dictionary Theology*. Downers Grove, Illinois: InterVarsity Press, 1988.
Finger, T. N. "Merit." In *Evangelical Dictionary of Theology*, ed. Walter A. Elwell, 709-10. Grand Rapids, Michigan: Baker Book House, 1984.
Flinn, P. Richard. "Baptism, Redemptive History, and Eschatology: The Parameters of Debate." *Christianity and Civilization* 1 (Spring 1982): 111-51.
Frame, John M. *Apologetics to the Glory of God: An Introduction*. Phillipsburg, New Jersey: Presbyterian and Reformed Publishing Company, 1994.
_____. *Cornelius Van Til: An Analysis of His Thought*. Phillipsburg : New Jersey: Presbyterian and Reformed Publishing Company, 1995.

_____. *The Doctrine of the Knowledge of God.* Phillipsburg, New Jersey: Presbyterian and Reformed Publishing Company, 1987.

Fuller, Daniel P. *Gospel and Law: Contrast or Continuum? The Hermeneutics of Dispensationalism and Covenant Theology.* Grand Rapids, Michigan: Eerdmans Publishing Company, 1980.

_____. "The Hermeneutics of Dispensationalism." Th.D. diss., Northern Baptist Theological Seminary, Chicago, Illinois, 1957.

_____. "A Response on the Subjects of Works and Grace." *Presbyterion* 9 (1983): 72-9.

Gaffin, Jr., Richard B. *The Centrality of the Resurrection: A Study in Paul's Soteriology.* Grand Rapids, Michigan: Baker Book House, 1978.

_____. "The Holy Spirit." *Westminster Theological Journal* 43 (1980): 58-78.

_____. *Perspectives on Pentecost: Studies in New Testament Teaching on the Gifts of the Holy Spirit.* Grand Rapids, Michigan: Baker Book House, 1979.

_____. "Systematic Theology and Biblical Theology." In *The New Testament Student and Theology.* vol.3. ed. John H. Skilton, 32-50. Philadelphia, Pennsylvania: Presbyterian and Reformed Publishing Company, 1976.

Garlington, D.B. "The Obedience of Faith in the Letter to the Romans; Part I: The Meaning of *hupakoen pisteos* (Rom 1:5; 16:26)." *Westminster Theological Journal* 52 (1990): 201-24.

_____. "The Obedience of Faith in the Letter to the Romans; Part II: The Obedience of Faith and Judgment by Works." *Westminster Theological Journal* 53 (1991): 47-72.

Garrett, Duane A. "Type, Typology." In *Evangelical Dictionary of Biblical Theology,* ed. Walter A. Elwell, 785-7. Grand Rapids, Michigan: Baker Book House, 1996.

Glenny, W. Edward. "Typology: A Summary of the Present Evangelical Discussion." *Journal of the Evangelical Theological Society* 40 (1997): 627-638.

Godfrey, W. Robert. "Back to Basics: A Response to the Robertson-Fuller Dialogue." *Presbyterion* 9 (1983): 80-4.

_____. "Law and Gospel." In *New Dictionary of Theology,* eds. Sinclair B. Ferguson & David F. Wright, 379-80. Downers Grove, Illinois / Leicester, England: InterVarsity Press, 1988.

_____. "What Really Caused the Great Divide?" In *Roman Catholicism: Evangelical Protestants Analyze What Divides and Unites Us*, ed. John Armstrong, 65-82. Chicago, Illinois: Moody Press, 1994.

Gordon, T. David. "Why Israel did not Obtain Torah-Righteousness: A Translation Note on Romans 9:32." *Westminster Theological Journal* 54 (1992): 163-66.

Grudem, Wayne. *Systematic Theology: An Introduction to Biblical Doctrine*. Grand Rapids, Michigan: Zondervan Publishing House, 1994.

Hagen, Kenneth. "From Testament to Covenant in the Early Sixteenth Century." *Sixteenth Century Journal* 3 (1972): 1-20.

Henderson, Ebenezer. *The Twelve Minor Prophets*. Thornapple Commentaries. Grand Rapids, Michigan: Baker Book House, 1980.

Heppe, Heinrich. *"Die Dogmatik: der Evangelisch-reformierten Kirche."* Neukirchen Kreis Moers: Neukirchener Verlag, 1958.

Hodge, A. A. *The Confession of Faith: A Handbook of Christian Doctrine Expounding The Westminster Confession*. Reprint, The Banner of Truth Trust, 1983.

Hoekema, Anthony A. "Calvin's Doctrine of the Covenant of Grace." *Reformed Review* 15 (1962): 1-12.

_____. "The Covenant of Grace in Calvin's Teaching." *Calvin Theological Journal* 2 (1967): 133-61.

Hoeksema, Herman. *Reformed Dogmatics*. Grand Rapids, Michigan: Reformed Free Publishing Association, 1985.

Horton, Michael. "What Still Keeps Us Apart?" In *Roman Catholicism: Evangelical Protestants Analyze What Divides and Unites Us*, ed. John Armstrong, 245-66. Chicago, Illinois: Moody Press, 1994.

Hubbard, David Allan. *Hosea*. Tyndale Old Testament Commentaries. Downers Grove, Illinois: InterVarsity Press, 1989.

Jensen, P. F. "Merit." In *New Dictionary of Theology*, eds. Sinclair B. Ferguson & David F. Wright, 422. Downers Grove, Illinois / Leicester, England: InterVarsity Press, 1988.

_____. Review of *Gospel and Law: Contrast or Continuum? The Hermeneutics of Dispensationalism and Covenant Theology*, by Daniel P. Fuller. *Calvin Theological Journal* 17 (1982): 109-12.

Johnson, Dennis E. *The Message of Acts in the History of Redemption.* Phillipsburg, New Jersey: Presbyterian and Reformed Publishing Company, 1997.
Kaiser, Walter C., Jr. "The Eschatological Hermeneutics of 'Epangelicalism': Promise Theology." *Journal of Evangelical Theological Society* 13 (1970), 91-100.
_____. "Leviticus 18:5 and Paul: Do This and You Shall Live (Eternally?)." *Journal of Evangelical Theological Society* 14 (1971), 19-28.
_____. "The Law As God's Gracious Guidance for the Promotion of Holiness." In *Five Views on Law and Gospel.* Grand Rapids, Michigan: Zondervan Publishing House, 1996.
Karlberg, Mark W. "Justification in Redemptive History." *Westminster Theological Journal* 43 (1981): 213-46.
_____. "Legitimate Discontinuities Between the Testaments." *Journal of the Evangelical Theological Society* 28 (1985): 9-20.
_____. *The Mosaic Covenant and the Concept of Works in Reformed Hermeneutics: A Historical Critical Analysis with Particular Attention to Early Covenant Eschatology.* Ph.D. diss., Westminster Theological Seminary, 1980.
_____. "The Original State of Adam: Tensions within Reformed Theology." *Evangelical Quarterly* 87 (1987): 291-309.
_____. "Reformed Interpretation of the Mosaic Covenant." *Westminster Theological Journal* 43 (1980): 1-57.
_____. "The Significance of Israel in Biblical Typology." *Journal of Evangelical Theological Society* 31/3 (1988): 257-69.
_____. "Works and Grace." *New Horizons* 18/9 (1997): 23.
Keil, Carl F. *The Twelve Minor Prophets.* vol. 1. Biblical Commentary on the Old Testament. tr. James Martin. London: Hamilton and Co., 1868.
Kim, Seyoon. *The Origin of Paul's Gospel.* 2nd ed. Tübingen: J. C. B. Mohr (Paul Siebeck), 1984.
Kevan, Ernest F. *The Grace of Law: A Study in Puritan Theology.* Reprint, Grand Rapids, Michigan: Baker Book House, 1976.
_____. *Moral Law.* Phillipsburg, New Jersey: Presbyterian and Reformed Publishing Company, 1991.
Klassen, William. *Covenant and Community.* Grand Rapids, Michigan : Eerdmans Publishing Company, 1968.

Knight, George A. F. *Hosea: God's Love*. Torch Bible Commentaries. London: SCM Press, 1967.
Küng, Hans. *Justification: The Doctrine of Karl Barth and a Catholic Reflection*. trans. Thomas Collins, Edmund E. Tolk, and David Granskou. Philadelphia, Pennsylvania: The Westminster Press, 1981.
Kuyper, Abraham. *The Work of the Holy Spirit*. trans. Henri De Vries. Chattanooga: AMG Publishers, 1995.
Ladd, George E. *Crucial Questions About the Kingdom of God*. Grand Rapids, Michigan: Eerdmans Publishing Company, 1952.
Laetsch, Theo. *The Minor Prophets*. Bible Commentary. Saint Louis, Missouri: Concordia Publishing House, 1956.
Lang, August. *Der Heidelberger Katechismus und vier verwandte Katechismen*. Reprint, Darmstadt: Wissenschaftliche Buchgesellachaft, 1967.
Lee, Irons. "Raised for Our Justification." *Modern Reformation* (March/April 1996): 25-8.
Letham, Robert W. A. "The *Foedus Operum*: Some Factors Accounting for Its Development." *Sixteenth Century Journal* 14 (1983): 457-67.
Lillback, Peter Alan. *The Binding of God: Calvin's Role in the Development of Covenant Theology*. Ph.D. diss., Westminster Theological Seminary, 1985.
_____. "Calvin's Covenantal Response to the Anabaptist View of Baptism." *Christianity and Civilization* 1 (1982): 185-232.
_____. "Ursinus' Development of the Covenant of Creation: A Debt to Melanchthon or Calvin?" *Westminster Theological Journal* 43 (1981): 247-88.
Longman III, Tremper & Reid, Daniel G. *God Is a Warrior*. Grand Rapids, Michigan: Zondervan Publishing House, 1995.
Luther, Martin. *Luther's Works,* 55 vols. eds. Jaroslav Pelikan and Helmut T. Lehmann. Philadelphia: Fortress Press / Muhlenberg Press, 1957-1986.
Machen, J. Gresham. *The Christian Faith and the Modern World*. London: Hodder and Stoughton Limited, 1936.
_____. *The Christian View of Man*. Reprint, Carlisle / Edinburgh: The Banner of Truth Trust, 1995.
_____. *Christianity and Culture*. Reprint, Carlisle / Edinburgh: The Banner of Truth Trust, 1969.

_____. *God Transcendent.* ed. Ned B. Stonehouse. Carlisle / Edinburgh: The Banner of Truth Trust, 1982.

_____. *Machen's Notes on Galatians.* ed. John H. Skilton. Philadelphia: Presbyterian and Reformed Publishing Company, 1972.

_____. *The New Testament: An Introduction to Its Literature and History.* ed. W. John Cook. Carlisle / Edinburgh: The Banner of Truth Trust, 1997.

_____. *The Origin of Paul's Religion.* Reprint, Grand Rapids, Michigan: Eerdmans Publishing Company, 1976.

_____. *What is Christianity?: And Other Addresses.* ed. Ned B. Stonehouse. Grand Rapids, Michigan: Eerdmans Publishing Company, 1951.

_____. *What is Faith?* New York: The Macmillan Company, 1925.

Macleod, Donald. "Covenant Theology." In *Dictionary of Scottish Church History & Theology*, ed. Nigel M. De S. Cameron, 214-18. Downers Grove, Illinois: InterVarsity Press, 1993.

Mays, James Luther. *Hosea.* The Old Testament Library. Philadelphia, Pennsylvania: The Westminster Press, 1969.

McComiskey, Thomas E. *The Covenant of Promise: A Theology of the Old Testament Covenants.* Grand Rapids, Michigan: Baker Book House, 1985.

_____. *The Minor Prophets: Hosea, Joel, and Amos.* vol. 1. Grand Rapids, Michigan: Baker Book House, 1992.

McConville, J. Gordon. *Grace in the End: A Study in Deuteronomic Theology.* Grand Rapids, Michigan: Zondervan Publishing House, 1993.

McCoy, Charles S. "The Covenant Theology of Johannes Cocceius." Ph.D. diss., Yale University, 1956.

McCoy, Charles S. and Baker, J. Wayne. *Fountainhead of Federalism: Heinrich Bullinger and the Covenant Tradition.* Louisville, Kentucky: Westminster/ John Knox Press, 1991.

McGiffert, Michael. "From Moses to Adam: the Making of the Covenant of Works." *Sixteenth Century Journal* 19/2 (1988): 131-55.

_____. "Grace and Works: the Rise and Division of Covenant Divinity in Elizabethan Puritanism." *Harvard Theological Review* 75/4 (1982): 463-502.

McGrath, Alister. *Iustitia Dei: A History of the Christian Doctrine of Justification*. 2 vols. Cambridge, London: Cambridge University Press, 1986.

_____. *Justification by Faith: What It Means for Us*. Grand Rapids, Michigan: Zondervan Publishing House, 1988.

McLelland, Joseph C. "Covenant Theology: A Re-evaluation." *Canadian Journal of Theology* 3 (1957): 184-97.

McWilliams, David B. "The Covenant Theology of the Westminster Confession of Faith and Recent Criticism." *Westminster Theological Journal* 53 (1991): 109-24.

Melanchthon, Philip. *Corpus Reformatorum: Philippi Melanchthonis Opera quae supersunt omnia*. eds. C. G. Bretschneider and H. E. Bindseil. Halle, 1834ff.

_____. *Loci Communes (1555)*. trans. Clyde L. Manschreck. Oxford, 1965.

Mendenhall, George E. "Ancient Oriental and Biblical Law." *The Biblical Archaeologist* 17/2 (1954): 26-46.

_____. "Covenant Forms in Israelite Tradition." *The Biblical Archaeologist* 17/3 (1954): 50-76.

Meyer, Heinrich A. W. *Critical and Exegetical Hand-Book to the Epistle to the Romans*. trans. John C Moore & Edwin Johnson. New York & London: Funk & Wagnalls Company, 1884.

Michaels, J. Ramsey. "The First Resurrection: a Response." *Westminster Theological Journal* 29 (1976/77): 100-09.

Milne, Douglas J. W. "A Barthian Stricture on Reformed Theology: The Unconditionality of the Covenant of Grace." *The Reformed Theological Review* 55/3 (1996): 121-33.

Moller, Jens G. "The Beginnings of Puritan Covenant Theology." *Journal of Ecclesiastical History* 14 (1963): 46-67.

Moltmann, Jürgen. "*Föderaltheologie*." In *Lexicon für Theologie und Kirche* 4:190-92. Freiburg: Verlag Herder, 1960.

_____. *God in Creation: A New Theology of Creation and the Spirit of God*. trans. Margaret Kohl. San Francisco, California: Harper and Row, 1985.

_____. *Theology of Hope*. trans. James W. Leitsch. New York: Harper and Row, 1967.

_____. *The Trinity and the Kingdom*. trans. Margaret Kohl. San Francisco, California: Harper and Row, 1981.

Moo, Douglas J. "Israel and Paul in Romans 7:7-12." *New Testament Studies* 32 (1986): 122-35.

_____. "'Law,' 'Works of the Law' and Legalism in Paul." *Westminster Theological Journal* 45 (1983): 73-100.

Muller, Richard A. "Calvin and the 'Calvinists': Assessing Continuities and Discontinuities Between the Reformation and Orthodoxy." *Calvin Theological Journal* 30 (1995): 345-75.

_____. "Covenant and Conscience in English Reformed Theology: Three Variations on a 17th Century Theme." *Westminster Theological Journal* 42 (1980): 308-34.

_____. "The Covenant of Works and the Stability of Divine Law in Seventeenth-Century Reformed Orthodoxy: A Study in the Theology of Herman Witsius and Wilhelmus À Brakel." *Calvin Theological Journal* 29 (1994): 75-101.

Nygren, Anders. *Commentary on Romans.* trans. Carl C. Rasmussen. Philadelphia, Pennsylvania: Muhlenberg Press, 1949.

Oberman, Heiko. *Forerunners of the Reformation.* Philadelphia, Pennsylvania: Fortress Press, 1981.

_____. *The Harvest of Medieval Theology: Gabriel Biel and the Late Medieval Nominalism* Cambridge: Harvard University Press, 1963.

_____. "The Tridentine Decree on Justification in the Light of Late Medieval Theology." In *Journal for Theology and the Church 3, Distinctive Protestant and Catholic Themes Revisited*, ed. Robert W. Funk, 28-54. New York: Harper & Row, 1967.

Ogilvie, Lloyd J. *Hosea, Joel, Amos, Obadiah, Jonah.* The Communicator's Commentary. vol. 20. Dallas, Texas: Word Books Publisher, 1990.

Orelli, C. Von. *The twelve Minor Prophets.* tr. J. S. Banks. Minneapolis, Minnesota: Klock & Klock Christian Publisher, 1977.

Osborne, G. R. "Type, Typology." In *Evangelical Dictionary of Theology*, ed. Walter A. Elwell, 1117-9. Grand Rapids, Michigan: Baker Book House, 1984.

Pelagius. *Pelagius's Expositions of Thirteen Epistles of St Paul: Text.* In *Texts and Studies: Contributions to Biblical and Patristic Literature*, vol. 9, ed. J. Armitage Robinson. 2 vols. London: Cambridge University Press, 1922, 1926.

Peter, Carl J. "Merit." In *The Dictionary of Theology*, eds. Joseph A. Komonchak, Mary Collins and Dermot A. Lane, 652-53. Wilmington, Delaware: Michael Glazier, Inc., 1987.

Piper, John. *Desiring God: Meditations of a Christian Hedonist.* Sisters, Oregon: Multnomah Books, 1996.

_____. *The Justification of God.* Grand Rapids, Michigan: Baker Book House, 1983.

_____. *Love Your Enemies: Jesus' Love Command in the Synoptic Gospels & the Early Christian Paraenesis.* Grand Rapids, Michigan: Baker Book House, 1991.

Poole, David N.J. *The History of the Covenant Concept from the Bible to Johannes Cloppenburg "De Foedere Dei."* San Francisco, California: Mellen Research University Press, 1992.

Pope, E. A. *New England Calvinism and the Disruption of the Presbyterian Church.* Ph.D. diss., Brown University, 1963.

Poythress, Vern S. *God-Centered Biblical Interpretation.* Phillipsburg, New Jersey: Presbyterian and Reformed Publishing Company, 1999.

_____. *The Shadow of Christ in the Law of Moses.* Phillipsburg, New Jersey: Presbyterian and Reformed Publishing Company, 1991.

_____. *Understanding Dispensationalists.* 2d. ed. Phillipsburg, New Jersey: Presbyterian and Reformed Publishing Company, 1994.

_____. *Using Multiple Thematic Centers in Theological Synthesis: Holiness as a Test Case in Developing a Pauline Theology.* Glenside, Pensylvania: Westminster Campus Bookstore, 1991.

Preus, James S. *From Shadow to Promise.* Cambridge: Belknap Press, 1969.

Pusey, E. B. *The Minor Prophets: A Commentary.* vol. 1. Grand Rapids, Michigan: Baker Book House, 1879.

Räisänen, Heikki. "Galatians 2:16 and Paul's Break with Judaism." *New Testament Studies* 31 (1985), 543-53.

_____. *Jesus, Paul and Torah: Collected Essays.* trans. David E. Orton. Journal for the Study of the New Testament Supplement Series 43. Sheffield: JSOT, 1992.

_____. "Legalism and Salvation by the Law: Paul's Portrayal of the Jewish Religion as a Historical and Theological Problem." In *The Pauline Literature and Theology*, ed. S. Pedersen, 63-83. Göttingen: Vandenhoeck and Ruprecht, 1980.

_____. *Paul and the Law*. 2nd. ed. Tübingen: J. C. B. Mohr (Paul Siebeck), 1983.
_____. "Paul's Conversion and the Development of His View of the Law." *New Testament Studies* 33 (1987): 404-19.
_____. *The Torah and Christ: Essays in German and English on the Problem of the Law in Early Christianity*. ed. Anne-Marit Enroth. Helsinki, 1986.
Reid, W. Stanford. "Justification by Faith According to John Calvin." *Westminster Theological Journal* 42 (1980): 290-307.
Ridderbos, Herman N. *The Coming of the Kingdom*. Philadelphia, Pennsylvania: Presbyterian and Reformed Publishing Company, 1962.
_____. *Paul: An Outline of His Theology*. Grand Rapids, Michigan: Eerdmans Publishing Company, 1975.
_____. *When the Time Had Fully Come: Studies in New Testament Theology*. Jordan Station, Ontario: Paideia Press, 1982.
Ritschl, Albrecht. *The Christian Doctrine of Justification and Reconciliation*. trans. H. R. Mackintosh and A. B. Macaulay. Edinburgh: T. & T. Clark, 1900.
Ritschl, Otto. *Dogmengeschichte des Protestantismus*. 4 vols. Göttingen: Vandenhoeck & Ruprecht, 1908-1927.
Robertson, O. Palmer. *The Christ of the Covenants*. Phillipsburg, New Jersey: Presbyterian and Reformed Publishing Company, 1980.
_____. "Current Reformed Thinking on the Nature of the Divine Covenants." *Westminster Theological Journal* 40 (1977): 63-76.
_____. "Genesis 15:6: New Covenant Expositions of an Old Covenant Text." *Westminster Theological Journal* 42 (1980): 259-89.
_____. Review of *Gospel and Law: Contrast or Continuum*, by O. Palmer Robertson. *Presbyterion* 8 (1982): 84-91.
Rohr, John v. "Covenant and Assurance in Early English Puritanism." *Church History* 34 (1965): 195-203.
_____. *The Covenant of Grace in Puritan Thought*. Atlanta, Georgia: Scholars Press, 1986.
Rolston, Holmes III. *John Calvin versus the Westminster Confession*. Richmond, Virginia: John Knox Press, 1972.
_____. "Responsible Man in Reformed Theology: Calvin Versus the Westminster Confession." *Scottish Journal of Theology* 23 (1970): 129-56.

Ryrie, Charles C. *Dispensationalism*. Revised and Expanded. Chicago, Illinois: Moody Press, 1995.
_____. *The Grace of God*. Chicago, Illinois: The Moody Bible Institute, 1963; Moody Press, 1975.
Sanders, E. P. "The Covenant as a Soteriological Category and the Nature of Salvation in Palestinian and Hellenistic Judaism." *Jews, Greeks and Christians: Religious Cultures in Late Antiquity*. ed. Robert Hamerton-Kelly and Robin Scroggs, 11-44. Leiden, 1976.
_____. *Jesus and Judaism*. Philadelphia, Pennsylvania: Fortress Press, 1985.
_____. *Jewish Law from Jesus to the Mishnah: Five Studies*. London: SCM Press / Philadelphia: Trinity Press International, 1990.
_____. *Paul*. Oxford / New York: Oxford University Press, 1992.
_____. *Paul and Palestinian Judaism*. Philadelphia, Pennsylvania: Fortress Press, 1977.
_____. *Paul, the Law and the Jewish People*. Philadelphia, Pennsylvania: Fortress Press, 1983.
Saucy, Robert L. *The Case for Progressive Dispensationalism: The Interface Between Dispensational & Non-Dispensational Theology*. Grand Rapids, Michigan: Zondervan Publishing House, 1993.
Schaff, Philip. *The Creeds of Christendom*. 3 vols. Grand Rapids, Michigan: Baker Book House, 1977.
Schenck, L. B. *The Presbyterian Doctrine of Children in the Covenant*. New Haven, Connecticut, 1940.
Schleiermacher, Friedrich. *The Christian Faith*. 2d ed. eds. H. R. Mackintosh and J. S. Stewart. Philadelphia, Pennsylvania: Fortress Press, 1928.
_____. *On Religion: Addresses in Response to its Cultured Critics*. trans. Terrence N. Tice. Richmond, Virginia: John Knox, 1969.
Schrenk, Gottlob. *Gottesreich und Bund im älteren Protestantismus, vornehmlich bei Johannes Cocceius*. Gütersloh: Bertelsmann, 1923.
Scofield, Cyrus I., ed. *The New Scofield Reference Bible. The Holy Bible Containing the Old and New Testaments. Authorized King James Version*, ed. E. Schuyler English. New York: Oxford, 1967.
_____., ed. *The Scofield Reference Bible. The Holy Bible Containing the Old and New Testaments. Authorized Version*. New and Improved ed. New York: Oxford, 1917.

Shedd, William G. T. *Dogmatic Theology*. 3 vols. New York: Charles Scribner's Sons, 1888.
Silva, Moisés. *Explorations in Exegetical Method: Galatians as a Test Case*. Grand Rapids, Michigan: Baker Book House, 1996.
_____. "Is the Law against the Promises? The Significance of the Galatians 3:21 for Covenant Continuity." In *Theonomy: A Reformed Critique*, eds. William S. Barker & W. Robert Godfrey, 153-67. Grand Rapids, Michigan: Zondervan Publishing House, 1990.
Sproul, R. C. *Faith Alone: Evangelical Doctrine of Justification*. 2d. Print. Grand Rapids, Michigan: Baker Book House, 1996.
_____. *Grace Unknown: The Heart of Reformed Theology*. Grand Rapids: Michigan, Baker Book House, 1997.
Stek, John H. "Biblical Typology Yesterday and Today." *Calvin Theological Journal* 5 (1970): 133-62.
_____. "'Covenant' Overload in Reformed Theology." 29 (1994): 12-41.
_____. "A New Theology of Baptism? Baptism: a Sign of Grace or Judgment?" *Calvin Theological Journal* 1 (1966): 69-73.
Stoute, D. A. "The Origins and Early Development of the Reformed Idea of Covenant." Ph.D. diss., Cambridge, 1979.
Strehle, Stephen. *Calvinism, Federalism, and Scholasticism: A Study of the Reformed Doctrine of the Covenant*. Basler und Berner Studien zur historischen und systematischen Theologie 58. Bern: Peter Lang, 1988.
Strickland, Wayne G. ed. *The Law, the Gospel and the Modern Christian: Five Views*. Grand Rapids, Michigan: Zondervan Publishing House, 1993.
Strimple, Robert B. "Roman Catholic Theology Today." In *Roman Catholicism: Evangelical Protestants Analyze What Divides and Unites Us*, ed. John Armstrong, 85-117. Chicago, Illinois: Moody Press, 1994.
Stuart, Douglas. *Word Biblical Commentary: Hosea-Jonah*. Vol. 31. eds. David A. Hubbard and Glenn W. Barker. Waco, Texas: Word Books Publisher, 1987.
Torrance, James B. "Calvin and Puritanism in England and Scotland - Some Basic Concepts in the Development of 'Federal Theology.'" In *Calvinus Reformator*, 264-277. Potchefstroom: Potchefstroom University for Christian Higher Education, 1982.

_____. "Covenant or Contract?: A Study of the Theological Background of Worship in Seventeenth-Century Scotland." *Scottish Journal of Theology* 23 (1970): 51-76.

_____. "The Covenant Concept in Scottish Theology and Politics and Its Legacy." *Scottish Journal of Theology* 34 (1981): 225-43.

_____. "Strengths and Weaknesses of the Westminster Theology." In *The Westminster Confession,* ed. Alisdair Heron, 40-54. Edinburgh: Saint Andrews Press, 1982.

Trinterud, Leonard J. "The Origins of Puritanism." *Church History* 20 (1951): 37-57.

Ursinus, Zacharias. "*Summa Theologiae.*" In *Der Heidelberger Katechismus,* ed. August Lang. Leipzig, 1907. Reprint, Darmstadt: Wissenschaftliche Buchgesellschaft, 1967.

Van Gemeren, Willem A. "Israel as the Hermeneutical Crux in the Interpretation of Prophecy." *Westminster Theological Journal* 45 (1983): 132-44.

_____. "Israel as the Hermeneutical Crux in the Interpretation of Prophecy, II." *Westminster Theological Journal* 46 (1984): 254-97.

_____. "The Law is the Perfection of Righteousness in Jesus Christ: A Reformed Perspective." In *Five Views on Law and Gospel,* ed. Wayne G. Strickland, 13-58. Grand Rapids, Michigan: Zondervan Publishing House, 1996.

Van Til, Cornelius. *Common Grace and The Gospel.* Phillipsburg, New Jersey: Presbyterian and Reformed Publishing Company, 1972.

_____. "Covenant Theology." In *New 20th- Century Encyclopedia of Religious Knowledge,* ed. J. D. Douglas, 240-41. 2d ed. Grand Rapids, Michigan, 1991.

_____. *The Defense of the Faith.* 3d. ed. Phillipsburg, New Jersey: Presbyterian and Reformed Publishing Company, 1967.

_____. *The Great Debate Today.* Nutley, New Jersey: Presbyterian and Reformed Publishing Company, 1971.

_____. *The Intellectual Challenge of the Gospel.* Phillipsburg, New Jersey: Presbyterian and Reformed Publishing Company, 1980.

_____. *An Introduction to Systematic Theology.* Phillipsburg, New Jersey: Presbyterian and Reformed Publishing Company, 1974.

_____. *The Sovereignty of Grace: An Appraisal of G. C. Berkouwer's View of Dordt.* New Jersey: Presbyterian and Reformed Publishing Company, 1969.

von Rad, Gerhard. *Genesis: A Commentary.* rev. ed. Philadelphia, Pennsylvania: The Westminster Press, 1972.

_____. *Theologie Des Alten Testaments.* Band I&II. München: Chr. Kaiser Verlag, 1958 & 1965.

Wallis, Wilber. Review of *Gospel and Law: Contrast or Continuum*, by Daniel P. Fuller. *Presbyterion* 8 (1982): 72-82.

Walton, John H. *Covenant.* Grand Rapids, Michigan: Zondervan Publishing House, 1994.

Watson, P. S. "Merit." In *A Dictionary of Christian Theology*, ed. Alan Richardson, Philadelphia, Pennsylvania: The Westminster Press, 1969.

Weir Daid A. *The Origins of the Federal Theology in Sixteenth-Century Reformation Thought.* Oxford: Clarendon Press, 1990.

Westerholm, Stephen. *Israel's Law and the Church's Faith: Paul and the Recent Interpreters.* Grand Rapids, Michigan: Eerdmans Publishing Company, 1988.

Westminster Theological Seminary. *Westminster Statement on Justification.* Unpublished Doctrinal Statement of Westminster Theological Seminary. Philadelphia, Pennsylvania, 1980.

Williams, George H. *The Radical Reformation.* Philadelphia, Pennsylvania: The Westminster Press, 1975.

Williamson, G. I. *The Westminster Confession of Faith: For Study Classes.* Presbyterian and Reformed Publishing Company, 1964.

Wingard, Charles. "The Doctrines of Grace." *New Horizons* 18/5 (1997): 6-9.

Witsius, Hermannus. *De Oeconomia Foederum Dei cum Homnibus Libri Quattuor.* Utrecht, 1694.

Wolff, Hans Walter. *Hosea.* trans. Gary Stansell & ed. Paul D. Hanson. Philadelphia, Pennsylvania: Fortress Press, 1974.

Wright, N. Thomas. *The Climax of the Covenant: Christ and the Law in Pauline Theology.* Minneapolis, Minnesota: Fortress Press, 1991.

_____. "The Paul of History and the Apostle of Faith." *Tyndale Bulletin* 29 (1978): 61-88.

_____. *What Saint Paul Really Said.* Grand Rapids, Michigan: Eerdmans Publishing Company, 1997.

Young, Edward J. "Confession and Covenant." In *Scripture and Confession: A Book about Confessions Old and New*, ed. John H.

Skilton, 31-66. Phillipsburg, New Jersey: Presbyterian and Reformed Publishing Company, 1973.

―――――. *Genesis 3: A Devotional and Expository Study.* Reprint, The Banner of Truth Trust, 1983.

―――――. *The Study of Old Testament Theology Today.* Westwood, New Jersey: Fleming H. Revell Company, 1959.

―――――. *The Study of Old Testament Today.* London: James Clarke, 1958.

―――――. "What is Old Testament Biblical Theology?" *Evangelical Quarterly* 31 (1959), 136-42.

Zuck, Lowell H. "Anabaptist Revolution Through the Covenant in Sixteenth Century Continental Protestantism." Ph.D. diss., Yale University, 1954.